Commander in Chief

Commander in Chief

How Truman, Johnson, and Bush Turned a Presidential
Power into a Threat to America's Future

Geoffrey Perret

Farrar, Straus and Giroux
New York

Farrar, Straus and Giroux
19 Union Square West, New York 10003

Copyright © 2007 by Geoffrey Perret
All rights reserved
Distributed in Canada by Douglas & McIntyre Ltd.
Printed in the United States of America
First edition, 2007

Library of Congress Cataloging-in-Publication Data
Perret, Geoffrey.
    Commander in chief : How Truman, Johnson, and Bush turned a presidential
power into a threat to America's future / by Geoffrey Perret.— 1st ed.
        p.   cm.
    Includes bibliographical references and index.
    ISBN-13: 978-0-374-10217-3 (hardcover : alk. paper)
    ISBN-10: 0-374-10217-1 (hardcover : alk. paper)
    1. United States—History, Military—20th century.   2. United States—History,
Military—21st century.   3. Intervention (International law)   4. Presidents—
United States—History.   5. Truman, Harry S., 1884–1972.   6. Korean War,
1950–1953.   7. Johnson, Lyndon B. (Lyndon Baines), 1908–1973.   8. Vietnamese
Conflict, 1961–1975.   9. Bush, George W. (George Walker), 1946–   10. Iraq War,
2003–   I. Title.

    E745.P395 2007
    355.020973'09045—dc22

                                                                2006009749

Designed by Debbie Glasserman

www.fsgbooks.com

10   9   8   7   6   5   4   3   2   1

To Jeffrey M. Flannery,
an archivist of rare talent,
acknowledged in a hundred
books, someone who has helped
countless researchers in the Library
of Congress Manuscript Reading
Room, and my dear friend,
this one's for you.

I saw askant the armies;
And I saw, as in noiseless dreams, hundreds of battle-flags;
Borne through the smoke of the battles, and pierc'd with missiles,
    I saw them, . . .
And at last but a few shreds left on the staffs, (and all in silence,)
And the staffs all splinter'd and broken.

                    —Walt Whitman, "Death Carol"

Contents

Introduction   3

Chapter 1   **Too Much Too Soon**   15

Chapter 2   **Man and Moment**   28

Chapter 3   **Position of Strength**   38

Chapter 4   **Location, Location, Location**   54

Chapter 5   **World Island**   67

Chapter 6   **Chinese Checkers**   79

Chapter 7   **National Home**   93

Chapter 8   **Panic Attack**   106

Chapter 9   **Talking Tough**   119

Chapter 10   **Zeitgeist Wins**   133

Chapter 11   **War of Maneuver**   149

Chapter 12   **What Goes Up . . .**   163

Chapter 13   **Wars of Choice**   176

Chapter 14   **Getting a Grip**   186

Chapter 15   **Hard Choices**   202

Chapter 16   **The Green Mountain**   211

Chapter 17   **Trading Places**   223

Chapter 18   **Thunder and Lightning**   235

Chapter 19   **All-Out Limited War**   246

Chapter 20   **Trapped**   257

Chapter 21   **Back to the Ranch**   272

Chapter 22   **The Nixinger War**   286

Chapter 23   **Futurismo**   299

Chapter 24   **Chances Are**   315

Chapter 25   **Targets**   326

Chapter 26   **Willful, Mendacious, Deluded**   339

Chapter 27   **Napoleon in Russia**   353

Chapter 28   **Armed Missionaries**   364

Chapter 29   **Iraq Syndrome**   375

Conclusion   391

Notes   393

Acknowledgments   417

Index   419

Commander in Chief

Introduction

THIS IS A STORY OF THREE UNWINNABLE WARS IN AN AGE OF UN-
winnable wars: Harry Truman and Korea, Lyndon Johnson and Vietnam, and George W. Bush and Iraq. The end result will be that in
another generation, roughly twenty-five years from now, the Global
War on Terror (or GWOT) will still be under way. The answer to the
suicide bomber will still be sought. When the inhabitants of John
Winthrop's "city upon a hill" gaze around from their place on the high
ground as the world burns, they will wonder, Whatever happened to
American power? They may well ask.

The last classical war was World War II. For more than two hundred years major wars had clear beginnings and clear endings. Since
1945, we have had a new kind of revolutionary war—wars that develop rather than erupt, wars without declarations of war, wars without surrenders. Their beginnings are murky, their conclusions unclear.
They are tests of stamina rather than strength, more likely than not to
sow the seeds of future wars. And since 1945 the United States has
chosen to place itself in the forefront of fighting them.

As it did so, the role of commander in chief was thrust at critical moments onto men who took counsel of their fears, beginning with Harry S. Truman. In three wars of choice, Truman, Johnson, and George W. Bush followed what was essentially the same script. At a time of high emotion they acted on their own visceral responses, ignoring the advice of the military and of major allies.

Truman made the decision to intervene in Korea without consulting anyone, and when he did so, he also intervened in the Chinese civil war, something he had vowed not to do. Why? Because in June 1950 the White House was facing something close to hysteria in the mainstream press and on Capitol Hill over "Who lost China?" and over Senator Joe McCarthy's claim that there were "205 known Communists" in the State Department. Truman was also under direct attack from Republicans in Congress for being indecisive in fighting the Cold War. When the North Koreans thrust across the 38th parallel, a deeply emotional president struck back, for all the wrong reasons.

Similarly, the assassination of John F. Kennedy had an impact on the American psyche that had to be lived through to be understood. That impact affected the emotionally volatile Lyndon Johnson as much as anyone. Without believing for a moment that the United States could win in Vietnam, Johnson chose to turn a small brushfire war into one of the twentieth century's biggest conflicts. Emotion was stronger than judgment, and in the end, not even Johnson could make sense of why he had done what he did. Yet the answer was not hard to find: once again domestic politics had overruled national security.

Finally, after September 11, Americans needed an Arab and Muslim country on which to take revenge. George W. Bush's visceral response was, "Can we attack Iraq?" For him, Saddam Hussein was a long-standing obsession, dating from before his presidency. He believed the story that Saddam had tried to assassinate his father during a visit George H. W. Bush made to Kuwait in 1993. Saddam, to him, became "the guy who tried to kill my dad."

He resented, too, the criticism of his father for leaving Saddam in power at the conclusion of the Gulf War. Overthrowing Saddam would, finally, put that right.

Bush was also trapped by an inflated paradigm. "We are at war," Dick Cheney and Donald Rumsfeld told him, and Bush agreed. A war in which America could bring all of its military power to bear would have appealed to any president at that moment. But not every president would have acted on it. Bush had trapped himself by believing in an assassination attempt that may have been manufactured by the Kuwaitis. Foiling an assassination plot—could gratitude be greater than this? George Herbert Walker Bush had saved Kuwait. That debt was paid because Kuwait had saved him. To the son, however, there was still a score to be settled.

Embracing the war paradigm, George W. Bush was playing to his enemy's strengths, not to his own. It meant that he had to promise "total victory" even though he was fighting what is a political and religious movement rather than a military force. Emotional and political realities pushed him into Afghanistan. Iraq would have to wait. But it would not have to wait for long.

Three wars—Korea, Vietnam, Iraq—all launched at moments of national crisis, all of them unwinnable.

They were unwinnable for many reasons, but the place to begin is this: in North Korea, North Vietnam, and Iraq, the enemy always held the strategic initiative. The most powerful country in the world found itself dancing to its enemy's tune, not its own. At times it was possible to seize the tactical initiative—crossing the 38th parallel, launching an aerial blitz against North Vietnam, flattening Fallujah. But the loss of the strategic initiative rules out the path to victory implicit in the military paradigm; namely, that one country imposes its will on another. Instead, the country that has chosen to wage the war finds itself wrestling with an insoluble challenge: a political victory requires a military victory first, because there can be no effective government without security and stability. But a military victory requires a political victory first, in the form of a government strong enough to establish a state monopoly on violence.

As commanders in chief seek military success, only to fail, then lurch off in search of political gains and fail again, time is used up. And time is not neutral. It strengthens the enemy. Knowing that, the enemy is never in a hurry. The longer the struggle lasts, the better their prospects. As America's distant wars grind on from year to year, internal divisions grow, nourishing a national debate that ultimately becomes acrimonious and divisive. Eventually, when public opinion realizes that a war is unwinnable, the war becomes unsustainable, whatever the party in power, whoever is commander in chief. If he won't end it, Congress will.

With commanders in chief, the political is always the personal. Truman's stormy relationship with MacArthur mattered in the Korean War. Lyndon Johnson's commitment to a war he did not believe in owed much to his desire not to be blamed for "losing" Vietnam—as Truman had been blamed for losing China—and to rivalry with the dead JFK, to prove that he was tougher than Kennedy.

George W. Bush—inheriting a war that his father had seemingly won yet could not conclude—sought to outdo his father and become, unlike Dad, a great president. What the first President Bush had failed to see was that the invasion and liberation of Kuwait was only the opening round in a fifty-year war. Liberating Kuwait meant that American troops would one day patrol the streets of Baghdad. It was only a matter of time. Still, it was the son's decision to invade Iraq. It was not a decision he had to make, and he was under no pressure to make it.

These modern wars are managed rather than won. It is possible to lose them, yet impossible to achieve victory. All have stubborn roots in the poisonous creeds of the nineteenth and early twentieth centuries: colonialism, nihilism, communism, and fascism. A decade ago, all four creeds appeared to have been vanquished, yet none of them had really gone away.

The turning point in the present struggle to maintain American power was Korea. This was the true curtain-raiser on the twenty-first-century challenge. Korea offered many wars in one—a war of aggression by one country against another; a war of national liberation; a civil war among the Koreans; a proxy war between the United States, the Soviet Union, and China; and a revolutionary war within Korean society. Above all, wars of national liberation are also identity wars. For many Koreans and for many Vietnamese, the whole meaning of being Korean or Vietnamese was to fight the Americans; for many a Muslim, being a Muslim means fighting the Americans, to the point of welcoming death. To die fighting the Americans has become the ultimate in identity politics.

The importance of identity in these liberation struggles was memorably expressed by Manuel Quezon, who spent his life trying to get the United States out of the Philippines and became the first president of an independent Philippines: "I would rather live in a hell ruled by Filipinos than in a heaven ruled by Americans."

The three major wars that this book considers were also wars against developing Third World birthrates. In Korea, the combined birthrates of China and North Korea meant that more than three million young men turned eighteen each year. Even though the United States killed more than a million Koreans and Chinese over the course of three years, it did not dent the inexorable rise in population.

In Vietnam, American intervention brought the deaths of more than a million Vietnamese, but the combined Chinese and North Vietnamese birthrate meant that the enemy could fight on despite horrendous losses. The Chinese deployed half a million troops in North Vietnam over the course of the war, and they were prepared to send many more. The prospect of using nuclear weapons was by then out of the question. The Chinese acquired their first usable nuclear weapons in 1965 and were already at work on a hydrogen bomb.

Finally, in Iraq, the United States is facing an insurgency that has widespread popular support. More than 250,000 young Iraqi males turn eighteen each year, and beyond Iraq, there is an aggrieved Sunni community of more than a billion people. The Iraq insurgency will never run short of manpower, money, or munitions; nor will terrorist groups across the Middle East.

There is a limit to the number of people that the United States can kill, capture, or incapacitate. In Iraq, it can kill tens of thousands, possibly more than a hundred thousand, but not millions, not in the name of liberation, not in the presence of television and camcorders. There are limits to what even a superpower can do without turning the entire civilized world against it.

International terrorism is only one head on the hydra that has America by the throat. The invasion of Iraq has created an insurgency that will increasingly link up with the world of international terrorism. Terrorism with a global reach is what Americans fear most, yet it is only one manifestation of the hydra. The global war on terror is another version of buy one war, get several more for free.

International terrorism makes sense only when viewed in the round, as one element in a global guerrilla war. Across the global south, we own the day, the guerillas own the night; we hold the cities, they hold the countryside; our firepower is always far greater, yet they have the strategic initiative; our military cannot be defeated, but our will can be eroded. Finally, we need to remember that guerrillas are notorious for losing every battle but winning the war.

This is also a struggle between cultures, a war between races, a war between the rich North and an impoverished South; a continuation of a 2,500-year-old struggle between East and West; a conflict that pits rich countries that are aging against poor ones where half the population is below the age of twenty-four. What is unique is not that such struggles are occurring, but that they are converging.

Fighting this new, multifaceted war, which manages to be both local and global, depends heavily on intelligence. Yet in the age of unwinnable wars, intelligence has been turned inside out. Traditionally, intelligence was about knowing an enemy's capabilities and unearthing his intentions. We knew how strong the Imperial Japanese Navy was on December 6, 1941, but we were not aware of its plan to attack Pearl Harbor. In 1962 the president's advisers knew the fine detail of Soviet military strength, but they were caught by surprise when Khrushchev put missiles into Cuba.

The most important intelligence—that on intentions—was always the hardest to find. Yet now we face an enemy whose intentions are obvious. What eludes us are his capabilities. These become apparent only when we sift through the debris of explosions.

The United States, like other nations, exercises its power in four ways. There is political power, which is the power of the state over its citizens, clients, and subjects. In a liberal democracy, where the power of the state is diffused throughout society, the result is political stability. Allied with political power is military power. The third type of power is economic, and the fourth is the power of culture. The great advantage of power, in its various guises, is the ability to shape events. Yet the historic moment when all four types of American power were at their peak has come and gone.

The start of America's comparative decline can be dated precisely. It began with Truman's succession to the presidency on the death of Franklin D. Roosevelt on April 12, 1945. When World War II ended four months later, the United States bestrode the world like a colossus in red, white, and blue. It accounted for at least half of the world economy. It possessed a monopoly on the atomic bomb. It was the most admired and envied country in the world, not only for its riches and military prowess but for its political stability and vibrant cultural life.

On becoming president, Truman had a clear idea of what his responsibility was: to keep the United States at its current peak of power. But that was impossible. As other countries recovered from the war, America's absolute supremacy would be eroded. Yet Truman, in trying to freeze a moment in time, had the encouragement of nearly all his advisers, the support of Congress, and the votes of the people.

America faced obvious limits. The Soviet Union was a barrier; so too was a band of impoverished states that formed a large arc from the Baltic to Egypt and from Egypt to Korea. The strategy for dealing with the Soviets was an atomic-armed alliance, NATO, plus a dominant American position in the United Nations. Truman abandoned Roosevelt's policy of nonintervention. Across the global south, his strategy for dealing with troublesome minor states was to try to control them by force.

The belief in frequent and sometimes massive American intervention created the intellectual framework for waging unwinnable wars. Since 1945 the United States has intervened nearly eighty times in more than a score of countries—on average, an intervention every nine months. Sometimes it was an operation to overthrow a government deemed a threat to American interests. At other times, it was to prop up a weak government that would advance those interests.

The cumulative risks were high, but the biggest risk of all was never anticipated. In the course of fighting three unwinnable major wars, the secret of American power has been given away. History turns on such revelations.

The Roman Empire was barely a hundred years old when, in the year A.D. 41, its most important secret was exposed. In a historic moment of confusion, the elite force that protected the emperor, the Praetorian Guard, proclaimed the timid, stuttering, and bookish Claudius the new emperor. From that moment, it was the Guard that held the supreme power in Rome. The old ruling families, in power for centuries, were powerless against the Praetorians.

In March and April 2003 the world discovered the secret of American military power: anarchy is stronger than any American president or any American army. There had been a glimpse of this truth in

Somalia in 1993–94, but Iraq was the ultimate demonstration. Shortly before the invasion of Iraq, Saddam Hussein is reported to have distributed thirty-five hundred copies of the film *Black Hawk Down* to senior officers in the Iraqi army, the Baath Party, and the secret police. The chaos from Iraq has spread, is spreading, and will continue to spread. In time, that ever-widening pool of chaos, striking deep roots in unstable parts of the world, will confound American power.

As the War on Terror lurches from decade to decade, it will distract attention from far greater threats. Nothing decisive can be done to combat global warming or curb nuclear proliferation without American leadership. These, not terrorism, are the dangers that threaten the survival of the human race.

The Global War on Terror is itself unwinnable. We cannot make terrorists stop; they must choose to stop. Major terrorist organizations such as the IRA, the Shining Path, and the Tamil Tigers became irrelevant without being defeated. War weariness affects guerrillas too. Even so, Americans will have to settle for a lot less than the "total victory" George W. Bush promised them.

The United States will also have to learn to live with being third in a global economy where the European Union and China are both richer than it is. There is also a fourth important player in the new Great Game—Russia.

As the world's largest producer of both oil and natural gas in an energy-desperate age, Russia's great power ambitions have come roaring back. Within a few years, most countries in the European Union will be so dependent on the Russians for their energy supplies that Moscow will have enormous leverage. China too will court the Russians for their oil.

Alone in the history of the world, the United States has a program for global supremacy. It can be found in the 2002 National Security Strategy (NSS) of the United States and in the governing doctrine of the United States military: "full-spectrum dominance."

American policy is to allow no rivals. That means that the Chinese will not be allowed to become dominant in East Asia, even if it means attacking China. The Russians will not be allowed to dominate Central Asia, even if it means going to war with Russia. Appearing to have learned nothing, President Bush laid out exactly the same program, full of menace and vainglory, in the National Security Strategy, 2006.

If this policy is pursued seriously, it will mean an America at war with most of the world. If, having been proclaimed, this dominance is not now pursued seriously, it will be seen as a bluff, and American influence will fall even faster.

However rich they become, neither the Europeans, the Russians, nor the Chinese will become direct rivals of the United States. They will nibble U.S. supremacy down to a nub, with American help: military interventions in poor countries pave the road to exhaustion. The NSS 2002 and 2006 provide the road map for getting there.

While the United States, with its post–9/11 sense of victimhood, trundles angrily down that road, the Europeans will devote themselves to shoring up what remains of the West while the Chinese continue to pursue what they see as their predestined role to dominate East Asia and recover Taiwan. The struggle for tomorrow's world will not be military, but political, cultural, and, above all, economic.

Americans are now almost alone in believing that war is a progressive force. There were fewer wars being waged by nation-states in 2006 than at any time since 1945. In fact, there was only one—the war in Iraq. Yet mired in the Iraqi morass, the United States continues to put its faith in military power as it struggles to defeat the Iraqi insurgency and prop up a weak government located mainly within an American military base—the Green Zone—and shielded from Iraq's people by American troops. As is commonplace across the Third World, this is a government that exists only on television. The real power in Iraq will therefore remain in the mosques.

The Europeans, the Russians, and the Chinese will not create an informal alliance to thwart American power. They don't have to. They will instead position themselves on each issue in accordance with what is good for Europe or Russia or China. There will be times when Europe has, in effect, the swing vote on American power. The United States and China may be on a collision course. The Europeans are not destined to clash with anyone. They will be free to support China against the United States if that serves their interests—for example, selling arms to China in exchange for multibillion-dollar Chinese purchases of Airbus aircraft. They will be free at the same time to support the United States against China if that serves their interests. Either way, the United States will have much less ability to shape events and to impose its will than it had before the invasion of Iraq.

The Iraqi blunder has accelerated America's comparative decline by at least a generation.

The old days are fast becoming a dream. American claims to being a benign superpower, acting for the good of the world, may have been plausible during the Cold War. But few people outside the United States now take them seriously, and over time, Western Europeans will replace governments that seem subservient to a fading and faltering United States.

The pursuit of unilateralism has not only done lasting damage to American credibility, but it has also split the West and undermined virtually every major global institution devoted to advancing the rule of law, beginning with the United Nations and reaching down to the latest creation, the International Criminal Court.

Great powers are always likely to follow the imperatives of power more often than the imperatives of law, yet the United States stands unique in its methods among modern empires. As the British Empire grew, it pursued the rule of law first and the planting of British values second. This was not wisdom at work, but pragmatism.

The British settled the areas they conquered. To make these dangerous places safe for British women and children, the force of law was the only realistic choice. There were too few soldiers to rely on the law of force. Over time, British values—representative democracy, entrepreneurship, freedom of speech and the press, an end to slavery—took root around the world, including in the United States.

As it pushed westward toward the Pacific, the United States began with the same approach. The American epic, played out in a thousand movies and novels, is of a nation bringing the law to an untamed frontier. In the law's wake came the schoolhouse, the newspaper, the labor union, and, eventually, McDonald's.

Beyond its shores, however, America inverted the formula: spread democratic values, and the rule of law will follow. Americans by and large had—and still have—little curiosity about the rest of the world and no intention of settling there. Rather than exporting its people, it exported its cultural and political values. The world readily embraced them. Jeans and baseball caps, the T-shirt and *Friends*, watching American movies and learning to play basketball became a new language of the world, the language of modernity.

But the rule of law did not follow. All too often, what small, poor countries got was the law of force, first from their own governments and then, in many parts of the world, from the United States.

As Europe, China, Russia, and the United States go their separate ways, American presidents will find themselves freer than ever to pursue unilateral action, including "preventive" wars. Ironically, however, an America that really is free to act alone probably won't—another manifestation of its increasing inability to shape events.

Thus irony rises on irony. The wars in Korea, Vietnam, and Iraq each began as a president lashed out at his foes, at home and abroad, but these soon became struggles to sustain American supremacy. Each venture ultimately failed, bringing the United States lower. And now, humanitarian disasters such as Haiti and Darfur—crises far short of fighting a war—advertise to the world how limited is the maneuvering room that the United States possesses. Once a superpower ceases to act like one, it soon ceases to be one.

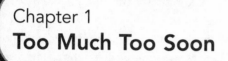

Chapter 1
Too Much Too Soon

ON AUGUST 18, 1944, HARRY S. TRUMAN LOOKED DEATH IN THE face, over lunch. This sunny afternoon, seated beneath his favorite tree, Truman was taking lunch with the president, Franklin D. Roosevelt, and although Truman at sixty brimmed with life, a deathly pallor darkened the sixty-two-year-old Roosevelt's famous face.

Senator Truman had arrived believing that the purpose of the lunch was to discuss his role as vice presidential nominee in the forthcoming election. And Roosevelt had evidently sought to please him by dining in the shade of what Truman called "the Andrew Jackson tree"—a splendid magnolia at the top of the South Lawn planted more than a hundred years earlier by his political hero.

Roosevelt told him there was a big experiment under way that could help win the war, but did not offer details. Truman chose not to press him for any. Instead, they turned their discussion to the upcoming campaign. It soon became clear, though, that Roosevelt did not expect Truman to do much, or even to add much to the ticket.[1]

There seemed to be only one thing Roosevelt wanted to convey, and that was a warning: "Harry, don't fly! You can't tell when you will have to take over this job." FDR's shaking hands made the same point: when Roosevelt tried to pour milk into his tea, most of it went into the saucer. His voice had lost its confident timbre, and he seemed to find even a brief conversation exhausting. When Truman returned to his office, he told his old friend Harry Vaughan, "Physically, he's going to pieces." And a few days later, when an old friend remarked that Roosevelt looked so ill that Truman might soon succeed him, Truman replied, "And it scares hell out of me."[2]

A month earlier, Truman had no intention of being on the ticket and had arrived at the Democratic convention in Chicago pledged to support James Byrnes of South Carolina for the vice presidency.

The current vice president, Henry Wallace, was too liberal for southern voters and too intellectual for the big-city bosses who dominated the party machine. Byrnes saw himself as the compromise candidate, but Roosevelt saw something else—Truman. As the chairman of a much-admired Senate committee dedicated to preventing corruption in wartime appropriations, Truman had won a national reputation.

He was also popular with other senators. Woodrow Wilson's dream at the end of World War I for a League of Nations that would enforce the peace had died in the Senate. Truman looked as though he might be just the man to see that Roosevelt's dreams for a new world body—the United Nations—did not die there too.[3]

The second day of the convention, the Democratic Party chairman, Robert Hannegan, got Truman together in a hotel room with some of the most powerful people in the party. We want you to be Roosevelt's running mate, they told him. And I don't want it, he told them. He was like a nail: the harder they hammered him, the deeper he dug in. Truman loved being a senator. There was not the remotest desire there to be president, still less to step into a dead man's shoes.

Hannegan finally put a call through to Roosevelt, in San Diego. The president was on his way to meet with MacArthur in Hawaii. Hannegan held up the telephone so that Truman could follow the conversation. "Bob, have you got that guy lined up yet on that vice presidency?" said Roosevelt.

"No," said Hannegan. "He's the contrariest goddam Missouri mule I ever saw."

The response came in those singular, patrician tones the whole country knew well: "You can tell him from me that if he wants to split the Democratic Party in the middle of a war and maybe lose that war, that's up to him."[4]

The threat of a split and the prospect of the Republican challenger, Thomas Dewey, replacing a giant such as Roosevelt was too serious to ignore. Truman agreed to run, provided Byrnes released him from his pledge, as Byrnes did.

"The week at Chicago was the most miserable I've ever spent, trying to prevent my own nomination to be vice president," he later told a family friend, Emmy Southern. "I was afraid of what would happen." Over lunch beneath the magnolia, those latent anxieties became powerful certainties. Roosevelt did not look like a man who could survive another four years as president.[5]

Soon after the inauguration in January, something happened to Roosevelt's signature. Once strong, even, and so stylish it looked worthy of gracing historic documents, it suddenly became a palsied scrawl, lacking energy and authority. If Truman saw it, and he may well have done so, seeing that he now presided over the Senate, it would have come as a shock to him, as it did to everyone else.[6]

Like many a southern or border state politician, Truman enjoyed hoisting a glass of bourbon around five o'clock almost any afternoon, which happened to be the hour when the Democratic speaker of the House, Sam Rayburn of Texas, held a soiree in his office for political friends and acolytes. Those invited knowingly and half-jokingly referred to these gatherings as "the Board of Education." After all, along with the booze, they imbibed Rayburn's political wisdom.

The afternoon of April 12, Truman had got his hand around a whiskey glass just as the Board went into session. Then Rayburn's phone rang. It was Steve Early, Roosevelt's press secretary, calling for Vice President Truman. "Come to the White House at once," said Early, "through the main gate."

Saying he'd probably be back in a few minutes, Truman returned to his office to collect his hat, and had his driver take him down Pennsylvania Avenue to the White House. When he reached the private quarters upstairs, Eleanor Roosevelt was waiting for him. She placed an arm around his shoulders. "Harry, the president is dead." A minute or so later the secretary of state, Edward Stettinius, arrived in tears.

No one seemed sure what to do next. Stettinius suggested a cabinet meeting be held immediately, and Truman reached, almost instinctively, for a gathering of other men around him. Truman was a joiner, a man who sat on a wallet stuffed with membership cards, and a member of the Masonic elite. He was rarely alone and then never for long.[7]

When the cabinet met at 6:00 p.m., it really had nothing much to discuss. There was too much grief. The purpose of this gathering was mutual support, not serious discussion, but they had to talk about something. Steve Early saved the moment. He came into the room and said the reporters outside wanted to know if there would be any change in the arrangements for the conference due to meet in San Francisco on April 25 to write a charter for the United Nations. "No," said Truman. "It will proceed as planned." In years to come, he would refer often to this moment as proof of two things—his commitment to world peace and the fact that he had been decisive from the first minutes of his presidency.

After the brief cabinet meeting broke up, Henry L. Stimson, the elderly secretary of war, asked for a word alone. He told Truman that the United States was developing a new kind of explosive. "It has almost unbelievable destructive power." Truman was physically and emotionally drained. It was too much to take in at such a moment.[8]

At 7:09 he was sworn in as President of the United States, in the Cabinet Room by the chief justice, Harlan Fisk Stone. Truman swore the oath on a red-edged Gideon Bible found after a brief, frantic search of West Wing bookcases and desks. When he reached the end of the oath, Truman bent over and kissed the Bible.

There were so many journalists and photographers, congressional leaders and White House staffers milling about in and around the Cabinet Room, it was a struggle getting out to where his car was waiting. He, Bess, and his daughter, Margaret, were driven back to their apartment at 4701 Connecticut Avenue, where dinner was a sandwich and a glass of milk. And then, he recalled, "Went to bed, went to sleep, did not worry any more."[9]

That was not true. In the morning he met with the leaders of Congress, and as they offered him their support, he burst into tears and wailed, "I am not big enough! I am not big enough!" And over the weeks that followed, Truman asked any number of people, "Pray for me." He assured others that he did not see how he could be president. "I'm the last man fitted to handle it," he told one. "If there ever was a man who was forced to be President, I'm that man," he told another.[10]

These outbursts expressed a characteristic humility, yet they were also an oblique reflection of crushing pressures suddenly brought to bear. Some hours after meeting with the leaders of Congress, Truman had recovered his composure and had a meeting with Byrnes. At Stimson's behest, Byrnes proceeded to give his old friend Harry an account of the Manhattan Project, the enormous secret program to build an atomic bomb. This time, Truman understood. By making atoms disintegrate and set off a chain reaction similar to the process that produced the light and energy of the sun, it would be possible to make a new kind of bomb. "It will be great enough to destroy the whole world," said Byrnes.[11]

What Truman had just been handed by Byrnes was not simply responsibility for the United States, great as that was, but responsibility for the future of the planet and the whole human race. How could he know he was up to it? Could anyone?

Less than two weeks into his presidency, Truman received a note from his secretary of war: "I think it is very important that I should have a talk with you as soon as possible on a highly secret matter." The bomb again. Stimson arrived the next day, bringing the director of the Manhattan Project, Major General Leslie Groves, with him.

Groves assured Truman that the first atomic bomb would be ready sometime in the summer. Stimson was confident that it would work. What troubled him was what might follow. The bomb would almost certainly force Japan to surrender, but then? It was only a matter of time before the Soviets produced one. There was a more worrying risk—some smaller nation might build a bomb in secret and use it against another country.

After Stimson and Groves departed, a deeply troubled Truman pushed his anxieties onto the next person he saw, J. Leonard Reinsch, a radio executive and political campaign adviser. "I am going to have to make a decision which no man in history has ever had to make," said Truman. What Reinsch made of this is unknown; sympathetic while mystified, probably. "I'll make the decision," Truman added, sounding resolute, "but it is terrifying to think about what I'll have to decide."[12]

Meanwhile, with the war in Europe drawing to a close, crucial decisions had to be made about America's future relationship with the Soviet Union. Shortly before he died, Roosevelt revealed that at Yalta he had agreed that the Soviet Union would have three seats in the United Nations General Assembly, and the British Commonwealth countries would have six. This revelation had astounded his new vice president. All the same, Truman told Stettinius, he intended to follow Roosevelt's lead. Any and every agreement the late president had made with the Soviets would be honored, whatever the consequences. As he explained to Averell Harriman, the U.S. ambassador to the Soviet Union, "Roosevelt was elected to the presidency, not me." It was his duty to carry out Roosevelt's policies and make good on his promises.[13]

First, though, he needed to find out what these promises were. Before he became president, Truman had not been shown a single secret war message between Roosevelt and the military or between Roosevelt and the Allies. In the first few months of his presidency, Truman spent hours each day reading these files, weighing their implications.[14]

Roosevelt's secret archive, crammed with messages to and from the Joint Chiefs, Churchill, Stalin, Jiang Jieshi (a.k.a. Chiang Kai-shek), Charles de Gaulle, American diplomats, and leading figures in the war industries—this was where the waters were deepest. At moments Truman felt that he risked drowning in them.

Having grown up disgusted, as most decent people were, at the crimes of Lenin and the Soviet system, Truman also lacked the intellectual sophistication of a Franklin Roosevelt, who could see possibilities beyond Communism. Truman's thinking was driven mainly by his emotions. When Hitler attacked the Soviet Union in June 1941, he was thrilled. "If we see Germany is winning, we ought to help Russia," Truman told a journalist. "And if Russia is winning, we ought to help Germany."[15]

The first test of how Truman would deal with Soviet Communists came early. On April 22 the Soviet foreign minister, Vyacheslav Molotov, stopped off to pay his respects to the new president. Molotov was on his way to the UN charter-writing conference in San Francisco. The dour Molotov—with his badly fitting serge suits, fedora, rimless spectacles, and slightly menacing air—was a figure familiar to millions of Americans from wartime newsreels that praised hard-fighting Ivan, impervious to snowdrifts and ice, advancing stolidly through Red Army artillery fire to defeat the German war machine.

Before Molotov arrived, Truman held a cabinet meeting to prepare for this, his first high-level diplomatic encounter. Stettinius said the Russians were trying to force a puppet government on Poland, in violation of the agreements Roosevelt had made with Stalin at Yalta. William D. Leahy, a five-star admiral who had served as Roosevelt's military chief of staff, disagreed.

With an office in the White House and an office in the Pentagon, Leahy had acted as the linchpin between Roosevelt and the senior military at a time when there was no chairman of the Joint Chiefs of Staff. And unlike Stettinius, Leahy had been present at Yalta. He told Truman there were two ways of interpreting the agreement on Poland. Stimson took the same view. Besides, great powers nearly always insisted on having friendly governments in states along their borders, said Stimson. In terms of great power politics, what the Soviets had demanded at Yalta was reasonable.

Truman was still trying to fathom what Yalta required. The borders of Poland had been the cause of wars and debates since before the United States came into existence, and for a time Poland had disappeared from the map. Establishing clear borders now meant casting them in an ambiguous language that drew on history, international law, and the facts of power on the ground—especially the presence across Eastern Europe of the Red Army. Ambiguity almost invariably brought Truman's excitable nature to the heights of impatience. He was being forced to state his position on the Yalta accords without feeling for a moment that he really understood them. "Every time I go over them, I find new meanings," he complained.

Yet a decision maker has to decide. He cannot retreat into general ignorance, but selective ignorance offers freedom of a kind. Whatever the deal at Yalta meant, however much Truman felt he ought to follow Roosevelt's policies, he still did not trust the Russians. He agreed

with Stettinius, said Truman. He also had some advice on how to deal
with Molotov if he caused any problems at the charter conference:
"Tell him he can go to hell."[16]

When Molotov arrived, there was an initial exchange of pleas-
antries. Truman said he would support Roosevelt's promise to allow
the Soviets to have three seats at the United Nations. Then, according to Truman's account, he tore into his visitor. So far, he said, every
agreement made between the United States and the Soviet Union
had turned out to be "a one-way street." The Americans had scrupulously adhered to every commitment, while the Soviets had violated
all of them. Molotov protested, "I have never been talked to like that
in my life." Truman brushed that aside. "Carry out your commitments
and you won't get talked to like that," he claims to have said, but
probably didn't.[17]

Molotov's recollection was different, as it was almost sure to be.
Rare is the diplomat who admits to losing an argument. "I cannot talk
with you if you take such a tone," Molotov responded, which brought
Truman up short. "Rather stupid to my mind . . . he wanted to show
who was boss," thought Molotov.[18]

Molotov had come only to pay a courtesy call on the president, but
Truman had been anything but courteous in return. A man shaped by
small-town friendliness and kindness had not only been aggressive
without provocation, but he gloated about it later. He told Joseph E.
Davies, a former ambassador to the Soviet Union, how he had humiliated Molotov. "I let him have it. It was the straight one-two to the
jaw."[19]

This was a different Truman—thrust onto the world stage, self-
conscious and unsure of himself despite a deep core of self-belief.
The president was not the same man as the senator. He described his
new, split existence to his staff, his family, or his friends. The old
Harry S. Truman they had always known was still much as before.
But now he found himself looking at a president of the United States
called Harry S. Truman and constantly asking himself, What should
the president do?[20]

Truman was relying for advice on Davies, a millionaire Democrat
whom Roosevelt had made ambassador to the Soviet Union, where
he'd gotten on well with Stalin. Davies was appalled at how Truman
had handled Molotov. Roosevelt had secured the respect of the Sovi-

ets by ignoring Communist ideology and Stalin's crimes for the sake of defeating Hitler. The war represented a chance for a fresh start in relations between the two countries, a chance that Davies and Roosevelt alike intended to seize if they could. They might not succeed, but they had a responsibility to try. Davies was hoping to bring Truman to the same realpolitik approach. Truman's temperament got in the way.

During a long talk at the White House on May 13, Davies and Truman held an earnest discussion about the Soviets. The two men were surrounded by piles of books that Truman had brought from his apartment and was putting on the shelves. The president was still in his shirtsleeves. If we pursue a tough policy, Davies told him, they will be just as tough in return. They will take it as proof that the capitalists are trying to encircle them. We must be realistic about this—push them too hard, and they won't hesitate to go it alone.[21]

Truman stayed up late at night reading and rereading the Yalta accords. Davies's successor as ambassador to the USSR, Averell Harriman, told him, wrongly, that they meant there had to be a completely independent Polish government, one that included members of the anti-Communist/anti-Soviet Polish government in exile in London, one that guaranteed a free press and free elections. Harriman allowed his emotions to dictate his views and offered himself as a counterweight to the older and wiser Davies and Stimson.

The London Poles were anathema to Stalin, for an obvious and widely publicized reason. When Hitler attacked Poland in September 1939, so did the Russians. Among their many prisoners were thousands of Polish officers, educated young men who, if they survived, would eventually become part of the Polish political and cultural elite. As ardent patriots, they could be expected to be equally ardent anti-Communists. In March 1940 Stalin reached out to shape the future by murdering nearly 26,000 Polish POWs.

Three years later, the Nazis came across one of the major Soviet execution sites, in the Katyn Forest, near Smolensk. The Germans made a propaganda coup out of these mass graves, as if they were not already murdering Jews and other prisoners by the thousands every week. The Russians tried to pin this atrocity on the Nazis. The London Poles placed the responsibility on Stalin.

After that, Stalin would never agree to allow any of these Polish political exiles to return and participate in government. Nor did the Yalta accords require him to do so. With calculated ambiguity, the accords squared what Roosevelt wanted and Stalin demanded. There was a text, crafted to satisfy public opinion in their respective countries, and a subtext that said that where the Soviets had the power, they would get their way. In all, a cynical agreement put together by two cynical men. Then one of them died.

As the Red Army advanced across Poland, a compliant provisional Polish government was established in Lublin in 1944. Harriman advised Truman to withhold recognition from the Lublin government.

The son of a railroad and shipping tycoon, Harriman had grown up in a hundred-room mansion, looked after by a hundred servants. An upper-class dilettante whose name and money had brought him an ambassadorship, he was almost a caricature of the anti-Communist plutocrat. Over time, he would come to understand the sheer complexity and messiness of the world, but for now his mind was made up. Yalta meant a free press and free elections for a free, anti-Communist Poland. Byrnes, like Leahy, had been at Yalta, and he too told Harriman, who had not been there, that he was completely wrong.[22]

Truman was showing signs of developing the "cushion effect"—bearing, that is, the impression of the last person to sit on him. When he was with Davies, he agreed with Davies; when he was with Harriman, he agreed with Harriman.

Even the German surrender, an event that ought to have marked the high point of alliance amity, had produced friction. After Hitler's suicide, his generals wanted to surrender to Eisenhower. Truman, Churchill, and Stalin rejected that. The surrender would take place in Reims at one minute past midnight, local time, the night of May 8–9. As the time approached, the Germans continued to fight hard in the east while ceasing fire in the west. Some members of the press, having been informed that the surrender would take place at one minute past midnight, couldn't keep their word, and broke the story. The Germans got what they wanted: they surrendered to Eisenhower. Infuriated, Stalin demanded that the German high command be ordered to surrender all over again, to a Soviet general, and they did so.

A few days after V-E Day, Truman received a gift from Eisenhower, one that may have raised a smile as well as gratitude at such thoughtfulness. As a former combat soldier and reserve colonel in the U.S. Army Reserve, Truman would have known the saying common in the wartime U.S. Army about what the ordinary soldier was fighting for: "The English fight for the king, the Germans fight for Hitler, the Japanese fight for the emperor . . . and Americans fight for souvenirs." Ike had sent him the pen used by the German generals to sign the instrument of surrender.[23]

He also received a hand-wringing telegram from Churchill. "I have always worked for friendship with Russia, but, like you, I feel deep anxiety because of their misinterpretation of the Yalta decisions, their attitude towards Poland, their overwhelming influence in the Balkans . . . the combination of Russian power and the territories under their control . . . above all their power to maintain very large armies in the field for a long time." And already, "an iron curtain is drawn down upon their front. We do not know what is going on behind."[24]

Truman replied that he shared Churchill's fears. The question was this: "whether our two countries are going to permit [the Russians] to engage in uncontrolled land grabbing and tactics which are all too reminiscent of those of Hitler and Japan."[25]

No one around Truman took a harder line than this, and if the president was serious, he would have a chance to express it directly to Stalin. Shortly before he died, Roosevelt had agreed to a meeting with Churchill and Stalin on July 15. Following the German surrender, Churchill suggested to Truman that the date be brought forward. Truman blandly replied that he could not leave Washington before June 30, the end of the fiscal year. In fact, he was stalling. What he intended, Truman told Davies, was to be in a position of strength when the victory meeting convened. What he did not tell Davies was that the strength he had in mind was radioactive.[26]

As the fighting came to a close in Europe, it was building to a crescendo in the Pacific. The campaign to take Okinawa had been launched on April 1. It ground on until June 28, producing 49,700 American dead and wounded, roughly 110,000 Japanese military casualties, and probably an even greater number of dead and wounded civilians.

The next big assault, Operation Olympic, would be mounted on November 1, against Kyushu, the southernmost of the home islands. The fighting was expected to be as savage as that on Okinawa, but on a much bigger scale. American ground forces had never had to fight a Japanese field army. There were two based in Manchuria and two based in Japan, still intact. The field armies in Japan could deploy up to 4 million men, armed with 3 million rifles, 90,000 fieldpieces and mortars, more than 100,000 machine guns, and at least a million tons of high explosives.

It had taken one American killed or wounded to kill or wound two Japanese soldiers and sailors on Okinawa. The army chief of staff, George C. Marshall, told Truman that on that basis, he could expect 250,000 American casualties to wrest Kyushu from its half a million defenders.[27]

The night of June 19, as the fighting on Okinawa drew to a close, Truman convened a meeting with the Joint Chiefs plus the secretaries of war and the navy. There was only one subject for discussion: What alternatives did he have to ordering the invasion of Kyushu? General Marshall and the chief of naval operations, Admiral Ernest J. King, told him that conventional bombing was not going to force the Japanese to surrender any more than it had forced the Germans to surrender. The assault would have to go ahead. The army was already moving veteran divisions from Europe to the Pacific.

Nearly everyone agreed with Marshall and King. Yet as the meeting moved toward its conclusion, it occurred to Truman that the assistant secretary of war, John J. McCloy, hadn't offered an opinion. "McCloy, you didn't express yourself, and nobody gets out of this room without standing up and being counted. Do you think I have a reasonable alternative to the decision that has just been made?"

"Mr. President, I think you have an alternative that ought to be fully explored." What McCloy was about to present to Truman was an idea that he and Stimson had discussed, but Stimson was feeling unwell this evening and preferred to have McCloy speak in his place.

McCloy said he thought the president ought to send a message to the emperor, calling on him to surrender, reminding him of America's overwhelming might; declaring that if Japan surrendered now, the nation would survive, but the emperor would have to become a constitutional monarch and Japanese industry would have access to the raw materials it needed, but on the same terms as all other countries.

If, despite these assurances, the Japanese did not surrender, the emperor should be informed that the United States possessed a new type of explosive. A single bomb based on it could destroy an entire city. If Japan refused the terms offered, such bombs would be employed to compel its unconditional surrender.

Truman said he'd been thinking along similar lines. He would like McCloy to talk it over with Mr. Byrnes. McCloy went straight to Byrnes's office. Byrnes dismissed the idea of anything short of unconditional and immediate surrender. Suppose the bomb did not work? What then? And how could the United States make its threat to use an atomic bomb credible? The Japanese, and the rest of the world, would probably think it was a bluff. They would then have to use the bomb anyway, but having given up the advantage of surprise. And finally, he said, if we appear to be seeking a deal at this stage, it will be taken as a sign of weakness. The Japanese will feel encouraged to fight on.[28]

A few days later, Truman was given a date for the test firing of an atomic device—July 16, 1945, New Mexico, the day provisionally set for the first plenary session at the conference in Berlin. Perfect timing.

Chapter 2
Man and Moment

WHEN HE FORCED TRUMAN TO ACCEPT THE NOMINATION AS VICE president, Roosevelt was pressing directly on the chord of Truman's character—loyalty. Truman remained loyal to everyone and everything that ever mattered to him. Unlike many a senator and more than a few presidents, he was not a man to betray his wife or a friend or any organization he belonged to. He was not only loyal up, but, a rarer trait, he was equally loyal toward subordinates.

A man entirely comfortable in the company of other men, there was nothing solitary or introspective about the new commander in chief. He was a 33rd-degree Mason and would one day be buried in his lambskin. When he sat at the cabinet table, there was invariably another Mason present. In the military, he found himself talking with five-star Masons such as General Marshall and Admiral Leahy. There were more than a few senior commanders he could address as "Brother."

Truman's wallet bulged with membership cards, such as the U.S. Chamber of Commerce and the American Legion. All were gold cards. The Legion card even had a small diamond set in it. This was the wallet of a man who belonged.[1]

Growing up on a hardscrabble farm in southwest Missouri, Truman hoped from an early age to escape into a military career. He saw himself as a greater natural commander than Napoleon. When West Point rejected his application, he tried Annapolis. Neither academy would take someone with a severe astigmatism. This failure, in which there was no disgrace, never ceased to rankle.

Truman was always slightly defensive about his adolescent ambition to go to West Point: "I needed to, wanted to, get a free education. I don't necessarily say it was a good one," he told an oral historian late in life. "It seems to give a man a narrow view of things, and if you're going to be a soldier and nothing else, that may work out all right. But not for any other line of work . . . They never seem to teach them anything at all about understanding people up there."[2]

Truman developed the kind of feelings toward the professional military that Andrew Jackson had possessed. A civilian soldier, Jackson treated career officers with suspicion, and was so hostile toward West Point that it was not expected to survive his presidency. And yet in his heart Jackson loved what he publicly scorned. He made sure that a nephew got an appointment.

Despite Truman's Jacksonian animadversions against West Point, he remained in thrall to Robert E. Lee and Stonewall Jackson, both of whom had graduated from the academy. During his time in the Senate, he spent hours studying applications for appointments to West Point and Annapolis, nearly always giving the nod to a bright but poor young man without political connections.

Truman's mixed emotions about the military were rooted in his army service. He joined the Missouri National Guard as a private before World War I, and when his unit was slated for deployment to France in 1918, the men of Battery D, 129th Artillery Regiment, 35th Division elected Truman their lieutenant. Before he shipped out, he had to complete an artillery course at Fort Sill, Oklahoma, where his free time was spent on what he coyly called "the study of probabilities," better known as poker.[3]

In France, the 35th was probably the most underperforming division in the American Expeditionary Forces, yet Battery D acquitted itself well. And Truman made his first venture as an entrepreneur. In partnership with another soldier, Eddie Jacobson, he set up a regimental canteen. There wasn't much for sale—toothpaste, razor blades and combs, handkerchiefs and soap, boxes of cookies and small bags of candy, and a near beer called Bevo. For men who were living in the mud and the cold, these were luxuries.[4]

After the war, Truman remained in the Army Reserve and founded the Missouri Reserve Officers' Association. He felt completely at home in a military setting, even a naval one. During the 1945 voyage to Europe aboard the cruiser *Augusta*, the gun crews held target practice. Truman stood on top of a turret during the firing, fascinated by naval gunnery techniques. "I'd still rather fire a battery than run a country," he told his diary.[5]

His poor eyesight did not hamper him as an artillery officer, but nearly all great commanders were in the branches that closed with the enemy—the infantry and the cavalry. The closest he might come to that was to join the Reserve Officers' Association pistol team. He was thwarted yet again: even with his spectacles, he couldn't see the target well enough to hit it. Competition made him perspire freely, and his glasses fogged up. In a desperate attempt to make his eyes stronger, Truman spent much of the night driving around in the dark. Fortunately, he did not kill himself or anyone else before he bowed to failure yet again and stopped.[6]

Truman loathed brass hats, especially flamboyant commanders such as MacArthur and Patton, yet his contempt for them—which may have contained a trace of envy—was balanced by his admiration for George Marshall and Dwight Eisenhower. Truman had first encountered Marshall in 1918 at an artillery school in France. Truman was an instructor there when Marshall came to conduct an inspection. Even then, Truman recalled, "everybody knew that he was just about the best of the young officers in France at the time."[7]

When Eisenhower came to see Truman at Potsdam, Truman told him, "You can have anything that's within my power to give and I'd be glad to support you for the presidency in 1948, if you have any such desire."

His admiration for Marshall was even greater. They had gotten to know each other in 1942, when Truman was chairing the wartime committee that policed defense contracts. Truman gave serious thought to resigning from the Senate and returning to active duty as a fifty-eight-year-old colonel of artillery.

Marshall's reply was, "Why, you're too old, Senator."

"Why, I'm not as old as you are by three years."

Marshall smiled rarely, but it isn't difficult to imagine the hint of a smile as he delivered the coup de grâce: "Yes, but I'm a general and I'm in and you're a colonel and you're not in."[8]

In 1944, when Truman was elected vice president, he had another request: Could his close friend Harry Vaughan be appointed his military aide? Marshall was probably surprised. Presidents had military aides, partly for ornamental reasons: they added a splash of color to social occasions and tended to be single and handsome. Vaughan was middle-aged, paunchy, and rough around the edges. Even so, Marshall granted the senator's wish this time, and Harry Vaughan became a military aide.

By the time the war ended, Truman had seen enough of Marshall to consider him the outstanding American of his generation. So when Marshall tried to resign after the Japanese surrender, Truman was astounded. Being president without Marshall to rely on was unimaginable. But just as the chord of Truman's character was loyalty, Marshall's was duty, and Truman played on it until he got Marshall to agree to stay on.[9]

Apart from Ike or Marshall, Truman found it impossible to warm to professional army officers. Maintaining a long tradition of low-grade disdain between the regulars and the rest, he never failed to identify with ordinary soldiers, especially those in combat units. Shortly after he became president, with the end of the war in Europe at hand, Truman made a broadcast to the armed forces, reminding them, "I know the strain, the mud, the misery, the utter weariness of the soldier in the field." He was declaring that he was one of them still; there are no *former* combat troops.[10]

His nephew, Lawrence Truman, was an enlisted sailor assigned to the *Missouri*. When Lawrence and his shipmates complained to the president about their terrible fare, Truman sampled it for himself. "There's no excuse," he concluded. "There's money enough, but it's just being stolen."[11]

Truman would not have been surprised by that. "You know what the military's like," he told his first budget director, Harold D. Smith. "They spend every nickel they can get their hands on."[12]

One of the ceremonies Truman enjoyed most was awarding the Congressional Medal of Honor. He personally decorated dozens of men, some of whom were horribly wounded and permanently scarred. The most moving of these ceremonies, and the one that created the greatest outpouring of public emotion, was held on September 10, 1945, when Truman awarded the Big Medal to General Jonathan Wainwright, still suffering both emotionally and physically after three years as a prisoner of the Japanese. Occasions such as this nourished Truman's deepest beliefs in the nobility of courage and sacrifice.[13]

Truman's formal education had ended in high school, and he was always defensive about that. He could neither speak nor read a foreign language, and he looked on the wider world with a xenophobe's eye. Even so, he told Dean Acheson, he had read every book in the Independence library, somewhere between 3,000 and 3,500 books.

He liked to think that years of reading had given him the equivalent of a college education, but he had missed out on the great advantage of higher education—learning to think analytically. Truman could not assemble information from a variety of sources, use it to formulate a coherent argument, and then offer it to other people who would criticize his reasoning and challenge his facts. Dean Acheson assured him that he had not missed out on anything. Wide reading and the school of hard knocks was better than anything provided by Harvard and Yale, he told Truman, and the president was happy to agree.[14]

The reading continued. There was always a pile of books on Truman's bedside table, mostly histories and biographies. He loved to talk about famous battles, and he had an almost encyclopedic knowledge of the Civil War. He was not, however, interested in twentieth-century political or economic history.[15]

Once he became a historical figure in his own right, he was defensive about what historians might make of his record. Truman derided them as "eggheads" and "contemplators 'after the fact.'" He convinced himself that the best history was written by the people who made it, men such as Julius Caesar and Cicero, and, by implication, himself.[16]

His character was solid and true, yet Truman's intellectual grasp often took the shape of a question mark. At times, he readily acknowledged this limitation, but it did not stop—and may even have encouraged—a desire to ridicule people known for their brains, such as Albert Einstein. "Needs a bath and a haircut" was Truman's opinion of the man often credited with being the most intelligent figure of the twentieth century.[17]

Truman took an interest in art and architecture, yet he despised modern art—"ham and eggs," he called it, meaning it looked as if someone had thrown ham and eggs at a wall. And just as he ridiculed the most famous thinker of the age, he also sneered at Pablo Picasso and said he should never be allowed into the United States because "he's a Communist."[18]

Here, then, was a man almost wholly of a particular time and a provincial place. Truman's world consisted of Jackson County, the Masonic lodge, Senate corridors and committee rooms, American Legion halls, the home he shared with his wife and daughter, and the landscape embedded in his imagination—southwestern Missouri, still loyal to the Confederacy, still suspicious of Yankees. His mother was as unreconstructed a rebel as anyone could meet. Before she would accept an invitation to stay at the White House, she told Truman that if he put her in the Lincoln bedroom, she would "sleep on the floor."[19]

Most journalists liked Truman, for his directness and his willingness to tolerate almost any criticism of himself. Yet there were limits. One day in 1946, when Drew Pearson went to the White House to talk about postwar demobilization, Truman told him he wasn't interested in discussing that. "You've been writing some nasty things about my family. And I want you to know something. Down in Missouri we put our women on a pedestal, and I'm going to keep them there. Now, over in that desk I've got a gold plated automatic pistol that was given to me for a present. And, you son of a bitch, if you write one more derogatory line about my women, I'm going to take that pistol and use it on you!"[20]

Truman could charm people by acknowledging his limitations: "I do the very best I can . . . and I talk to the good Lord, and that's all there is to it." Yet he could not stand to be compared with his towering predecessor. Once, when he was criticized for not being big enough to be president, Truman snapped, "Well, who is big enough?" The shadow of FDR fell over the White House far into the Truman presidency.[21]

To sustain him as he struggled to fulfill his role as commander in chief at a time filled with challenges short of war and a long way from peace, Truman turned for encouragement to his wife, to poetry, to religion, to iconography, and to medication.

Although Truman spent many hours working on speeches and public announcements with his cabinet and the White House staff, in the end Bess Wallace Truman read the nearly finished drafts. If Bess did not like something, out it went.[22]

The president also drew for support on great verse, and it was not only membership cards that strained his wallet. There was a quotation that he had written out from "Locksley Hall," by Alfred, Lord Tennyson:

> *For I dipt into the future, far as human eye*
> *could see,*
> *Saw the Vision of the world, and all*
> *the wonder that would be;*
>
> *Saw the heavens fill with commerce,*
> *argosies of magic sails,*
> *Pilots of the purple twilight dropping*
> *down with costly bales;*
>
> *Heard the heavens fill with shouting,*
> *and there rain'd a ghastly dew*
> *From the nations' airy navies grappling*
> *in the central blue;*
>
> *Far along the world-wide whisper of the*
> *south-wind rushing warm,*
> *With the standards of the peoples plunging*
> *thro' the thunder-storm;*
>
> *Till the war-drum throbb'd no longer,*
> *and the battle-flags were furl'd . . .*

Truman reread this passage so often that over his life, he estimated, he had copied it out more than twenty times. Tennyson's poem, published in 1842, offered Truman an assurance that a man *could* look far into the future and find promise there: commerce in the skies, war in the skies, and, beyond that, peace on Earth.[23]

Truman was also a deeply religious man, attending church regularly without need of prodding. In his first appearance before Congress, four days after becoming president, he quoted 1 Kings 3:9: "Give therefore thy servant an understanding heart to judge thy people, that I may discern between good and the bad; for who is able to judge this thy so great a people?" And this, from 2 Chronicles 1:10: "Give me now wisdom and knowledge, that I may go out and come in before this people: for who can judge this thy people, that is so great?" While Truman ridiculed the idea that the Jews were God's chosen people, he seemed willing to extend that idea to Americans.

He had been convinced since 1920 that God intended the United States to break with its isolationist past and assume the leading role in maintaining world peace. The League of Nations project had foundered, to Truman's dismay, but with the end of the Second World War, he was certain that God's plan for America could finally be put into action.[24]

And Truman's God was not just watching, but acting. At the end of May 1945, he saw the hand of providence at work "since becoming Chief Executive and Commander in Chief. Things have gone so well that I can't understand it—except to attribute it to God. He guides me."[25]

The iconography that sustained him was mainly in the Oval Office. Three pictures faced Truman from the opposite wall as he sat at his desk. In the center, above the mantel, was a painting of the frigate *Constitution* in action. To its left was a Rembrandt Peale portrait of George Washington; to the right was a portrait of Simon Bolívar, the Washington-style hero of South American history. Back when Truman was a judge in Jackson County, Missouri, he had the county pay to erect a life-size statue of Andrew Jackson on horseback, and on his Oval Office desk was a miniature version of the same. There was also a small gift from an admirer—a sign showing a bucking Missouri mule and the now famous legend, in gold letters, THE BUCK STOPS HERE. The American flag was a few feet from the desk, and for Truman the flag was both imago and icon. He liked to assure people that the most beautiful sight an American could ever see was Old Glory flying over foreign soil.

And finally, there was the medication. During Truman's eight years in the Senate he had proved to be one of its worst public speakers. He couldn't wait to put the ordeal of a speech behind him and rushed through every sentence and into the next. It was hard to follow what he was saying. He was a man who expressed himself far better in the corridors and cloakrooms and the Board of Education.

At some point he evidently sought medical advice on why he became panicky before giving a speech. His lungs filled with fluid, impairing his breathing and reducing the oxygen flow to the brain. The navy doctor assigned to look after the health of members of the Senate diagnosed Truman as suffering from pulmonary edema, which is often the result of a heart attack. Even when there is no history of heart failure, pulmonary edema is nevertheless a life-threatening condition; all the more reason, then, to avoid giving speeches.

When he came under pressure, Truman feared that his nerves were about to get the better of him. He called his illness "the old-lady reaction." Yet he could not afford to be paralyzed by it if he was going to function as president. In August 1945 he took on a new doctor, Wallace H. Graham, the son of a doctor Truman had served with in the Army Reserve for more than twenty years. He finally received medical help for the old-lady reaction, but its existence and the treatment for it would be the most deeply held secret of his presidency.

Graham feared that the truth about Truman's health might somehow get out. To prepare the ground, he talked in a roundabout way with Eben Ayers, the assistant press secretary. The president has a persistent health problem, said Graham, but he was not going to explain it or go into the details. It was enough for Ayers to know that the problem could be controlled with medication. He had not even told Truman just what it was, said Graham. "It will be time enough to tell the president when he is about to end his term of office." Ayers was bewildered, but at least he now knew there was a health story that might break at any time—if, say, Truman had a heart attack.[26]

Besides treating Truman as he would any other patient with pulmonary edema, such as giving him diuretics, Dr. Graham also relied on a medication that his doctor father concocted. Just what was in it remains a mystery. It must have been a drug that would engender a sense of being in control, of being on top of almost any situation.

Truman's need for mood-enhancing drugs to see him through times of crisis did not fade. If anything, it increased. His political foes liked to imagine that he was reaching for the bourbon when the pressure was on, but he had evidently tried that and found that at the commander in chief level, the old cures didn't work. Instead, he sent for the doctor. "Got any of that damn snake oil, doc?" he'd ask. "It works!"[27]

When Truman went to war, some of it was Harry. The rest was chemistry.

Chapter 3
Position of Strength

TRUMAN HAD KNOWN SINCE THE GERMAN SURRENDER WHAT HE wanted from the victory meeting. "The Russians are like people from across the tracks whose manners are very bad," he told Henry Wallace, but the long journey to Potsdam would be worth it if he returned with only a single agreement: "To be sure to get Russia into the Japanese war and save the lives of 100,000 American boys." Stalin had agreed at Yalta to enter the war in exchange for the Kuril Islands and Japanese possessions along the periphery of East Asia. Truman intended to hold Stalin to that pledge.[1]

Part of his preparation involved selective amnesia. "I'm not afraid of Russia," he wrote in his diary shortly before he departed for Berlin. "They've always been our friends and I can't see any reason why they shouldn't always be." He was choosing to forget American military intervention in the Russian civil war in the early 1920s. Relations between the two countries had been adversarial until Roosevelt became president in 1933 and the United States finally recognized the Soviet government.[2]

Truman journeyed to Europe aboard the cruiser *Augusta* rather than fly: there was no vice president to step into his place should he perish in an airplane disaster over the Atlantic. The sea air was invigorating, the pace aboard ship relaxing, and in obedience to what was considered the first duty of a soldier—looking after his body—Truman took his usual brisk morning walk. He traveled around the top deck at 120 paces to the minute, the quick march speed of the army.[3]

The *Augusta* docked in Antwerp on July 15, and a beaming Eisenhower welcomed him to Europe. The presidential party was then driven through Flanders fields carpeted with bright red poppies. In Brussels they boarded the presidential airplane, *The Sacred Cow*, its name a testament to Roosevelt's whimsical sense of humor. Above Frankfurt, it was met by an escort of P-47 fighters. Truman would arrive at Berlin's Gatow Airport as a conqueror should, with a military flourish.[4]

As Truman, Byrnes, and Leahy disembarked, a Soviet diplomatic delegation waited to greet them on the tarmac. Dressed in gray uniforms with gold buttons and gold braid, they looked as if they had gathered for a doormen's convention. Their presence nevertheless had a serious side—they were a white-glove reminder that the president was now in the Soviet zone.

Truman was driven the twelve miles to Babelsberg, a suburb that had suffered only minor damage. Soviet military outriders and a truckload of American troops escorted his limousine. For the entire journey a Red Army soldier was posted every fifty feet or so, on both sides of the road. Many wore the green hats of frontier troops from Central Asia and the Soviet far east, their Asiatic appearance guaranteed to terrify and humiliate the Germans.

Code-named Terminal, the meeting would take place in the vicinity of Sans Souci, Frederick the Great's summer palace in Potsdam. On Truman's first morning there, he found himself with time on his hands. As he awaited the arrival of Stalin, there came the sound of huge explosions, as if the war still raged. Only later did he learn that the explosions were the work of Red Army demolition squads blowing up German mines.

Seizing the opportunity, Truman went to take a look at Berlin and what war had wrought. Along the way into the city, Truman's motorcade halted so that he could review the 2nd Armored Division (Rein-forced), drawn up along one side of the deserted four-lane autobahn. With five thousand vehicles and twenty thousand soldiers, there seemed to be tanks, command cars, half-tracks, jeeps, tank destroy-ers, self-propelled howitzers, and two-and-a-half-ton trucks stretching to the horizon. Overstrength and over here.

Truman pinned a Presidential Unit Citation to the guidon of an ar-mored engineer company and made a short impromptu speech. He could not resist adding a personal note: "I only wish I could have played a more active part in the war myself." Seeing these men—battle-hardened veterans with the adamantine confidence that only victory confers—left the colonel in Truman deeply moved and slightly envious.

What walls remained standing in Berlin, whether of brick or stone, were streaked with sooty black lines, the signature of flamethrowers. Truman gazed on the ruins of the Reichschancellery and what was left of the balcony from which Hitler had addressed huge adoring crowds. "It is a terrible thing," Truman told the journalists crowding around, "but they brought it on themselves. That's what happens when a man overreaches himself."[5]

The ruins of Berlin left him in a melancholy and ruminative mood. When he returned to his villa, Truman's thoughts turned to other proud cities reduced by war to shattered walls and gaping roofs—Carthage, Rome, Jerusalem. And for good measure, he threw in At-lantis. The future suddenly looked bleak. "I hope for some sort of peace," he wrote in his diary, "but I fear that machines are ahead of morals by some centuries . . ."[6]

That evening, as Truman finished dinner, Stimson and Marshall ar-rived with news. Truman took them upstairs to the library. The atomic bomb test in the New Mexico desert had been a huge success, they said—every bit as powerful, as stunningly devastating as anyone had dared hope for.

Truman went back downstairs a man transformed. The gloominess that had enveloped him since the visit to the bunker was gone. His step was lighter. The smile was back. He informed the others gath-ered at the dinner table—Byrnes, Leahy, Joe Davies, et al.—that what Stimson and Marshall had reported just now reminded him of a story about a young girl who told her boyfriend she thought she was pregnant. If the doctor confirmed it, she added, she would drown herself in the lake. The boyfriend sighed and said, "Dearest, that takes a great load off my mind." And that was just how Truman said he felt: "A great load has been taken off my mind."[7]

Stalin arrived that same evening, a mass murderer, but not trailing clouds of sulfur or dragging a tail. He had suffered a heart attack a few days earlier, and he began his relationship with the new president by telling Truman when they met up that his doctors had forbidden him to fly, which explained his tardy arrival by train. In truth, Stalin—a self-bestowed name that meant "man of steel"—was terrified of flying. Aloft, it was always a white-knuckle ride and an ashen face.

At that first meeting, Truman and Stalin talked for two hours. Truman was fascinated by this quasi-legendary figure. Only five feet four inches tall, his teeth brown from smoking fifty or sixty cigarettes a day, his face covered with small scars from a childhood illness, his left hand always tucked into a pocket to disguise a crippled arm, this short, stocky man exuded power and had cultivated a direct manner and unaffected charm, such as an impressionable westerner might expect—even hope for—from a warmhearted Russian peasant. Truman fell for it, but so, too, had Churchill and Roosevelt. Knowing what they hoped to see, Stalin did not disappoint.

The two leaders also had a fair amount in common. Neither had been to college, and both felt defensive about it; both had grown up in struggling families; both retained provincial accents and provincial ways that brought ridicule from the more worldly-wise; both spent much of their free time reading history and biography.

At this first meeting, they discussed a mutual enemy—Hitler. Stalin said he was convinced that Hitler was still alive. The Soviets had searched Berlin for him, or his remains, and found nothing. He was no doubt alive somewhere. Stalin's bet was Argentina.

This was bizarre. Soviet soldiers had disinterred Hitler's charred remains from the grounds of the Führerbunker, identified them from dental records, and interviewed the SS soldier who had thrown gasoline on the bodies of Hitler and Eva Braun before setting them ablaze. What was left of Hitler was now in a small box at a hospital only a few miles from Potsdam. Stalin, however, refused to believe that Hitler was dead, and never changed his mind, which may not have been so surprising.

As one of Stalin's modern biographers, Edvard Radzinsky, noticed, "if Hitler had not existed, Stalin would have had to invent him." Without Hitler, Stalin would have been little more than a despotic mass murderer. It was Hitler who made it possible for Stalin to present himself to the world—and to himself—as the savior of Communism and the Soviet Union.[8]

Having performed his principal duty at Potsdam, Stimson found himself with nothing much to do, and to help fill the time, he asked Truman if he could meet Stalin. A day or two later, Stalin invited him to call. The Stalin charm worked yet again. Stimson emerged more inclined than ever to give the Russians the benefit of the doubt.[9]

Stalin did not sway everyone, though. The more Admiral Leahy saw of Stalin at Potsdam, the deeper his disdain. Leahy told Truman, "Stalin is a liar and a crook."[10]

For the moment, Truman chose to go with his instincts. After their initial two-hour meeting, he informed his diary, "I can deal with Stalin. He is honest—but smart as hell." He was delighted when Stalin said, without any prompting, that the Soviets would declare war on Japan by the middle of August.

Truman was curious to know what had really happened to the Polish officers in the Katyn Forest, after all the claims and counterclaims. Stalin made a dismissive gesture: a man of steel does not waste his time on trivia. "Oh," Stalin replied, "they went away."[11]

After this meeting, Truman told Joe Davies, who had come to Potsdam as an unofficial adviser, "I could go home now. I got what I came for."[12]

The Potsdam Conference was meant to be merely the first rung of a three-rung ladder to international peace, a peace that would be secured by the United Nations. The second rung would be the creation of a Council of Foreign Ministers (CFM). The foreign ministers of the five permanent members of the UN Security Council would meet in a few months and resolve whatever important issues remained between them. And finally, a peace conference would bring the victorious allies together with the defeated enemy nations and hammer out peace treaties based on the agreements reached by the CFM.

The whole scheme, when taken at face value, seemed wonderfully harmonious and forward-looking. The first full session at Potsdam, on July 17, 1945, exposed the gap between promise and reality. There was an undercurrent of tension that was never absent, even at the most harmonious sessions. Stalin said he thought they ought to deal with the difficult matters first, and proceeded to complain bitterly over the way the Germans had been able to take advantage of surrender talks while the Soviets were frozen out. Although the Allies had agreed not to negotiate separately with the Germans, in Italy the Russians had been excluded from the surrender talks and the Germans were allowed to prolong the discussions long enough to transfer entire divisions over to the eastern front, where they continued to fight.[13]

The next day was devoted to Poland. Churchill launched into a heartfelt and eloquent disquisition that moved Stalin at one point to interject with a compliment: *"Horoshiro!"* meaning "excellent."

Truman was being overshadowed by Churchill and Stalin even though he had been chosen to serve as the presiding officer. He passed a note to Davies: "Joe, how am I doing?" Davies scribbled a reply: "You are batting 1000%. You are holding your own with the best at this table."[14]

The Polish question dogged the discussions from beginning to end. Churchill reminded everyone at the conference table that Britain had gone to war with Germany in September 1939 over Poland, even though it had no treaty obligation to do so. It was honor bound to see that Poland emerged from the war with a government its people supported. Truman reminded Stalin that he could not ignore the views of the five or six million Americans of Polish descent who wanted a truly free Poland.

Stalin responded that as the Red Army advanced, it had to install friendly and cooperative governments in its rear, for security reasons. Having done so, it could not now abandon those Poles who had been willing to help Russia when it was fighting for its life.

There was also the problematic question of redrawing the boundaries of Poland so that parts of eastern Poland would be granted to Russia. Poland would make up for its loss by gaining parts of eastern Germany. The net result, as Churchill complained to Truman, was that the Soviets had advanced into the heart of Western Europe.[15]

During a leisurely lunch with Churchill on July 18, Truman showed him the messages from New Mexico. Obviously I have to tell the Russians at some point, Truman acknowledged—but when? Churchill advised him to do it soon.

Although Truman had come to Germany wary of Churchill, seeing himself as something of a mediator between Churchill and Stalin, the two men took a liking to each other from the moment they met. Each spoke frankly, freely, and flatteringly. The United States owed a debt to the British, Truman said, for holding Hitler at bay despite all the odds. "If you had gone down like France, we might be fighting the Germans on the American coast at the present time."

While Truman looked to the future, feeling hopeful, Churchill looked to the present, with dread. Ever since the Athenian golden age, the threat to Europe had always come from the East. The Greeks had defeated the Persians, but after them came the Huns, the Vandals and the Goths, the Moors, the Tartars and the Turks, and now it was the turn of the Russians, who were as much Asiatic as European.

The only reliable counter to the new threat, Churchill said, was to continue the Anglo-American alliance. They should not only continue to use each other's air and naval bases all over the world, but they should cooperate more closely than ever. "Why should an American battleship calling at Gibraltar not find the torpedoes to fit her tubes, and the shells to fit her guns, deposited there?"

"Your language is very near my own heart," said Truman.[16]

Three days later, when Truman awoke from the long nap that he took after lunch each day, Stimson came to him with a detailed account of the atomic test. It had generated the explosive power of fifteen thousand to twenty thousand tons of TNT. Enough, that is, to destroy a large city. Truman had wanted to believe this weapon would force the Japanese to surrender. Now he knew for certain.

And yet . . . second thoughts. Too late, though, like most second thoughts. There would be a usable bomb by August 1, and another, even more powerful, would be ready soon after. Truman's desires went into reverse. Suddenly he did not want the Soviets to get into the war with Japan. They were no longer needed to save American lives, and Stalin would probably demand a role in the occupation. And what else? Bases on Japanese soil?

The physicist who directed scientific research on the Manhattan Project, J. Robert Oppenheimer, had recalled an expression from the Bhagavad Gita—"Brighter than a thousand suns"—when the device strapped to a hundred-foot tower in the desert exploded. The bomb's dazzling power had blinded Truman, Stimson, and Marshall to its implications for the endgame. They had got the Russians to promise to declare war on Japan, only to wish fervently that they hadn't done so. Here was one agreement they wanted Stalin to break. And Truman still had not informed Stalin about the bomb.

When the formal session on July 24 broke up, he went over to Stalin and Molotov and, through Stalin's interpreter, Vladimir Pavlov, told them that the United States had developed a new, unusually powerful explosive. Stalin merely nodded and was studiously incurious. He could not have seemed more unimpressed without yawning. Molotov remained stony-faced. Truman, having hoped to get a reaction, turned away disappointed.[17]

He decided that Stalin had no inkling of what kind of explosive he was talking about. But the Soviets had been working on an atomic bomb for more than two years, and among those who advised Stalin on it was Molotov. There were also Soviet sympathizers and Communists passing technical and scientific reports on the Manhattan Project to Soviet handlers. "They neatly stole just what we needed," Molotov recalled. It had been a success twice over—first the espionage, then the bomb.[18]

Stalin had known about the Manhattan Project long before Truman did, and he knew there was going to be a test firing in New Mexico. Even so, he had been indignant at Roosevelt's silence, and now he had to listen to Truman's pretense of openness. "Roosevelt could have done it at Yalta. He could simply have told me the atom bomb was going through its experimental stages. We were supposed to be allies," Stalin complained to Molotov.[19]

Byrnes was taken aback that the Soviets were so unimpressed by news of the atomic bomb test. Why were they being so stubborn? "You're reckoning without the Russians," said Davies. The president had to forget about using the bomb to pressure them. Not only would it fail; it would probably lead to another world war.[20]

Byrnes, a neophyte in foreign policy and national security, was seemingly the principal adviser to a president who was also a neophyte on the world stage. Truman had appointed him secretary of state not for any experience he had in world affairs—he had virtually none—but as a counterweight to an awkward fact: there was no vice president. Byrnes might not be able to contribute much as secretary of state, but he was well qualified to be president—better qualified in many respects than Truman. "Able and conniving" was how Truman described him. "My but he has a keen mind!" Even so, Truman was making himself what Roosevelt had been, his own secretary of state.[21]

He would also have to act as his own ambassador to the Russians. Harriman was at Potsdam but had destroyed whatever effectiveness he might have had by calling the Russians "barbarians." Stalin and Molotov, certain to hear of it, would resent it as a racist slur. Harriman had also remarked during the UN conference in San Francisco that war with the Soviet Union was inevitable. There were reports, too, that he was one of those who had the president's ear and used it to urge that he wage "a preventive war" against the Soviet Union. Recognizing that he had become a liability, Harriman resigned shortly after the conference ended.[22]

Truman had arrived at Potsdam with a big idea of his own—free navigation rights on international rivers and straits. The Montreux Convention of 1936 governed passage between the Mediterranean and the Black Sea via the Dardanelles. Now that convention stood in need of revision: among its ten signatories were Nazi Germany and the Japanese Empire. Truman proposed that any major waterway that ran between two or more countries should be internationalized and open to all the ships of the world. "I do not want to fight another war in twenty years because of a quarrel on the Danube," he said.[23]

Churchill did not consider the proposal worth spending much time on, and Stalin brushed it aside as irrelevant. What Stalin wanted was a naval base on Turkish territory close to the Dardanelles, with an explicit right for Soviet ships to pass through in times of peace or war without any interference from the Turks. Under the Montreux Convention, any ship carrying any cargo was allowed to pass through, and in war, so were the warships of any country not at war with Turkey. The Turks, however, had refused to allow Soviet warships through during World War II, and they blocked Lend-Lease shipping as well rather than risk infuriating the Germans.

To Truman's astonishment, when Stalin talked about the straits, years of pent-up fury poured out. The Russians had a naval base on the straits in the nineteenth century, he said. Britain and France had also promised them a base during World War I, when Turkey was allied with Germany. That promise had been broken. Russia was only demanding the restoration of a former right and the fulfillment of a solemn promise. Truman cannot have imagined, as he listened to Stalin talk about gaining a naval base on the straits, that this issue would go far toward shaping his presidency and defining his legacy.

The American agenda for Potsdam consisted of thirteen items, including the Dardanelles, as well as Korea and "Oil Resources in the Middle East." At the top of Stalin's agenda came reparations, which did not appear on Truman's list. The Polish question was going to be resolved in Stalin's favor, and everyone knew it. The Red Army, with its tanks and artillery, would ultimately give him nearly everything he wanted in Poland. Reparations, though, depended on American and British agreement, and he thought he had achieved an agreement in principle at Yalta to $10 billion from the Germans.[24]

Compared with the cost of World War II to all those involved—at least a trillion dollars and probably a lot more—the $10 billion was small change. It barely touched on the destruction done to Soviet factories, homes, railroads, government property, and economic output. Stalin had asked Ivan Maisky, a well-known Russian politician, diplomat, and writer, to make an estimate of how long it would take for the economy to recover. Maisky's estimate was twenty years. In effect, the Soviet Union would not be able to afford to fight another major war for a generation. Stalin did not worry about that. No one was going to start another war for fifteen to twenty years, he told a gathering of Communist leaders shortly after the German surrender.[25]

But who would truly be paying reparations? The British had discovered after World War I that the reparations forced on Germany by the French were paid for in large part by British taxpayers. It was the victors who fed the vanquished, the victors who financed reconstruction. That was the only way the Germans could be kept from starving to death, the only way that reparations were paid. The British had no intention of paying for German reparations again, and Truman was not going to pay for them either.

As he sat at the huge conference table beneath two enormous and ugly iron chandeliers, Truman saw nothing but trouble ahead. How was he going to sell whatever came out of these meetings to a Congress mainly under Republican control?

"The Constitution contemplates cooperation in foreign affairs between the Executive and the Legislature," he told Davies. "I'm thinking of asking for Byrnes's resignation, making Joe Martin [the

Republican speaker of the House] the Secretary of State, and then resigning myself. That would make Martin President and create a Republican President for a Republican Congress. That would bring this situation to a head." That was never going to happen, of course, but it caught his mood and his imagination. Too many boring meetings, and his thoughts drifted into fantasies of masterly control that would astound and amaze.[26]

Time and again at Potsdam, agreement was out of reach, even though the world's three most powerful men sat at the table. One issue after another was set aside, to be dealt with by the Council of Foreign Ministers. How should the German fleet be divided up? Should the pro-Communist governments of Bulgaria and Romania be recognized? Should the United Nations deny membership to Spain so long as Francisco Franco, who was practically a fascist, ruled it?

Throughout these discussions, Churchill had a shadow—Clement Attlee, leader of the Labour Party. A British general election had been called for the end of July. In case Churchill and the Conservative Party were ousted, Attlee could return to Potsdam and maintain the continuity of a British prime ministerial presence. Truman persuaded Churchill to sign a surrender demand to the Japanese before he returned to London. As Churchill walked away from the table for the last time, his eyes glistened with emotion, but his head remained high, his chin thrust out in best British bulldog style. He knew he might not be coming back.

In his haste to secure Churchill's signature, Truman either forgot to tell Stalin about it or chose not to do so. Either way, Stalin was bound to consider it a case of the Americans and the British slighting the Soviets, and he resented it deeply, doubly so when he learned that the Chinese government had also been allowed to sign the surrender demand.

Truman wanted to give the Japanese one last chance before the atomic bomb was unleashed. On July 26, the day after Churchill's departure, the Potsdam Declaration was submitted to the Japanese government and the world's press. It was couched more as a list of promises than as a manifesto of threats. Unconditional surrender would offer the chance of a new beginning. Japan would survive as a nation, its people would survive as a race, their religion would be guaranteed along with a free press, and military occupation would last only as long as it took to install a democratic government. The future of the emperor was left ambiguous, but if the war continued, one thing was certain—"prompt and utter destruction."[27]

While the declaration was being read around the world, so were the results of the British election. To the astonishment of Truman and most Americans, Churchill was voted out of office. British voters remembered Churchill as Americans did not—a man who had been the worst chancellor of the exchequer in living memory, a foe of organized labor, and an ardent imperialist. He was a man for the drama of war, not the prosaic domestic narratives of a country scarred by rubble and bomb craters, its savings gone, its debts crushing, its exhausted, demoralized citizens struggling to rebuild their lives.

Two days after the election, Attlee returned to Potsdam. There was still no response from the Japanese to the call for unconditional surrender. But, Stalin announced, the Japanese ambassador to the Soviet Union had requested that the Soviets act as mediators to end the war in the Pacific. An emissary from the emperor was prepared to leave for Moscow at once to discuss terms and conditions of surrender. Truman and Attlee and everyone with them waited in suspense as Stalin dragged out the moment. "To this statement there is nothing to add—except our reply. The answer to Japan is . . . No."[28]

With Churchill gone, never to return, Truman lost interest in the conference. Why couldn't the outstanding matters be settled by the Council of Foreign Ministers? There seemed no point in sitting at the table any longer. Besides, he had come to loathe Molotov, whose answer to everything seemed to be *nyet*.

Truman's impatience to go home set Joe Davies thinking, and Davies sensed that Stalin too was looking for a way to speed things along. "Now is the time to get down to some horse trading," Davies told Byrnes. "Why not tie up reparations, the satellite states, the Polish border in a package proposal and secure an agreement through simultaneous concessions, and dispose of all of them together?"

"I think you've got something there," Byrnes replied. The next day, he suggested to Molotov that the two most difficult issues—Poland and reparations—should be resolved in a single deal. The Russians weren't going to get everything they wanted on reparations any more than the Americans could get everything they wanted on Poland. Give us a break on the borders, Byrnes told them, and we'll give you a break on reparations. The impasse was broken, and Stalin complimented Byrnes. "You are the most honest horse thief I have ever met!" Truman thought that was hilarious.[29]

On August 2, the conference broke up, having resolved almost nothing. Yet it had served as a classroom for Truman. This was where he began his education in world statesmanship and discovered that he could hold his own. "I feel comfortable with Churchill and Stalin," he told Joe Davies a week into the conference. "It is always easier to get along with big men."[30]

On August 6, 1945, as the *Augusta* made flank speed toward Norfolk, Virginia, Truman was having lunch with the crew. Captain Frank A. Graham, an army officer assigned to the White House message center, handed him a telegram. Truman scanned it. The first atomic bomb had been dropped, on Hiroshima. Initial reports indicated complete success.

Truman's plain features broke into a huge smile. Jumping to his feet, he shook the officer's hand. "This is the greatest thing in History! Show it to the Secretary of State."[31]

He then turned back to the crew, now agog with anticipation. "Please keep your seats and listen for a moment," said their commander in chief. "We have just dropped a new bomb on Japan that has more power than twenty thousand tons of TNT. It has been an overwhelming success!" The crew—from the humblest swabbie to the most senior officer present—let out a football crowd roar. One sailor was heard to shout, "I guess I'll get home sooner now!"[32]

A public statement, composed some days earlier in the Pentagon, was released in Truman's name from the *Augusta*. It began, "Sixteen hours ago an American airplane dropped one bomb on Hiroshima, an important Japanese army base. That bomb had more power than 20,000 tons of TNT." The description of an entire city of 350,000 people being a military base was an interesting example of judicious phraseology. What haunted Truman was that he knew better. The statement went on to give a brief general history of the bomb's development, but it also sounded a flourishing note: "We have spent two billion dollars on the greatest scientific gamble in history—and won."[33]

The military leaders who governed Japan voted 6–0 to continue fighting the war, in hopes of better surrender terms if they appeared resolute. Besides, the Americans might not have any more of these terrible bombs. The Russians had no such illusions. They were not expected to declare war on Japan until August 15. Hiroshima changed their minds. They declared war on Japan on August 8.

The second bomb was based on plutonium instead of uranium. It would be four times more powerful than the bomb that had killed seventy thousand people in Hiroshima, and it would be dropped as a matter of course. Truman did not have to make a second decision. It was employed against the city of Nagasaki on August 9, and the toll of dead and injured was more than double that at Hiroshima.

The Japanese military government was split 3–3 this time, which allowed the emperor to cast what amounted to the tie-breaking vote: "We must endure the unendurable," said Hirohito. Even so, the Japanese sought clarification on the position of the emperor. Truman assured them that they would choose their own form of government—an indirect guarantee, but acceptable. On August 14 Truman announced the surrender of Japan.

Even before then, he had instructed Stimson and Marshall not to drop any more atomic bombs without his specific authorization. What troubled him, he told the cabinet, was "all those kids."[34]

MacArthur insisted that the Japanese must surrender to him. The navy, taking what amounted to a proprietary view of the war in the Pacific, was indignant. Truman, however, was gracious enough to let MacArthur have his way. To appease the sailors, the ceremony would take place aboard a warship, and to please the president, the navy selected the battleship *Missouri*.

After the surrender in Tokyo Bay, Stalin sent Truman an autographed photograph, which he had framed and placed on his desk. Eisenhower gave him the globe that he had used as supreme Allied commander in fighting the war, and MacArthur sent him . . . nothing.[35]

Truman faced a world finally at peace, but not at peace with itself. On his return from Potsdam, he had issued a lengthy anodyne statement, but in two places he expressed something of his true feelings: "How glad I am to be home again!" and "How grateful I am to Almighty God that this land of ours has been spared!"[36]

The ruins of Europe, and the sight of streams of refugees carrying their possessions in handcarts or on their backs, were as depressing as they were unforgettable. "I would not want to live in Europe," he told his staff, "and I never want to go back." But he had gained something from the trip to Potsdam. He liked Stalin and was ready to trust him. Truman declared, "He is one of those people who, if he says something one time will say it the next time. In other words, he can be depended upon."[37]

The most pressing problem he confronted was getting control over the atomic bomb. If it did not happen now, it never would. The ability to release atomic energy was going to be an irresistible lure. Nuclear fuel could be used to generate electricity; refine it even further, and it could be used in a bomb. How would the world get the benefits of the one and avoid the dangers of the other?

Truman convened a cabinet meeting on September 21 to discuss nothing but the atomic bomb. This would be the day when Henry Stimson's long public service came to a close. He would step down as secretary of the army. Truman asked him to open the meeting.

Stimson read out a memorandum that he had shown Truman more than a week earlier. Truman had tacitly agreed with its main argument—there was no way of keeping "the secret" of the bomb, because in science nothing remains secret for long. It was also inevitable that future bombs would be much more powerful, and some scientists feared that they might even ignite the oxygen in the atmosphere, destroying all life on Earth. Controlling the bomb meant talking to the Russians and working through the United Nations.[38]

Truman reminded his cabinet that he wasn't proposing that they tell anybody how to make an atomic bomb. What was under discussion here was what should be done about sharing scientific knowledge in a way that would direct atomic energy into peaceful uses only.

Byrnes was in London for a meeting of the Council of Foreign Ministers, but his deputy, Dean Acheson, said that he agreed with Secretary Stimson. So did Henry Wallace, a member of the five-man committee that had launched the bomb project back in 1941. The idea that the only people who possessed this knowledge were Americans was wrong, said Wallace: "The whole approach originated in Europe. It would be impossible to bottle the thing up no matter how hard we try."[39]

The secretary of the navy, James Forrestal, disagreed emphatically. The Russians were just like the Japanese, he said—"Oriental in their thinking." They could not be trusted or won over. "We tried that once with Hitler. There are no returns on appeasement." The bomb must be used to advance American security and force the Soviets to abandon their imperialistic ambitions. "It's the gun behind the door." Most of the cabinet supported Forrestal.[40]

Truman had been advised by Major General Leslie Groves that it would take the Russians twenty years to build their own bomb, but what Groves knew about atomic physics was close to zero. Vannevar Bush, director of the wartime Office of Scientific Research and Development and a founding father of computing, told Truman that the Russians could do it in five or six years.[41]

Two days after the bomb was dropped on Hiroshima, Stalin admitted to Harriman that the Soviets had tried to build an atomic bomb, but had failed. He did not say they had given up, and they hadn't. Now, in exploding an atomic bomb, the United States had just given away the most important secret of all—the fact that it could be done. Truman ignored what amounted to a signal that a nuclear arms race had already begun. Instead, he clung to Groves's prognostication. Stalin meanwhile gave an order to his scientists: speed up.[42]

Sometime after the September 21 cabinet meeting, J. Robert Oppenheimer came to talk to the president about the atomic bomb. "There is blood on my hands," he lamented.

Disgusted at such maudlin weakness, Truman shifted instantly into stern commander in chief mode: "The blood is on *my* hands. Let me worry about that," he said. Relating this episode to other people, he derided the agonized Oppenheimer as "a cry baby."

That was unjust, and slightly dishonest, for Truman too was deeply, perpetually troubled. He remained so to the end. As he lay dying almost his last words, his last thoughts, were about the bomb. Was that how he'd be remembered—the man who dropped the atomic bomb, twice?[43]

Chapter 4
Location, Location, Location

ONE DAY IN OCTOBER 1945, HARRY VAUGHAN POKED HIS HEAD INTO the Oval Office. "I've got a guy here from Missouri who wants to see you." The visitor was tiny, go-getting Franc L. McCluer, president of Westminster College, Missouri, Vaughan's alma mater. Thanks to his slightly pointed head, McCluer was known to his friends—including Truman—as Bullet.

Harry and Bullet wanted the president to get Winston Churchill to come out to Westminster College, in Fulton, Missouri, and give a speech. After all, it said in the newspapers that Churchill was going to spend the winter in Florida. Bullet had written an invitation to the great man. What did the president think? Truman read it. "That might work. Wait a minute." He reached for a pen and wrote on the back of the invitation, "Dear Winston: This is a wonderful school in my home State. Hope you can make it. I'll introduce you. Harry S. Truman." He handed it back to McCluer. "Now, you send him that." Churchill accepted the offer. He would do it in March, when his sunshine sojourn ended.[1]

In the meantime, Truman seemed unable to make up his mind just what to do about the Russians. One day he sounded conciliatory, the next uncompromising. His commitment to follow Roosevelt's path was faltering. What could be justified in war could be impossible to sell now, like the deal over the Kuril Islands. Under Secretary of State Dean Acheson denied that the United States had agreed at Yalta to allow the Soviets to take the Kuril Islands from Japan as their reward for joining the Pacific war. The Russians' response was to publish the secret protocol that gave them the Kurils.[2]

Truman had come into the presidency with a disdain for the State Department—common then, common still. A secretary of state's journeys crank up the cynicism: when he departs for another country, fellow citizens regard it as a mission to sell out America, and when his plane arrives, the people he's visiting assume he's on a mission to bribe or bully them. "The smart boys in the State Department, as usual, are against the best interest of the United States," Truman grumbled to his diary shortly before he had left for Potsdam.[3]

He hoped for something better when he made James Byrnes secretary of state, but Byrnes was a wheeler-dealer, not an ideologue. He had arrived at Potsdam willing to talk tough, and he left willing to talk turkey. Stalin, almost as unsure as Truman about what to do in the postwar world, was resorting to the traditional European and Russian answer to the problem of national security—seizing and controlling contiguous territory. That was the default setting for Russia, but in the age of long-range bombers, fast carrier task forces, and fleet submarines, territory was a poor substitute for technology.

Byrnes had come to see the Communism threat for what it was—not a military challenge, but a political one. And politicians are always looking for a deal. He knew how to do that.

At the second Council of Foreign Ministers meeting, in Moscow in December 1945, Byrnes tried to move toward recognition of Bulgaria and Romania in exchange for getting the Soviets out of northwestern Iran. To Truman's irritation, he did not receive regular and timely reports from Moscow as negotiations progressed. Was Byrnes high-hatting him, still resentful that it was Truman sitting in the Oval Office rather than someone with the brains and experience to be president?

To Truman, Bulgaria and Romania were "police states," yet he never told Byrnes that the United States intended to withhold diplomatic recognition. Lacking that, Byrnes was entitled to assume that recognition would be granted to them, as it was to most other police states. Truman's indecisiveness was the problem, not Byrnes's vanity.

When Truman did hear from Byrnes, it was in a radio interview that Byrnes had given. "These countries are neighbors of the Soviet Union," Byrnes said. It was a remark that seemed to be aimed straight at Truman. "And they were involved in the war against the Soviet Union. It is to be expected that the withdrawal of Soviet troops from these countries may depend on the Soviet government's confidence in [their] peaceful character . . ."

As for Iran, Byrnes once again got neither strong support nor clear instructions from the president. Instead, Truman sounded off within the Oval Office like a man looking for a fight. "We, with the British, are in difficulties with the Soviets over Iran," he told Averell Harriman. "They are refusing to carry out their treaty obligations to withdraw their troops. This may lead to war."[4]

The Soviet republics of Azerbaijan and Armenia were making territorial claims in northwestern Iran. Stalin was prepared to support them, if only to get the benefit of Iranian oil. During the war, the British had exercised their legal right to station troops in Iran. They had also extended their privileged position to cover the deployment of thirty thousand American soldiers and airmen to move Lend-Lease supplies across Iran and into Russia. The Russians meanwhile were moving thousands of troops into northwest Iran to protect Lend-Lease operations. Nearly all the British and American troops departed in the fall of 1945, but Stalin was trying to foment an insurgency in the northwest. He showed no signs of leaving, despite his pledge to do so.[5]

When Byrnes returned from Moscow, he headed straight to his South Carolina home, in a failed effort to reach it in time for Christmas. He did not report to the president first, and when it was announced that the secretary of state would be making a radio address on what had happened at the Moscow meeting, Truman was enraged.

He demanded that Byrnes come and meet with him aboard the presidential yacht, the *Williamsburg*. When Byrnes arrived, he and Truman spent more than an hour in the stateroom, with no one else present. Truman said that he should have been informed regularly on what was happening at the CFM meeting. Byrnes told him that the communications problem wasn't his fault. The secure message center at the Moscow embassy was gripped by bureaucratic inertia. That was why Truman often had received news from the conference over commercial radio before he heard it from Byrnes.

Why hadn't Byrnes come to the White House to make his report? "I wasn't invited," said Byrnes, which must have seemed evasive to Truman.

The real clash was what to do about the Soviets. Truman seemed unable to make up his mind—talking tough, followed by talking more reasonably; setting a priority objective one day, then setting something else as the priority a few days later. "In this world today," Byrnes told Truman, "you've got to pick a goal and you'll never get there unless you just trample right through all the underbrush to get it."

"Well," Truman replied, "it all depends on what the underbrush is"—a feeble response that may help explain Truman's lingering irritation at what transpired on the *Williamsburg*.[6]

When the meeting broke up and they went to join the other guests, mostly senior officials and staff, Truman was all smiles and bonhomie, his usual self with his pals. Byrnes wanted to leave, but Truman insisted that he stay for dinner. Over the meal, Admiral Leahy said that he thought Byrnes had not handled the Romanian and Bulgarian situations well.

Byrnes replied, "What would you have done?" After all, Leahy had never criticized Roosevelt for taking the same approach to the same problem. Continuing the Roosevelt policy was the stated aim of this administration, wasn't it? Rebuked by a master of intellectual cut and thrust, Leahy retreated into a stony silence.[7]

Truman returned to Washington determined to have the last word. Six days after the meeting on the *Williamsburg* he penned an angry rebuke to Byrnes: anything less than telling the Soviets where to get off would only strengthen Stalin and harm the United States. Truman concluded with a flourish: "I'm tired of babying the Soviets." The letter was never sent. According to Truman, he read it to Byrnes in the Oval Office; and according to Byrnes, he would have resigned on the spot if it had been sent. It seems likely that Truman gave him the gist of the letter verbally, without the hectoring tone, and counted that as reading the whole thing aloud. The least likely scenario is that he tore into Byrnes, for Byrnes's resignation would have been accompanied by a scathing public critique and created a political crisis.[8]

What happened next showed, in fact, that Byrnes had won the argument. The United States recognized Bulgaria and Romania, but by then Byrnes had taken the Iranian issue to the United Nations. It was the first time that the UN was asked to resolve a major international dispute.

Stalin's insurgency was failing to generate local support in northwestern Iran, and Byrnes personally placed the Iranian problem before the Security Council. The consequent propaganda beating the Russians took and the indignation that Iran aroused in the General Assembly gave the American and British delegations the moral high ground. Stalin ordered the insurgents to abandon the struggle. He cut his losses, and in the spring of 1946 he removed his troops. Byrnes's methods had worked, as had the UN's.[9]

In the meantime, the tension between the two superpowers shifted to the airwaves. In a speech to party functionaries on February 9, 1946, shortly before elections to the Supreme Soviet, Stalin promised better times for the long-suffering people of the Soviet empire, but not yet. Victory over the Nazis had vindicated the Soviet political system and Soviet economic policy, but the Soviet Union must remain militarily strong. The forces of capitalism and imperialism were still a threat to the Soviet Union and world peace. Even so, Stalin remarked, it should be possible for the leading nations of the world to settle their differences "by taking concerted and peaceful decisions." What he was hinting at was a willingness to seek mutual recognition of spheres of influence. For some reason, that part of the speech did not appear in the version transmitted from the embassy in Moscow to the State Department and offered to the Western media. Without it, Dean Acheson and James Forrestal and much of the press were quick to assert that Stalin had virtually declared war on the United States.[10]

Russians noticed something else: Stalin had addressed them as "comrades," but during the war they had been "brothers, sisters, my friends, my countrymen." And he sounded angry and bitter. During that winter, Stalin had been seriously ill. When he shook off his illness, he seemed to his daughter to be in the grip of paranoid terrors, seeing enemies everywhere. Not long after this speech, the greatest Soviet soldier of the war, Georgy Zhukov, was sent into what amounted to internal exile, as if he were a potential threat. Zhukov was lucky. Other generals were shot. The Allies forcibly returned Russians who had found their way to the West during the upheavals of war. Many thousands were executed. Hundreds of thousands more vanished into the huge and metastasizing "gulag archipelago." Stalin was reverting to his old political philosophy—"No man, no problem."[11]

Yet Stalin's speech did not represent the hurling of a gauntlet or a gloved hand smiting the president's cheek. Not even Harriman, contemptuous as he was of Stalin and the Soviet state, saw anything menacing in Stalin's February 9 speech. It was obvious to him that as always, the Communists needed an enemy to hold their empire together and get their people to accept a life of grinding poverty and fear. Truman too recognized it for what it was and said it reminded him of what another senator had once told him: "Well, you know, we always have to demagogue a little before elections."[12]

While Truman was pondering Stalin's speech, the deputy chief of mission at the Moscow embassy, George Kennan, was writing an eight-thousand-word telegram to James Byrnes. Truman may never have seen it, but the Long Telegram, as it became known, was about to provide the leitmotif for the mood music wafting toward the White House from the Pentagon and the State Department.

It seemed to Kennan that much of the time and in many places the Soviets were bluffing. Behind the bluster, their position was politically weak and their military power exaggerated. They also had a blinkered view, for obvious reasons, of what was happening beyond their borders. Even so, the present balance of forces in the world favored the Soviets rather than the United States. A strong but not rigid policy could change that. It would buy time for the Russians to develop a more advanced society, with a more sophisticated outlook. As the Soviet Union matured into a modern state, it would become less threatening. Eventually the Russians might evolve into reliable partners in the search for world peace.

Nevertheless, Soviet power had to be matched wherever it threatened American security. Stalin's military might was not as daunting as it appeared: "Impervious to logic of reason, it is highly sensitive to logic of force. For this reason it can easily withdraw—and usually does—when strong resistance is encountered at any point."[13]

Kennan's telegram reached Washington while it was still digesting Stalin's February 9 speech. "My voice now carried," said Kennan. All the same, he had very mixed feelings about the Long Telegram. When he read it again some years later, it occasioned "a horrified amusement. Much of it reads exactly like one of those primers put out by alarmed congressional committees of the Daughters of the American Revolution, designed to arouse the citizenry to the dangers of the Communist conspiracy."[14]

For all Kennan's efforts to get the administration to take a long view, Truman was so excitable and irritable that he could never do so for long. Instead, he kept coming back to his default setting, the hard line. That was not just *his* default setting; it applied to the country as a whole. Roosevelt may have been hoping to change that, but he would surely have failed. There was always going to be a battle of wits and wills between the United States and the Soviet Union.

In February 1946, with the pressure building at home and abroad, Truman told his cabinet that no one should doubt his determination. "I am going to be President of this country for the next three and a half years, and by God I am going to make it click." And at a White House staff meeting in his office that same month he took some secret cables out of a folder and placed them on his desk. What did they mean? "We are going to have a war with Russia," said Truman. It could break out anywhere from Germany to Korea.[15]

By this time, Churchill's Florida vacation was drawing to a close. Fulton beckoned. On the twenty-four-hour train ride to Jefferson City, Missouri, Truman and Churchill established a relationship of mutual liking and trust, something there had been little time for at Potsdam.

Truman drew his attention to the new presidential seal. The original design went back to 1912, and Truman felt it looked dated. He had redesigned it. The seal now had a blue background, with a large circle of white stars, and in the center, a bald eagle spread its wings. Above the starry ring were clouds, and the eagle was repositioned. It now faced the olive branch, symbol of peace, instead of the bundle of fasces, symbol of war. What did Winston think?

"The eagle's head should be on a swivel, so that it can turn from the fasces to the olive branch as the occasion warrants," said Churchill. "And the berries, or whatever they are, on the olive branch, they look suspiciously like atom bombs."[16]

Churchill finished working on his speech as the train rattled westward. He had crafted it as a response to Stalin's February 9 address. A mimeographed copy of the final draft was handed to Truman around the middle of the journey. He was not going to read it, he told his staff; otherwise, people would say he had endorsed it. Then his curiosity got the better of him, and he read the smudgy purple ink product from the mimeograph machine. He told Churchill it was "admirable. It will create quite a stir."

The next day, Churchill said what he had to say at the Westminster College gymnasium. It was a beautiful spring afternoon, and all the windows were open, a hopeful day for a troubling message. Churchill had a powerful sense of himself as a historical figure, and he dressed the part despite an unhelpful physiognomy. In the billowing scarlet and gold academic gown of an honorary doctor of laws from Oxford University, he looked as theatrical and memorable a sight as anything Bullet could have hoped for.

Churchill had faith in the United Nations, provided it had a strong air force to uphold peace and resist aggression. He spoke warmly, too, of the heroic and long-suffering Russian people and of his wartime comrade, Marshal Stalin. Nonetheless, he had come to deliver a call to the battlements, but not yet to battle.

"From Stettin in the Baltic to Trieste in the Adriatic, an iron curtain has descended across the continent. Behind that line lie all the capitals of the ancient states of Central and Eastern Europe . . . The Communist parties, which were very small in all these Eastern states of Europe, have been raised to pre-eminence and power far beyond their numbers and are seeking everywhere to obtain totalitarian control." Nor did Communist depredations end there. Even on the Western side of this iron curtain, in France and Italy, the Communist menace loomed. "Throughout the world," in fact, the Communists "constitute a growing challenge and peril to Christian civilization." Unless a strong and united front was established against this peril, "indeed catastrophe may overwhelm us all."

There was hope, however. "I do not believe that Soviet Russia wants war." There was a burst of relieved applause. Then he shifted into an ominous key: "What they desire is the fruits of war . . . [and] there is nothing they admire so much as strength." If the United States and the British Commonwealth combined their efforts and worked through the United Nations to resist the spread of Communism, the world might yet be saved.[17]

Back on the train, Truman held a brief press conference. Had he read the speech in advance? "No," said Truman, "I did not."

Stalin responded to Churchill's speech with an interview. He angrily compared Churchill to Hitler and denounced what he portrayed as an Anglo-American capitalist plot to launch a new crusade against the Soviet Union. They attacked us after World War I, Stalin reminded his interviewer. We defeated them before. We will do so again.[18]

With Churchill's "iron curtain" speech raising tensions and doubts, Truman toyed with the idea of reducing both by a grand gesture. Maybe he could get Stalin to visit the United States. He sent an invitation to Stalin to come with him to Missouri, where the marshal could make a similar speech and was sure to enjoy "exactly the same kind of reception." The answer was *nyet*.[19]

The Fulton speech generated a critical response—in Congress, in the Democratic Party, and in the press. Why should the United States ride to the rescue of the British Empire once again? Wasn't the war over? Truman wouldn't be drawn into arguing about the Fulton speech, but his mind had been made up long before Churchill delivered it. "I want the support of Great Britain in anything we do so far as peace is concerned," he had told Joe Davies only a month into his presidency. That wasn't about to change. If anything, events were moving swiftly toward an informal alliance.[20]

After reading George Kennan's Long Telegram, Secretary of the Navy James Forrestal thrust it on other people, telling them that they had to read it, and then, "We must prepare for war." It was often assumed that this was the view of the military chiefs, but it was not. The War Department calculated that the Soviet Union's military was so threadbare and its industrial base so damaged that it would take the Soviets at least fifteen years before they could fight another major war. Stalin had arrived at the same conclusion. All war planning on the Soviet side before the 1960s was based on an assumption of an American attack, and it called for pulling back to the borders of the Soviet Union, if war broke out in Europe, and digging in. There were no plans to launch an offensive.[21]

Truman too was convinced that the Soviet Union could not pose a threat to the United States anytime soon. "Russia couldn't turn a wheel in the next ten years without our aid," he told his staff.[22]

Nothing, though, was going to change Forrestal's mind. He was a much-misunderstood man. A broken nose, the legacy of the college boxing ring, merged with scowling Black Irish features to give him the look of a bruiser. This was one investment banker you probably would not want to encounter late at night in a dark alley. Yet the real Forrestal was introspective, emotionally confused about his working-class origins and his Catholic faith—a man whose relationships with women were shabby and cruel, a man of energy and ambition who worked sixteen hours a day, hoping to be taken seriously as a thinker and a decision maker, two things he happened not to be good at. He eventually subcontracted the intellectual challenge. Someone he hired to make sense from his rambling, disjointed utterances described the problem this way: the Princeton-educated Forrestal could not "drive his thoughts from his mind into the outer world in any coherent form."

Instead, he was reduced to glib formulations, reinforced by bewilderment at the complexities of European politics. Even after it became evident that Tito was a Yugoslav nationalist and not a Croatian Stalinist, Forrestal refused to believe that Tito was anything but a Soviet puppet. "Tito is in fact Russia," Forrestal asserted. To him, the Soviet Union was not Churchill's "riddle wrapped in a mystery inside an enigma." It was much simpler than that. "The fundamental question is whether we are dealing with a nation or a religion." Personally, as a lapsed but troubled Catholic, he gravitated effortlessly into religious explanation. It was a perverse mysticism that explained the appeal of Communism, he assured people.[23]

Forrestal swooped down on Kennan, as if he were the man he had been looking for these many years, and scooped him up. He arranged for Kennan to be brought to Washington and made vice commandant of the National Defense University. Here was an intellectual who thought as he did, that Western civilization was losing its force and confidence. Back in Washington, Kennan used the Long Telegram as the foundation stone for an article titled "The Sources of Soviet Conduct," published in *Foreign Affairs* and attributed to "X," which gave it an air of mystery. Reproduced in *Life* and *Reader's Digest*, the X article became the Apostles' Creed of the Cold War.

There was an important difference between the telegram and the article. The subtlety and shading of the Long Telegram seemed to have evaporated. In their place was a clarion call to a life-or-death struggle with evil—something that anyone, Democrat or Republican, would understand. Communism was portrayed as a menace akin to a virus, likely to spread by close contact. The answer to it was implicit in Kennan's article: containment—a kind of military quarantine based on bombers and bayonets wherever the infection took hold. Do it right, Kennan promised, and "the Russians will never challenge us to an open war."

The article had been written at Forrestal's urging, and as a man with a patron will, Kennan had just torn a piece from himself and sold it. He would soon regret the militarization of his ideas. Kennan protested, unheeded, that he never intended to portray the challenge as a military one, calling for a military response; he had known all along that it was a political one, calling for political responses. It made no difference. George Kennan is regularly lauded as the mastermind behind a policy that held the Soviet Union in check for another forty-three years and culminated in the fall of the Berlin Wall.[24]

As thinkers such as Kennan fed their ideas into the policy debate, Stalin and Truman preferred, as commanders do, to reach for their maps, the material manifestations of abstract facts—power, will, danger, history. When the war ended, Molotov brought Stalin a new map. Stalin pinned it to a wall of his dacha with thumbtacks and stepped back. It showed the Soviet Union as it now was, bigger than ever. "Let's see what we've got then," said Stalin. "In the north everything's all right. Finland greatly wronged us, so we've moved her frontier farther from Leningrad. The Baltic States were Russian territory from ancient times and are ours again. All of the Belorussians are ours now, the Ukrainians also, and the Moldavians are back with us. So to the west, everything is normal."

He gazed at the eastern side of the map. "What have we got here? The Kuril Islands are ours, and the whole of Sakhalin. Port Arthur [in Manchuria] is also ours." He moved his pipe over the map. "China, Mongolia, all as it should be."

Stalin pointed at the southern edge of the map. "Now, this frontier I don't like at all. The Dardanelles. We have claims to Turkish territory."[25]

Truman's map was a large foldout that he kept in a desk drawer for ready reference. It showed the world from the eastern Mediterranean to the Bay of Bengal. He looked at it so often there was black tape along the creases to keep it from falling apart. To help him understand the remorseless nature of Soviet Communism, Admiral Leahy gave Truman a copy of the "political testament" of Peter the Great. In his will, Peter called on his countrymen to follow a program of ruthless expansion after his death. The country should be placed on a permanent war footing. It would have to bring the rulers of the various German states to heel, dominate the political life of Poland, take control of the Baltic States, conquer Persia and Turkey and bring them into the Russian Empire, and with its borders reaching deep into the Middle East, it would be ready for the greatest of all military campaigns—the conquest of Western Europe. A new Russia would arise, one that ruled from the Atlantic to the Urals, from the Arctic Circle to the Persian Gulf. Truman, with his interest in the history of this part of the world, was fascinated: he believed every word, especially when he looked at the map.

At the time of Churchill's Fulton speech, the Turks were under intense pressure. Not only was Stalin demanding a base on the Dardanelles, but the supposedly "autonomous" republics of Georgia and Armenia were claiming parts of western Turkey. These lands had been fought over and haggled over for centuries, but Truman wanted to show support for the Turks, whose public stance was that they were prepared to fight rather than submit to Soviet pressure. Why not, Forrestal suggested, send them a corpse? The wartime Turkish ambassador to the United States, Mehmet Munir Ertegun, had died in 1944 and was interred at Arlington National Cemetery. We could disinter Ertegun, said Forrestal, and ship him home on the *Missouri*. That would be a show of force and a gesture of solidarity. Once the *Missouri* reached Turkish waters, it remained there for several weeks, and the pressure seemed to abate. In August 1946, however, the Soviets renewed their demands for a base.

Let's send a naval task force this time, Forrestal advised, something with plenty of muscle—a battleship, a carrier, two cruisers, and five destroyers. Truman convened a meeting in his office with Acheson, Forrestal, the under secretary of war, and the Joint Chiefs of Staff on August 15. Acheson said that the Russians were only using the demand for a base as a way of getting control over Turkey. "We must take a firm position," said Truman, "and we might as well find out now as in five or ten years whether the Russians are bent on world conquest."

Eisenhower leaned over to Acheson, who was sitting next to him, and said he hoped the president understood that this kind of talk could lead to war. Truman told Eisenhower to speak up. The general repeated what he had just said to Acheson. What did Acheson think? asked Truman. Acheson repeated what he'd said earlier about the dire effects of a Soviet base on the straits. Truman then opened a drawer of his desk, took out the map, and unfolded it.

He launched into a lecture on the history of this part of the world as it was set out in the will of Peter the Great. "Satisfied now?" Truman asked Eisenhower. Laughing, Ike said he was. Several days later the Soviet government was officially informed that the United States supported the Turkish position on the Dardanelles, and if Turkey was attacked or even threatened with an attack, "the resulting situation would constitute a threat to international security." This thinly veiled hint of military intervention was reinforced by a similar note from the British. To back it up, the proposed naval task force was sent to the eastern Mediterranean.[26]

The political testament of Peter the Great had a more immediate and profound effect on Truman's way of measuring the Soviet challenge than anything George Kennan ever wrote. Truman took to telling people that there was no difference between Stalin's ambitions and those of Peter. When his foreign policy came under attack, Truman sometimes resorted to telling his critics, "The Russians have fixed ideas and those ideas were set out by Peter the Great in his will—I suggest you read it."

He'd been had. The political testament of Peter the Great was a forgery, produced nearly a hundred years after Peter's death by Polish émigrés in Paris and a group of Bonapartists seeking to justify war with Russia.[27]

The chances of Truman's using it to justify another attack on Russia were small, not to say remote. Nonetheless, in moments of stress he was fantasizing in his diary: "Got plenty of atomic bombs . . . might drop one on Stalin."[28]

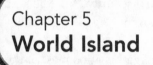

Chapter 5
World Island

CONVIVIAL AND CHATTY, TRUMAN LIKED TO HAVE A DRINK WITH HIS aides at the end of the workday. At times like these he could chat, gossip, wisecrack, relate amusing anecdotes, reminisce, be himself, shake off President Harry S. Truman for a while. Sometimes, though, the problems weighed so heavily that he could not shrug them off despite the lift of bourbon and bonhomie.

July 12, 1946, had been one of those days. Glass in hand, frustration in mind, he damned the Russians. These past few weeks he had been pestered by influential columnists and important scientists to make an agreement with the Soviet Union to control the atomic bomb, but what was the point? To Truman, Russians were "Orientals," meaning cruel, perfidious, and backward. All of these traits were being turned to the perverse ends of Communist ideology, making them more sinister still. "The great task that lies before me," he said, "is to find the answer of how we and the world can conduct ourselves *vis à vis* the Soviets."

There were moments when Truman liked to believe that while Stalin was a tough negotiator, he could be flexible and frank. The problem wasn't the marshal—it was the people around him, such as Molotov. Truman feared for Stalin's health, as if Stalin were the one reasonable man in the Soviet leadership. Even though he privately called the Soviet Union "a police state," Truman refused to accept the logic of his own argument: Molotov's *nyet* was Stalin's *nyet*.

And so on this balmy evening he turned to Clark Clifford, recently appointed his general counsel, and told him what he wanted: a report giving chapter and verse on how the Soviets had broken every agreement they had signed since 1941. The report should weigh the implications of Soviet treachery for U.S. national security. What he seemed to be looking for was a good excuse for not making any agreement for controlling the Bomb.[1]

Clifford had his youthful assistant, George Elsey, do most of the research. After all, the twenty-six-year-old Elsey had a master's degree in history from Harvard. Proximity to power had convinced Elsey that history was valuable only as a tool for winning an argument. Historians were ridiculous figures who "lie on the psychoanalytic couch and try to figure out how things might have been done differently . . . interesting but quite irrelevant."[2]

Truman had to wait more than two months for the report, but on September 24 Clifford handed him a printed copy. It was titled "American Relations with the Soviet Union." Truman took it to bed with him.

The postwar clash of wills and interests between the United States and the Soviet Union was presented by Clifford and Elsey as a menace spawned by the malevolence, ignorance, and ambition of a power-crazed Soviet elite. Truman was inclined to the same view; what Clifford and Elsey did was hold a mirror up to Truman's mind and reflect his limited understanding straight back to him, but reified.

Somehow, in all his reading of history, Truman seems to have skipped de Tocqueville's *Democracy in America*, published in 1835. The concluding paragraph of de Tocqueville's first volume looks into the future and focuses on two rising powers, Russia and the United States. They were already set on a collision course for the twentieth century, concluded de Tocqueville.

Instead of opting for the correct and obvious explanation, that as the United States advanced westward and Russia expanded eastward, they were destined to become rivals, Clifford and Elsey presented Soviet behavior as a drive for world domination. That was the goal of Soviet foreign policy. By implication, unless the United States intervened—and soon—every one of the world's 150-plus countries was doomed to Stalinist enslavement. What price security then?

Odd, then, that the Soviets were presently struggling to impose their will on Eastern Europe and could not even impose it on Yugoslavia. Stranger still, the Red Army was rapidly demobilizing. Clifford and Elsey ignored such trifles. Blessed like many a good lawyer with paraphrastic gifts, Clifford could reduce the most complicated or open-ended struggle to a few simple words and phrases. Truman liked that. World domination had a compelling quality, evoking something terrifying and evil.

The proof of Soviet wickedness, said Clifford and Elsey, was to be found in the way they broke their agreements, especially those with the United States, much as the president said they did. Curiously, though, the report contained a frank admission, one that Truman seems to have missed: although the report based its entire case on Soviet failure to live up to its formal obligations, "it is difficult to adduce direct evidence of literal violations."

There was also some strong evidence to the contrary. Stalin had followed the terms of the Nazi-Soviet Pact of 1939 scrupulously, delivering foodstuffs and raw materials to the German war machine right up until Hitler attacked Russia in June 1941. Stalin had also kept his word to declare war on Japan in August 1945. However reluctantly, he had pulled his troops out of Iran. None of these was mentioned in the report.

Instead, Clifford and Elsey crafted their report as a clarion call to action: the United States should "support and assist all democratic countries which are in any way menaced or endangered by the USSR," it declared. This was a formula for wars without end, for if this report were accurate, more than a hundred countries were already menaced or endangered in some way by Communists, world domination being what it was. Clifford and Elsey were setting the threshold for intervention so low that a bump in the road might be enough.

A letter from Clifford accompanied the report. In it, he assured

Truman that there was a consensus among senior foreign policy and military advisers on what the Soviets had done, were doing, and could be expected to do. This was untrue, but that never bothered Clifford. He was telling Truman what Truman wanted to hear. James Byrnes, the secretary of state, did not support the Clifford-Elsey thesis, nor did the Joint Chiefs, nor did Robert Patterson, the secretary of war. James Forrestal alone in the military-diplomatic top tier supported the line that Clifford and Elsey pursued, but that was not mentioned.

Enthralled, Truman spent much of the night reading and pondering. In the morning, following his customary brisk walk through the half-deserted streets of Washington, he called Clifford. "Powerful stuff."

"Thank you, Mr. President."

"Clark, how many copies of this memorandum do you have?"

"Twenty," said Clifford.

"Have any been distributed yet?"

"No, sir. They are all in my safe at the office."

Truman told him to come to the White House immediately and bring every copy.

When Clifford came into the Oval Office a few hours later, Truman said, "I read your report with care last night. It is very valuable to me. But if it leaked it would blow the roof off the White House. It would blow the roof off the Kremlin. We'd have the most serious situation on our hands that has yet occurred in my Administration." Clifford handed over all twenty printed copies, but he kept a draft copy of this 26,000-word document for future use.[3]

Truman was determined to shelve the report, not because it did not reflect his own thinking, but because it captured it perfectly. To have such a bald statement on the public record would alarm too many people and cause an outcry from the Rooseveltian wing of the Democratic Party. It sounded like a call to rearm, if not yet a call to arms. Coming out of its biggest war, the country was not ready to give serious thought to another.

In the meantime, though, he could do the preparatory work. Several weeks after he read Clifford's report, Truman addressed the United Nations General Assembly. History, he told the world, had conferred on the United States the right to respond to aggression everywhere. In some countries that sounded like a promise; in others, a threat.[4]

An opportunity to act was already at hand. The Japanese had wrested Indochina from the French, to the fury of many Vietnamese. Being colonized first by the French was bad enough, but to be colonized again, by the Japanese, was even worse. A Communist-led insurgency took root. Following Japan's surrender, the French came back, and the Vietnamese found themselves being colonized for the third time.

Given this stimulus, the insurgency grew exponentially. The insurgents called themselves the Vietminh, and their leader was Ho Chi Minh. There was nothing to show that the Soviets were aiding the Vietminh, and not even the French claimed that Stalin was pulling Ho's strings. Yet the French felt they had no choice but to fight, for reasons that had nothing to do with Communism.

It was not a region that meant much to them. The great fear was that if an insurgency wrested Indochina away, it would encourage a similar revolt in Algeria, which had a population of more than a million *pieds noirs*—Algerian-born French citizens.

France was broke in 1946. There was no money for fighting a major war ten thousand miles away. Broke, but not without hope.

In the first fifteen years after World War II, government in France was a revolving door. Some governments lasted only a few weeks before being forced to resign, and some French governments contained Communist cabinet members. This was enough to convince Truman and the State Department that unless the United States aided France in its war in Indochina, the whole country would fall to the Communists.

The chances of France going Communist were between zero and nil. France was a deeply conservative, petit bourgeois society. The occasional Communist cabinet minister was an inevitable part of coalition building in the National Assembly, because the French Communist Party was the largest single party in France, but it accounted for less than 25 percent of the electorate. The coalitions that governed France were center-right. Had the Communists had any real weight in any French government, France would never have sought American help to defeat a Communist-led insurgency in a colonial possession.[5]

Truman responded with alacrity to French demands for money and arms, even though his military chiefs told him that the French could defeat the Vietminh with what they had. In the guise of helping France rebuild Europe to face up to the Red Army, he was, by a sleight of hand, intervening in a colonial war on behalf of the coloniz- ers. Clifford boasted for years that although Truman chose to keep his report in a safe, the president told him many times that it governed his actions.[6]

As Truman moved away from Roosevelt, James Byrnes moved away from Truman. In January 1947 Byrnes resigned. It was his heart, he told Truman. If he stayed in government, he'd soon be dead. Truman let him go, with regret, and Byrnes lived for another twenty-five years. Truman prevailed on George Marshall to become secretary of state.

Marshall had hardly found his way around his new office before a new crisis broke. The unpopular Greek government seemed to be los- ing the fight against Communist insurgents, and the British were muttering darkly about not being able to prop up Greece much longer. The solution, Truman was advised, was to oust the current Greek government and bring in a coalition that would undercut sup- port for the Communists. Marshall had his staff begin work on a pro- gram of military and economic aid. They had barely begun before Truman received a call from Dean Acheson, the under secretary of state: the British had just informed the State Department that all aid to Greece and Turkey would end on March 1, barely three weeks away.

There was no cause for alarm, Acheson reassured him. Marshall was out of town, but Acheson had already arranged meetings of mili- tary, economic, and political experts. Reports were being written on how money could be found in a hurry, how people could be found in a hurry, how supplies could be found in a hurry. Did the president approve? All the president had to do was say yes.

Here was a crisis that stirred a particular fear that Truman had cul- tivated in recent months: a domino effect. If Greece fell under Com- munist rule, the effects would be felt in countries such as Italy and France, with their large Communist parties. All of Europe—Eastern and Western—would then fall into Stalin's clutches. With so much economic and political power under Soviet control, the dominoes would keep falling until more than half the world became Communist. At that point, the Soviet Union would be strong enough to conquer the United States, the biggest domino of all.[7]

On February 27, 1947, Truman met with the congressional leadership at Blair House to set out the case for military aid to Greece and financial help to Turkey, which was still under Soviet pressure. He knew it was going to be a tough sell. Most Americans who took any interest were scornful of the reactionary and undemocratic Greek monarchy, forced on the Greeks by the British a generation earlier and then legitimized at the end of World War II by a dubious referendum.

As for Turkey, it was a primitive Islamic land run by the military. During World War I it had been allied with Germany, and during World War II it had refused to take sides. Turkey had never been democratic, and it showed no signs of becoming so.

Marshall offered a brief and lackluster account of recent events. He was famously meticulous in preparing for important briefings, and more experienced in dealing with national security challenges than anyone else in the room, but there was a good reason for his mediocre presentation: he was not convinced by the argument he was making. Acheson, however, believed in it heart and soul, and he interrupted Marshall before too much damage was done. "Might I speak?" Marshall sat down, Acheson stood up.[8]

Acheson's mind turned to the apocalyptic as easily, if not as often, as other men's thoughts turn toward money or sex. It was a mind shaped in considerable part by two seminal figures, one English, the other German—two men whose thinking was on a global scale and had millennial reach.

The Englishman was an Oxford professor, Sir Halford Mackinder, originator of the idea of geopolitics, who in 1904 offered a paper to the Royal Geographical Society. "The joint continent of Europe, Africa and Asia [is] the World Island." Within that, stretching from Poland to Central Asia, was "the Heartland." The World Island was too big to be conquered outright, but bordering the Heartland, from Lithuania to Korea, was more than a score of weak, potentially unstable countries, every one of them a battlefield for more powerful neighbors.

The influence of Mackinder could not be avoided in seats of power following World War II. Acheson was far from unique. From the

1920s to the 1960s nearly all of the leading liberal arts colleges—starting with Columbia—required their graduates to complete a course in the history of Western civilization. Truman was surrounded by advisers such as Elsey, George Kennan, and Dean Acheson, who looked to Mackinder's ideas for inspiration, clues, patterns.

What did Mackinder's geography mean for aspiring powers? "Who rules East Europe commands the Heartland; Who rules the Heartland commands the World Island; Who rules the World Island commands the World." By 1946 Mackinder seemed to have been vindicated by the titanic struggle of the Soviets and the Nazis for control of the Heartland, beginning with Hitler's conquest of Poland and Stalin's simultaneous invasion of the Baltic States in the fall of 1939.

Acheson's German influence was a philosopher and mathematician, Oswald Spengler, whose *The Decline of the West* claimed that all great civilizations follow a similar path of ascension, fruition, and ultimate fall.

History is not linear, proclaimed Spengler. It operates in cycles. There had been twenty major civilizations, and nearly all had tracked the same narrative arc: heroic rise, golden age, inexorable decline, eventual fall. The only two that remained were those of China and the West. China might survive, Spengler concluded, but Western civilization had already gone into decline, and in a century or so it too would fall.

Toward the end of World War II, Acheson saw the future as a titanic struggle between Islam and the West. By the time of this meeting at Blair House, however, the apocalypse had become a life-or-death showdown between the Soviet Union and the West. This, he informed the congressmen, was the greatest challenge to Western civilization since Rome had fought Carthage.[9]

And now the ancient struggle came down to the fate of Greece and Turkey. If they fell under Soviet domination, three regions—Europe, Africa, and the Middle East—would be on the line. If the Soviets got control of Turkey, they would pick up Greece and Iran too. And if the large Italian Communist Party came to power, the Soviets would be able to seize the entire Middle East. And once Stalin had a hammerlock on the eastern Mediterranean and Middle East, both South Asia and all of Africa were theirs for the taking. It was a desperate situation, relieved by a single ray of hope. "We and we alone are in a position to break up the play," said Acheson.[10]

When he sat down, a long, troubled silence filled the room. Then Arthur Vandenberg, chairman of the Senate Foreign Relations Committee, broke it. He addressed Truman directly. "Mr. President, the only way you are ever going to get this is to make a speech and scare the hell out of the country." By "this" Vandenberg meant an open-ended commitment to assert American control over the eastern Mediterranean, across Asia Minor, and deep into the Persian Gulf. Reason could never sell "this." Fear was Truman's only hope.[11]

As Acheson and Clark Clifford worked on the address that Truman would give to both houses of Congress, the president received a visit from the spiritual leader of the Greek Orthodox Church in the United States, Archbishop Athenagoras. The archbishop planted a kiss on the presidential forehead, and the *Life* magazine picture of the kiss charmed and amused millions of Americans.

Poised to make what would be the most important speech he had ever delivered, Truman redefined the national mission and, by extension, the nature of the country. Roosevelt had promoted the "Four Freedoms" as the pillars of democratic government: freedom from fear, freedom from want, freedom of speech, and freedom of worship.

Truman decided to jettison freedom from want and freedom from fear. These were just the kinds of goals that Communists pushed. Instead, there would be only three freedoms: freedom of speech, freedom of worship, and freedom of enterprise. "It must be true," he told a gathering at Baylor University, "that the first two of these freedoms are related to the third." In effect, he had reverted to the national creed from back when he was working in a bank, twenty years before the New Deal.[12]

By the time Truman made his appearance before Congress, Clifford had drafted three key sentences that served as a preamble. Clifford knew only the small world of the St. Louis legal and financial elite and almost nothing about the world beyond. He looked and sounded sophisticated, but it was only a provincial lawyer's sophistication in pleading a case.

Striving for effect, Clifford wrote and Truman spoke the following: "I believe that it must be the policy of the United States to support free peoples who are resisting subjugation by armed minorities or by outside pressure. I believe that we must assist free peoples to work out their destinies in their own way. I believe that our help should be primarily through economic and financial aid which is essential to economic stability and orderly political processes." These assertions became known almost at once as the Truman Doctrine.[13]

The speech combined elements of Acheson's fears, Clifford's intellectual shallows, and Truman's excitability. He did not say outright that the Soviets were behind Greek and Turkish woes; he didn't have to. Everyone knew whom he held responsible.

Besides, he was going to blurt it out at some point. Like Martin Luther, he could do no other. When a group of radio journalists came to see him shortly after the Truman Doctrine speech, he told them that he had tried to get along with the Russians, but they had betrayed his trust every time. "I have got to use other methods. They understand one language, and that is the language they are going to get from me from this point."[14]

He might have gone to the United Nations and invoked the machinery that Roosevelt had gone to so much trouble to create and Byrnes had shown could be made to work. Truman never considered it. The United States would act alone. Isolationism had not gone away, merely underground. The deep and tenacious American incuriosity about the rest of the planet was ever the heart and soul of isolationism. This was the modern version, willing to take on the world in order to bring to it American values—not run away from it the way the old, discredited isolationism did.

Even so, the debate in Congress was long and often sharp. The $250 million for Greece and $150 million for Turkey that the president was asking for was a large sum but manageable in the context of a $41 billion federal budget. Nevertheless, on its first outing, the domino theory generated skepticism. The president's thinking—today Greece, tomorrow the world—was dangerously like a proposal to intervene in countries around the globe. It was not only people on the Hill who feared that. So did George Kennan.

Acheson sent the assistant secretary of state, Will Clayton, to tell the senators there was nothing to fear. Clayton told them, "I do not think it would be wise to [conclude] that this is just the first step in a great, big program." Yet Acheson was assuring Truman that if the bill went through, it would "cover other countries." Truman was encouraged by the thought of being able to challenge the Communist menace all over the world. "This is only the beginning," he told the cabinet. In the end, Congress passed the administration's bill by big margins in both houses.[15]

So far, the Soviets had given more moral than material support to the Communist insurgency in Greece. What outside support the guerrillas received came mainly from Yugoslavia and Bulgaria. With the Greek government coming under the effective control of a U.S. Military Advisory Group, headed by Lieutenant General James Van Fleet, the whole character of the struggle was transformed. Van Fleet tripled the size of the Greek army, until it numbered more than 250,000 men. That gave him an advantage of more than ten to one over the guerrillas. The Greek army was also modernized with American weaponry, communications gear, and transportation. And it was transformed by infusing the officer corps with a belief that *they* were Greece. The way was opened for the eventual overthrow of the monarchy and the imposition of a military dictatorship.

Stalin saw the Balkans as a potential trap. In October 1946 he had told a gathering of journalists that the Red Army was demobilizing rapidly. Its strength in Eastern Europe and the Balkans was about to fall from nearly sixty divisions to forty. No one in Washington believed it, including George Kennan. But what Stalin said happened to be true.[16]

When this message failed to have the desired effect, he summoned the Bulgarian and Yugoslavian Communist leaders to Moscow and berated them. "What do you think, that Great Britain and the United States—the United States, the most powerful state in the world—will permit you to break their line of communication in the Mediterranean Sea! Nonsense. And we have no navy. The uprising in Greece must be stopped as quickly as possible."[17]

The Greek civil war fizzled out, but the Truman Doctrine had paradoxically worked to Stalin's advantage. The Soviet hold on Eastern Europe was far from solid, and the threat of American intervention pushed the new and unpopular leaders of Eastern Europe, from Poland to Romania, into a deeper embrace with the Soviets. The great holdout was Tito, someone Truman viewed with the deepest suspicion.

James Byrnes, gazing on what Truman had wrought, was filled with a sense of foreboding. The United States was threatening armed intervention around the globe. Byrnes was working on his memoirs when the Truman Doctrine was proclaimed. This was his response: "We need not fear the result if we use our power but we must fear the unnecessary use of our power." He saw what Truman did not. The United States was going to run out of money, troops, and allies long before it ran out of enemies.[18]

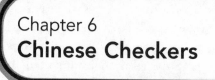

Chapter 6
Chinese Checkers

THERE IS A LINE IN TRUMAN'S FAVORITE POEM, "LOCKSLEY Hall," that expressed nineteenth-century feelings about China— weak, humiliated, backward, strange:

> *Better fifty years of Europe than a cycle of Cathay . . .*

Truman felt much the same, but on becoming president, he inherited Roosevelt's China legacy, a fantasy based on a sentimental notion that the United States was China's only true friend among the great powers, its sole defender against the rapacious Europeans, and its ally in fighting Japan. Churchill had insisted that France be made a permanent member of the UN Security Council, even though France had failed to put up much of a fight against Hitler. This left Roosevelt free to argue that China must be a permanent member too, even though it hadn't put up much of a fight against the Japanese.

Millions of Americans shared Roosevelt's romantic view that the United States was the one nation that wanted to help China get off its knees and onto the road to prosperity. American missionaries in China had spread this idea, as did the writings of Pearl Buck, winner of the Nobel Prize. Chinese politicians and thinkers, on the other hand, never saw much to choose from between Americans and Europeans. Both had taken unfair advantage of a prostrate China, brought low by the Big Noses and their modern weapons.

In the first year of his presidency, Truman overcame his doubts about Roosevelt's commitment by convincing himself that he could create a stable, democratic China. To arrive at this delusion, he first had to ignore the fact that his chosen instrument—the existing Guo Min Dang (GMD), or "Nationalist" government—had only a theoretical interest in democracy and a clear hands-on interest in bribery. The Nationalist leader, Generalissimo Jiang Jieshi, may have been personally honest, within limits, but he chose to surround himself with people whose greed knew no bounds. So long as they supported Jiang politically, he protected them. This arrangement bore more than a passing resemblance to politics in Missouri, where Truman's mentor, Thomas Prendergast, had overseen a crooked political machine based on patronage and pilferage.

Even before World War II ended, China was slipping into a civil war between Jiang's GMD armies and the Communist guerrilla armies of Mao Zedong. At Potsdam, Truman had asked Stalin to recognize the Nationalist government. Stalin not only agreed, but to Truman's immense delight, he ridiculed Mao's followers as "a bunch of fascists." The Nationalists and Communists had sometimes cooperated in resisting the Japanese invasion that had begun in 1937, but those days were fading fast.[1]

It never occurred to Truman that Stalin's contempt for Chinese Communists was rooted in their reluctance to take instructions from Moscow. The only good Communist in Stalin's world was one who defended Soviet interests. Mao and his followers seemed more interested in defending China's.

Truman soon discovered that however scornful Stalin was of the Chinese Communists, the Russians were seeking to replace the Japanese as the bullyboys of the western Pacific. Stalin, like the Japanese before him, was striving to keep China permanently weak and divided. And then, on November 27, 1945, the China problem seemed to spin out of control.

That evening, the American ambassador to China, Patrick J. Hurley, delivered a speech at the National Press Club, four blocks from the White House. A rich oilman from Oklahoma, Hurley was also a former secretary of war, a self-important figure with a deserved reputation for fleecing poor and gullible Oklahomans who happened to find oil on their land. At the Press Club, he proceeded to make a root and branch attack on Truman's China policy.

With the end of the war, the United States had abruptly ended Lend-Lease to all its wartime allies, including China. Hurley now denounced this as a betrayal of one of the world's greatest men, Jiang Jieshi, and one of its most noble causes. There were also more than 110,000 American troops stationed in China when the war ended, but they were departing eagerly, even though China was still in peril.

Hurley was not alone in fawning on Jiang, a devout Methodist who read his Bible daily. Mike Mansfield, congressman from Montana, was an acknowledged authority on the Far East. Mansfield lauded Jiang as more than just a general and more than a politician. He towered above mere mortals, Mansfield declared, because "he *is* China."[2]

In northern China, the Japanese were moving out, the Russians were moving in, the Nationalists were moving in circles, and the Communists were moving toward power. Truman wanted to pull out, but he was assured by the State Department that the GMD government would then collapse and he would be blamed for it.[3]

News of Hurley's speech flashed over the wires. The next morning, clutching a long piece of yellow Teletype paper in his hand, Truman stalked into a cabinet meeting. "See what that son of a bitch did to me!"[4]

He would have to send someone to China to replace Hurley and put a stop to its biggest problem—the unfolding civil war. The man he decided to send was George Marshall, not as the ambassador, but as something more exalted—the president's personal representative. After six years as chief of staff, Marshall was about to retire from the army and become president of the American Red Cross. Truman went straight for Marshall's one known weakness—an exalted sense of duty—and prevailed on him to try to save China from Mao.

This is what I want, Truman told him: organize a cease-fire, put together a Communist-GMD coalition government, make Jiang the superior partner, and tell him that even if the coalition collapses, he will continue to receive American aid. At the same time, make it clear to Mao that even if he is willing to be the junior partner, the Communists will not get so much as a nickel out of the American taxpayer.

Marshall departed for China in January 1946, and within a couple of months he had some good news for Truman: Jiang said he would form a coalition that included the Communists. But then, when it appeared that Mao might actually agree to Truman's plan, Jiang changed his mind and told Marshall that the GMD was going to destroy Mao's forces and rid China of the Communist menace once and for all. Marshall told him that was going to prove impossible.[5]

All the proof anyone needed was to be found in Manchuria, an area bigger than Texas. A million-man Japanese field army had been deployed across Manchuria since 1937. In the closing days of the war, the GMD was too poorly organized and too weakly led to take control of so large a region. The result was a decision at Potsdam to have the Russians move into Manchuria, impose order, and disarm the Japanese. By the spring of 1946, the Japanese were gone and the Russians were leaving, having dismantled their factories and shipped them to the USSR.

Both the GMD and the Chinese Communists rushed in. Jiang's troops seized the Manchurian capital, Changchun, and the principal port, Harbin, but Mao's forces, traveling mostly on foot for want of anything better, got control of the countryside and, with it, most of the population. The way this would end was obvious to Mao and to Marshall, but not to Jiang.

Truman stopped military assistance to the GMD that summer, in the vain hope that it might make Jiang do something about his corrupt and ineffectual regime, but after Marshall returned home in the fall, military assistance resumed. By this time there was a China bloc busy within the halls of Congress, and a China lobby outside the halls, with much mutual admiration in between. Truman found the self-righteous bloc frustrating, the corrupt lobby nauseating.

The China bloc's leading figure in the Senate was William F. Knowland, a mentally unstable California publisher, of dubious ethics and execrable judgment. Knowland was known among political journalists as "the Senator from Formosa."[6]

His counterpart in the House was Congressman Walter Judd of

Minnesota, a former medical missionary in China. What would be the consequences of a hostile China? Judd asked. "Who would hold the balance of power? Not we. The billion and a quarter people who live in Asia would have the balance of power . . . Their immediate fate, especially China's, is in our hands; but in the long run, our fate is in their hands." For that reason, Judd argued, the United States had to support Jiang, because the alternative was Mao.[7]

Stopping aid to China was never going to be easy, and keeping it flowing was not much of a problem. As the U.S. military presence in China was reduced to sixty thousand men, departing units handed over nearly six thousand tons of ammunition to Jiang's forces. The GMD was also given hundreds of millions of dollars in the form of American government property suddenly declared surplus.

Even within the cabinet, Truman found himself facing pressure to give Jiang Jieshi more money, more armaments. At a cabinet meeting in March 1947, Truman's secretary of the interior, Julius Krug, said there was something wrong when the government was asserting a set of principles that justified intervening in Greece and Turkey yet sought to ignore those same principles to avoid intervening in China.

Marshall was now the secretary of state, but at this meeting he was represented by his deputy, Dean Acheson, who told Krug, "The fundamentals are the same, but the incidences are different." Truman waved Acheson's sophistry aside. The problem was simple: "Chiang Kai-shek [Jiang Jieshi] will not fight it out. The Communists will fight it out—they are fanatical. Giving more aid to Chiang would be pouring sand in a rat hole under the present situation."[8]

Marshall was reduced to hand-wringing as more provinces, more towns and cities, more millions of people fell to the advancing Communists in 1947. "I wash my hands of the problem, which has passed beyond my comprehension," he told his staff.[9]

As 1947 turned into 1948 and minds turned to the presidential election, Truman's China trap yawned ever wider. He threw money into it, hoping. He came up with an extra $570 million for Jiang's ineffectual government. There was no more money for the army, the navy, the air force, or the Marine Corps, all of which were under intense budget pressure from the president, while there seemed to be no limit to what Truman would pony up for Jiang Jieshi. Yet he and the Republican "Asialationists" were alike in wanting a balanced budget. Jiang's money had to come out of other parts of the federal budget, including the military.

Truman did not even attempt to justify his largesse. As he moved toward involving the United States in China's civil war, he simply did not want to talk about it. There was no mention in his speeches or press conferences of the Communist armies that every month were forcing Jiang's troops to retreat, surrender, or die. Between February and November the president made only one fleeting public reference to the Chinese civil war.

In May 1948, Communist troops were moving toward the Shantung Peninsula and its principal city, Qingdao. James Forrestal, elevated from secretary of the navy to secretary of defense, urged Truman to allow the thousands of marines still in China to defend it. The peninsula was long and narrow and could be dominated by naval gunfire and airpower. The marines could not be driven out. But fighting for the Shantung Peninsula would have thrust the United States directly into the Chinese civil war.

Marshall told Truman, "That would be a terrible mistake," and Truman hesitated. As word spread to Capitol Hill that the marines might be evacuated, Jiang's admirers and defenders screamed "Appeasement!" Truman stalled, and Mao's troops obliged by not attacking the marines. Like Truman, Mao seemed to be waiting to see how the November election turned out.[10]

The China lobby was giving unstinting support to the Republican candidate, Governor Thomas Dewey of New York. They expected that a Dewey administration would rule out disengagement from China. Truman, they guessed, was hoping to get out, and they were right.

Much of the press was vehemently hostile to Truman over China, not because he wasn't providing military and economic aid, but because he wasn't providing enough and quickly enough. Jiang's failings were almost never discussed; Truman's were dissected with the patience and care of a first-rate autopsy.

Acheson had the State Department prepare an authoritative defense. Known as the China White Paper, it comprised four hundred pages of history and commentary, supported and explicated by more than a thousand pages of official documents. It was published as *United States Relations with China, with Special Reference to the*

Period 1944–1949. This door-stopping tome proved a boon to historians, and nobody else. Its message—that there was nothing the U.S. government could have done to stop Mao's advances and Jiang's retreats—was true, but the truth was not enough. The rising "Who lost China?" furor grew and blended seamlessly with a tidal wave of anger, raised high by revelations of Soviet espionage.

Meanwhile, with the election out of the way and Truman re-elected, Marshall put the China issue squarely to the cabinet. The president could tell the country the truth, which was that Jiang's government was doomed. "Or we can play along with the existing government and keep the facts from the American people and thereby not be accused later of playing into the hands of the Communists." No decision was made then and there, because Truman still could not make up his mind about China.[11]

Marshall was meanwhile telling Truman that the United States should do nothing to defend Formosa. The Joint Chiefs agreed, advising him that the United States should make a complete withdrawal from China.[12]

By the end of the year, the marines had departed Qingdao and Mao's troops had arrived. With the prospect of pinning the responsibility on the military, Truman decided to act on the advice from Marshall and the Joint Chiefs.[13]

Less than a month after his inauguration, he informed the congressional leadership that he was going to stop propping up Jiang Jieshi. The generalissimo had just decamped to Taiwan, leaving one of his potential rivals, the Virginia Military Institute–trained Li Zongren, to face Mao's all-conquering armies. Yet before long, Li, too, quit China, heading for the United States to seek medical treatment for a mysterious illness that was never diagnosed. It would be sixteen years before he returned to China, receiving a hero's welcome from its Communist government.

The congressmen were shocked at Truman's announcement that the Nationalist gravy train was about to stop. Arthur Vandenberg, the Republican chairman of the Senate Foreign Relations Committee, said that stopping aid to Jiang was unthinkable. Even if collapse was inevitable, "this blood must not be on our hands." Virtually the entire Senate leadership was on the Foreign Relations Committee. It was difficult enough to deal with a Senate under Republican control. To get into a fight with the leadership at the start of a four-year term was going to mean four tough years. Was China worth it? Truman decided it was not.

He knew that Jiang's regime could not be saved, and that knowledge ought to have guided his actions. He could be sure of being hounded and damned by the China bloc and the China lobby no matter what he did. Truman should have opted to take the pain, knowing that a clean break was best for the country.

Besides, Truman had told his staff that there was at least one thing he'd learned from reading history and from serving in the Senate: "No President ever lost anything in a fight with Congress." That genially feisty style had also given rise to another piece of pithy advice: "If you can't stand the heat, stay out of the kitchen." But it was all bluster. Within twenty-four hours he was reassuring the Republicans in Congress that he was never going to withdraw from China, would never give up on Jiang.[14]

Acheson tried to get a group of Republican congressmen to understand just what the administration was up against. How could anyone deal with a country like this? he wanted to know. "China is not a modern, centralized state—China even under Communism cannot become a springboard for attack. The Communists face a morass in China. Until some of the smoke and dust of the disaster clear away we must wait and see." He did not change a single mind.[15]

It was inevitable by now that there would be a Communist government in China before the year was out. Truman approved a National Security Council paper that said once that happened, it should be American policy to exploit every opportunity to encourage a Sino-Soviet split. This sensible idea lasted all of three months, until June 1949, when Mao announced that China would make a formal alliance with the Soviet Union. The choice was either to go with the Soviets or with the capitalists, said Mao. "We must lean to one side . . . Sitting on the fence is not possible; nor is there a third road."

In truth, though, what Mao was looking for was economic assistance from the Soviets and a trading relationship with the Americans. He could not have that now, but it was worth aiming for over time. Mao's closest adviser and mouthpiece, Zhou Enlai (a.k.a. Chou En-lai) had signaled the shift in a recent speech: "No force can prevent China from having two friends at once." Nobody in the State Department or the White House paid any heed. While Stalin's utterances and Molotov's were scrutinized intensely, Mao's and Zhou's were ignored.[16]

At the same time, Truman received a letter signed by sixteen Republican and six Democratic senators. They implored him not to recognize the coming Communist government of China. Vandenberg, speaking on behalf of the Foreign Relations Committee, said much the same.

What the Chinese got from their treaty of friendship with Stalin was a promise to help China industrialize, $300 million in economic assistance, plus some German machinery taken by the Russians as reparations.[17] What the Soviets got was billions of dollars' worth of strategic raw materials from China. For Stalin, it was the bargain of the century. And he never followed through on his pledge to help China create an industrial economy—for obvious reasons.

Acheson advised Truman that the Chinese Communists had just sold their country to Moscow. But it was only a matter of time before the Chinese people woke up to this betrayal, ousted the Communists, and installed a different government, said Acheson. The United States should withhold recognition until that happened.

On coming to power in Beijing, the Chinese Communists had only two demands on the United States: that China be accepted as a great power, and that China's traditional sphere of influence be respected: the Korean Peninsula, Vietnam, Laos, Cambodia, Thailand, Burma, Tibet. Formosa was a renegade province with a rival government. That made it a special case. Everywhere else—Hong Kong, Macao, Outer Mongolia, Kowloon—China would wait for national reunification.

Because Mao would not give ground over Formosa, the China tangle became knottier than ever. Jiang and his troops spent 1949 wresting the island from the Formosans in a struggle that cost more than one hundred thousand Formosans their lives. A Chinese government had not ruled it since the Japanese conquest of 1895.

At the Cairo Conference in 1943, Roosevelt had promised that Formosa would be returned to China. Truman had repeated that promise at Potsdam. It seemed easy and right at the time. Formosa was important, not to the security of the United States, but to the economic revival of Japan. During fifty years of occupation, it had become a major exporter of food and raw materials to Japan and an important importer of Japanese goods. The sole strategic interest that the United States might have was an indirect one: promoting a revival of Formosa-Japanese trade.

Even before the People's Republic of China was proclaimed, in October 1949, the CIA was forecasting that within a year or so, Mao's forces would capture Formosa. Once installed in Beijing, Mao's generals began amassing a junk fleet of more than twenty-five hundred vessels for an invasion in the summer of 1950.

On the face of it, Jiang had more than enough arms, ammunition, and troops to hold Formosa. He even had a five-hundred-plane air force. What he lacked was commanders willing to fight and leaders able to lead. The only action that could prevent Formosa falling to Mao's invasion, said the CIA, was American military intervention.[18]

Even without that, there was a serious risk that if Jiang tried to set up a rival Chinese government on Formosa, and the United States recognized it, Mao would see that as American intervention in China's civil war. Truman would be pushing the Chinese into a tighter Soviet embrace and postponing the day when the Communist regime fell. Nor would the United States gain any security advantage from defending Formosa. The Joint Chiefs were sticking to their preferred strategy—avoid any ground war in East Asia and rely on an offshore chain of island bases from the Aleutians, through Japan and Okinawa, down to the Philippines. American airpower and naval power made such a defensive perimeter impregnable while securing America's strategic interests.

Truman hesitated. He told Acheson that he did not want to get involved with the defense of Formosa, but how could he sell an offshore, hands-off policy to Congress? He could not think of a way to do it; nor could Acheson. Instead, the Chiefs were told in effect to change the offshore strategy, for short-term political reasons. Truman wanted them to send a team of military advisers to Formosa and reconsider whether it ought to be included in the defensive perimeter. The Chiefs balked: no fact-finding necessary, they responded.

The Chiefs, however, had a new boss, with a new agenda. James Forrestal had committed suicide, and Truman's new secretary of defense, Louis Johnson, ordered the Chiefs to think again, without bothering with the fact-finding smoke screen, and they did so.[19]

In appointing Louis Johnson to be secretary of defense, Truman had invited the China lobby into the executive branch. Johnson was close to important figures in the China lobby, including Jiang's brother-in-law, H. H. Kung, who had become one of the richest men in the world in an impressively short period of time. Johnson and Acheson clashed often and fiercely over Johnson's desire to provide whatever it took to keep Jiang in power and Mao in the rice paddies. And when Acheson tried to raise the question of Guo Min Dang criminality in the China White Paper, Johnson demanded that every mention or hint of corruption be struck out before publication. Truman supported him in this whitewashing enterprise.[20]

Meanwhile, from his supreme allied commander's office in Tokyo, Douglas MacArthur was asserting that the "loss" of Formosa would somehow outflank the American defense perimeter in the Far East. His personal preferences were proving stronger than his professional judgment, further proof that Truman should have retired him long before.

MacArthur had supported the existing offshore defense strategy when it was formulated shortly after World War II. Besides, the irrelevance of Formosa had been demonstrated during the war: Formosa had been neutralized by airpower and naval power. It was not necessary to invade Formosa to defeat Japan. Unfortunately, MacArthur's emotional attachment to Jiang, Madame Jiang, and almost anyone else who was being attacked by Chinese Communists meant that they could count on his support. MacArthur was also convinced that East Asia would determine the history of the world and, consequently, the fate of the United States. One way or another, Americans would eventually find themselves fighting against Mao's China and alongside the troops of the GMD.

Acheson advised Truman not to get more entangled than he already was in the Chinese morass, but Truman pushed the United States ever deeper in China's civil war. He knew that what he was doing would alarm the vast majority of Americans, so plain-speaking Harry threw dust in their eyes. He invented a China that was a menace to international peace and stability, bent on conquering its neighbors. No mean goal, given that China shares a border with fourteen countries. Truman was scraping the Yellow Peril barrel with an enthusiasm for scaremongering that he would have found intolerable in anyone else.

Apart from Taiwan and Tibet, Mao was willing to wait for national reunification with Hong Kong, Macao, Outer Mongolia, and Kowloon. Formosa in GMD hands was different: it would pose a military threat to the mainland for years to come. Tibet was different too. China and India had been in dispute over Tibet for generations. As Indian influence grew, it was taken as a geostrategic threat in an area where China felt almost as vulnerable as in the Taiwan Strait.

When Mao proclaimed the establishment of the People's Republic of China in Beijing in October 1949, there was a chance for a fresh start. Truman chose to put a national security problem in its place. He was looking for a little domestic tranquillity, but he was not going to find it.

Truman could have extended de facto recognition to the new government, a step that does nothing more than recognize a government as being in control of its territory. It simply says that a new crowd of gangsters has taken over from another gang. De facto recognition does not require full diplomatic relations, such as exchanging ambassadors and opening an embassy.

What it does offer is a chance to establish a small diplomatic mission in order to reduce friction, avoid misunderstandings, and manage whatever crises come along. In the meantime, the United States could have continued to offer economic and political support to the GMD, meaning it was recognized as the legal government of China even if it did not control all of China's territory. Flexibility is the backbone of great power diplomacy. Truman rejected flexibility. He was tying the United States so tightly to Jiang that if the GMD lost Formosa, it would do so at America's expense.

Here was a challenge to presidential leadership and an eye on the future, not fixation on the moment. Truman was not going to seek reelection in 1952, and de facto recognition did not require Senate approval. Instead of leading, he followed. Former president Herbert Hoover and "Mr. Republican"—Senator Robert Taft—were demanding that he commit American forces to the defense of Formosa.

Most Americans would not support that, but Truman could not remain silent. He had his staff prepare a statement that declared, "The United States has no desire to obtain special rights or privileges or to establish military bases on Formosa at this time." His staff advised him to say that the United States would not "interfere in the present civil war or to detach Formosa from China." Truman crossed that out. And even as he spoke, Truman continued to finance Jiang's government and Jiang's brutal conquest of Formosa, rhetorically claiming the sensible policy, pursuing the foolish one.[21]

Like Acheson, Truman looked on China and saw a country so weak, economically and militarily, that there wasn't anything the Chinese could do, no matter what the United States did—not now, maybe not ever. China's weakness looked like an invitation to them.

The British, the French, and more than a dozen other countries took a different view. They extended de facto recognition during the winter of 1949. Mao, in turn, recognized the Communist regime of Ho Chi Minh as the legitimate government of Vietnam. Infuriated, Truman granted full recognition to the puppet regime the French had established under a fat, youthful, and not overly bright "emperor," Bao Dai. A Buddha in a trademark white suit, always genial, always pliable, Bao Dai was a stooge's stooge. He had served as Japan's puppet, and was happy to change paymasters. The French duly organized a fake referendum showing that virtually the entire population of Indochina supported the new emperor.

As Mao's junk fleet grew in the spring of 1950, so did the pressure on the United States to defend Formosa. It came not only from Herbert Hoover, Robert Taft, the China bloc, the China lobby, and the secretary of defense. It started coming from the State Department too. At the end of May 1950, Dean Rusk, the assistant secretary of state for Far Eastern affairs, solemnly informed Acheson and, through him, the president that the Sino-Soviet alliance "marks a shift in the balance of power in favor of Soviet Russia and to the disfavor of the United States."

What the rest of the world was wondering now, said Rusk, was what the United States would do. "If our conduct indicates a continuing disposition to fall back and allow doubtful areas to fall under Soviet Communist control," the results would be terrifying: Western Europe would fall under Soviet domination; the Monroe Doctrine would become untenable, putting all of Central and South America at risk; Japan, the Philippines, and Indonesia would probably fold "and the oil of the Middle East will be in jeopardy."

The only solution was to pick a fight somewhere; it hardly mattered where. "This series of disasters can probably be prevented if at some doubtful point we quickly take a dramatic and strong stand." The place to stand, and fight, said Rusk, was Formosa.[22]

After direct intervention and war with China were ruled out, Rusk had another suggestion: let's stage a coup d'état, overthrow Jiang, and put Li Zongren in his place. Acheson told Truman what Rusk was thinking, and Truman said he'd give it some thought.

By this time, Truman had been drawn so deeply into China affairs that he had a pair of Chinese-American businessmen, Albert and William Chow, sending him private reports on the situation of Formosa. He also had an old family friend, Karl W. V. Nix, who conducted a lot of business in the Far East, acting as the president's unofficial observer. Nix told him that Jiang was prepared to resign, if a face-saving way could be found. And that was how things stood on June 24, 1950. Should Truman okay a coup, or ask Jiang to go quietly?[23]

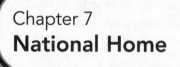

Chapter 7
National Home

IN THE AFTERMATH OF WORLD WAR II, THE SYSTEMATIC MURDER OF
six million Jews was a crime almost beyond comprehension. The
bloodshed and suffering the war had brought to humanity exceeded
every war that had gone before, yet the Holocaust weighed heavily on
the conscience of the liberal democracies. It seemed to be less a
product of the war than a product of human wickedness.

Governments and people alike were agreed that something had to
be done, yet there was no agreement among ordinary citizens or their
governments as to just what that something should be. The majority
of Jews, however, had a clear idea: a Jewish state, in Palestine; a return to the land their ancestors had departed nearly two thousand
years before. After all, they insisted, that was what they had been
promised by Britain back in 1917.

The British foreign secretary at the time was Arthur Balfour, a former
Oxford professor and philosopher. In November of that year he had
written to Lord Rothschild, Britain's most prominent Zionist, to clarify
British intentions toward the Jews. Britain was clearly going to drive the

Turks out of Palestine, and the British government was seeking financial support for its war effort from the Jews of Britain and beyond.

Balfour informed Rothschild, "His Majesty's Government view with favour the establishment in Palestine of a national home for the Jewish people, and will use their best endeavors to facilitate the achievement of this object, it being clearly understood that nothing shall be done which may prejudice the civil and religious rights of existing non-Jewish communities in Palestine . . ."

Jews tended to quote only the first part of this conditional pledge, while Palestinians were likely to emphasize the second. Nor did it offer to help create a Jewish state, but only "a national home," which implied an autonomous Jewish region or province within Palestine. In 1946, the newly created United Nations took that as the basis for providing dispossessed and suffering Holocaust survivors with a place they might call their own.

Truman had no prejudice against individual Jews. During World War I he had gone into partnership with one, Eddie Jacobson, to operate a canteen for soldiers in France. After the war ended, the two of them established a haberdashery in Kansas City. The business failed, but the friendship did not.

Yet, like many another American, Truman was not immune to casual anti-Semitism. People are always going to be mocked or scorned for whatever it is that makes them different, and Truman didn't spare his pal Eddie's coreligionists. "The Jews claim God Almighty picked 'em out for special privilege. Well, I'm sure He had better judgment," Truman wrote in his diary as the Jewish homeland problem landed on his desk.[1]

His frustration at the Zionist lobby came out at a cabinet meeting in July 1946. "Jesus Christ couldn't please them when he was here on Earth, so how could anyone else expect that I would have better luck?" He did not like them, said Truman, did not have any use for them, and did not care what happened to them.

Henry Wallace, his secretary of commerce, reminded him of the Holocaust. "No other people have suffered this way." Truman ignored Wallace's implied rebuke.[2]

Despite this, Truman became as much a creator of Israel as its two earliest advocates, Moses Hess and Theodor Herzl. It seems unlikely that Israel would have survived its critical first year without him; it might not even have come into existence at all. The United States could have vetoed it in the Security Council, which is what Acheson, Marshall, and Forrestal wanted. The State Department thought that American security would suffer from the establishment of a Jewish state in the Middle East, and the Pentagon agreed. Truman seemed to be working alone to bring it about, but at his elbow, urging him on, stood Clark Clifford.

Truman had inherited Judge Samuel Rosenman from Roosevelt. Rosenman was the first special counsel in the history of the presidency, and he was a Zionist. Rosenman in turn had brought Clifford into the White House to serve as his assistant, and when Rosenman departed, in 1946, Clifford was elevated to take his place.

Clifford had risen like a rocket because he possessed an ability that Truman prized: he could write a speech that sounded as Trumanesque as if the president himself had produced it. Truman felt comfortable reading aloud almost anything that Clifford had written. Clifford worked mainly on the foreign policy speeches, for which he had no special qualifications at all. It was Clifford who wrote the preamble to the Truman Doctrine speech and provided its tone. In writing important speeches, Clifford also shaped some of their content, infuriating Marshall and Acheson.

Clifford had a second, equally important ability. Truman had a habit of talking tough, then wondering if he might have gone too far, and proclaiming his belief in cooperation the next day, only to change his mind a few days later and then change his mind all over again. In all this emotional and intellectual gyration, Clifford could divine just what it was that Truman really wanted. This is the supreme gift of the courtier, and Clifford knew how to use it.[3]

There was something else besides, something hinted at in Truman's need for Dr. Wallace Graham's "snake oil." Truman had an abundance of self-belief: he knew just who he was and what he was. But self-belief is not the same as self-confidence. The foreign policy questions he had to decide were so complex, the risks so great, the lobbying so intense, that he needed Dr. Graham's secret preparation to see him through. The self-confidence just wasn't there, even though self-belief was.

Clifford, though—there was self-confidence on legs. Truman made up for his deficit by drawing on Clifford's abundance. And although Truman readily claimed responsibility for the decisions he made, he could not always claim as much for the thinking behind them.

Clifford found poker boring, but he knew how important it was to Truman, so it was Clifford who organized the poker sessions aboard the presidential yacht, the *Williamsburg*, and down at Key West or up at Shangri-La. Clifford did not court publicity for himself, and Truman appreciated that. The two of them had lunch several times a week, alone.

Other members of the staff tended to consider Clifford a little too smooth, a little too pleased with himself, a little too close to Truman. This may have been jealousy in part, but Margaret Truman did not like or trust him any more than the staff did.[4]

Movies were shown about once a week in the small theater in the White House basement. Clifford would appear just as the lights were about to be dimmed and the projector started. He would stand in the doorway, impeccably and expensively dressed, handsome in a slightly lounge lizard way. After making a small bow, he proceeded regally to his seat, the cynosure of every eye. Clifford needed to be noticed, and he made sure he was.

Once Truman had made up his mind on a major issue, there were only two people who could make him think again. Bess was one. The other was Clark Clifford. What was missing in both cases, though, was political experience. Like Bess, Clifford had never run for office, never held an executive position, never been immersed in political life. Clifford was a phrasemaker, not a deal maker, and the only politics that seemed to interest him was the lowest common denominator variety: get tough with the Russians, don't let the Republicans win Jewish votes, crush the Communist guerrillas in Vietnam. Clifford lacked the temperament and the grasp of politics to think through the implications of the policies he argued for. Like Truman, he lived in the moment and only the moment, assuming he'd be able to handle whatever followed. Which was why he would get involved one day with a bank that was a criminal enterprise and fail to see it for what it was, the money to be made being so impressive. Clifford would have ended his life in a federal prison had it not been for a merciful judge and a helpful doctor's report. As it turned out, he matched Napoleon's description of Talleyrand, *"Merde dans un bas de soie"*—shit in a silk stocking.

Although Truman had originally expected to be a one-term president and had no desire to be anything else, by 1947 he had changed his mind. He decided to run in his own right, and one day, Clifford handed him a memo. It set out a campaign strategy that he could not possibly have crafted.

The memo had actually been produced by James Rowe, a longtime Democratic Party strategist. Clifford had appropriated it and presented it to the president as if it were his own creation. It would be more than twenty years before Rowe got any of the credit he deserved. Across the decades, Clifford lied prodigiously about his role in the 1948 campaign, gave ground only under intense pressure, and revised his version of events. Even as he was dying, he would only grudgingly admit the irrefutable truth.[5]

Clifford's one important contribution to Truman's campaign was to focus on Palestine, an issue where Truman's sympathies were obvious. Henry Wallace made this note in his diary after talking to Truman about Palestine in July 1946: "I emphasized the political angle because that is the one angle on Palestine which has a really deep interest for Truman."[6]

At about the same time, Truman told Marshall and Acheson that he was going to speak out in favor of the Zionist project. "I have to answer to hundreds of thousands who are anxious for the success of Zionism; I do not have hundreds of thousands of Arabs among my constituents."[7]

What he did have, though, was a letter, written by Roosevelt shortly before his death, to Ibn Sa'ūd, the ruler of Saudi Arabia. In it, Roosevelt had addressed Ibn Sa'ūd as "Great and Good Friend," a traditional form of address used by presidents when writing to foreign rulers, whether or not the president had ever met them. Ibn Sa'ūd was a ruler who had two interests of consequence: one was opposing a Jewish state in the Arab world; the other was sex with girls as young as twelve or thirteen, hence the three thousand Saudi princes a generation after his death. In his letter, Roosevelt pledged to take no action on Palestine without consulting Ibn Sa'ūd first. "I wish that 'Great and Good' letter had never been found," Truman told his staff.[8]

The prime minister and the foreign minister of Iraq meanwhile informed the State Department that if the United States imposed a Zionist state on Palestine, the entire Arab world would be enraged, and the Soviets would be able to take advantage of that even though the Russians were currently supporting the Zionists. Countries that were now pro-American would become anti-American, until the entire Middle East was hostile. American ambassadors from across the region reported the same thing.[9]

Marshall, Acheson, and Forrestal and their principal assistants all saw a Zionist state as posing a permanent danger to national security. The United States imported hardly any foreign oil; it was almost self-sufficient and would remain so for at least another decade. It was Europe that was vulnerable, as was Japan. Any serious disruption would create turmoil across the globe. It was Truman's responsibility to ensure that that didn't happen.

The State Department official responsible for the Middle East, Loy Henderson, advised Truman that the right response to the challenge was for the United States, the United Kingdom, Canada, Australia, and New Zealand to lower their immigration barriers. Every Jew who wanted to move away from Europe to start a new life in a stable liberal democracy should be helped and encouraged to do so. The national home they wanted to build in Palestine would not be the peaceful, happy place that Zionists imagined. And what would become of the Palestinians who were displaced? They would trade places with the Jews and become refugees, a people without a land to call their own.

An Anglo-American Committee was formed, with the blessing of the UN, to study the challenge of creating a Jewish homeland. For a time, the committee thought the best thing would be a two-state solution. But for every problem that seemed solved, another sprang up in its place. There were enclaves of Jews in the projected Palestinian state, enclaves of Palestinians in the Jewish state. Connecting them up was impossible, but leaving them as enclaves was also impossible, and how they could be made economically viable was beyond anyone's comprehension. After nearly a year of talking to experts and interested parties, the committee recommended creating a new state in Palestine, one that embraced Palestinians and Jews, Muslims and Christians, and guaranteed equal rights to all. Most Zionists would not even consider it. They demanded their own state, a Zionist state, and nothing less.

Forrestal held up an apocalyptic picture of the future for Truman to contemplate. Creating a small state that would be surrounded by enemies for the next hundred years, in a region as unstable as the Middle East, would only lead to one war after another, he told Truman. Yet the United States was becoming so involved in the Zionist enterprise that it would become the guarantor of Israel's security. One day, the United States would be called on to make good on that pledge, said Forrestal.[10]

Truman paid little attention to such warnings. Instead, he listened to Clifford and to David Niles, one of his presidential aides. Niles was the presidential assistant for minorities, meaning Jews and blacks. There is no record of Niles ever doing much for blacks, but as an observant Jew, he devoted much of his energies to the creation of Israel. The Zionist lobby had someone in the White House who kept it informed of every impending executive branch action. Niles went even further. He told politicians at home and abroad that he was speaking to them on behalf of Truman, who was demanding their support for a Jewish state.[11]

There was also Judge Rosenman. He and Clifford remained close, and in the fall of 1947 Rosenman and Clifford together held a long talk with Truman over American policy toward the attempt to establish a Jewish homeland in Palestine. They reminded him that Roosevelt had promised to press the British to live up to the 1917 Balfour Declaration. How could he not do the same?

As the election year approached, the pressure on Truman mounted inexorably. What about the pledge to Ibn Sa'ūd? What about the Balfour pledge to protect the rights of the Palestinians? At times he felt helpless. At a meeting with his staff early in 1948, he said he didn't know what else to do. "I've done everything I can, short of putting the country back on a war footing to bring about a Jewish homeland."[12]

Emanuel Celler, a progressive congressman from New York who was also the chairman of the House Judiciary Committee, led a delegation of Jewish leaders into the Oval Office. "We have been talking to Tom Dewey," said Celler. "He is going to declare for a Jewish state and we are going to turn our money over and urge Jews to vote for him unless you beat him to it." Celler pounded on Truman's desk. "And if you don't come out for a Jewish state we'll run you out of town!"

Dewey was certain to be the Republican nominee, and although the Jewish vote amounted to only 4 percent of the total vote, that 4 percent was heavily concentrated in New York City. There was also the question of campaign funding. Clifford told Truman that Dewey could persuade American Jews to vote Republican with both ballots and wallets.

Robert Hannegan, the chairman of the Democratic National Committee, assured Truman that Clifford was spouting nonsense. The vast majority of Jews would remain loyal to the party of Roosevelt. Even worse, said Hannegan, taking such a strong stand on a Jewish homeland might cost him the election. Although it might win some Jewish votes, it would be easily offset by alienating a lot of non-Jewish votes.

Hannegan was right. Nothing was going to get the bulk of Jewish voters to switch parties. They were not going to do it in 1948, and they have never done it since. Yet between Clifford's amateurish analysis and Hannegan's professional judgment, Truman took Clifford's advice. "We're going to have a country for these Jews and that's the end of it," said Truman.[13]

With the failure of the Anglo-American Committee's search for a solution, the problem was handed off to the UN. There seemed only two possibilities now: a partition of Palestine, or a trusteeship under the Security Council, an arrangement that would embrace both Jews and Palestinians.

Zionists were vehemently opposed to trusteeship. It meant that the major powers would try to impose their own solution on what the Palestinians would have to surrender and what the Jewish state would gain. Partition was a much better option; then the issue would be settled by force, and nobody, Zionist or not, believed that the Arabs could fight their way out of a wet paper bag. Yet there was strong opposition to partition within the Security Council.

In March 1948, with the UN heading for deadlock over the question of partition, Truman received a request for a meeting from Chaim Weizmann, the erstwhile leader of the Zionist movement. A distinguished chemist and an engaging man, Weizmann had traveled from his home in London, hoping. Truman replied that he was too busy.

The real reason for Truman's refusal was the impending deadlock at the UN. Marshall had told Truman that the alternative to partition—trusteeship—would have to be considered, and there might still be enough time to get a truce in place, preventing fighting before it could get started. Marshall showed Truman a telegram that contained the necessary instructions to Warren Austin, the U.S. representative at the UN. Truman told Marshall to send it, and Marshall scrawled on the telegram, "Approved by the President." With the United States about to make a fundamental change in its position, Truman was not going to discuss it with Weizmann before it became public.

And then he received a call from Eddie Jacobson, his old pal and partner in the failed haberdashery business. Eddie was begging for a meeting. "Eddie, I'm always glad to see old friends," Truman told him, "but there's one thing you've got to promise me. I don't want you to say a word about what's going on over there in the Middle East." Jacobson so promised.

When he was shown into the Oval Office the next day, Jacobson had tears running down his cheeks. "Eddie, you son of a bitch," said Truman.

"Every time I think of the homeless Jews, homeless for thousands of years . . ." What else could he do but cry? He begged Truman to see Chaim Weizmann. "I ought to have you thrown out of here," said Truman. "You knew damn good and well that I couldn't stand seeing you cry." Rather than endure more tears, he agreed to see Weizmann.[14]

When Truman met with Weizmann a few days later, he assured him that he would support the establishment of a national home for the Jews, which to Weizmann meant support for partition. It seems that Truman had forgotten the telegram.[15]

The very next day, Warren Austin told the UN Security Council, "My government believes that a temporary trusteeship of the United Nations should be established to maintain the peace and afford the Jews and Arabs of Palestine, who must live together, further opportunity to reach agreement . . ."[16]

The first Truman heard about it was in *The New York Times* the next morning, as he was having breakfast. He called Clifford immediately. "There's a story in the papers on Palestine and I don't know what's happened."

When Clifford reached the White House, Truman was in an emotional state, wailing, "How could this have happened? I assured Chaim Weizmann we would stick to it. He must think I'm a shitass!"[17]

Clifford told him that he'd been betrayed by the State Department. There was a widespread feeling among American Jews that people who were pro-Arab and anti-Zionist ran the department. Given Truman's long-standing contempt for State, he was inclined to agree.

The president might admire George Marshall above everyone else in the government, but Clifford persuaded him that there were rogue elements a couple of tiers below the secretary's office. They were the ones to blame for making him look like a shitass.[18] A meeting was held in the Cabinet Room, and it rapidly degenerated into a heated argument between Loy Henderson, the assistant secretary of state for Near Eastern affairs, and Clark Clifford.

Henderson said that a trusteeship offered a good chance of securing a truce, and without a truce, there was no way of stabilizing Palestine once the British pulled out. Partition would make a truce impossible, and the country would fall almost at once into what amounted to a war between Jews and Palestinians. He wasn't expressing only his own views, he said, but those of every U.S. consulate or legation in the Middle East and of every Arab expert in the department. Clifford was a lawyer; he had never set foot in the Middle East. He turned the argument into an impromptu trial in which a hostile witness's veracity was the issue, not the merits of an argument about policy. Fast losing interest, Truman stood up. "Oh, hell," he muttered. "I'm leaving."[19]

Clifford provided the only official account of this meeting, an account so slanted it verged on crooked. Marshall saw it coming and gave an extensive briefing, without attribution, to *The New York Times*, which made the State Department's case also a matter of record.[20]

The next day, Truman told a packed press conference that trusteeship was essential to prevent a power vacuum when the British withdrew. "Partition could not be carried out by peaceful means," Truman said, "and we could not impose this solution on the people of Palestine by use of American troops."[21]

The British planned to leave Palestine at midnight on May 14,

1948. Five Arab armies were getting ready to move in. Clifford and David Niles were eager to know just what the president would do. Was he going to recognize the nascent Zionist state, name still unknown? "Prepare a statement for me," Truman told Clifford. On May 12, Clifford handed it to him. It made the case for immediate recognition.

A meeting was convened in Truman's office two days later to discuss it. Clifford read out the statement. First, he ridiculed the State Department's belief that a truce was possible. Then he argued for prompt recognition, so the Soviet Union would not be the first state to offer it. Finally, he said that the government should use the UN to pressure other countries into recognizing the new country. These were the arguments that Zionists were making, and they served only to show that Clifford could not see beyond the next election.

George Marshall was unable to contemplate the present without giving thought to the future. He had begun preparing the army to fight World War II more than ten years before Pearl Harbor. Marshall could hardly stand to listen to anything so shortsighted or so base as what Clifford proposed. It amounted to grubbing for votes at a critical moment in American history, and to hell with everything else.[22]

Marshall turned to Truman. "Speaking objectively, I cannot help but think that the suggestions made by Clifford are wrong." He denounced them as "a transparent dodge to win a few votes." Clifford protested that he had not said anything about politics, and that was so. Yet Clifford was running a campaign for Truman's election and a campaign for recognition of a Zionist state. Having told Truman and many others that the two amounted to a single campaign, his protestations fell flat.

Marshall responded, "This is a serious matter of foreign policy determination and the question of politics and political opinion does not enter into it." Tall and solidly built, he towered over everyone else in the room. Normally, he was a master at concealing his emotions behind a perpetual hangdog expression. He was a man who kept his distance, no matter whom he was dealing with. He called everyone, even those for whom he felt a great fondness, by their surnames, and rarely smiled. He was impersonal with all save Mrs. Marshall. Now, though, his famously frosty demeanor was turning to fire; his face and neck were turning brick red, and for once, he reverted to the personal.

"In an effort to let you know how strongly I feel about this issue," he told Truman, "if you were to adopt the policy that is recommended by Clifford, I would be unable to vote for you in this fall's election. What is Clifford doing here anyway?" A good question, one that Truman brushed off rather than addressed. "He's here because I asked him," said Truman.

To make sure that this time Clifford did not get to write the official account, Marshall wrote it himself.[23]

Truman felt uncomfortable about pursuing a foreign policy against Marshall's advice, but Clifford convinced him that he could do it, provided Marshall did not resign or denounce the decision. In the end, Marshall agreed to say nothing publicly, but he never spoke of or to Clifford again, and following Truman's reelection, he resigned almost immediately.

When the British mandate expired at midnight on May 14, 1948, in Tel Aviv, it was 6:00 p.m. in Washington. No one in the White House knew what the new state would be called until shortly before its existence was proclaimed. Eleven minutes later, Truman extended recognition to the new provisional government. The statement issued on May 14 reads: "This Government has been informed that a Jewish state has been proclaimed in Palestine, and recognition has been requested by the provisional government thereof. The United States recognizes the provisional government as the de facto authority of the new State of Israel."

The United States had never before recognized a country that lacked well-defined boundaries. The State Department thought the government should at least wait a few weeks until the Israelis told them what its territory comprised, or at least what it was they were claiming.

Egypt, Syria, Jordan, and other Arab countries were already deploying their armies to intervene. Clifford said that these were empty threats. Who were these Arabs anyway? "A few nomadic tribes," he told Truman. Nothing to worry about. The Arabic and Muslim world did not matter. What mattered was the Jewish vote in November, and that had just been secured.[24]

Truman, nevertheless, had been looking beyond the election. Although Marshall and Forrestal prophesied a future of wars for both the Jews and the United States, people such as David Niles, Manny

Celler, and Chaim Weizmann offered a different prospect. Imagine a future in which a Jewish state, established by able and intelligent people fleeing pogroms and genocide, would one day blaze like a beacon in a stygian night. "Zionism is a humanitarian movement," they told him. "It's liberal, it's progressive."

From his reading of history, Truman believed the Middle East had never had anything resembling democracy. There had been rule only by despots—some benevolent, most not—or by colonial powers. Zionists he had spoken to between his accession to the presidency and the creation of Israel convinced him that a Jewish state would represent liberal democracy in a poor and backward part of the world.

Once it took root, that country would create sparks that jumped across frontiers, igniting a passion for change. The poor Arabs, downtrodden for a thousand years, would finally be free and prosperous. For the rest of his life Truman spoke proudly of his part in the foundation of Israel. You'll see, he liked to say, this is going to make the world a safer and happier place, spreading democracy from the Levant to the Gulf.[25]

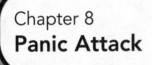

Chapter 8
Panic Attack

A YEAR BEFORE THE 1948 ELECTION, TRUMAN SEEMED DOOMED. HIS job approval rating fell below 50 percent and continued to fall. All was not lost, though, because there was one sure way to engineer a reversal of fortune—a good war scare. Clark Clifford helpfully pointed out to Truman that "the worse matters get, up to a fairly certain point— real danger of imminent war—the more there is a sense of crisis. In times of crisis, the American citizen tends to back up his President."[1]

The military was as ready as the president for a war scare. Truman was still slashing military budgets, convinced that the armed forces were as profligate as they were patriotic. *The Wall Street Journal* anticipated what the response would be: "a Russian Scare will be used to prod more Army-Navy money out of Congress."[2]

Marshall too was ready for a war scare. Congress was resisting the European Recovery Program, better known in later years as the Marshall Plan. Yet the omens at the start of the new year weren't promising. "The Soviet Union is in no position to support a global war," Dwight Eisenhower told a reporter for *The New York Times* in February 1948. And then Stalin and a group of Czech Communists came providentially to Truman's and Marshall's and the Pentagon's assistance.[3]

The government of Czechoslovakia had been under Soviet control for more than a year. Communists held all of the important ministries—Interior, Finance, Foreign Affairs, National Defense. They also controlled the press and the trade unions. All of which had been reported to the State Department by the U.S. ambassador to Czechoslovakia, Laurence A. Steinhardt. The Soviets had been restrained in using the powers they possessed, Steinhardt had recently informed Marshall. There were no large Soviet troop concentrations on Czech soil and "no direct evidence of Soviet interference."[4]

Everything changed in February 1948, when a power struggle erupted between the members of the Czech government who were trying to keep the police out of politics and the hard-line Communists who demanded that the police come under their direct control. The hard-liners won the argument by ousting the moderates.

Events were also moving in Truman's favor in Finland. Stalin was pressing the Finnish government to join in a treaty of friendship and mutual security with the Soviet Union. The Finns agreed, reluctantly.

Here was something to work with, something that played directly into a ploy crafted by Walter Bedell Smith, the ambassador to the Soviet Union. FULL INFORMATION AND EXPLANATION TO OUR OWN CONGRESS OF SIGNIFICANCE OF RECENT SOVIET MOVES IN CZECHOSLOVAKIA AND FINLAND MAY RESULT IN SPEEDING CONSIDERATION AND ADOPTION OF UNIVERSAL MILITARY TRAINING AND BUILDING PROGRAMS FOR ARMY, NAVY, AND PARTICULARLY AIR FORCE, Smith had advised Marshall in a telegram on March 1. The very next day, a full-blown war scare was put together over lunch by Marshall and Secretary of Defense Forrestal.[5]

The Finnish-Soviet pact was described by the administration as being a replay of the Hitler-Stalin Pact of August 1939—the precursor of a new world war. Truman and Marshall sedulously ignored the reports from American diplomats in Finland and from the CIA, who insisted there was nothing sinister about it.[6]

The sense of crisis over Czechoslavakia rose sharply when, on the night of March 9–10, the leading anti-Communist politician in Czechoslovakia, Jan Masaryk, jumped or was pushed from a window and died a few hours later. When news reached Washington of Masaryk's death, Marshall had his staff organize a press conference.

The director of the CIA, R. H. Hillenkoetter, assured Truman that the recent installation of a Communist government in Czechoslovakia had almost nothing to do with the Russians. "We do not believe," Hillenkoetter's analysis read, "that this event reflects any sudden increase in Soviet capabilities, more aggressive intentions, or any change in current Soviet policy and tactics."[7]

Marshall ignored Hillenkoetter's report. Czechoslovakia was now, he solemnly declared, suffering "a reign of terror." The Soviet threat had never been more threatening; the dangerous parts of the world were more dangerous than ever. But there was one thing people needed to understand: Americans must remain calm.

It was a bizarre attempt to whip up the war scare for the benefit of Congress, without frightening voters into looking for a peace candidate and consumers into closing their wallets. As James Reston described it in *The New York Times* two days later, "The Secretary's performance was like a man getting up in a theatre and announcing, 'I advise everybody here to be very calm because the whole block around this theatre is on fire.' "[8]

In the months that followed, Marshall talked about how the installation of a hard-line Communist government in Prague foreshadowed Communist attempts at seizing power across Western Europe, but he knew that was nonsense. As he told Jefferson Caffrey, the U.S. ambassador to France, there was nothing to worry about. "In the last three years Czechoslovakia has faithfully followed the Soviet policy . . . a Communist regime would merely crystallize and confirm for the future previous Czech policy."[9]

On March 5, General Lucius D. Clay, the commander of U.S. forces in Europe and military governor of the U.S. zone of occupation in Germany, had obligingly sent a telegram to Forrestal that overflowed with menace and dread: FOR MANY MONTHS, BASED ON LOGICAL ANALYSIS, I HAVE FELT AND HELD THAT WAR WAS UNLIKELY FOR AT LEAST TEN YEARS. WITHIN THE LAST FEW WEEKS, I HAVE FELT A SUBTLE CHANGE IN SOVIET ATTITUDE WHICH I CANNOT DEFINE, BUT WHICH NOW GIVES ME A FEELING THAT IT MAY COME WITH DRAMATIC SUDDENNESS.[10]

It was all fiction. Clay did not believe a word of what he had written. A week earlier he had received a visit from Lieutenant General

Stephen J. Chamberlain, the head of army intelligence. Chamberlain said that Congress was resisting Truman's proposal to bring back the draft. Could Clay do anything to help? Clay sent the telegram to Chamberlain, who in turn passed it on to Forrestal instead of to Omar Bradley, the army chief of staff. What Bradley would have done with it wasn't certain, but Forrestal made sure not only that it was shown to the congressional leadership but also that it was leaked. Some newspapers obligingly played it up as a dire and imminent warning of an impending Soviet attack.[11]

Truman was ready, possibly eager, to play his part. At his press conference on March 10 he declared that recent events had left his confidence that the world would remain at peace "somewhat shaken." As Forrestal noted with satisfaction in his diary six days later, "Papers this morning full of rumors and portents of war."[12]

On March 17 Truman addressed Congress on the current crisis. Stewart and Joseph Alsop's column in *The Washington Post* that day announced, "The atmosphere in Washington today is no longer a postwar atmosphere. It is, to put it bluntly, a prewar atmosphere."[13]

In his address, Truman told Congress that the situation the United States now faced was critical. Everything wrong in the world was entirely the fault of the Soviets, the need to stop their evil designs was urgent, and the place to begin was by funding the Marshall Plan, instituting universal military training (UMT), and reenacting the draft, temporarily, while a UMT program was being established. Both houses swiftly came up with the money he wanted for the Marshall Plan. The war scare was working, partly. Congress balked at UMT and at a renewed draft.

Marshall swung into action with speeches at UC Berkeley and UCLA. Stalin, he informed his audiences, was the new Hitler. As army chief of staff, he recalled, "I watched the Nazi government take control of one country after another until finally Poland was invaded." He portrayed the Soviets as being poised to unleash a blitzkrieg offensive to conquer Western Europe, yet while the situation he saw unfolding now was "disturbingly similar," it was also alarmingly new: "Never before in history has the world situation been more threatening to our ideals and interests than at the present time." The United States had to act, and act now, before it was too late.[14]

The secretary of the navy, John L. Sullivan, made his own contribution by revealing that "submarines not belonging to any nation west of the iron curtain have been sighted off our shores." For anyone who might manage to miss the point, he added, "We all recall that an early step of the Germans in 1917 and in 1941 was to deploy submarines off our coasts." All of which came as news to the Office of Naval Intelligence, which had no confirmed sightings of Russian submarines within three thousand miles of American shores.[15]

Strangely, during this time of imminent peril, sinister Soviet moves, and blatant provocations, the administration was selling war surplus to Poland and the Soviet Union. The surplus included brand-new engines powerful enough for heavy bombers, as well as thousands of combat aircraft, well preserved and as deadly as their designers intended.

A congressional subcommittee happened to be holding hearings on the disposal of surplus property, and one of its expert witnesses told them what he'd seen. In New York, he said, "there are boxes and cases marked 'For Russia' lying all over the waterfront. They are being loaded every day. They've brought sixty Soviet-flag ships into New York harbor and loaded them with material for Russia since the first of the year." Here was a consequence that Truman had not anticipated. Congress demanded that he stop selling war surplus to the Soviet Union, or to any Communist country. With the war scare coming to its feverish peak, he had to change course, at least on the sales: "Russia is, at the present time, a friendly nation and has been buying goods from us right along." The previous week, in addressing Congress, this "friendly nation" had been, in his words, "a growing menace."[16]

Even before the war scare, Congress and the president did not seem willing to boost the air force budget, and the air force secretary, Stuart Symington, was becoming frustrated. He thought a shocking revelation might help. In February he had informed the country that the Soviets were now the world leaders in airpower. They were currently turning out up to two thousand combat aircraft a week. Asked by the Senate Armed Services Committee how he knew this, he claimed that there was intelligence to substantiate it. Forrestal told the committee that was simply not true. There was no intelligence that justified Symington's claims. Even so, the war scare offered new possibilities. In a speech in Denver in April, Symington warned Colorado Rotarians, "We are not at peace . . . the threat of the Red Army and the Red Air Force" menaced America. It might have surprised the Rotarians to know that a recent Defense Department study had concluded that the Soviets were years away from being able to create and deploy a heavy bomber force in major combat operations. It also found that the Soviets would not be capable of effective naval operations far from Russian waters for at least a decade. Symington, like Sullivan, was inventing intelligence claims to mislead Congress and the public.[17]

It worked. One predictable result of the war scare was pressure on Truman from the army, the navy, and the air force to stop cutting their budgets and to find more money for them. Predictable, but he did not see it coming, while those who did, such as Forrestal, chose to keep their foresight to themselves. Once the scare took off, Forrestal could hardly wait to get up to Capitol Hill and tell the Senate Armed Services Committee that a supplemental appropriation of $3 billion was needed immediately, an increase in the defense budget of nearly 30 percent.

Truman was shocked, telling his chief economic adviser, Edwin G. Nourse, "We must be careful that the military does not overstep the bounds from an economic standpoint . . . Most of them would like to go back to a war footing."[18]

At a meeting with Forrestal and the Joint Chiefs he told them to stop pushing so hard. "I want a peace program, not a war program." They more or less ignored him. Truman's control over the military was less than total, partly because he had to work through Forrestal. Six weeks after this meeting, the military services got their extra $3 billion. In percentage terms, this was and remains the biggest one-year increase in Pentagon spending. For every dollar the war scare had produced for the Marshall Plan, it produced even more for the Pentagon.[19]

Even after the Pentagon got its $3 billion, Forrestal was reluctant to let the war scare fade away. He went back to the Senate Armed Services Committee to reveal that there was still a crisis. "The problem is, we set up a plan last year based on the assumption of no immediate danger of war." Well, that was then. Right now, "we have to contemplate the possibility of war."[20]

His moment had passed. Truman was trying to ratchet the scare down. He didn't want to provoke the Russians into some kind of dangerous riposte. A message was duly composed and delivered to Molotov. In it, Walter Bedell Smith said that he wanted the Soviet Union to understand "that the United States has no hostile or aggressive design whatever with respect to the Soviet Union." Any and all contrary views were "falsehoods," based on "complete misunderstanding or malicious motives."

Having reached out a hand, though, Truman could not resist talking tough. There were serious problems with the current U.S.-Soviet relationship, the message acknowledged, but these were due entirely to "Soviet and world Communist policy." Stalin's response was two notes that were equally equivocal—sounding positive here, negative there, and clear nowhere. The Americans would get his real reply soon enough, in Berlin.[21]

One of Truman's creations was the Central Intelligence Agency. Established in 1947, the CIA was and is usually described as a direct descendant of the wartime Office of Strategic Services, but that wasn't how its first director, R. H. Hillenkoetter, saw it; nor was it how Truman saw it. The core activity of the OSS under its Medal of Honor–winning founder, William Donovan, had been operations behind enemy lines. Collecting information was a secondary role.

Hillenkoetter wanted the CIA to devote itself to unearthing the capabilities and intentions of other countries and analyzing the resulting haul. Covert operations were out. All of which came as a major disappointment to George Kennan, famous author of the Long Telegram and putative father of the policy of containing the Soviet Union.[22]

Even so, containment was never going to be enough for peace, Kennan decided. It was not in the nature of the Russian people or the Soviet government to be contained for long without seeking to strike back. Kennan's Policy Planning Staff turned its thoughts toward launching a campaign of psychological warfare against the Soviet Union. That soon became only one element in a broader, even more ambitious design—rolling back Communism across Eastern Europe. Kennan the intellectual was morphing into Kennan the thinking man of action. He began itching to create trouble for the Russians, with sabotage, partisan attacks, guerrilla warfare, popular insurrections, black propaganda, and, if necessary, assassination. He persuaded Marshall, and Marshall in turn persuaded Truman that if the CIA would not try to undermine Soviet rule, then the State Department must.[23]

A new body was created in the spring of 1948, the Office of Policy Coordination (OPC). In keeping with the opaque moniker, its purpose was left deliberately vague. It aimed to draw upon the large population of refugees and displaced persons from Russia and Eastern Europe that had become established in the United States. It would also draw on other refugees and DPs in Western Europe; on former fascist groups in Eastern Europe that had gone underground as the Red Army moved in; on Hitler's chief of military intelligence on the eastern front, Reinhard Gehlen; and on the intelligence assets that Britain's Secret Intelligence Service (SIS) had developed from Gibraltar to Lithuania.

The British were already trying to undermine Stalin's hold on his new satellites. The United States and Britain agreed to pool their covert operations. On June 18, 1948, as the war scare was winding down, Truman authorized National Security Council Directive 10/2. This directive put the presidential seal on Operation Rollback. Stalin almost certainly knew it was coming, and he would have known within days that Truman had approved it. After all, he had an impeccable source. The first secretary at the British embassy in Washington was Donald McLean, a charming young Englishman with a Cambridge degree, an excellent pedigree, and a Soviet handler. McLean was the Secret Intelligence Service's man in the District. For the past four years he had been reporting to Moscow.

There was also someone else. The SIS's man in Ankara was Kim Philby, formerly the head of Section IX and thereby responsible for SIS plans to make life difficult for the Soviets if, at the end of the war, Stalin sought to make life difficult for the West. Philby seemed to be the best person for the OPC to turn to for advice now, but with McLean and Philby spying for Soviet military intelligence, Stalin had little to fear from Operation Rollback.

In 1949 Philby became the principal figure in the secret offensive. Its biggest success was getting Radio Free Europe established. Its biggest failure was an attempt in 1949 to overthrow Enver Hoxha, the Communist ruler of Albania. Nearly every Albanian involved was arrested and executed, thanks to Kim Philby, who was directly responsible for organizing this putative coup. The Albanian mission was his way of flushing out Albanian subversives and getting them eliminated.

Every major venture that Rollback launched failed, as did nearly all the minor ones. The members of a partisan group in the Baltic States—called the Forest Brothers—were tracked down and killed. Reinhard Gehlen's spies died in droves. The principal effect of Rollback was to make Communist rule, repressive under almost any circumstances, even harsher.

The principle behind every OPC operation was "plausible deniability." Whatever story the government provided—on the rare occasions where it was compelled to say anything—had to be merely plausible; it did not have to be true. What mattered most was that the president not be implicated—but Truman being Truman, he could not be counted on to keep his mouth shut. Shortly before an operation was mounted in Romania, he told a group of Romanian refugees, "If I can continue our program which I have inaugurated, you are going to be a free country again." The Romanian operation failed.[24]

Six days after Truman authorized a campaign of covert operations behind the iron curtain, Stalin imposed a blockade on civilian road and rail traffic into Berlin. The city was currently divided into four zones, under U.S., Soviet, British, and French control. Berlin itself was within the Soviet occupation zone and two hundred miles east of the three Allied zones. The Allied military was allowed to cross the Soviet occupation zone—the future East Germany—by road and rail. Civilian passenger and freight traffic had no such rights, to either the highway or the railroads.

In March 1948, Stalin held conversations with East German leaders who had told him that something had to be done about the continued Allied presence in Berlin. "Let's join our efforts," said Stalin. "Maybe we'll drive them out." This was at a time when Operation Rollback was being pushed on Truman by Kennan and Marshall.

By June, the Americans, British, and French were preparing to introduce a new currency, the deutsche mark, in their zones of occupation. This currency would be the first step in creating a government of West Germany, and West Germany would inevitably be encouraged to raise an army. The usual interpretation of the blockade was that Stalin was trying to discourage or delay introduction of the new currency. It seems even more likely, however, that the blockade was his response to Operation Rollback. Stalin was not the kind of megalomaniacal tyrant who would allow challenges to his rule to go unanswered.

Forrestal was of two minds about how to respond to the blockade. Truman was of one. "We'll stay in Berlin," Truman informed his diary, "come what may."[25]

Every C-47 that the United States and Britain had available was pitched into keeping Berliners fed. Lucius Clay wanted to supplement these aircraft with armed convoys traveling the two hundred miles across East Germany, something the Allied military had a legal right to do. Truman feared that an overly aggressive officer on one side or the other might start a shooting war on a stretch of autobahn. No armed convoys.

Four weeks into the blockade, with the Berlin airlift well under way, he convened a National Security Council meeting in the Cabinet Room. Clay made a pitch for control of all the air force's C-54s, four-engine aircraft that could carry substantially bigger loads than the two-engine C-47s. The Joint Chiefs said they could not approve it. Suppose an emergency broke out somewhere else—a military emergency, not a civilian one?

Truman told Clay to come into the Oval Office. "You're not feeling very happy about this, are you, Clay?"

"No, sir, I'm not. I think this is going to make our efforts a failure, and I'm afraid of what will happen to Europe if it does fail."

"Don't you worry," said Truman. "You're going to get your airplanes."[26]

Truman also had Stuart Symington come to his office. Truman told Symington that the air force had to cooperate on the airlift, and if the C-54s did not make the airlift a success, he was going to commandeer civilian aircraft and use them to break the blockade. Whatever happened, the airlift had to succeed. The airlift continued, with the British relying mainly on C-47s and the Americans on C-54s.[27]

The blockade created its own war scare, which served Truman's election purposes even better than the phony one. This time, though, Walter Bedell Smith was eager to damp down feverish speculation. Three months into the blockade, he informed Marshall that he was certain the Soviets were not gearing up for war. "I feel so confident they would not now undertake a deliberate military attack on, say, one of our concentrations of aircraft at Wiesbaden, that I would not hesitate to go there and sit on the field myself."[28]

Truman nevertheless needed to reassure public opinion. He moved sixty B-29s to Britain. The press reported that they were capable of carrying atomic bombs. It is likely, too, that this muscle flexing was also meant to impress Stalin, but it probably did not. Although the United States had approximately one hundred atomic bombs at the time, whether it would have been able to strike major Russian cities is open to question.[29]

The B-29 could not fly as high or as fast as the Soviet MiG-15 fighters that came into frontline service in 1948. Fighter escorts for the B-29 bombers might cover them deep into Poland, but the industrial centers of Russia and most of its major military installations were far to the east.

As the Berlin airlift came up against its biggest challenge—winter weather, winter nights—Truman was elected president. Marshall promptly retired, and Truman turned immediately to Marshall's deputy, Dean Acheson. Over the past few years the two men had formed a mutual admiration society. That was to prove only the beginning of what would become the closest relationship between any president and his secretary of state.

Acheson was always going to stand out. The beaky nose conferred a predatory look, like a hawk about to stoop on a mouse. The Brigade of Guards mustache and solid build conjured up the stereotypical roast beef Englishman, an impression only heightened by the tweedy *Country Life* wardrobe. The son of an Episcopalian bishop, Acheson cultivated the English upper-class affectation of being at heart a gentleman farmer. Not surprisingly, then, he called his modest Maryland farm Harewood, after one of the stateliest of Yorkshire's stately homes. His every attempt to deny that he wanted the United States to assume the role and responsibilities of the fast-fading British Empire was doomed to fail.

On the face of it, Acheson seemed exactly the kind of eastern prep school and Ivy League product Truman was primed to despise. Yet, beneath his sophisticated veneer, Acheson looked at the world much as Truman did. His was an understanding mediated by ill-informed guesses and unexamined assumptions about the fundamental forces that were currently shaping great nations and great events.

Acheson defended the overly simplistic, sometimes misleading, and on occasion blatantly untrue statements that he and Truman resorted to as being "clearer than truth . . . and could hardly be otherwise." This relativistic view of truth claimed superiority—greater clarity—over the genuine, unvarnished article and at the same time tried to avoid moral responsibility for the result by claiming that there was no alternative.

This kind of ethics—which claims that truth not being used in the service of political ends is inherently inferior—is well known. Without even realizing it, Acheson was rejecting the morality of Washington and Lincoln in favor of the strictly utilitarian morality that characterized Communism, Fascism, and National Socialism. To Stalin, Mussolini, and Hitler, truth was never more than a means to an end, a plastic thing, ready to be manipulated, never an end in itself.

Together, Truman and Acheson were clinging to a fictive scrim of perpetual American supremacy and unlimited benevolence. Even if this was rooted in patriotic imaginings, their interpretation nevertheless conferred a freedom that was beyond price to national leaders in moments of crisis: it enabled them to act on the basis of imperfect information. There was no analysis paralysis in Truman's White House, but there was an abundance of short-term imperatives and missed opportunities.

Shaped as they were by World War II, Truman and Acheson believed in acting with allies, and they created alliances such as the North Atlantic Treaty Organization to wage the Cold War. Yet outside of Europe, they believed in intervention and unilateralism. The United States had the right to intervene and should be ready to do so whether or not it had the support of other liberal democracies.

Acheson conceded that this policy of regular intervention in the Third World was a form of imperialism and colonialism. But those on the receiving end ought to consider themselves fortunate, he argued, because it was not "imperialism in the Russian style."[30]

This embrace of interventionism marked a sharp departure from the Rooseveltian approach, which had put a stop to military interventions in Latin America and, by implication, almost anywhere else. After Acheson left office, he began to have doubts about the wisdom of major interventions, yet even then he lacked the imaginative power to think of anything better. Intervention, especially in the early stages, creates a feeling—or only a hope—of control, and he could not let that go.[31]

Finally, Acheson placed a primary value on prestige in international relations. He defined prestige as "the shadow cast by power." Over time, he persuaded Truman to see prestige in the same way—two men, then, chasing shadows. But at home, in the world of domestic politics, where Truman knew just what he was dealing with and did not have to resort to chasing shadows, the president was always the pragmatic politician.

With the Berlin airlift's crowning achievement—flying enough coal into West Berlin to keep its three million people warm through the winter—Stalin called a halt. Had he really wanted to stop the airlift, he could have done so, by jamming the radio transmitters used for air-ground communications. Without the signals, especially in winter weather or at night, the airlift would have been reduced to a few flights in clear weather. West Berlin would have faced starvation and many thousands of deaths from hypothermia. Not only did Stalin refrain from jamming the transmitters, he never even threatened to do so.[32]

The Allies had not been driven out, but he had shown that if they wanted to create problems for him, he could always make problems for them. He was playing a weak hand strongly, and he had another surprise up his sleeve for the American president—a radioactive surprise this time.

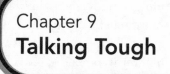

Chapter 9
Talking Tough

MAYBE IT WENT WITH HAVING TO LIVE UP TO BEING COMMANDER IN chief, but Truman loved talking tough. Even after he stepped down as president, he claimed that he had told the Secret Service he would deal with would-be assassins his own way: "Any son of a bitch tries to shoot me, I'll take the gun away from him, stick it up his ass and pull the trigger."[1]

He yearned to show that despite the poor eyesight and the taunts of "sissy" casting a shadow over his boyhood, he was as tough a kid as any on the block. He claimed he would rather win the Medal of Honor than be president and routinely identified with the serving military. Whenever he inscribed a photograph to someone in uniform, he was likely to write, "Your Commander in Chief, Harry S Truman," as if to emphasize a special bond between commander and commanded.[2]

Yet none of that altered his jaundiced view of the professional military, the brass hats. Seven years as commander in chief left him as suspicious of them as before. "You have got to keep an eye on the military at all times," Truman told Merle Miller.[3]

His own military service in the National Guard, along with the thwarted ambition of the adolescent Harry Truman to attend West Point, had left him convinced that he was something of an expert in how the modern military needed to be trained, commanded, and organized. One of the few things he did while campaigning for the vice presidency was to turn his mind to an idea that was spreading rapidly across the top tier of the army—service unification.

It was obvious in the White House and the Pentagon during the last year of the war that there was going to be a new, independent military service, the United States Air Force. The airmen, frustrated at serving in wartime under nominal army command, were pushing hard to be cut loose, and Congress and the public were ready to do it. The army, about to lose its formal link with the airmen but desperate to secure future air-ground cooperation, began talking up the merits of unification. Army generals such as Eisenhower were mockingly called "the purple-suiters." Supposedly that would be the resulting color if all the military's uniforms were thrown together into the wash, although no one seems to have conducted the research.

To Truman, as to many others, it was obviously wasteful and inefficient to continue to maintain two armies (the army and the Marine Corps), two navies (the navy and the coast guard), and three air forces (army air forces, navy air, and marine air). Shortly after being nominated for the vice presidency, he offered his thoughts on the subject to readers of *Collier's* magazine, under the title "Our Armed Forces Must Be Unified."[4]

The unification debate also revived his thinking on national defense policy, a topic that had interested him since enlisting in the National Guard back in 1905. The United States would never maintain a large standing army in peacetime, so it would always have to fall back on the citizen soldier. Truman's preferred option was universal military training. That meant putting every able-bodied male who reached eighteen through three months of military training, then calling them back each year for a further sixty days of training. A peacetime draft would be unnecessary, huge amounts of taxpayer money would be saved, and millions of men would be ready to spring to arms, much like the Minutemen of old.

And there was the politico-spiritual dimension. Truman feared for what postwar prosperity might do to the nation's moral fiber. Sloth and immorality threatened to ruin the great republic. It had happened once before. Isn't that what had happened to Rome?[5]

To round out his program, Truman would abolish West Point and Annapolis. He nursed a forty-year grudge against the snobbish attitude of academy graduates. They almost invariably looked down on soldiers such as Harry S. Truman, weekend warrior. The army was sure to resist, and the navy would resist ever harder, but "the present clique of Annapolis graduates must be broken up," he informed the cabinet.[6]

Truman's plan for UMT would find the military's officers from the more quick-witted and mature teenagers in the ranks. This would democratize defense, Truman told his staff, and there was absolutely nothing that he might accomplish as president that would be more important than UMT.[7]

Both Marshall and Eisenhower urged Congress to introduce UMT, but it is inconceivable that they took seriously his proposal to abolish the military academies. More likely, they were willing to back his idea as a way of encouraging him to adopt unification. The fight to save West Point could be left for later.

One thing that he shared with Marshall and Eisenhower was the simmering army indignation at the Marine Corps. During the war, the army had conducted many more amphibious assaults than the marines, including the biggest of all, D-day. Yet the public seemed more interested in Tarawa and Iwo Jima. Truman famously described a marine squad as "twelve riflemen and a photographer." For a time, he entertained a fantasy that under the guise of unification he might get the Marine Corps reduced to the bandsmen who played at the White House and the guards posted at U.S. embassies. James Forrestal blocked that. The Marine Corps remained much as it was, the navy's ground force.

Truman also issued an order to put an end to segregation in the military. He was highly praised for striking a blow for racial equality. The truth was something else. Apart from the 82nd Airborne Division, which happened to have a commander, James M. Gavin, who agreed with Truman's policy, the order was ignored. The desegregation of the military came some years later, on the battlefield, and had virtually nothing to do with him.[8]

Truman never managed to get a firm grip on the military. The navy torpedoed every attempt to push service unification through Congress. He could not even secure UMT, which was strenuously resisted by the air force. The postwar military, having defeated Germany and Japan, had at least as many supporters in Congress and the press as Truman could claim.

He was left with only one way to impose his will on the Pentagon—cutting defense budgets to the bone and threatening the marrow. The military that came out of the war, however, was more politically astute than the military that Truman had served in during the previous war. The Pentagon was rapidly becoming as good as the White House at cultivating friends in Congress, and those friends passed defense budgets bigger than Truman asked for. He refused to spend the extra money. The army then began drawing up plans to pull troops out of occupied peripheral areas, such as South Korea, and to hand responsibility for them over to the State Department.[9]

There was also a major disagreement over control of nuclear weapons. During and after World War II, the Atomic Energy Commission (AEC), a civilian agency, kept all of the components of atomic bombs. The components were delivered to the air force only on orders from the president. In 1948 Truman was informed that the military was trying to undermine this policy and secure direct control of nuclear weapons. He responded by sticking out his chin and declaring, "Well, I'm the Commander in Chief . . . [and] Papa won't hesitate to use the strap if that's what it takes." He was still the commander in chief, and the strap was still dangling, unused, when the military wrested control away from the AEC.[10]

At times his frustration at the complexity of these national security and foreign policy problems came out in self-pitying outbursts. "I'm not a superman like my predecessor. I can't do everything myself," he lamented one day. And instead of creating a single service of purple-suiters under a single military department, Truman was forced to compromise all down the line. He got three military departments (Army, Navy, Air Force) where before there were only two. The secretaries of war and the navy were no longer in the cabinet, which only encouraged them to cultivate close ties with defense contractors and lobbyists, having lost direct access to the White House.[11]

Truman's original intention was to create a position of supreme military commander, someone who would control all the armed forces. He was talked out of it by Clark Clifford, who said giving that much military power to someone could make him more powerful than the president and might even lead to dictatorship. Truman settled instead for a secretary of defense and a chairman of the Joint Chiefs of Staff (JCS), splitting the powers that would have gone to a supreme military commander.[12]

It delighted Truman to appoint Omar Bradley, a fellow Missourian, to fill the role of chairman of the JCS, but the Unification Act did not unify the military. Its main accomplishment was creating an additional service, the air force, which was going to spend nearly half the entire defense budget. The airmen secured the lion's share because they could do something the army, navy, and Marine Corps combined could not—raise mushroom clouds over Moscow.

At the apex of the new structure was the secretary of defense. Truman chose James Forrestal to fill it, even though he knew that Forrestal was disloyal. He regularly received reports of Forrestal's providing Republican congressmen with inside information that could be used against the administration in the 1948 election. That did not stop Truman from railing at "the muttonheads" running Defense, every one of them his own appointment.[13]

Truman squared these contradictions by persuading himself that with the aid of a small staff of expert advisers, and by holding regular consultations with the secretaries of the army, navy, and air force, Forrestal was going to create a lean, mean fighting machine. The mechanism began to jam almost as soon as it went into operation.

Forrestal was swamped with memos, recommendations, and requests pushed up to him by the service secretaries. That may have been their way of keeping the defense secretary so busy that he would have to leave them to run their fiefdoms as they preferred. Truman had so little experience with bureaucratic infighting and high-level turf wars that he had never anticipated this, and he had no idea what to do when it happened. Forrestal meanwhile continued along a path of self-destruction limned with depressing class anxieties and a squalid private life. He rejected Truman's offer to create a deputy secretary of defense who would relieve him of some of his burdens. Working up to eighteen hours a day, Forrestal was killing himself— a slow-motion suicide, and nobody who dealt with him regularly, including Truman, even noticed.[14]

By the time he became secretary of defense, Forrestal was incapable of making decisions, even on routine and relatively mundane matters. Every day, and several times a day, Truman was taking calls from him. What should he do about this? How would the president want him to deal with that?

At the cabinet table, Forrestal was the toughest talker there, a quality Truman invariably responded to. Yet the great proponent of toughness in dealing with the Soviets could not make a hard decision and then ride out the criticism or override resistance. Under pressure, he reversed himself, then spiraled away into indecision. Here was a man too thin-skinned and too emotional to be a good office secretary, let alone a secretary of defense.[15]

Truman failed to see that Forrestal had not run the wartime Navy Department. Roosevelt had left the War Department to Stimson and Marshall, but he was too interested in the navy to leave it to Forrestal and the chief of naval operations, Admiral Ernest King. It was Roosevelt who ran it, just as he ran the State Department. Forrestal got Defense not because he was the right man for it, but because he was in the right position when it came along.

To Truman, though, his election in November 1948, confounding the polls and the pundits, was all the proof he needed that he was fighting the Cold War the way it needed to be fought. The people had spoken. What the people did not see coming any more than the president did was that in August 1949 the Soviets would conduct an atomic test in Siberia. An air force reconnaissance plane picked up some of the radioactive debris high in the atmosphere a few days later.

The twenty-year projection Truman had been clinging to since 1945 collapsed on him. It was more than two weeks before he could bring himself to inform the cabinet and the country.

Stimson and at least half a dozen of the leading scientists on the Manhattan Project had tried to get Truman to prepare for this day. It might just be possible to draw the Soviets into an agreement to control nuclear weapons, they told him. If the attempt failed, as it well might, nothing important would be lost by trying, but if it succeeded, there would be no nuclear arms race.

Truman had briefly seemed on the verge of seeking an agreement back in September 1945, then changed his mind. Even if they knew the theory, the Russians would not be able to build a bomb, he told his staff. "Other countries have been able to make automobiles and airplanes," he pointed out, "but they haven't been able to make them equal to ours," even though they had seen how Americans made them.[16]

His natural position was talking tough. During an ad hoc press conference in Tennessee in October 1945, Truman had dismissed all thought of seeking an agreement. America's big advantage was "know-how," he said, and that applied to the atomic bomb as it did to just about everything else. The United States was not going to share its atomic know-how with anybody. "If they want to catch up with us, they will have to do it on their own hook, just as we did."[17]

American scientists knew that countries around the world were already hoping to harness the atom for peaceful purposes. Some, inevitably, would want to build atomic bombs. The best way to support peaceful uses while curbing weapons production, they argued, was for the United Nations to put the world's supplies of uranium under international supervision.

Instead of supporting this idea, Truman created a small advisory group headed by Bernard Baruch, sometime Wall Street operator and, in World War I, the man Woodrow Wilson had chosen to oversee the mobilization of the economy, a project he bungled. Baruch was well connected but had no knowledge of physics. The intellectual achievement he was proudest of was an ability to read Latin. The elderly Baruch was to be found several days each week, weather permitting, on a park bench in Lafayette Square, holding forth to journalists, the idle, and the curious about what an important person he was. Baruch came up with a proposal for controlling the bomb by preventing the Soviets from building one.

Before delivering his opening address on the subject to the United Nations, Baruch showed Truman a copy. The method of control that Baruch was advocating was "swift and sure punishment" of any country that resisted a putative UN atomic energy agency established along similar lines to the Atomic Energy Commission.

Acheson was appalled. That phrase about swift and sure punishment has to come out, he told Truman. Only the United States had the power to deliver the kind of punishment Baruch was proposing. The Russians would see this as a threat to use the UN as cover for launching an attack. Truman asked Baruch to spell out exactly what he meant by "swift and sure punishment." Simple, said Baruch. "I mean war." And, he added, if the phrase came out, "I will resign."

Truman approved swift and sure punishment, dooming Baruch's plan to failure, something that did not seem to trouble either Truman or Baruch. When the Security Council voted on it, in December 1946, the Soviet Union did not use its veto; it abstained. The Baruch Plan was passed on a vote of 10 to 0, but without Soviet acceptance, it could never be implemented.[18]

After the American nuclear monopoly was broken, Truman created a committee, chaired by Dean Acheson, to advise him on building something much more powerful than an atomic bomb—a hydrogen bomb. Instead of splitting atoms, as the atomic bomb did, a hydrogen bomb would fuse them, the way the sun does, releasing much more energy.

The potential destructive power of hydrogen bombs was apocalyptic. Some of the scientists who were consulted urged Truman to seek an agreement with the Russians that neither the United States nor the Soviet Union would build a thermonuclear weapon. There was a moral side to such arms, they argued. J. Robert Oppenheimer directly urged Truman not to build a hydrogen bomb. If it was discovered that the Soviets were building one (and they were), the United States could launch its own program and almost certainly beat them to it.

Acheson ridiculed the scientists' scruples. Morality was irrelevant to national security, he assured Truman. Until now, morality had been at the heart of the administration's statements on the evils of Communism. Suddenly, amorality was the position to embrace. Truman had been troubled for years about the morality of nuclear weapons, which were area weapons. They would always kill far more women, children, and old men than military personnel or workers in defense plants. But, determined to show toughness in the dazzling light of the Soviet test, Truman intended to escalate the arms race, convincing himself that there was a race waiting to be won. He did not need to be persuaded; there was no shortage of people who were pressing for the hydrogen bomb, including the Joint Chiefs of Staff. At the decisive meeting of the National Security Council, Truman had only one question: "Can the Russians do it?"

All of the experts present nodded. Then one of them, David Lilienthal, began raising some questions about the wisdom of relying so heavily on nuclear weapons. Truman cut him short. "What the hell are we waiting for? Let's get on with it." The meeting had taken all of seven minutes.[19]

At times appalled by the Bomb, Truman was at other times, such as now, seduced by it. Even scientists who had worked on the Manhattan Project were susceptible. In the words of one of them, Freeman Dyson, "I have felt it myself—the glitter of nuclear weapons. It is irresistible . . . it is something that gives people the illusion of illimitable power . . . when they can see what they can do with their minds."[20]

Truman also had another, related response to the Soviet atomic explosion. He wanted a completely fresh look at national security in a world where the United States no longer had a nuclear monopoly. The bulk of this assignment devolved on Paul Nitze, who had recently succeeded George Kennan as head of the Policy Planning Staff.

Nitze was a Forrestal protégé and another Ivy League graduate who had become rich and bored on Wall Street. In his youth he had studied Spengler's *Decline of the West* closely, thought about it at length, and brooded over it since. Nitze recruited experts from across the executive branch and academia to measure the scale, the nature, and the immediacy of the Soviet threat, and to devise a strategy to counter it. The result was a proposed new directive, NSC-68, which carried a price tag of $187 billion over four years. That was enough to make Truman, or almost anyone else, rub his eyes. It was nearly fourteen times the entire defense budget for 1950.[21]

NSC-68 had that "clearer than truth" quality that Acheson so admired. It was one of the most important documents of the Cold War, and when one reads it now, it has an almost cartoonlike quality, offering a world populated entirely by American heroes and Communist villains locked in a life-or-death struggle, where ultimately, justice must destroy a great evil, or that evil would triumph and Western civilization would be swept away along with the Incas and the Etruscans.

The Truman Doctrine had been based on containment of the Soviet Union along its periphery. Nitze was proposing to expand containment to every corner of the world. He cranked up the drama even more by invoking the specter of nuclear war. There would be "the hour of maximum danger," arriving like a train on schedule in 1954, when the Soviets would have enough nuclear weapons to hit the United States with an atomic blitz. The Russians were working on designs for a jet bomber, but their record in bomber design was abysmal.

Their heavy bomber fleet in 1950 consisted entirely of Tupolev Tu-4 aircraft, rivet-for-rivet copies of the obsolescent B-29. The chances that they might beat the United States in the design and construction of jet bombers were zero. In fact, they would never be able to put heavy bombers over the White House or Edwards Air Force Base. The real threat would be long-range missiles, something Nitze did not even consider, even though the air force, the army, and the navy all saw nuclear-armed missiles as the ultimate deterrent and had done so since 1945.

Nitze brought a moral fury to his efforts that Forrestal would have been proud of. The way to defeat the wicked plots of the enemy, he informed the president, was by ramping up military spending, at the same time aggressively pushing democracy across all the unstable parts of the world until, ultimately, it reached the Soviet Union itself. Such was "our national destiny." As for where the money would come from, Nitze believed that the United States could afford anything, once it had a clear objective in mind.

One of Truman's outside advisers, James Bryant Conant, the president of Harvard, was dismayed. If this program was seriously pursued, he warned, "we might be risking our freedom." Truman tried to bury NSC-68 in a specially created committee. The committee was under no pressure to provide a speedy evaluation; it might conceivably have still been deliberating when his presidency ended, had not other events intervened.[22]

By this time, Forrestal had been replaced. Truman had grown weary of Forrestal's indecisiveness and his failure to impose his stamp on Defense. One day in March 1949 he had picked up the telephone on his desk and put a call through to the Pentagon to demand Forrestal's resignation. Forrestal could hardly believe what he was hearing. Did the president really mean it? "Yes, Jim. That's the way I want it." A few weeks later Forrestal suffered a nervous breakdown, was admitted to Bethesda Naval Hospital, and shortly afterward committed suicide.[23]

His replacement as secretary of defense was a large, paunchy, balding figure, Louis Johnson, who had served as assistant secretary of war a decade earlier. More recently, Johnson had taken charge of the Democratic Party's finance committee for Truman's 1948 campaign, and he was rumored to have contributed a large amount of his own money.[24]

Johnson inherited a defense budget of $13 billion, which could be implemented only by making large cuts in warships and airplanes. Truman had decided on the $13 billion figure, but Johnson was loyally and zealously taking the flak with an eye to becoming the Democratic presidential nominee in 1952.

Johnson's fights over the budget soon turned into a major struggle with Acheson, and the issue was South Korea. The army wanted to leave, and Acheson insisted it stay, not because it was essential to American security, but because the United States had already made a major political investment there. To pull out now would be bad for American prestige—the shadow of power again.

At the Cairo Conference in 1943, Roosevelt, Churchill, and Jiang had issued a declaration that "in due course Korea shall become free and independent." This was vague, but at Yalta two years later, Roosevelt, Churchill, and Stalin agreed that there would be a trusteeship of Korea, exercised by China, the United States, Britain, and the USSR. There was a State-War-Navy Coordinating Committee (a.k.a. Swink) that was currently working out demarcation lines for Japanese surrenders across East Asia. Two army colonels assigned to Swink— Dean Rusk and Charles Bonesteel—late one night took a close look at the 38th parallel. Why not have the Russians take Japanese surrenders north of the parallel and American forces take the surrenders south of it? And so it was, and thus did Dean Rusk enter the world of international politics.

Even as the surrenders were being taken, Truman was worrying that the Communists might gain control of a united Korea. During the war, in Korea as in Greece, Communists and Communist sympathizers led resistance to the occupation in many areas. With Japan's defeat, there was a serious risk of civil war between former collaborators and resistance fighters. Truman's fears seemed confirmed when a provisional government, calling itself the Korean People's Republic (KPR), was established, although, despite the name, it was a broad-based coalition.

Acheson persuaded him that Korea was too important to the economic recovery of Japan to let the Communists have it. Truman asked Congress for $575 million in aid to South Korea and placed his hopes in Syngman Rhee. Neither a collaborator nor a resistance fighter, Rhee had spent the past twenty years living mainly in the United

States, not Korea. He solemnly invoked the Truman Doctrine, informing Truman, "Korea is located in a strategic area similar to that of Greece." Congress wasn't persuaded. It declined to lavish large amounts of money on South Korea.

Rhee meanwhile was making progress without it. When he returned to Korea, he had been given a prominent place in the KPR: he became its chairman. Lieutenant General John R. Hodge, the general in command of U.S. forces in Korea, nevertheless seemed convinced that any entity with "People's Republic" in its name was Communist or about to turn Communist. Hodge and Rhee began to purge those of its members who had fought the Japanese. In a matter of months, they had destroyed the KPR. Hodge's civil affairs adviser, Alfred Crofts, could hardly credit what he was witnessing: "A potential unifying agency thus became one of the fifty-four splinter groups in Korean political life." A country with a plethora of political splinter groups is a standing invitation to any ambitious local strongman, and Rhee was ready. Thousands of Rhee's opponents were murdered, and up to fourteen thousand more were imprisoned. The Japanese collaborators he gathered around him comprised the government, including men who had trafficked Korean girls as sex slaves for the Imperial Japanese Army. Not surprisingly, this fraudulent and exploitative bunch could not have survived a free and fair election, and they made sure that no such thing was possible. Rhee's government of collaborators left a wound in South Korean life that festers to this day.[25]

The UN had planned to conduct nationwide elections to unify Korea, but there was no need for an election: with two-thirds of the population living in the South, the result was a foregone conclusion. North Korea blocked unification by referendum. Its own strongman, Kim Il Sung, had a simple plan for bringing the two Koreas together. Rhee too had a plan, and it was identical to Kim's—unity by force of arms.

Events seemed to be moving toward just that result. In 1948 there were still forty-five thousand American troops in South Korea, and the army had plans for all to be withdrawn, soon. The Joint Chiefs of Staff had concluded, "The United States has little strategic interest in maintaining the present troops and bases in Korea." The Chiefs had no illusions about what the consequences were likely to be: "the eventual domination of Korea by the U.S.S.R." That was unfortunate, but economic aid and military support should be devoted to countries that had something to contribute to American security. South Korea contributed nothing. The United States should create a properly trained and equipped army of 65,000 men and a paramilitary police force of 35,000 to enable the country to defend itself.[26]

American troops were withdrawing when, in January 1949, Dean Acheson became secretary of state. He soon found himself in a ferocious struggle with Louis Johnson and, by extension, with the Joint Chiefs. Acheson persuaded Truman to slow the pullout from South Korea. The army nevertheless managed to get nearly all of its troops out, and by the spring of 1950 the State Department, not the Pentagon, had the lead role in South Korea. There were only five hundred American soldiers left, there to train the Republic of Korea Army, an army designed to be strong enough to defend South Korea, but not so strong it could conquer North Korea.[27]

Acheson asked Congress for $150 million in economic and military aid for South Korea. It was a way of keeping the United States committed even after its troops were out. Congress did not see the point of spending so much money for a place that Marshall did not think was worth defending, and Acheson seemed to be coming at last to the same view. He made a speech at the National Press Club on January 12, 1950, and he described an American security perimeter in the Far East in which South Korea and Formosa were both outside that perimeter.

What he was presenting was the Joint Chiefs' offshore strategy for East and Southeast Asia, with an American military presence based in Alaska, the islands of Japan, including Okinawa, and the Philippines. From these positions American air and naval power would be dominant from the Bering Strait down to Australia. It offered effective defense at minimum cost, and it would be generations, if not centuries, before its offshore position might be seriously threatened. It was a sensible, sustainable policy. A week after Acheson's speech, the House rejected the Korea aid request by 192 votes to 191.

A month later, in February 1950, Stalin and Mao signed a treaty of Sino-Soviet friendship and mutual security. In itself, this was not particularly ominous. Acheson still ridiculed Mao as being little more than Stalin's glove puppet, which would have astonished and possibly amused Stalin if he had learned of it.

The new Sino-Soviet relationship was a wary one from the beginning. The overwhelming sense of destiny that the Chinese carried,
even when they were poor and weak, meant that they would always go
their own way. Stalin called them "radishes—red only on the outside.
Yet he also knew that if Communism made any headway in Asia, it
would have to be under the aegis of China, not the Soviet Union.
What Stalin needed now was something that might cement the treaty
before it turned into a dead letter—something dramatic and bound to
arouse Mao's anger, such as having the United States make itself the
defender of Formosa. Then Mao would need the Soviet Union.
Meanwhile, he could only wait, and hope.

On June 24 Truman flew home to Independence aboard the new
presidential airplane, *Independence*, to deal with some family business. When his airplane landed at Kansas City that afternoon, his sister and other family members were at the airport to greet him. After
he had gone to bed, the wire services began clattering with reports of
fighting breaking out along the demarcation line between North and
South Korea. No one on Truman's staff was going to wake him up for
what might be a minor incident exaggerated in the telling. A telegram
from Acheson arrived in the early hours. Something was happening in
Korea. Either the North was attacking the South, or the South was attacking the North. Truman was woken up this time, and he held a
brief conversation by telephone with Acheson. Until the picture became clearer, he and Acheson agreed, there was not much the president could do.

By noon, though, Acheson had more to report. "The news is bad,"
he said. "The attack is all along the parallel."

"Dean, we've got to stop the sons of bitches, no matter what." At
2:00 p.m. Truman was airborne again, on his way back to Washington.[28]

During a cabinet meeting shortly after World War II ended, the
question had been raised, Was it really the responsibility of the
United States to police the world? Truman had no doubt about it—
"The courts must have marshals"—and now there was shooting in a
rough part of town.[29]

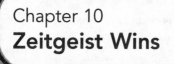

Chapter 10
Zeitgeist Wins

TRUMAN HAD STRONG, FIXED VIEWS ON WAR, AND ONE OF THEM was a belief in preventive war. "It is no longer enough to say, 'We don't want war,' " he had told a Jefferson-Jackson Day audience in April 1947. "We must act in time—ahead of time—to stamp out the smoldering beginnings of any conflict that may threaten to spread." In his implacable pursuit of a balanced budget, though, he had tied his own hands. Time and again he talked about how tough he was going to be, only to compromise or back off. The military was too small for a preventive war strategy.

On the flight back to Washington on June 25, 1950, Truman's thoughts turned yet again to the merits of preventive war. He mused aloud that the news from Korea reminded him of the 1930s, when Britain and France had failed to stand up to Hitler. They had tried to appease his demands for territory and had done nothing when he swallowed Czechoslovakia. The result was World War II. Hitler could have been stopped if only the British and French had stood firm.

Truman's interpretation of the 1930s was so commonplace it was hardly ever challenged, despite the fact that it was a view formed at the time in almost total ignorance of what had happened, at least in Britain. The British cabinet had concluded, three weeks after Hitler came to power in 1933, that Germany would start another war, probably in 1940 but possibly in 1939. Its strategy to meet that challenge was to strive for air superiority by 1939.

Detailed design work was begun on Spitfires to take on German fighters and Hurricanes to take on German bombers. Research into long-distance detection led to the development of radar. Provided the Royal Air Force could defend the skies over England and the English Channel, no invasion of Britain would be possible.

Instead of achieving the quick knockout the Germans needed, Hitler would then be drawn into a long war. The longer it lasted, major powers, such as the United States and Russia, would be drawn in. Over time, the weight of the alliance opposing Germany would doom it to yet another defeat.[1]

The French, meanwhile, were mounting the kind of rearmament program that Winston Churchill was demanding for Britain. They built a huge fighter arm, creating a force of five thousand fighters in the mid-1930s that were obsolescent in 1940; they began the Maginot Line, but could not finish it because of the cost; and they created an army even bigger than Hitler's, but it lacked mobility and firepower. Like the British, the French were intending to fight, but they prepared in the wrong way, for the wrong war, at the wrong time.[2]

The British strategy for defeating Hitler was more successful than Hitler's strategy for defeating Britain, but British governments of the 1930s wisely refused to talk about their strategy for meeting the German threat. That left their critics, led by Churchill, free to denounce them, on the basis of almost total ignorance—hence the myth of appeasement. Only when he became prime minister, in June 1940, did Churchill discover what the true strategy was. As he described it to the prime minister of South Africa, Jan Smuts, "I see only one sure way through now—to wit, that Hitler should attack this country, and in so doing break his air weapon." This quotation and more of the same kind appeared in Churchill's lengthy account of World War II, the second volume of which was published in Boston in 1949. Even so, Truman and those around him never questioned the conventional wisdom and got maximum mileage from a myth.[3]

When the *Independence* arrived back in Washington, Dean Acheson and Louis Johnson were both on hand to greet Truman. Once they were all in the official limousine, Truman told them he'd been thinking on the plane about how reckless the Russians were. They were obviously behind this attack, but they could not sustain it. What fools. Their war industries were in eastern Russia, but to support a war in Korea, they would be dependent on the four-thousand-mile Trans-Siberian Railway, which boasted only a single track. If the United States rose to the challenge, the North Korean army would fall apart for want of arms and ammunition. It was like the 1930s all over again. The difference was, he was going to stand firm. "By God, I'm going to let them have it!"

Johnson reached over to shake his hand. "I'm with you, Mr. President!"

Acheson told him there had been developments at the UN. It had just approved a resolution calling on both sides to return to their original borders. The vote was 9–0. The Soviets might have vetoed it, but they were still boycotting the UN over its failure to allow the Chinese Communists to take the Security Council seat reserved for China.

What amounted to a council of war had been hastily arranged for that evening at Blair House. There was a fried chicken dinner with hot biscuits, followed by discussion. Once the dishes had been cleared away, Truman had five documents placed where he could reach them, beginning with a telegram from the ambassador to South Korea, John J. Muccio.

ACCORDING KOREAN ARMY REPORTS WHICH PARTLY CONFIRMED . . . NORTH KOREAN FORCES INVADED ROK [REPUBLIC OF KOREA] TERRITORY AT SEVERAL POINTS . . . IT WOULD APPEAR FROM NATURE OF ATTACK AND MANNER IN WHICH IT WAS LAUNCHED THAT IT CONSTITUTES ALL OUT OFFENSIVE AGAINST ROK.[4]

Truman asked Acheson to speak first. Acheson had four ideas to offer. First, additional weapons and military assistance must be sent from Japan to the South Korea army immediately; second, air force and navy combat aircraft ought to be free to attack North Korean tanks and troop concentrations during the evacuation of American dependents; third, the Seventh Fleet should be ordered to steam north from its base in the Philippines and place itself between Formosa and the mainland; and finally, the French effort to defeat the Communist insurgency in Indochina should receive more support, including a large American military advisory mission.[5]

Louis Johnson and Omar Bradley had returned only the previous day from Japan, and before they left, Douglas MacArthur, supreme commander of the Allied Powers in the occupation of Japan, had given them a memorandum addressed to the Joint Chiefs. Bradley read it aloud to the gathering at Blair House: "The western strategic frontier of the United States rests today on the littoral islands extending through the Aleutians to the Philippine Archipelago. Geographically and strategically, Formosa is an integral part of this offshore position."[6]

MacArthur seemed to have forgotten that some months earlier he had endorsed the existing strategic posture, which left Formosa out of the offshore strategy. A huge junk fleet was currently being assembled in Chinese ports, and an army of two hundred thousand men was preparing for the invasion of Formosa. Overly emotional and always likely to allow his emotions to cloud his judgment, MacArthur was deeply attached to Jiang Jieshi—"My old comrade in arms"—and Madame Jiang. He placed the blame for Jiang's defeat by Mao's armies on George Marshall and the State Department.[7]

With the junk fleet expected to set sail in a matter of weeks, MacArthur could not bear the thought of what might happen to Jiang and the Madame. Besides which, MacArthur had always believed that even if China did not figure in American national security now, the day would come when it would. Dean Acheson was convinced that not only was China under Stalin's control, but it could not amount to anything much because it would never, ever be an industrial country.

Within hours of the North Koreans breaching the parallel, MacArthur received urgent pleas for ammunition and military equipment from the Republic of Korea Army, and he had already received Truman's approval to meet these requests from army depots in Japan. Truman now told the other people around the large mahogany table in the Blair House dining room that additional military assistance would be provided to South Korea. He approved the suggestion of air cover for the evacuation, but he hesitated before getting directly involved in the Chinese civil war. The Seventh Fleet could steam toward the Taiwan Strait, he said, but not into it.

The Joint Chiefs had evidently reminded Johnson before he departed for dinner that they were still opposed to fighting a major war for Korea. Johnson now said that he was adamantly against committing American ground units. Bradley said, "We have to draw the line somewhere," and what had happened in Korea "offers as good an occasion for drawing the line as anywhere else." But, Truman asked, just what are the Russians up to, attacking South Korea? Bradley and the army chief of staff, J. Lawton Collins, said that the present balance of forces was so unfavorable to the Soviets that Stalin would not commit troops to Korea. Similarly, to put American soldiers onto the mainland of Asia would be a mistake.[8]

A second war council was held at Blair House the next evening. Acheson reiterated his demand to expand a war the United States had not yet joined. He wanted significantly more support for the French attempt to recolonize Vietnam; close air support for South Korean ground units; another UN resolution, this one calling on all UN members to come to the aid of South Korea; and an order for the Seventh Fleet, most of which was in the Philippines, to steam north and defend Formosa. This time Truman agreed to everything Acheson asked for. There was no serious discussion of the wisdom, or unwisdom, of becoming party to the Chinese civil war. On the contrary, Truman not only approved Acheson's recommendation to use the Seventh Fleet to stop any Chinese invasion, but he also wanted Formosa to revert to being a Japanese colony once again.[9]

There was no commitment yet of ground troops for Korea. It was still all air and navy, in keeping with the offshore strategy. The chances of that lasting much longer, though, were slim. After four days of the kind of tension that only war generates, Truman was so ready to fight the Russians, the Chinese, and the North Koreans that he seemed at moments almost to welcome the chance. There was no shortage of reasons for it, including Dr. Graham's snake oil. Here was the kind of pressure guaranteed to stir up the Old Lady Reflex. How much of Truman's famous decisiveness was Harry and how much was a mood-enhancing drug? Obvious question; unknowable answer.

But there were other factors too. Truman did not need to be president long to discover how limited his powers really were. The pomp, the deference, the mystique that enveloped a president disguised a truth he had to confront every day. "The people can never understand why the President does not use his supposedly great power to make 'em behave. Well, all the President is, is a glorified public relations man who spends his time flattering, kissing and kicking people to get them to do what they were supposed to do anyway," he told his sister, Mary Jane.[10]

That was only at home, though. Abroad, it was different. There he was not a public relations man, but a commander possessed of awesome military might and great economic power, able to raise up a nation, or bring one down.

But what Truman faced in Korea was more than a military challenge to the postwar order that the United States had tried to create. He was up against a force of immeasurable power for good or bad— the zeitgeist, the spirit of the time. The 1949–1950 zeitgeist was one of fear and alarm, of conspiracies and treachery, of hidden enemies and nuclear weapons.

If Truman did not fight a war in Korea, what he had dreaded for the past three years would happen: he would be outflanked on the right. That shadow had fallen across his path ever since the election of the Republican-dominated 80th Congress, in 1946.

The Republicans came to Washington for the 80th Congress committed to rolling back the New Deal. They found that was impossible. People liked having Social Security and government-supported mortgages. The Republicans settled for containment. And although Truman excoriated the "Do-Nothing 80th Congress," in truth he sought a modus vivendi.

He was proud of forging the bipartisan consensus that produced the Truman Doctrine and the Marshall Plan, but remained wary of the anti-Communist ultras clustered in the China bloc and on the House Un-American Activities Committee. Shortly after the 80th Congress was sworn in, Truman yielded to pressure from the House Un-American Activities Committee and its legman, J. Edgar Hoover, and created the Federal Loyalty-Security Program.

There was already legislation that barred the employment of people with subversive opinions, and the Civil Service Commission had ruled years earlier that anyone holding Communist views was "potentially disloyal." Truman's executive order was an attempt to appease the Republican right early in their relationship.

As his election campaign got under way, he announced, "I do not want and will not accept the political support of Henry Wallace and his Communists." This scurrilous attack hardly brought credit to Truman the man or Truman the president. Wallace was no more a Communist than Truman was. As if to underline Truman's point, though, eleven leaders of the Communist Party were indicted three months before the 1948 election on charges of harboring subversive thoughts and reading disloyal literature. Much of Truman's determination to stand up to Communism abroad—and, more, to be seen standing up to it—was driven by persistent anxieties about his right flank.

Nevertheless, the pressure only grew as Communist spies in the New Deal and the Manhattan Project were unearthed. Then, during the winter of 1949, the State Department came under heavy bombardment. In January 1950 Alger Hiss, once one of its brightest stars, was convicted of perjury. He was really guilty of treason, but the statute of limitations had run out before his treachery was discovered. Hiss's perjury conviction raised serious doubts about loyalty in the State Department.

Hiss had hardly begun his five-year sentence before news broke of a Lincoln's Birthday speech in Wheeling, West Virginia, delivered by the junior senator from Wisconsin, Joseph McCarthy. Toward the end of his speech, McCarthy held up a sheet of paper. Here, he announced, are the names of 205 known Communists presently employed by the State Department.[11]

Acheson and the State Department were still reeling from "Who lost China?" But that was mild compared with the second wave of attacks that now erupted in Congress, in much of the press, and across the country. And while Hiss's perjury conviction was taken as proof of something far more sinister, so was McCarthy's list taken as proof of Communist penetration reaching into the heart of government. Senator Taft, a.k.a. "Mr. Republican," had some advice for McCarthy: "Keep talking, and if one case doesn't work out, proceed with another."[12]

When the North Korean People's Army crossed the 38th parallel, the mood in the United States was so febrile the response to this attack was more likely to be shaped by atmospherics than by the long-term security needs of the country.

There was already a clear agreement, from the president down, that the United States would not fight a ground war on the Asian mainland, nor would it go to war over Formosa. The primary role of the UN as envisaged by its founding fathers, Roosevelt and Churchill, was to prevent or resolve conflicts between nation-states. Formosa was considered an entirely Chinese affair. It was not only Mao who claimed that Formosa was an integral part of China; Jiang made exactly the same claim. Formosa was, as the Cairo Declaration put it, "stolen" from China by Japan.

In 1947 the UN had promoted reunification talks for Korea, but Truman allowed Syngman Rhee to block them. The UN had then organized elections, but the North refused to take part. The result, in 1948, was the establishment of the Republic of Korea in the South. Although it was receiving economic and military assistance from the United States, if it came under attack, South Korea was expected to defend itself long enough for the UN to intervene diplomatically and, if necessary, militarily. MacArthur's initial reaction when he heard of the North Korean attack was to inform one of his subordinates, "Enemy effort . . . is an undisguised act of war and subject to United Nations censure."[13]

MacArthur was right, but Truman had long since lost what limited faith he had in diplomacy. What the Communists understood was divisions, he told his staff, and he offered a telling anecdote. Dr. Wallace Graham had overheard Churchill telling Stalin at Potsdam that it was important to have the support of the pope in the postwar settlement. Stalin seemed amused. "And how many divisions does the Pope have?" he wanted to know. Divisions—infantry, armored, airborne—that was the only language the Communists understood.[14]

Having been through the "Who lost China?" hysteria, Truman may have thought the sequel, "Who lost Korea?", would be unendurable. Like Acheson, he had no doubt that the Soviets had instigated the North Korean attack and the North Koreans were merely puppets.

In fact, the North Koreans were anything but. The attack on South Korea could not have been mounted without Stalin's approval and active assistance. All the same, this was not a case of pulling the North Koreans' strings.

The original impetus came from Kim Il Sung, not Stalin. He had sent nearly fifty telegrams to Stalin between 1946 and 1950, urging him to support a war that would unify the Korean Peninsula. Stalin's unvarying response was *nyet*, even though Kim was his kind of Korean Communist—one who had fought with the Red Army against the Japanese, who spoke Russian, looked to Moscow for inspiration, and shared the traditional Korean suspicion of China.

There was already a de facto civil war under way. In the North, anti-Communist bands were fighting Kim's army and police; in the South, pro-Communist groups could call on thousands of guerrillas, some of them infiltrators from the North. Border clashes were also commonplace, but in the summer of 1949 South Korean troops, or ROKs, had mounted a major offensive, thanks partly to Dean Rusk's midnight inspiration to draw a boundary that favored an attack from South to North.

When Japan surrendered, on August 14, 1945, the secretary of state, James Byrnes, ordered two army colonels to find or devise a line across the Korean Peninsula for the purpose of organizing Japanese surrenders. The two colonels, Dean Rusk and Charles Bonesteel, decided to work from a *National Geographic* map of Korea. They chose not to call on the large map collections of either the Pentagon or the State Department.[15]

Byrnes had instructed them to place the line as far north as possible. Instead, they opted for the 38th parallel, which made no sense politically or militarily. The place to draw the line fairly leaps off almost any map of Korea—the narrow waist between Songming on the west coast and Wonsan, a major port, on the east. Pyongyang, the second largest city on the peninsula, would be north of the line, as is nearly half the total area of the peninsula. Russians would have the honor of taking the largest number of Japanese prisoners and would almost certainly have accepted this arrangement. Rusk and Bonesteel were both former Rhodes scholars and were therefore presumed to be brilliant, but it was late at night when they drew a line along the parallel for no reason but a desire to go home.

They had ignored their instructions and bungled the work. The Ongjin Peninsula begins north of the parallel, but most of it is south of the parallel, jutting into the Yellow Sea. This peninsula has no military value except as a jumping-off point for an advance northward toward Pyongyang, the inevitable capital of North Korea.

Similarly, the town of Kaesong sits astride the 38th parallel. The hills behind the town dominate the road and the railroad linking

Seoul and Pyongyang. Taking the northern end of the Ongjin Peninsula and the high ground at Kaesong would make Pyongyang vulnerable to a lightning attack, and that is what the South Koreans
attempted to do in the summer of 1949—conquer the whole of the
peninsula and grab the highest hill near Kaesong. The North Koreans
beat back these attacks, and Kim sent Stalin even more telegrams.[16]

This time, Kim struck lucky because events in the Far East seemed
to be moving in Stalin's favor. There had been the successful atomic
test, China had come under Communist rule, and the last American
combat troops had been removed from South Korea in June 1949. In
January 1950 Kim was invited to Moscow.

During his conversations with Stalin, Kim said he could conquer
the South in three days. Once the attack began, he boasted, the people of South Korea would rise in revolt, overthrow their evil pro-
American masters, and welcome the soldiers of North Korea as their
liberators. Stalin was not impressed by bluster. "If you get kicked in
the teeth," he warned, "I shall not lift a finger." Even so, he was willing to agree in principle, provided two conditions were met. First, he
wanted an assurance that the Americans would not intervene. Second, Mao had to offer troops. The Soviet Union would not provide
any of its own, but the possibility of air support was left open.

A few weeks later, Kim secured a promise of assistance from Mao,
who dismissed the risk of American intervention. "They will not go to
war for such a small territory as Korea," he said.[17]

Truman and Acheson had by this time infuriated Mao, and here
was his opportunity to settle some scores. Truman had not only refused to recognize China but had blocked it from claiming its seat on
the Security Council. Acheson's public statements that China was
merely an appendage to Soviet Communism were almost calculated
to wound Chinese feelings. Mao wrote no fewer than five magazine
articles rebuking Acheson and protesting American hostility since the
creation of the Chinese People's Republic. One way or another, Mao
intended to force Truman and Acheson to show some respect.[18]

After talking to Mao, Kim assured Stalin that with both China and
Russia offering fraternal support, the Americans would not dare to intervene, for to do so might ignite a world war. Red Army officers were
ordered to Pyongyang to help the North Koreans plan their invasion
of the South.[19]

At this point Stalin probably realized that he held a winning hand. If the North Koreans won the war quickly, his status as "pontiff to all the world's revolutionaries" would be greater than ever. And if the North Koreans got into trouble, the Chinese would intervene, which meant a protracted war, a war that would bedevil anti-Communist forces led by the United States for years to come.

Had the Chinese planned the North Korean attack, the result would have been the creation of a guerrilla army of South Koreans, supplemented by armed and trained bands of fighters from the North and a long war, much like the one that had brought victory to Mao and his generals. There would have been little risk of outside intervention, only a lot of hand-wringing at the UN. Instead, the Red Army planners crafted a tank-led mini-blitzkrieg, the kind of operation they had used to drive the Germans out of the Ukraine.

The next day, George Elsey was in the Oval Office, and he asked Truman what he thought was going to happen now. Would Formosa be the next target? Truman walked over to the globe that Eisenhower had sent him as a World War II souvenir. He put his finger on Iran. "Here is where they will start trouble if we aren't careful. Korea is the Greece of the Far East. If we are tough enough now, they won't take any next step. But if we just stand by, they'll move into Iran and take over the whole Middle East. There's no telling what they'll do, if we don't put up a fight now."[20]

When Truman met again with his Pentagon and State Department advisers at Blair House the evening of June 26, 1950, J. Lawton Collins, the army chief of staff, said the latest reports from Korea were bad. The South Korean army seemed to be falling apart, and he blamed it on its chief of staff. "There's no fight left in him," said Collins.

Louis Johnson and Omar Bradley repeated their opposition to committing American ground units. But if that became necessary, they advised Truman, he would have to order a general mobilization. Now it seemed real. "I don't want to go to war," said Truman. That was doubtless true, but even as he spoke, Truman may have realized that he had left himself little room for maneuver.[21]

Truman realized how stark the choice was: either the United States would abandon South Korea or it would have to put an army onto the Asian mainland. Yet he refused to see that if it put in ground forces, the United States would use what was at root a civil war to justify a major international war that would in turn magnify the civil war. The fundamental problem would not be resolved. It would almost certainly be passed on to future generations.

Neither Truman nor Acheson seemed able to see that the chances of winning were not merely slim, but possibly nonexistent. If things went badly for them, the North Koreans would not be forced to quit. They could revert to a guerrilla struggle, going back to where they began. A commander in chief is expected to think seriously about the implications of any major war, yet there is no evidence that Truman did so. He clung instead to the appeasement myth. This meant that he had already taken a long step toward committing ground troops several days before he had to announce his decision.

Robert Taft anticipated as much. On June 28 he made a speech in the Senate demanding that Truman seek a congressional resolution that supported American intervention in Korea. Do that, said Taft, and I will vote for it.

That same day, the Democratic leadership of the House and Senate came to the White House. They wanted to know what the president was going to do about Taft's call for a congressional resolution. The Democrats held narrow majorities in both houses, which in normal times would have settled the issue. Yet the temper of the times was so agitated and Truman's actions and statements on Far Eastern policy so confused, there was little trust left in his judgment.

The Democratic leader in the Senate, Scott Lucas of Illinois, wasn't encouraging. One reason Truman couldn't be sure of getting a congressional resolution was that few Republicans had any interest in defending Korea. What most of them wanted was a commitment to the defense of Formosa. And even after he gave them that, he still could not count on their support for a war in Korea. Any attempt to secure a resolution would be opposed, said Lucas, and the debate might be prolonged, sowing doubts about the wisdom of the president's action even if a resolution was eventually secured.

Acheson told Truman that he didn't really need one anyway—the country would swing behind the president in time of war. The State Department helpfully produced a list of eighty-seven occasions when a president, acting as commander in chief, had committed American forces to combat without seeking congressional approval either before or after the fact. Nearly all were trifling incidents in places from China to the Caribbean, where Americans had got themselves into a jam and a corporal's guard of soldiers or marines got them out of it. Not one of them was, or even approached becoming, a major war. It was as spurious a document as Acheson ever concocted.[22] McCarthy's attacks on the State Department were scurrilous and inexcusable, but there was an integrity deficit there.

Truman's solution was not going to be Acheson's list. Congress and the press would never accept something so flimsy. Instead, Truman got a firm grip on another document: the Constitution. Article II, Section 2 reads, "The president shall be commander in chief of the army and navy of the United States, and of the militia of the Several states, when called into the actual service of the United States." The title itself was a British creation, and the monarch had been the traditional commander in chief of British military forces. If a male, the monarch was even expected to lead troops into battle. George II had done so at the Battle of Minden in 1759. Female monarchs delegated their CinC powers to generals such as Churchill's great ancestor, John Churchill, Duke of Marlborough.

Well aware of the dangers this precedent might create for the new republic, the Founders had given the great issues of war and peace to Congress, not the president. It was Congress that declared war, Congress that raised and supported armies, Congress that would provide and maintain a navy, Congress that would draw up the regulations that governed the military. As Alexander Hamilton explained it in Federalist Paper 69, being commander in chief "would amount to nothing more than the supreme command and direction of the military and naval forces."

Article II, Section 2 had been written with George Washington in mind, and in 1794 Washington, as president, had taken an army of thirteen thousand militia into western Pennsylvania to suppress the Whiskey Rebellion. And in 1798, during the Quasi-War with France, John Adams had delegated his powers as commander in chief to Washington. The Senate duly ratified the appointment.

Sixteen years later, with a British army closing in on Washington, the decidedly unmilitary James Madison felt it was his duty as commander in chief to do as Washington had done. He strapped on a sword and mounted a war steed. On the northern outskirts of the District, his army broke after a few musket volleys and a British bayonet charge. What happened next stands in that space where history holds hands with folklore: Bladensburg Races, Washington's portrait, White House ablaze, and Congress ransacked.

With Madison's almost comical retreat, the exact responsibilities of the commander in chief were in flux. They remained so until 1846, when James K. Polk stretched the envelope by provoking a war with Mexico and personally choosing the generals who would fight it. But because it was Mexico that declared war on the United States, not the other way around, Polk claimed that nothing he did had produced a fundamental change in the president's war-making powers or the role of Congress. By and large, Polk was right, and in 1857 James Buchanan declined to join the British in suppressing Chinese pirates preying on shipping in the western Pacific, because to do so would mean "usurping the warmaking power which . . . belongs exclusively to Congress."

That was why during the Civil War there were many in Congress who believed that it was for them to direct the war, not the president. Lincoln disagreed. He created a whole new, unwritten addition to Article II, Section 2: "war powers." They are mentioned nowhere in the Constitution, and what they are and what limits there may be to their use is up for debate in every war. Congress has never provided a definitive judgment; nor has the Supreme Court. Lincoln used his war powers to do many things that Congress would probably not have supported, such as instituting the draft. He demanded that the states implement conscription, but there was hardly a Northern governor who believed that what he was doing was legal.

Lincoln's slighting of Congress had a price. It created the Joint Committee on the Conduct of the War, which tried repeatedly to dictate war policy, telling the president what strategy to pursue, which generals to promote and which to dismiss, and using the press to undermine his decisions. In the end, however, nearly everything Lincoln had done in the name of his war powers was accepted, for one overriding reason: the North won.

Since then, the United States had fought major wars with Spain, Germany, Italy, and Japan, and all four had declared war on the United States. Except for the Spanish-American War, Americans had never launched a major war without first being attacked. A congressional declaration of war was axiomatic when that happened.

North Korea, however, had not attacked the United States, nor was it making any evident effort to kill or capture the five hundred American military advisers. This was something new.

At Truman's weekly press conference that same day, June 28, a journalist wanted to know if the current fighting in Korea amounted to "a police action." Truman said it did. Among his advisers he had referred to it as a war many times, yet he could not bring himself to tell that to the country.[23]

Even as Truman was meeting with the congressional leaders, Seoul was under direct assault by leading elements of the North Korean People's Army, or Inmun Gun. Rhee departed in haste for Pusan, a port at the southeastern tip of the peninsula, more than two hundred miles away. MacArthur meanwhile arrived in Korea to make a command reconnaissance. What he saw was thousands of South Korean soldiers, or ROKs, heading south. Few of them had been wounded or looked like men who had been through the fire of close combat. Rhee's army, like its president, was scuttling to safety.

Truman shunned both Congress and the Security Council before intervening in Korea. Plain-speaking, direct Harry also embraced casuistry when he called it "a police action." Had he acknowledged the simple and irrefutable truth—that he was taking the nation to war—he would have been under pressure from Congress to seek a declaration of war.

At 5:00 a.m. on June 30, the secretary of the army, Frank Pace, came to the White House to tell Truman that MacArthur wanted to send a regimental combat team (roughly thirty-five hundred men) to secure Pusan, and to send two of the four divisions currently on occupation duty in Japan to launch a counteroffensive. If he did not get these troops, MacArthur said, "The fighting will be terminated within 10 days . . . a clear-cut decision is imperative."[24]

Truman was proud of his decisiveness, and the people who worked for him were proud of it too. Even experienced political journalists were impressed. One of them, Richard Lee Strout, described Truman's way of making a decision as being "like a man driving in a nail."[25]

All the same, Korea was about to demonstrate that although Truman appeared free to make a tough decision, he had already blocked or avoided every road that might have taken him in a different direction. He was careful throughout his presidency to avoid doing anything that might limit the powers of a future president. Yet he had limited his own. All American forces, including military advisers, would on any rational calculus have been out of South Korea by 1949, as the Joint Chiefs wanted. The country would then have been unified under Syngman Rhee or, more likely, under Kim Il Sung. The result would have been an impoverished autocratic state of some kind, but not a threat to any of its neighbors. It would have been much like Vietnam these past thirty years. When the crisis came, with no maneuver room left, Truman was blown by the zeitgeist into an unwinnable war, no more the master of his fate than a leaf tumbling down the street in the wind.

Truman's principal foreign policy advisers were, from left to right, Dean Acheson, the under secretary of state; the ambassador to the Soviet Union, Averell Harriman; and George C. Marshall, former army chief of staff but now secretary of state. The ideological Acheson and Harriman never ceased to play on Truman's simplistic conception of the Red Menace, and, although Truman claimed to admire Marshall above all other men, he routinely ignored the general's pragmatic advice. (*National Park Service photograph by Abbie Rowe, courtesy Harry S. Truman Library*)

Truman's eagerness to get away from Potsdam, Stalin, and Europe can be read in his stride as the 1945 conference broke up. Nothing was achieved at Potsdam that could not have been achieved without it. (*U.S. Army, courtesy Harry S. Truman Library*)

The medieval notion that "the King can do no wrong" was based on the idea that if anything went awry, it was due to the king's evil counsellors. Clark Clifford was Truman's evil counsellor. Here he stands between Truman and Churchill in Fulton, Missouri, for Churchill's "iron curtain" speech. (*Terry Savage, courtesy Harry S. Truman Library*)

From left to right are Truman's World War I buddy and military aide, Harry Vaughan; Clark Clifford, still in naval uniform; the president; his doctor and "snake oil" provider, Dr. Wallace Graham; and Truman's high school classmate and press secretary, Charlie Ross. (*U.S. Marine Corps, courtesy Harry S. Truman Library*)

A strong and wise president would have ordered MacArthur to return home
following the 1948 election. But Truman lacked the nerve. Two years
later, in 1950, he pinned on MacArthur's fourth Distinguished
Service Medal when the two met on Wake Island.
Behind the smiles, bottomless contempt.
(U.S. Army, courtesy Harry S. Truman Library)

Johnson wanted to be able to say that his decisions on Vietnam were based on wide consultation, yet the people he actually listened to were inveterate hawks such as, from left to right, his ambassador to Saigon, Maxwell Taylor; his director of intelligence, Richard Helms; and his secretary of state, Dean Rusk—all highly intelligent and all deficient in judgment.

(LBJ Library photograph by Yoichi Okamoto)

In August 1964, LBJ signed the Tonkin Gulf resolution in the presence of the Washington political elite and the national press. Johnson knew even as he signed the resolution that there had been no unprovoked attack on American warships. Even so, he now had a legal fig leaf that he could use to justify making war against North Vietnam.

(LBJ Library photograph by Cecil Stoughton)

From 1964 to 1969, public opinion strongly supported the war. Johnson was even able to use Vietnam to his advantage in the 1964 election campaign, running as the peace candidate while he prepared for a major escalation once the election was over.

(LBJ Library photograph by Yoichi Okamoto)

Nguyen Cao Ky was a flamboyant fighter pilot: purple silk scarf wound around his neck, Colt .45 slapping against his thigh. He was too flashy ever to be a credible political leader of a traditional and conservative people such as the Vietnamese. At this meeting in Honolulu, Ky pretended to consult with the president while Johnson pretended to pay attention.
(LBJ Library photograph by Yoichi Okamoto)

William Westmoreland, the general chosen by Johnson to take command in Vietnam in 1964. Westy looked like Central Casting's idea of a general. An able soldier, Westmoreland would probably have succeeded in any assignment but this one. *(LBJ Library photograph by Yoichi Okamoto)*

ABOVE: On his one trip to South Vietnam, Johnson visited Cam Ranh Bay and took this soldier's salute. Johnson's emotions are all over his face, but the person he really felt sorry for was himself. (*LBJ Library photograph by Yoichi Okamoto*).

BELOW: This photograph, taken in February 1968, shows Johnson and McNamara's despairing reaction to news of the Tet Offensive in Vietnam. (*LBJ Library photograph by Yoichi Okamoto*)

On March 31, 1968, Johnson announced that he would not seek reelection. He also halted the bombing of North Vietnam, hoping that might bring the North Vietnamese into serious talks about peace. Yet so long as they had the support of the Soviet Union and China, the North Vietnamese had nothing to lose by fighting, and nothing to gain by quitting.

(LBJ Library photograph by Yoichi Okamoto)

Narrowly having won the presidency in 1968 by suggesting he had a secret plan for ending the war, Nixon paid a fleeting, highly publicized visit to an American base in South Vietnam in June 1969. "Magical Mystery Tour" struck the right note: Nixon had no idea how to end the war but was tempted to make a nuclear attack on North Vietnam.

(National Archives)

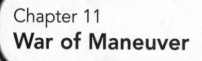

Chapter 11
War of Maneuver

WHEN KIM IL SUNG PROMISED STALIN AND MAO A KNOCKOUT BLOW
that would conquer South Korea before the Americans could intervene, it seemed more than realistic—it seemed inevitable. Kim's army,
the Inmun Gun, numbered 135,000 men organized in seven infantry
divisions, plus an armored brigade that was equipped with 150 obsolescent but still potent T-34 tanks. In its ranks were 30,000 Koreans
who had served in Mao's victorious armies. The Inmun Gun's firepower was impressive, especially for a force of its size: 2,000 artillery
pieces, many self-propelled. There were also more than a hundred
fighters and light bombers for close air support.

The Republic of Korea's forces consisted of 95,000 men, a handful
of tanks, and only 90 pieces of artillery. There was no ROK air force
to speak of, and the South's lightly armed troops were little more than
a paramilitary force maintained not for war, but for domestic repression and raids into the North. There were invasion scares along the
border every spring or summer, but few took them seriously.

The Inmun Gun's 1950 attack was the real thing. It went straight for Seoul, like a tiger going for its prey's throat. Led by its T-34s, it covered the forty miles from the 38th parallel to the northern outskirts of Seoul in only forty-eight hours. The ROK army dissolved before it. On June 29 the Inmun Gun paraded through the streets of Seoul, looking unstoppable. And then it stopped. American F-80 jet fighters and B-26 bombers were bombing, strafing, and rocketing the troop and truck columns that were now clogging the roads and railroad lines north and northwest of the city. They ignited fuel trucks in fireballs, blew up locomotives in huge clouds of steam, and forced the North Koreans to spend a week picking up the pieces. That gave MacArthur time to start feeding ground units into South Korea piecemeal, and for him to become what he had never expected to be again—a field commander with a war to fight.

Within twenty-four hours of the North Korean attack, Acheson had placed a resolution in front of the Security Council that called on North Korea to pull its troops back to the 38th parallel and cease hostilities. So far, so predictable. The resolution was quickly adopted, but the North Koreans did not respond. Two days later the United States submitted a second resolution, this time calling on "members of the United Nations to furnish such assistance to the Republic of Korea as may be necessary to repel the armed attack and restore international peace and security to the area."

The UN was useful but not essential to Truman's purposes. If the UN had not fallen into line, he was going to fight in Korea anyway. Truman was hoping, in fact, that the Soviet representative, Yakov Malik, would show up and veto the resolution. If Malik had done that, the United States would be free to act unilaterally in Korea, aided by whatever countries were willing to join it in a coalition of the willing.[1]

One thing would not have been changed: Truman felt he had no option but to put MacArthur in command. To pick anyone else would be to start a fight with virtually every Republican in Congress, and with more than a few Democrats. Truman's antipathy for the general went back many years: the colonel in the army reserve had loathed the flamboyant West Pointer ever since World War I, during which MacArthur—with his grommetless cap, riding crop under one arm, gleaming riding boots, and seven-foot hand-knitted purple scarf from Mother—had emerged as the beau ideal of American soldiering.

When MacArthur's campaign to liberate the Philippines had come to a close in 1945, Truman had taken up his diary to vent his bile at "Mr. Prima Donna, Brass Hat, Five Star McArthur [*sic*]. He is worse than the Cabots and the Lodges. They at least talked to one another before they told God what to do. Mc tells God what to do right off. It is a very great pity we have to have stuffed shirts like that in key positions." MacArthur was nothing but "a play actor and bunko man."[2]

Truman's disdain was so comprehensive it included contempt for the most obvious of MacArthur's military attributes—his physical courage. Truman derisively referred to MacArthur as "Dugout Doug." It counted for nothing that MacArthur held a dozen medals for gallantry and two Purple Hearts. To Truman, everything about MacArthur was fake, including his bravery. Yet Truman loved to award the Medal of Honor and craved a combat decoration for himself. For many years he tried to secure a Purple Heart for his service in World War I, even though he had never been wounded.[3]

A few months after the Japanese surrender, Truman told MacArthur he ought to come home to receive the accolades of a grateful nation. He did not say so, but he intended to award MacArthur a third oak-leaf cluster to his Distinguished Service Medal, and he probably hoped to persuade MacArthur to go into retirement. That was what MacArthur half expected to happen. However, Truman did not give a direct order. Commanders in chief rarely give direct orders to five-star generals except in emergencies. Besides, in the army, any suggestion or request from a superior is considered an order, be it ever so politely phrased.

Truman's courtesy provided all the leeway MacArthur needed. He declined the invitation, claiming that if he left Japan now, the occupation might fail. This was ridiculous, given that the emperor had ordered his people to obey the occupation authorities. Truman should have reissued the invitation, buttressed by a direct order to accept it from the army chief of staff, Dwight Eisenhower. In failing to do so Truman had shown weakness, something that could only increase MacArthur's scorn.

Truman's distaste for MacArthur bore fruit, however. MacArthur received his oak-leaf cluster in a brown paper bag. Word seeped back to the White House from Tokyo that the oversensitive MacArthur was deeply hurt at being treated this way. Was he being mocked?[4]

Before long, Truman began fantasizing about ridding himself of Mr.

Prima Donna. He devised a plan to replace MacArthur after the 1948 election, assuming he was elected. The replacement he had in mind was Lucius Clay. After his success running the occupation of Germany, Clay was a credible candidate for Japan. Once Truman was duly elected, he offered Clay the assignment, but Clay turned him down. He was about to leave the army to become president of a major corporation, and he would not be dissuaded. Truman gave up, showing timidity again.[5]

On becoming UN commander, MacArthur had something he had not possessed as supreme allied commander in Japan: he was now responsible for the defense of South Korea. He also had a new demand from his commander in chief. The Joint Chiefs ordered him to report to the president every day on current operations. During the last war, Truman explained to the NSC, "I practically had to telephone General MacArthur to get information from him." It wasn't going to happen again.[6]

After its weeklong pause in Seoul to reorganize its logistics, the Inmun Gun began moving south toward Pusan at six miles a day. For a tank-led offensive, this was hardly lightning war. On July 19, MacArthur informed Truman, "The enemy has had his chance and failed to exploit it." He credited the troops he had deployed from Japan with the slow rate of the enemy's advance.[7]

It owed much more to inexperience with combined arms operations and to the failure of one key element in Kim's plan and promise: there was no popular uprising, no ardent embrace by ordinary Koreans of their northern brothers, few flowers and kisses for the liberators. Without an uprising to aid their advance, Kim's field commanders spread their forces out to seize control of all of South Korea instead of putting everything into taking Pusan.

The result of these misjudgments was that MacArthur's Eighth Army, flabby from prolonged occupation duty in Japan, was granted enough time and more than a month of the military's best academy—being shot at. Men and equipment were landed at Pusan and carved a defensive perimeter that would keep enemy artillery at least thirty miles from the city's docks, harbor, and ammunition depots. By early August, when the Inmun Gun's leading elements reached the defensive perimeter, the Eighth Army had nearly two hundred thousand troops, six times as many tanks, far more artillery, and nearly all the high ground.

Truman was nevertheless feeling the strain. His famous ability to fall asleep almost on command failed him. It troubled him deeply to ask young Americans to fight and die in a faraway place, and he knew, as all combat veterans do, that mistakes higher up the line mean death or crippling wounds for the soldier in the rifle pit or tank. If he got it wrong, not only would the cost be high, but mainly others would pay it.[8]

As the Inmun Gun closed on Pusan, he felt the need to unburden himself to Arthur Krock, one of the country's premier political columnists. "We have decided to retake Korea even if we are forced off the beaches and back to Japan," said Truman. The Joint Chiefs weren't happy about fighting there, he conceded. Korea was Stalin's backyard, not America's. "We want any showdown to come in Western Europe, where we can use the Bomb . . . But it happens that the weakest of the Communist satellites [North Korea] is licking the hell out of us, which is very bad from a propaganda point of view." The other thing that worried him was "the Trojan Horse Commies" in the United States. Truman estimated there were fifty thousand secret party members poised to strike while the United States had a war on its hands. If the country was vulnerable anywhere, it was vulnerable at home, and if there was a vulnerable time, this was it.[9]

Truman and Acheson had also convinced themselves that Stalin was using Korea as a diversion before making his real move somewhere in Western Europe or the Middle East. They were playing baseball while Stalin played football. In the 1930s Stalin had abandoned the idea of world revolution and adopted "Socialism in One Country." This change in Soviet policy had never been a secret, and any attempt to foment insurrectionism in the postwar years was more dangerous for Stalin than it had ever been, given the American military presence across Western Europe. In Asia, however, where there was a new, powerful partner that was wedded to the doctrine of insurrectionism, risk taking was possible without igniting a world war. Yet when George Kennan tried to get Acheson to see the war on the Korean peninsula for what it was, a war unconnected to Europe or the Middle East, Acheson refused to believe it.[10]

Truman similarly told anyone who questioned what he'd done or why he'd done it that they were missing the point: by fighting in Korea, he had prevented World War III. The Soviets were in no shape to fight a global war, but having repeatedly portrayed Stalin as the new Hitler and Russia as the Third Reich reborn under a red star, Truman was fenced in by the intellectual boundaries of the incoherent paradigm he had created.

While Truman and Acheson liked to believe that the Soviet Union dogmatically followed the same strategy of conquest all over the world, Stalin remained what he had always been—an opportunist. By providing support to insurgencies in Malaya and Indochina, he was going to make it more difficult for Britain and France to fulfill their commitments to NATO. And by aiding a North Korean attack on South Korea, he was hoping to provoke the Americans into blocking a Communist invasion of Formosa. For him, the Korean War was off to a promising start, despite the failings of the Inmun Gun.

By the end of July, MacArthur was so confident about Pusan that he felt free to make a trip to Formosa. In the early days of the fighting, Jiang Jieshi had offered to send 33,000 soldiers to fight under MacArthur's command. Truman wanted to accept them. Acheson had a struggle talking him out of doing so. One, to accept them would weaken the defenses of Formosa at a time when up to 3,000 wooden junks—almost unsinkable vessels—were being assembled for an invasion of Formosa. Two, Chinese Nationalist troops had shown that they could not defend their homeland; it was impossible to believe they would do any better defending South Korea.[11]

Having spurned the offer, Truman nevertheless increased the American commitment to the defense of Jiang's regime. A month after sending the Seventh Fleet into the Formosa Strait, Truman provided Jiang with $125 million in military and economic assistance. The mission of the Seventh Fleet was also broadened, to defend not only Formosa but also the sixty-four small islands within the Strait, including those that were within China's three-mile limit.

To Truman's astonishment, MacArthur made an unannounced visit to Formosa on July 31, accompanied by a personal retinue that filled one transport plane and a press contingent that filled another. In front of the cameras he threw his arms around Jiang, whom he had not met until now. When the general departed the next day, he took the hand of Madame Jiang, bent low, and kissed it like a true *galant*. No one paid much attention to the embrace of Jiang, but there was fury in Washington over the kissing of the hand, even if it was attached to a Wellesley graduate.[12]

As the Inmun Gun set about its hopeless task of breaking through the Pusan perimeter, MacArthur's fertile mind turned to mounting a counteroffensive. He informed the Joint Chiefs that once the enemy had exhausted itself, he wanted to make an amphibious assault at Inchon, halfway up the west coast of Korea. Inchon was only thirty miles from Seoul. If the assault was timed to coincide with a breakout from the perimeter, the North Koreans could be annihilated.

The Joint Chiefs flew to Tokyo to discuss the Inchon plan with its author. Truman had two other people travel with them: Averell Harriman and Edwin Lowe. Truman wanted Harriman, who had known MacArthur for three years, to convey a two-part message: one, he must not encourage Jiang to get involved in the war; two, if he lets me know just what he needs, I'll do everything I can to provide it.[13]

Lowe was an old Truman friend, a colonel in the army reserve and a courtly gent. He was to stay in Tokyo as Truman's personal representative at MacArthur's headquarters, and he too brought a message from the president: "I have never had anything but the utmost confidence in the general's ability to do that Far Eastern job."[14]

The Joint Chiefs could hardly credit MacArthur's proposed assault at Inchon. The tides were all wrong, the topography was all wrong, and it would not be possible to put more than half the assaulting force ashore in the initial attack. MacArthur was also demanding the 1st Marine Division, which was at little more than half its authorized strength. It would have to be reinforced with marines from other divisions and shipped on short notice across the Pacific. Yet everything depended on that.

MacArthur told Harriman there was something the president needed to understand: if the general got command of the 1st Marine Division, "I will on the rising tide of fifteenth of September, land at Inchon, and between the hammer of this landing and the anvil of the Eighth Army, I will crush and destroy the enemy armies of North Korea."[15]

Harriman found it spine-tingling, but there was something else, he told Truman; something that he found troubling: MacArthur seemed to think the United States had to defend the regime of Jiang Jieshi because "he has the strange idea that we should back anybody who will fight Communism." Why Harriman was puzzled is hard to fathom. MacArthur's strange idea was known as the Truman Doctrine—i.e., "I believe that it must be the policy of the United States to support free peoples who are resisting subjugation by armed minorities or by outside pressure."[16]

Less than three weeks later Harriman brought Truman something else. MacArthur had composed a message to be read out at a gathering of the Veterans of Foreign Wars. A friendly journalist had passed on a copy of the press release that contained MacArthur's message. Acheson had passed it on to Harriman. There were some references to "the Oriental mind," but the gist of what MacArthur had to say was that Formosa was so vital to American security that it had to be defended from a Communist attack.

Half an hour after Harriman showed Truman the press release, Omar Bradley gave his daily White House briefing on the past twenty-four hours in Korea. The other Chiefs were also there, as were Louis Johnson and Dean Acheson. When Bradley, a former schoolteacher and always at home with a pointer and an easel, finished his presentation, Truman said, "I have just come across something rather interesting." He proceeded to read the press release to them. When he finished, he turned to Johnson. "Louis, I want you to direct General MacArthur to withdraw that statement." Johnson squirmed at the thought of rebuking MacArthur, a man he admired. He went back to his office and wrestled, unsuccessfully, with a response that might keep Truman happy without triggering MacArthur's resignation.

Irritated, Truman ordered Johnson to get the message withdrawn, and dictated a telegram that Johnson would send to MacArthur:

THE PRESIDENT OF THE UNITED STATES DIRECTS THAT YOU WITHDRAW YOUR MESSAGE FOR THE VETERANS OF FOREIGN WARS BECAUSE VARIOUS FEATURES WITH RESPECT TO FORMOSA ARE IN CONFLICT WITH THE POLICY OF THE U.S. AND ITS POSITION IN THE U.N.

MacArthur issued a statement disavowing the offending remarks, but with the wire services already distributing his VFW message all over the planet, he could no more withdraw it than he could repeal yesterday.[17]

Truman's patience these days was so thin it was virtually gone. The Joint Chiefs had come home, thought about things, sent the army chief of staff, J. Lawton Collins, to discuss Inchon some more, and finally given the operation their blessing, fervently praying it would not prove a disaster. At almost the same time, though, a congressman from California, Gordon L. McDonough, began demanding in Congress and the press that Truman get the Marine Corps into Korea.

The marines, Truman informed McDonough, were little more than a police force for the navy, "and they have a propaganda machine that is almost equal to Stalin's." A few days later Truman's letter was reprinted in the New York *Daily News*. The old army vs. marine antipathy was still strong in Colonel Truman, but he was obliged by the storm that ensued to write a fawning, if not groveling, letter about how he'd always admired the Marine Corps and how determined he was to protect it from its critics.

Meanwhile, the Inmun Gun launched its do-or-die offensive to break through the Pusan perimeter. Instead of concentrating their attack, they spread it far and wide, hoping to find a weak spot. On the few occasions they managed to find one, Far East Air Force appeared the next morning and bombed them off it. MacArthur had his commanders prepare for the breakout and organized them into a new formation, X Corps, to be commanded by his chief of staff, Edward Almond.

As the assault force prepared to set sail from ports in Japan, there were developments in Washington. When Harriman returned from Tokyo, Truman had told him, "Dean's in trouble and I want you to help him." The Korean War had only exacerbated the power struggle between Acheson and Johnson, and as always happens in wartime, the Pentagon was gaining the upper hand over the Department of State.[18]

This was a problem that had weighed on Truman since the war began, but after talking to Marshall at the end of June, Truman had glimpsed a possible solution to the infighting between Acheson and Johnson. Maybe he could get Marshall to come back, this time in charge of the Pentagon. By early September, with the situation around Pusan finally secured, Truman told Marshall he had to remove Johnson, but it all hinged on whether the general would take Johnson's place. Marshall, the good soldier always, replied, "You know, Mr. President, I'll do whatever you think is necessary."[19]

A few days later, word got into the newspapers that Louis Johnson was about to be dismissed. Johnson asked Truman to let him have a couple of days to think about resigning, and wrote a letter of resignation. At the end of the cabinet meeting on September 16, he followed Truman into the Oval Office. Clutching the letter, he burst into tears and begged for a second chance. Truman scanned the letter. "Louis, you haven't signed this—sign it." More tears, but Johnson signed. Truman found dismissing Johnson deeply upsetting, however necessary it might be. "This is the toughest job I ever had to do," he told Charlie Ross, his press secretary and friend from high school days. "I feel as if I had just whipped my daughter, Margaret."[20]

Three days later, marines hit the beach at Inchon. Tens of thousands more troops from allied countries followed. The port was as lightly defended as MacArthur anticipated. The main shipping channel was clear of mines, and there were only 2,500 North Koreans to resist the assault. Inchon was taken in less than twenty-four hours. It was a dazzling victory, and having grasped it, MacArthur went after Seoul.

The North Koreans pushed 25,000 green troops into the city to defend it, and two weeks later it fell. Meanwhile, some Inmun Gun commanders failed or refused to retreat across the 38th parallel, allowing the X Corps, moving north, to kill or capture thousands. Those who did recross the parallel became guerrillas. The North Korean People's Army had been destroyed. Then and after, Inchon was hailed as a brilliant feat of arms, not a hollow victory, and MacArthur's stock was so high that for many people he might as well have been God's right-hand man.

To George Elsey, one of the youngest people on Truman's staff, the timing of MacArthur's Inchon counterstroke and the emotional ceremony in Seoul at which MacArthur restored Syngman Rhee to power could not have been more fortuitous. The midterm congressional election was in its closing stages, and the Democrats had looked set to be trounced. Wouldn't a meeting between the president and the general go a long way toward helping deserving Democrats at the polls? wondered Elsey.[21]

The logical place for the encounter was Hawaii, but Elsey soon discovered that MacArthur hated flying at night. MacArthur suggested
Wake Island instead, which he could reach in nine daylight hours
from Japan. Truman accepted Wake, even though it would take him
two days to get there and two days to come back. That was an indica-
tion of the potential electoral payoff.

Truman may have offered some pro forma objections to this cynical
ploy. If so, he evidently did not need a lot of persuading. The White
House press machine strenuously denied that Truman's trip to meet
with MacArthur had anything to do with politics and everything to do
with the war, but Marshall wasn't consulted in advance, and when he
found out about it, he declined to take part.

MacArthur considered it yet another intrusion of party politics
onto the battlefield, deeply resented it, and despised Truman all the
more. Just another cheapjack politician.[22]

The meeting was arranged for October 15. MacArthur arrived the
evening of the 14th, flying only in daylight, and was up early the next
morning for Truman's arrival. When the *Independence* landed, Truman was slightly surprised to see MacArthur waiting in a jeep some
distance away. As the ramp was pushed up to the airplane and Truman appeared in the doorway, MacArthur walked briskly over to the
foot of the ramp, arriving at the bottom at almost the same instant as
the president. To Truman's surprise, MacArthur did not bother to
salute his commander in chief. Instead, he stuck out his right hand.

Truman understandably saw this as disdain, but he was probably
wrong. MacArthur had strong views on the rituals of military po-
litesse. He considered saluting a relic of a bygone era, along with the
surrender of swords and kissing the regimental flag. The aristocratic
Roosevelt had not been bothered about not being saluted. A hand-
shake was good enough. It did not occur to MacArthur that the petit
bourgeois Truman would be affronted.[23] As they shook hands, Truman forced a smile. "How are you, General? I'm glad you are here. I
have been a long time meeting you."

MacArthur responded, "I hope it won't be so long next time."[24]

The only automobile on the island, a battered old Chevrolet sedan,
ferried them the hundred yards to a small building where they could
have a chat without anyone else present. Meanwhile, a bus took Truman's entourage over to the main building where the conference

would be held. Five large folding tables had been pushed together to create a conference table, and the room, having been repainted easy-eye green the previous day, still reeked of paint.

When Truman and MacArthur entered after their forty minutes of private conversation, Truman strode to the head of the table and pointed to the chair next to his. "You sit there." MacArthur proceeded to give a comprehensive account of how operations were unfolding in Korea.

As the general spoke, Truman had one question above all that he wanted to ask: What about China? There were intelligence reports of Chinese troops being moved in large numbers into Manchuria, and on October 3, the Chinese foreign minister, Zhou Enlai, had invited the Indian ambassador to China, K. M. Pannikar, to his office. Zhou said he had a message he wanted Pannikar to convey to the Americans: if American troops crossed the 38th parallel, China would enter the war.

Acheson dismissed it out of hand. "Zhou's words were a warning," he decided, "but not an authoritative statement of policy." Zhou was only Acheson's equivalent in the government of China. When Acheson spoke, his words were presented and accepted as authoritative statements of American policy. But in Acheson's world, it was Stalin who told the Chinese what they could or could not do. Acheson thus portrayed Zhou as a nobody, while Truman scorned Pannikar as "a fellow traveler."[25]

Even so, when MacArthur finished his briefing, Truman said, "General, all of our intelligence sources indicate that the Chinese Communists are about to enter this war. What are the chances of Soviet or Chinese intervention?"

"Very little, Mr. President," MacArthur replied. "Had they interfered in the first or second month it would have been decisive. We are no longer fearful of their intervention. Only fifty to sixty thousand could be gotten across the Yalu river. If the Chinese Communists cross the Yalu, I shall make of them the greatest slaughter in the history of mankind."

MacArthur did not claim that the Chinese would not enter the war. What he was emphasizing was Chinese capabilities. He wisely avoided guessing at their intentions. They had no air cover, he explained, and that would expose them to the full ferocity of the Far

East Air Force. The Russians might try to provide air cover, but close air support required exceptional coordination between air and ground units, a level of coordination that was simply beyond Russian airplanes and Chinese infantry hugging the ground. Chinese units would be bombed and strafed on such a scale it sickened him even to contemplate it.[26]

In the course of a ninety-minute meeting, MacArthur dealt with thirty-four questions. Most were banal. Dean Rusk was dismayed at the inanity of many of them and the speed with which Truman was asking them, clearly impatient with anything more than snappy answers. Rusk pushed a note over to Truman, who glanced at it. Rusk wanted him to slow down, "to lend a note of seriousness to the meeting." Truman scribbled on the note, "Hell, no! I want to get out of here before we get into trouble!"[27] Apart from Truman's initial question about China, only one other serious issue was addressed. The French had 150,000 soldiers in Indochina, fighting the Vietminh. Truman wanted them to continue doing that, even though he and Eisenhower were pressing the French to increase their commitments to NATO. A month before this meeting, the Vietminh had launched a major offensive and were currently driving the French back from the Vietnamese-Chinese border and inflicting serious losses. Truman wanted to know what MacArthur made of the news from Indochina? The Vietminh seemed to be becoming bolder and stronger. Were they being pushed into this offensive by the Chinese to divert American attention—and possibly troops—from Korea?

"It's puzzling," said MacArthur.

"This is the most discouraging thing we face," said Truman.

"We must stiffen the backbone of the French," MacArthur responded.[28]

There was some good news to offset it. The war in Korea, MacArthur said, would be over by Thanksgiving whether the Chinese intervened or not. He would be able to release an entire division—possibly two—before Christmas, to bolster NATO. And there would be more divisions available for deployment to Europe in the New Year.[29] As the meeting broke up, MacArthur told Charlie Ross that he could quote the general in these words: "No field commander in the history of warfare has had more complete and admirable support than I have had during the Korean operation."[30]

Truman awarded a fourth oak-leaf cluster to MacArthur's Distinguished Service Medal on the top row of ribbons that decorated MacArthur's open-necked shirt. No paper bag this time.

As MacArthur flew north to Tokyo and Truman flew east to Hawaii, nine divisions of Chinese People's Volunteers were moving south from Manchuria.

Chapter 12
What Goes Up . . .

COLONEL TRUMAN WAS ITCHING TO HIT BACK. EVEN BEFORE THE landing at Inchon, he and the National Security Council drafted a resolution that would authorize MacArthur to cross the 38th parallel. By the time the resolution was passed by the UN, MacArthur had taken Inchon. He was instructed to move north, but Truman was still worried about the Chinese and the Russians. MacArthur was told to keep his non-Korean troops away from the Yalu River. Only the ROKs could go all the way.[1]

On October 1, 1950, with Seoul retaken, ROK units had begun crossing the 38th parallel. Acheson, meanwhile, was thrilled at the prospects he saw opening up. "Korea is a stage to prove to the world what Western democracy can do to help underprivileged countries." Containment was about to give way to something more glorious, said Acheson: liberation. The North Koreans would surely rejoice as their liberators appeared.[2]

The number of Chinese troops in Manchuria had doubled in recent weeks, and a new army, devoted to border defense, was being created. Truman tried to reassure the Chinese of his intentions, declaring publicly that Americans were their friends; a fatuous claim given all that he had done to undermine and humiliate China in recent years. Even so, Truman almost certainly believed what he was saying was true. At the same time, Acheson chose to threaten China with "dismemberment and destruction" if it dared to intervene in Korea.[3]

MacArthur's instructions to cross the parallel had been issued by the Joint Chiefs, but they reflected the full range of Truman's and Acheson's confusion on the kind of war they were fighting, the role of the Soviets, and the risk of Chinese intervention. The orders struck the right martial note—"Your objective is the destruction of the North Korean Armed Forces"—and thereafter crashed into the implications. What about North Korean guerrillas? Was MacArthur to go after them too? Even at the risk of being drawn into fighting a nationalistic insurgency? No guidance there.

MacArthur was to cross the 38th parallel provided the Soviets and Chinese had not already entered North Korea or threatened to do so, yet "if the Soviet Union or Chinese Communists should announce in advance their intention to reoccupy North Korea and give warning, either explicitly or implicitly, that their forces should not be attacked you should refer the matter to Washington." The contention that the Chinese People's Republic had at one time occupied North Korea was wrong. And just what was an implicit warning—shots fired over the heads of American troops? One of the most famous of military aphorisms had been crafted by the elder von Moltke nearly a century earlier: "Any order that can be misunderstood will be misunderstood." The order that unleashed the charge of the Light Brigade in the Crimean War was a model of clarity compared with MacArthur's instructions for taking the war into North Korea.[4]

Both Acheson and Marshall approved the order before it went to Truman. These days, Marshall was an exhausted man, taking frequent breaks and long naps. To a large degree, the Defense Department was left to his deputy, Robert Lovett, who had served as assistant secretary of war but had spent much longer on Wall Street. Marshall had certainly passed his peak by 1950, and he compounded his folly with a loosely worded message to MacArthur after Truman approved the order: "We want you to feel unhampered tactically and strategically to proceed north of the 38th parallel." This was hardly the Marshall who was at pains not to give MacArthur free rein during World War II.[5]

As MacArthur moved north, Kim Il Sung was begging Stalin to send troops into North Korea. Stalin's chilly response was, go see Mao. He backed up this advice with a telegram to Mao telling him to "move at least five or six divisions toward the 38th parallel," or the war would be lost. Mao responded that China would have to commit huge forces if it was to stop the Americans. The result was likely to be a war between the United States and China, and such a conflict would inevitably draw in the Soviets. "The question would thus become extremely large. Therefore it is better to show patience now."

Stalin was emotionally all over the map. At first he was alarmed at the prospect of American troops on the Soviet border, but he soon seemed resigned to that possibility. On October 2, the Soviets placed a resolution before the UN that called for a cease-fire, the withdrawal of all foreign forces from the peninsula, and a general election under UN supervision that would produce a united Korea. If it passed, Syngman Rhee would win the election and rule a united Korea. Stalin told his entourage that he was prepared to live with a capitalist Korea, and the Americans were sure to keep their forces on the Korean peninsula. "So what?" said Stalin. "Let the United States be our neighbors in the Far East. They will come here, but we shall not fight them now. We are not ready to fight." Two days later, the UN rejected the Soviets' call for a cease-fire.[6]

While the resolution was being introduced to—and rejected by—the UN, Stalin was pressing China to intervene immediately, otherwise North Korea would be wiped out, he informed Mao, and that would put the Americans on China's borders.

He shrugged off Mao's warning that Chinese intervention might ignite a global war. "Should we fear this?" Stalin asked. "In my opinion we should not, because together we shall be stronger than the United States and Great Britain . . . If war is inevitable, let us wage it now."[7]

Mao had been bluffing, calling Stalin's hand. He had already concluded that China would have to intervene. It was his colleagues on the Central Committee who needed to be convinced, starting with

Zhou Enlai. Over several days of impassioned debate, while Stalin waited for word from the UN, Mao was arguing with the doubters that China could not stand by and watch North Korea, its neighbor, destroyed. If the Americans crossed the 38th parallel, China would have to intervene. Mao did not know that American troops had already crossed it. By the time he learned they had done so, Chinese divisions were already in motion.

There was also something missing from Stalin's telegram: no mention of the Red Air Force providing cover for the Chinese troops he was so eager to push into North Korea. Only after Zhou went to see Stalin and Stalin promised Soviet fighters and air defense units did Mao inform the Russians that China would intervene.[8]

For all his bellicosity that October, it was not MacArthur who spurned Stalin's offer of a peaceful settlement, it was Truman. Had the United States chosen to put the Soviets' sincerity to the test, the UN would have passed the resolution and the war really might have been over by Christmas. Truman was so dazzled by the prospect of outright victory—and personal vindication—that he gave peaceful settlement not a moment's thought. A united, pro-Western Korea was within his grasp, and he threw it away. Once again the question arises: Was it Harry, or was it the pep pills?

At the very least, he was becoming hubristic. Following the meeting on Wake Island, he informed MacArthur that even if the Chinese intervened, he was to continue to advance, provided "in your judgment, action by forces now under your control offers a reasonable chance of success." MacArthur was capable of generating his own hubris. He did not need to lean on Truman's, and the day after receiving Truman's message, he called on the North Koreans to "forthwith lay down your arms and cease hostilities."

Overconfident to the point of complacency, MacArthur had divided his forces in the face of the enemy. He had done the same at Inchon and got away with it. Grant had done it repeatedly during the Civil War. Napoleon, too, had done it many times, but at Waterloo doing so led to the destruction of his army. MacArthur had the 200,000-strong Eighth Army, commanded by Lieutenant General Walton Walker, advancing up the western side of the peninsula, while the X Corps moved along the eastern side. In between was a gap seventy miles wide consisting of mountainous terrain. Their operations were virtually independent.

Walton Walker was a cigar-smoking fireplug of a man, his sallow features characterized by a ferocious scowl. MacArthur did not think Walker was bright enough to command an army in combat, despite his fine record as an armor commander in World War II. Rather than put everything under Walker, MacArthur chose to create a second formation, the X Corps, and put his former chief of staff, Edward Almond, in command. Having failed as an infantry division commander back in 1944, Almond should probably have been left at a desk in Tokyo.

On his return from Wake, a buoyed-up MacArthur instructed Walker and Almond "to drive forward with all speed and . . . use any and all ground forces . . . to secure all of North Korea." He had just overturned the barrier to putting American troops along China's border. The Joint Chiefs sent a telegram: YOUR ACTION IS A MATTER OF SOME CONCERN HERE. MacArthur's response was that General Marshall's message authorized the freedom of action that he was now exercising. Besides, he added, TACTICAL HAZARDS MIGHT EVEN RESULT FROM OTHER ACTION THAN THAT WHICH I HAVE DIRECTED.[9]

The Joint Chiefs were also unhappy about MacArthur's decision to split his forces, but they'd been doubtful about Inchon and he'd proved them wrong. So they allowed MacArthur to fight the next phase of the war his way.

On October 25, nearly a hundred thousand Chinese troops struck the advance units of the ROK 1st and 6th Divisions, inflicting more than a thousand casualties and prompting thousands of survivors to flee. It was a rout.

MacArthur damned the Chinese intervention—"outrageous international lawlessness"—and sought permission to order air attacks on the bridges over the Yalu. MacArthur, Truman, and the Far East Air Force debated whether to bomb the bridges, but it would have been more fruitful to discuss weather. The Yalu flows through mountainous terrain that rises to more than nine thousand feet. The river begins to freeze around November 1, allowing soldiers to cross on foot. By mid-November, the ice would support towed artillery and supply trucks.

The Chinese divisions that had repelled the ROKs retreated into the mountains. As they waited for the main UN force to cross the river, Mao was giving Truman a second chance to take Zhou's warning seriously at last and pull MacArthur back to the 38th parallel. Truman, however, proved as bemused and complacent as MacArthur when the Chinese seemed to vanish in the night. There were only sixteen thousand Chinese troops in North Korea, MacArthur assured Washington—one-sixth the true number—and there cannot be much doubt that Truman wanted to believe him.

The next day, Truman told a press conference that only ROK troops would approach the Yalu. He was trying to tell the Chinese that they had nothing to fear: please, no more attacks. MacArthur contradicted him almost at once at a press conference of his own, saying, "The mission of the UN force is to clear Korea." He was placing no restraint on American units. He too was trying to send a signal: back off.

Both of them soon got a signal in return. On November 1, Soviet MiG-15s appeared over the Yalu, providing air cover for the Chinese who were preparing to cross. The MiG-15 was faster and more maneuverable than the P-51 Mustangs and F-80 jet fighters, and for six crucial weeks the Soviets achieved air superiority where the Chinese needed it most. After that, the Yalu was frozen so hard that tanks, trucks, and towed artillery could be pushed across even if every bridge was destroyed. The river would remain frozen until April.[10]

For Mao, this was a heady moment. The main military project planned for 1950 had been to take Formosa. The huge junk armada had been assembled by June, and the invasion would have been mounted in July or August had it not been for the outbreak of the war in Korea. Kim did not bother to tell Mao the date of the North Korean attack. Chinese troops had seized Hainan Island in April, and Mao pushed more than a hundred thousand troops into Tibet in October, just as a much larger force prepared to cross into Korea, twenty-five hundred miles away.

The military operation Mao had been counting on for the Chinese People's Republic to command the world's attention was to have been Formosa. The American decision to defend Formosa was a major setback, but intervening in Korea offered Mao a chance to repay the Americans for their intervention in China. The result was likely to be an unwinnable war for the Americans and their South Korean protégés. The Russians could not lose in Korea once China was involved, and the Chinese knew they could not be nuked so long as the Russians were involved.

On November 24 MacArthur launched his win-the-war offensive. This would be the final push to the Yalu. Intensive bombing and strafing had isolated the battlefield. There was nothing now to hold him back, and once he reached the river, the war would be as good as over. All that would remain would be mopping up operations to destroy the guerrilla bands in his rear.

Within twenty-four hours, more than 200,000 Chinese and some 50,000 North Korean troops launched their own win-the-war offensive. They had moved into the gap between the Eighth Army and the X Corps, and they now hurled themselves, bugles blaring, on MacArthur's leading elements. MacArthur sent the Pentagon a panicky telegram:

> MEN AND MATERIEL IN LARGE FORCE ARE POURING ACROSS ALL BRIDGES OVER THE YALU FROM MANCHURIA. THIS MOVEMENT NOT ONLY JEOPARDIZES BUT THREATENS THE ULTIMATE DESTRUCTION OF THE FORCES UNDER MY COMMAND . . . I TRUST THE MATTER BE IMMEDIATELY BROUGHT TO THE ATTENTION OF THE PRESIDENT . . .[11]

The morning of November 28, Truman was about to have his after-breakfast walk when he received a call from Bradley. MacArthur had just reported to the Joint Chiefs, WE FACE AN ENTIRELY NEW WAR. A Chinese army numbering 260,000 men had launched a ferocious attack, forcing him to halt his advance and assume the defensive.

"It's no longer a question of a few so-called volunteers," Truman told his staff. "The Chinese have come in with both feet." This was followed by a little bluster, saying that he was sure the Chinese attack would fail, then falling into self-pity, like a man who feared it was going to succeed. "Well, the liars have accomplished their purpose," said Truman. "This whole campaign of lies we have been seeing in this country has brought about this result . . . What has appeared in our press has made the world believe that the American people are not behind our foreign policy. I don't think the Communists would have ever dared to do this thing in Korea if it hadn't been for that belief."[12]

He called a cabinet meeting. The mood was grim, and Truman's distress was obvious. This was not the "police action" he had claimed it was, nor was the decision to fight in Korea any longer the only way to prevent a world conflagration. The Chinese intervention made Truman finally realize that the United States could not fight and win a major war on its own. It needed strong support from the other liberal democracies, not token forces in an ad hoc coalition. His belief in unilateralism collided with reality in Korea. "The situation is very serious. It can develop into complete involvement in total war."[13]

At his press conference on November 30, Truman tried to sound confident. "We will take whatever steps are necessary to meet the military situation, just as we always have."

Jack Doherty, a journalist from the New York *Daily News*, wanted to know, "Will that include the atomic bomb?"

"That includes every weapon we have."

A reporter from a Chicago newspaper followed up: "Does that mean that there is active consideration of the use of the atomic bomb?"

This was an invitation to the kind of tough talk that Truman loved, as if talking tough might make a man so. "There has always been active consideration of its use." This provoked even more questions, but Truman tried to bring the discussion to an end by saying that it would be up to MacArthur to decide whether to use nuclear weapons: "The military commander in the field will have charge of the use of the weapons, as he always has." More bluster. At no time did MacArthur have authority for using the atomic bomb or physical control of any.

When exaggerated news stories reached London that MacArthur could use the atomic bomb to stop the Chinese onslaught, Churchill urged the prime minister, Clement Attlee, to head for Washington at once. The United States seemed about to wage an all-out war with China and the Soviet Union. A few days later Attlee was on his way.

The British had opposed any attempt to take the war into North Korea. A bigger war, they argued, guaranteed bigger risks without any guarantee of bigger gains. And now Attlee advised Truman to bring it to a close by offering to establish normal relations with China and revoke its commitment to defend Formosa. The quid pro quo from the Chinese side would have to be a cease-fire in Korea. Ridiculous, said Truman: China wasn't China anymore. "It's Russian and nothing else." Marshall too thought it was an absurd idea. Didn't the British prime minister realize that the Chinese and the Russians were "coreligionists"? When Attlee declared that it was important to persuade the people of Asia that the West was not an enemy, Acheson dismissed it. What would impress them even more, he said, was to see America's military might being used.[14]

Attlee returned home without any commitment not to use nuclear weapons in Korea. Whether they were used, Truman assured him, was entirely an American question and would remain so. The most the British should expect was to be consulted in advance, but only if that was deemed possible. The Truman-Attlee conversations established a precedent that would continue for more than fifty years within NATO—multilateral discussions, unilateral decisions.[15]

The Eighth Army and X Corps had retreated so rapidly they had broken contact with the enemy, and continued to fall back. They were followed rather than pursued by the Chinese. On December 23 Walton Walker was killed on the outskirts of Seoul when a ROK (pronounced "rock") weapons carrier hit his jeep.

During these dispiriting days, with the Eighth Army still retreating, MacArthur sent a message saying that morale was poor. During a meeting at the White House, General Matthew Ridgway, the man who had created and led the 82nd Airborne Division in World War II, told Truman, "When an American general loses confidence in the morale of his own troops, the problem of morale is with the general."[16]

In January 1951 the Eighth Army's retreat ended fifty miles south of Seoul. The Chinese had taken both the capital and Inchon, erasing all of MacArthur's gains. Ridgway was sent to Korea to take command of the Eighth Army. In February he launched a series of punishing attacks aptly called Operation Killer. Drawing heavily on the air force and on thousands of artillery pieces, Ridgway inflicted heavy losses before following up with infantry and armor attacks that forced the Chinese back to Seoul, then up to the 38th parallel, more or less.

Truman and Acheson agreed that if the Chinese were ever going to be ready to negotiate a cease-fire, the moment was now. When MacArthur learned that the president was about to seek a negotiated settlement, he undercut Truman by publicly demanding that the Chinese leadership admit defeat or risk "a decision by the United Nations to depart from its tolerant effort to contain the war to the area of Korea, through an expansion of our military operations to [China's] coastal areas and interior bases, [which] would doom Red China to the risk of complete military collapse"—i.e., quit now, before we destroy you.[17]

MacArthur and all other senior officers had recently been ordered to clear their public statements in advance by submitting them to the Joint Chiefs of Staff. Truman was incandescent with rage. MacArthur's demand for surrender had not been cleared, but his ultimatum was so widely acclaimed that Truman was hesitant to fire him.

MacArthur's recent statements and actions were those of someone who wanted out. The war was obviously not going to be won, and he was the last man in the world who would engage in prolonged negotiations with Chinese or North Korean Communists over who would get what. Better to be a martyr and leave a legend than be a politician's thing and live a lie.[18]

MacArthur's call on the Chinese to surrender was soon followed by a letter to Joseph Martin, the Republican speaker of the House of Representatives. MacArthur damned the administration's Eurocentric foreign policy. What mattered was the Far East. "If we lose this war to Communism in Asia, the fall of Europe is inevitable; win it, and Europe most probably would avoid war and yet preserve freedom." What truly galled him, though, was the prospect of a war that would end only when the enemy chose to end it. "There is no substitute for victory," he declared, his rage almost palpable. MacArthur made sure that copies of his message to Martin were distributed to the press, and he attached a statement describing American strategy in Korea as "ludicrous."[19]

Marshall told Truman, "Mr. President, General MacArthur is an American general on active duty. You are entitled to have the recommendation of your Joint Chiefs of Staff on this matter. I would ask them for one." Truman soon had their advice: a unanimous recommendation that MacArthur be relieved of his commands in both Korea and Japan.[20]

Late at night, as Truman was trying to decide what to do about MacArthur, Dean Rusk arrived from the State Department. The *Chicago Tribune* had received a message from the general asking this rock-ribbed Republican publication—an inveterate critic of Truman—to hold space on the front page for a major announcement from the general the next day. Truman signed the necessary orders and told

Frank Pace, the secretary of the army, to leave at once for Tokyo and inform MacArthur that he was about to be relieved.

The next evening, Omar Bradley arrived at the White House. The wire services were already carrying the story, said Bradley, and MacArthur was likely to quit before Pace arrived. Truman's temper flared. "The son of a bitch isn't going to resign on me. I want him fired!" A press conference was called at 1:00 a.m. to announce the president's decision—the general had been summarily relieved of his commands.[21]

For all the discourtesy and vainglory that MacArthur had exhibited, Truman felt that he deserved a hero's homecoming for his victories in World War II. Their grateful countrymen had regaled Patton and Eisenhower. MacArthur deserved the same. "I don't want anyone to interfere with the welcome he will get when he comes home," Truman told his staff. And true to form, when MacArthur arrived back in Washington, he did not pay a courtesy call on his commander in chief. Instead, he headed straight for Congress, to denounce the way Truman was fighting the war.[22]

With MacArthur gone and Ridgway still inflicting heavy losses, Stalin sent Mao a telegram obviously intended to encourage him to look beyond his mounting casualties. There were significant advantages to fighting a protracted war in Korea, said Stalin: the Chinese army was receiving an invaluable education in modern warfare, while at the same time "it harms the military prestige of the Anglo-American troops."[23]

Mao didn't disagree with Stalin's message, but he did want to buy time for the Chinese troops in Korea to dig in and prepare for a long war. His timing could hardly have been better. Truman was desperate to secure a cease-fire. The Joint Chiefs and others said that any overture now was a sign that the enemy was hurting; let's hurt him some more. Truman ignored them, and truce talks began in July, at Panmunjom. Both sides were prepared to continue fighting while negotiating, but the tempo diminished dramatically. By the end of the summer, Chinese defenses were so strong that not even Ridgway could blast them out. The tempo of fighting picked up again.[24]

Eventually the negotiation bogged down over the question of returning POWs to their respective countries. Under the Geneva Conventions, a cease-fire required a swift exchange of prisoners. Large

numbers of Chinese and North Koreans rioted at the prospect of being sent back to the poverty and repression of life under Communism.
There were also feelings of guilt in Washington and London over the
forced repatriation of Russian POWs at the end of the previous war.
Tens of thousands had been murdered by the paranoid Stalin, and
hundreds of thousands more had been sentenced to long stretches in
the gulag archipelago, where many died from hunger and disease.

Truman, who had from the earliest days of his presidency boasted
that the United States scrupulously abided by its international agreements, rejected the Geneva Conventions. In their place he put his
own personal morality. He refused to agree to forced repatriation. His
stance was estimable, in principle, but his true motives were mixed.
Having fought a war that ended so anticlimactically after so many
deaths, he needed to claim a victory of some kind. Morality was on
his side . . . maybe. Yet Truman was not only rejecting the Geneva
Convention on prisoners of war; he might have been prolonging the
war unnecessarily, which meant prolonging the hardship of prisoners
whether in North or South Korea. The number who died in captivity
or had their health destroyed as a result is incalculable, but it probably ran into the thousands.

The true author of their fate, however, was not Truman, but Stalin.
Even if Truman had agreed to forced repatriation, Stalin would have
rejected a settlement. When, in the fall of 1952, it seemed that Mao
might yield on repatriation, Stalin played his trump, telling Zhou Enlai, "The Chinese comrades must know that if America does not lose
this war, then China will never recapture Taiwan." Stalin was never
going to agree to a settlement. He would have to die before an
armistice was possible, which was how it turned out.[25]

Following Stalin's death, in March 1953, the new Soviet leadership, headed by Georgy Malenkov and Nikita Khrushchev, agreed to
seek a cease-fire. Mao raised no objections. Rebuilding China's economy and reviving the revolutionary spirit of the Chinese could not
wait any longer. Nor would Kim Il Sung be an obstacle. He had been
willing to settle for a truce since the negotiations began.

When armistice terms were finally agreed at Panmunjom, Mao
boasted that the war had been a victory for China. "From a purely military point of view," he told the Russians, "it would not be bad to continue to strike the Americans for approximately another year." The war

had achieved everything Mao sought—recognition that there was a new China, a China that was a great power. This was not the pathetic basket-case China of the past hundred years. After Korea, the whole world would take China seriously.[26]

Korea had been five wars in one: a civil war between those who had collaborated with the Japanese and those in the anti-Japanese resistance; a revolutionary war to bring about a new social order; a nationalistic war to unite a divided Korea; a proxy war within the Cold War, with the ROKs as America's proxy forces and the Inmun Gun as Stalin's; and a war for prestige.

No one made the prestige argument more often or forcefully than Dean Acheson. Ironic, that. The net winners in the prestige war were Stalin, Mao, and Kim Il Sung. The net loser was Truman. American prestige stood higher on June 24, 1950, than it did on July 27, 1953, when the armistice was agreed.

Those such as Acheson and Rusk, who had favored fighting in Korea from the beginning, sought what consolation they could by extolling the new line that divided the Korean peninsula. This had been, in military parlance, the MLR, or main line of resistance, the line that divided the opposing forces when the armistice took effect. Much better than the parallel, said the admirers. South Korea had gained more than five thousand square miles of territory northeast of Seoul.

It may seem odd, then, that the North Koreans liked the new line even more. The 38th parallel ran through the Ongjin Peninsula and the town of Kaesong, northwest of Seoul, making Pyongyang vulnerable to a surprise attack. Now, though, the entire Ongjin Peninsula and all of Kaesong were well within North Korean territory.[27]

From his tomb, Stalin too would have counted the way the war ended—ambiguously suspended between peace and war—as a victory. He had brought the Americans and Chinese into open conflict, prevented the reunification of Korea under the pro-Western Syngman Rhee, and caught the United States in the toils of Korean nationalism. Stalin, Lenin's commissar for nationalities, knew only too well that nationalism was more tenacious than Communism. The thought that more than fifty years later Korea would still be divided—and the United States would have to deal with a North Korea that had become a nuclear power—would have filled his psychopathic soul with delight and got him puffing hard on his pipe.

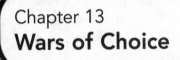

Chapter 13
Wars of Choice

WHEN EISENHOWER WAS INAUGURATED ON A COLD AND BLUSTERY day in January 1953, it took the parade six hours to pass the reviewing stand, instead of the allotted four. Almost at the end, a large, ungainly object slowly trundled past—a 280-mm atomic cannon. This enormous weapon, called a Long Tom (for Tomahawk), was a triumph of miniaturization and, Eisenhower believed, his best chance of ending the Korean War. No matter how deeply the Chinese and North Koreans dug in, the Long Tom threatened to blast them out. And when, six months later, an armistice was agreed at Panmunjom, Eisenhower was convinced that the threat of atomic artillery coming onto the battlefield had brought the breakthrough.

He was wrong. What made the difference was Stalin's death in March 1953 and Mao's intention to move on from a battlefield where he had gained more than any of his colleagues had dared hope for. Before the guns fell silent in Korea Mao was already looking at another, even more promising war, in Indochina. The new Soviet leaders, Georgy Malenkov and Nikita Khrushchev, presented themselves as men eager to break with the worst of Stalinism while remaining true to the brightest hopes of Communism. They proclaimed a policy of peaceful coexistence with the West and claimed to welcome the chance to turn the fundamental challenge of the Cold War away from atomic might and into an economic competition. Mao was disgusted. To him, they were little more than the stunted descendants of revolutionary heroes.[1]

Meanwhile, the main provisions of NSC-68 were already reshaping American policy. Military spending during the Korean War tripled, and Eisenhower came to the presidency having accepted its fundamental argument. Paul Nitze had shrewdly presented NSC-68 as the sensible middle way between appeasement and preventive war. Since the end of World War II, there had been hawkish senators and representatives on Capitol Hill who had demanded war with the Soviet Union while the United States still had its nuclear monopoly. Not even the Soviet development of nuclear weapons had stilled this chorus, and Truman's secretary of the navy, Francis B. Matthews, had added his own voice to the demand for an immediate "preventive" war.[2]

Yet for all Nitze's alarmist talk of 1954 being "the hour of maximum danger"—the moment the Soviets would feel strong enough to launch World War III—NSC-68 did not rule out negotiations to avert that disaster. But it did not put much faith in them. What Nitze was really looking for was a trial of strength stretching across decades, using all means short of war—a Soviet Union encircled by bomber bases, a large and growing nuclear arsenal, and a much larger peacetime military. The United States would then be ready for every military challenge, from small conventional wars to an all-out nuclear showdown. In adopting NSC-68, Eisenhower positioned himself to promote the militant interventionism of the Truman Doctrine on a scale that Truman could only dream about.

The place Eisenhower began was in the Middle East. *Time* magazine's Man of the Year for 1951 was Dr. Mohammad Mossadeq, prime minister of Iran, a politician with idiosyncrasies that Americans found childish and foolish. Mossadeq was as likely to give a major speech wearing his pajamas as dressed in a suit and tie. He was a semi-invalid who spent a lot of time in bed, yet seemed capable of bouncing out of it when the spirit moved him. His habits included bursting into tears as readily as a small child, and *Time* put him on its cover as a warning that Iran was heading over the cliff. Waiting at the bottom to scoop up Iran's oil wealth was the sinister figure of Stalin, and it was true that Mossadeq was already courting Iran's minuscule Communist Party.

Modern Iran was created by Britain, mostly to control the oil fields. Part of the control mechanism was a royal family minted in London and installed in Tehran. Mossadeq had made a political career out of resisting British interference and undermining the youthful shah of Iran, Reza Pahlavi, who was as ineffectual as he was self-absorbed. The shah was isolated in his palace, afraid of the mobs in the streets calling for his overthrow. When, in 1951, Mossadeq played his trump card—a threat to nationalize the oil—the British shut down the wells and organized an international boycott of Iranian oil.

All of which gave British intelligence agents an idea: let's organize a coup and get rid of Mossadeq, boost the power of the shah and run things through him, and get the oil flowing again. The British spooks asked their friends in the CIA if they would like to help them remove the odious Dr. Mossadeq. The answer was a swift and enthusiastic yes.

The coup would be directed by Kermit "Kim" Roosevelt, grandson of the more famous Teddy and a highly experienced veteran of the wartime Office of Strategic Services, the forerunner of the CIA. The shah was persuaded to take a sudden vacation in Italy, and in August 1953 a million dollars in CIA money was spent organizing street mobs that agitated for the shah and against Mossadeq. The capital was paralyzed by the mobs, the national treasury was empty thanks to the oil boycott, and to save the nation, the Iranian army arrested the weeping Mossadeq in his pajamas.

The shah returned from Italy grateful for American help and dependent on more of the same for the rest of his life. Ordinary Iranians refused to give their loyalty to a government imposed on them by Britain and the United States. To hold on to his throne, Pahlavi built up an enormous force of secret police, the *savak*, who murdered and tortured with impunity, piling physical pain atop national humiliation. The people of Iran, famously entrepreneurial and outgoing, now seethed with a desire for revenge.

Eisenhower was oblivious to all that. In the White House, he decorated Kim Roosevelt with the National Security Medal and listened in rapt fascination to his account of the Iranian coup. "It seemed like a dime novel," Ike informed his diary, still enthralled.[3]

This was only the start of Eisenhower's anxieties over oil. In 1954 the military dictator of Syria, Colonel Adib Shishakli, was overthrown by pro-Egyptian Baathists and Communists. They installed a figurehead president. By 1957 Eisenhower was worried that the Syrian Communists, under Moscow's direction, would threaten the pipeline that brought oil from northern Iraq into Turkey, from where it was shipped to Western Europe.

Kermit Roosevelt had another venture to propose. He and his friends in MI6 thought it would be possible to stage border incidents in Turkey, Iraq, and Lebanon. These could then be blamed on Syrian Communists and used to justify joint American and British military intervention. The current rulers of Syria would be ousted and an anti-Communist, pro-Western government would take their place. Eisenhower gave it his approval, but Roosevelt's scenario fell at the first hurdle, when the Lebanese and Iraqis refused to take part.[4]

This aborted venture was not the end of the story. In 1957 there was a general election in Lebanon, a country split four ways: Maronite Christian, Druze (a Shiite sect with its own branch of Islam), Sunni Muslim, and Shia. The Christians accounted for roughly one-third of the population, the Shiites maybe slightly more, with the Druze and the Sunnis accounting for the rest. The French had held the League of Nations' trusteeship of Lebanon between the two world wars and had installed the Christians to run it. Although the French were gone, the Maronite political and economic elites still felt they had the right to govern the country, but they faced a rising threat from Arab nationalism, fomented by Syria and Egypt.

The Maronites portrayed the threat to their power as Communism, not nationalism, knowing this was sure to secure the attention of Washington. Eisenhower's solution was to ensure that millions of dollars in cash were delivered to the Maronite leader, Camille Chamoun, by American diplomats and CIA operatives. That provided enough electoral fraud to secure the election. The losers, however, became restive, knowing they had been swindled, and in 1958 Lebanon seemed poised to descend into civil war—or so Chamoun claimed. And those behind the present unrest were, of course, Communists.

This time Eisenhower's response was to put five thousand marines ashore on the beaches of Beirut, where they landed among girls in bikinis and startled swimmers. This show of force cowed Chamoun's critics, and whatever threat there was seemed to vanish whence it had come.[5]

While he was intervening forcibly in the Middle East, Eisenhower was also overturning Franklin Roosevelt's Good Neighbor Policy in Latin America. In 1950 a young army officer, Jacobo Arbenz, had been elected president of Guatemala in the first free and fair election that country had enjoyed in many years.[6]

Determined to carry out land reform, Arbenz turned to advisers who believed in reform as much as he did, and some of them were, inevitably, Communists. Eisenhower's brother Milton returned from a fact-finding mission to Latin America and informed him that "the Guatemalan government has succumbed to Communist infiltration." Eisenhower was alarmed. Suppose Guatemala went under? What then for its neighbors? "My God," he exclaimed during a cabinet meeting, "just think what it would mean if Mexico went Communist!" He could see dominoes toppling.[7]

The CIA trained a force of disaffected Guatemalans who mounted an attack, and the fiercely anti-Communist Guatemalan army, recognizing that the Americans were behind this attempted coup, forced Arbenz to flee. A Guatemalan army colonel was then installed in the presidential palace.[8]

Following the signing of the armistice in Korea, Eisenhower pulled the Seventh Fleet out of the Taiwan Strait. This allowed Jiang Jieshi to deploy 58,000 troops to Quemoy and 15,000 to Matsu in the summer of 1954, two islands within artillery range of the mainland. Holding Quemoy and Matsu would allow him to blockade two important Chinese ports, Amoy and Foochow. The Chinese response was to bombard the islands, and the Nationalists shot back. Most Americans could not comprehend what all the shooting was about, and Walter Robertson, the assistant secretary of state for Far Eastern affairs, had to explain it to Congress. "There is to be kept alive a constant threat of military action vis-à-vis Red China, in the hope that at some future point there will be an internal breakdown." Now it made sense.[9]

While artillery shells were filling the air, Zhou Enlai appeared to raise the stakes by declaring that Taiwan must be liberated. Eisenhower had a ready answer to that. "What would happen is this: any invasion of Taiwan would have to run over the Seventh Fleet."[10]

On December 2, 1954, with artillery exchanges still reverberating all the way to Washington, the United States and Taiwan signed a mutual defense treaty, but there was no clear commitment to defend Quemoy and Matsu. To put some muscle behind the new treaty, three carriers moved into the Taiwan Strait in January, and Eisenhower asked Congress for a joint resolution that would allow him to use force "for the purpose of securing and protecting Formosa." Secretary of State John Foster Dulles announced that the United States was prepared to use nuclear weapons. Eisenhower said much the same thing, which created consternation among America's principal allies, such as Britain, to whom nuclear weapons had to be a last resort, not just another option.

Eisenhower was also upping the ante, telling a press conference that if the crisis in the strait produced a major war, "the logical enemy will be Russia, not China." He had accepted without question the Truman-Acheson notion that China was not really China, but a Soviet puppet. Even so, once the shelling stopped, the administration was willing to open secret talks in Warsaw with the puppet in the hope of avoiding any more dangerous confrontations over small islands devoid of strategic significance.[11] Yet in August 1958 there was another crisis in the straits, this one provoked by Mao Zedong.

The Soviets had reneged on their commitment to help China become a nuclear power. Khrushchev had also rejected Mao's personal plea to start a war with the United States. The orbiting of the first Sputnik, in October 1957, had convinced Mao that, with Soviet technology and Chinese manpower, it was finally possible to defeat the United States.

Khrushchev knew better, and returned to Moscow to inform the Soviet leadership that Mao was insane. Mao in turn rejected Khrushchev's policy of peaceful coexistence, and one way of showing he meant it was to start bombarding Quemoy and Matsu again. He also had a flotilla of torpedo boats blockading these islands, until ships from the Seventh Fleet broke the blockade. Khrushchev meanwhile made it clear that the Soviet Union would not fight a war with the United States over Quemoy and Matsu.

Mao ordered the bombardment to cease. As he mulled over the

meaning of what had just happened, the lesson he drew was that from now on, China would have to go its own way. It could not rely on the Russians for anything.

Eisenhower's other Far Eastern challenge was Indochina, where the French had suffered a major defeat. Even before Pearl Harbor, the French had surrendered their colonies in Indochina to the Japanese. The resistance to occupation was led mainly by Vietnamese Communists, yet Stalin never trusted them. As Lenin's original commissar for nationalities, he thought he could smell the enduring nationalist lurking within the modern Communist. He never trusted either Chinese Communists or Vietnamese Communists to be much more than patriotic peasants. And when the Japanese were defeated, the leader of the Vietnamese insurgents, Ho Chi Minh, seemed to prove him right. Ho wrote a declaration of Vietnamese independence that was almost a straight copy of Jefferson's.

Ho had worked in conjunction with the OSS during the war, and considered Americans potential allies even after the Japanese departed. He wrote two letters to Truman seeking American support in securing the independence of Vietnam, but received no reply. Instead, when the French returned to colonize Indochina all over again, Truman provided them with money and arms.[12]

The Vietnamese insurgency against the Japanese morphed into an insurgency against the French. With the establishment of the People's Republic of China, in October 1949, the French were doomed. Mao saw any Western army on China's southern border as a threat to national security. Mao promised Ho, "Whatever China has and Vietnam needs, we will provide it."[13]

As negotiations in Korea moved toward a truce, the Chinese were free to pour men and weapons into Vietnam. Truman did the same. The United States underwrote the French war in Vietnam and provided virtually all the arms and ammunition the French could use. What the Americans could not provide was fighting spirit and advice to match. Mao advised the Vietnamese to make a killing ground of a French base at Dien Bien Phu, on the mountainous border between North Vietnam and Laos. The Vietminh, Ho's guerrilla army, hauled American howitzers captured in Korea onto the high ground and pounded the beleaguered French garrison below.

The French pleaded with Eisenhower to intervene. He offered only a token force of obsolescent B-26 bombers and the mechanics needed to keep 'em flying. When a senator complained that the United States was edging into the Indochinese war, Eisenhower told him, "Every move I authorize is calculated to make sure that doesn't happen." And it didn't. Eisenhower knew that the current war could not be waged without the Chinese. That meant it could not be won without defeating China. No one in his right mind would support a war with China in order to help the French hold on to a colony.[14]

Besides, a conference had already been arranged, to take place in Geneva. The Russians and the British would cohost the talks, but it was the Chinese who more or less swaggered onto the world stage in Geneva. They had arrived, and they knew it. Ho's soldiers also did what was expected of them. Down to their last artillery shells, scraping the last reserves of strength from his troops, the Vietminh commander, General Vo Nguyen Giap, mounted a final attack. Dien Bien Phu fell the day after the conference opened.[15]

The 1954 Geneva Accords created a temporary demarcation line across Vietnam, with a Communist regime to the north of it and a non-Communist regime to the south. Elections were to be held under UN supervision in two years as a first step toward unification. The United States chose not to be a signatory to the Geneva Accords, but pledged it would do nothing to undermine them.

The Republic of South Vietnam was ruled by Ngo Dinh Diem, a Catholic who had spent many years in the United States. Eisenhower wrote Diem a letter pledging American help in building a viable country. That help would be conditional, however, on the South Vietnamese embracing democratic values and political reform.

Diem's government was anything but democratic. It was based on the Catholic minority that had collaborated with the French and enjoyed a privileged position even after the French departed. The Catholics ruled a predominantly Buddhist country and could maintain their power only in the same way the French had, by ready recourse to widespread killings and overflowing prisons.

Diem was a megalomaniac. On one of his periodic trips to Washington to demand more money, more arms, more political support, he was given an hour with Dulles. From the moment the two men sat down, Diem talked nonstop. When he finished, he stood up and departed. Dulles wondered aloud to an aide, "Wouldn't you think that here in Washington he might be interested in what our Secretary of State had to say?"[16]

Diem refused to hold the elections that the Geneva Accords promised, claiming that any election in the North would be rigged, but the real reason was that he was bound to lose even in a scrupulously honest ballot. North Vietnam had a significantly larger population than South Vietnam. It was also the case that Ho Chi Minh was admired across Indochina in a way, and for reasons, that Diem—who had never struck a blow against the Japanese or the French—was not. Diem's was a government filled with people who had spent much of their lives serving another country, France, in preference to their own.

Meanwhile, the resistance fighters who composed the government in the North were nursing a profound sense of betrayal. With the Geneva Accords signed, China seemed to lose interest in Vietnam. Instead, it entered into secret talks with the Americans in Warsaw—talks that went on for years. The Russians were not much help either. They were devoting their energies to trying to create a robust Soviet economy, a doomed venture, but Marxism-Leninism disdained everyday realities.

Diem meanwhile was trying to uproot every last Vietminh political officer or fighter who remained in the South, and everyone else who opposed his dictatorial regime. More than ten thousand people were imprisoned, and thousands more were executed. By 1959, organized resistance was beginning to spread, with no practical encouragement from North Vietnam.

Eisenhower poured money and weapons in for Diem as he had done earlier for the French. And in 1960 he renewed his pledge of support, but once again he qualified it: Diem had to accept democratic norms and institute the rule of law. As the number one man in his class at the Command and General Staff College in the 1930s, Eisenhower had long since absorbed one of its principal tactical precepts: to mount an attack, a commander needs two secure routes of advance, while maintaining at least one secure line of retreat, just in case. He was not a commander in chief who would make a major commitment without leaving a way out if everything failed.

By 1961 Eisenhower had funneled more than $2 billion into South Vietnam, and the government there was more unpopular than ever. Following the creation of the National Liberation Front (NLF), Diem disparaged its members as Vietcong—for Vietnamese Communists. While he chose to belittle them, the number of South Vietnamese officials, police, and troops being killed each month rose from 100 to nearly 400. An American official working in Saigon offered a brief account of the unfolding challenge:

> Like the police in Harlem, the government forces go freely wherever they want through the countryside, as long as they move in sufficient force. But a single Vietnamese Army vehicle, or a small patrol, invites sudden ambush, just as a single patrolman in Harlem risks being attacked in a dark alley. Also as in Harlem, reinforcements arrive to find a neighborhood of blank faces. Nobody saw it happen. Nobody heard any shooting. Nobody ever, ever knows anybody who conceivably might be a Viet Cong.[17]

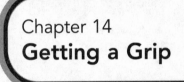

Chapter 14
Getting a Grip

IN DECEMBER 1960 A CANADIAN DIPLOMAT ASSIGNED TO THE International Control Commission, the body created to monitor the Geneva Accords, reported to his government that Soviet transport planes were flying into Hanoi, refueling, and then flying west, toward Laos. After the Canadian government passed this information to Washington, unmarked C-47s started flying over northwest Laos. They soon found they were sharing the sky with Soviet Ilyushin-14 transports dropping weapons and ammunition.

A C-47 pilot even filmed them bringing in a small bulldozer to a remote grass airstrip. During the fight for Dien Bien Phu, the Vietminh had infiltrated into Laos along narrow and mountainous jungle paths. With a bulldozer they could now make a road, allowing them to take over the sparsely populated and virtually undefended northern half of the country. A year later, they were nearly there.[1]

On January 19, 1961, the day before his inauguration, John F. Kennedy met with Eisenhower and the cabinet. Kennedy wanted to talk about Berlin and Cuba, about how the National Security Council worked, about foreign leaders, what they were really like as allies or adversaries. What Eisenhower wanted to talk about was Laos.

Communist forces, backed by North Vietnam, were now on the verge of seizing power in Laos, said Eisenhower. If that happened, four neighboring countries—South Vietnam, Thailand, Burma, and Cambodia—would eventually fall to Communist pressure. "Unilateral intervention would be our last desperate hope . . . We may have to fight."[2]

The government of Laos in recent years had consisted of an anti-Communist general, Phoumi Nosavan, who had received money, arms, and twenty-two military advisers from the United States. But when Eisenhower met with Kennedy, the Royal Lao Army had just broken into three mutually antagonistic factions. One of these factions decided to join forces with the Pathet Lao, a group of insurgents led by a former Royal Lao Army officer, Kong Le. The Pathet Lao was nationalist and neutralist, but some of those who joined were avowed Communists. Kong Le's troops were also receiving the benefits of weapons from the Soviets and advisers from the battle-hardened Vietminh.

When Kennedy asked Eisenhower directly just what the United States could do to stop the Pathet Lao, Eisenhower did not reply: a soldier with nothing to say is conceding defeat.

Kennedy soon discovered why. The maximum force that could be put into Laos at short notice amounted to fewer than ten thousand men. The Pathet Lao did not command large numbers, but it was moving swiftly toward one of Laos's two capitals, Vientiane, situated on the main highway of Southeast Asia, the Mekong River. Even if Kennedy managed to get a bigger force in there, northern Laos was so remote it was virtually immune to American air and naval power. Kennedy had been in Vietnam at the time Dien Bien Phu fell. What happens, he asked the Joint Chiefs, if our troops find themselves besieged and we have to get them out? Easy, was the answer: we use nuclear weapons.

After telling his friend Ben Bradlee, "General Phoumi is a total shit," Kennedy appeared on television with a pointer and three large maps. "We strongly and unreservedly support the goal of a neutral and independent Lay-os," he declared. He was rejecting Eisenhower's policy of destroying the Pathet Lao and keeping Phoumi Nosavan in power. First, though, the Pathet Lao and their Vietminh allies had to be stopped from taking Vientiane. If they reached the Mekong, there would be nothing much left to negotiate. For several months of the year, parts of the Mekong are so shallow an army could walk across it into Thailand.

Special Forces and other troops were flown into Laos to stiffen the Royal Lao Army units that remained loyal to Phoumi Nosavan and to organize Hmong tribesmen into pro-government guerrillas. The Hmong had a long history of fighting the Chinese and the Vietnamese. The Pathet Lao's advance was slowed, giving Khrushchev and Kennedy time to decide that Laos was not worth fighting for. Another Geneva conference would meet, to install a neutral coalition government in Laos.

The Joint Chiefs were disgusted. They knew, as Kennedy probably did, that a neutralist government that included the Pathet Lao would never prevent the North Vietnamese from using eastern Laos as a highway into South Vietnam. The chief of naval operations, Arleigh Burke, told Kennedy, "If you don't stand in Laos, you're going to have to stand someplace else. If it's not Laos, is it going to be South Vietnam? And if it's not South Vietnam, is it going to be Thailand?"[3]

Kennedy had believed in fighting for South Vietnam throughout his years in the Senate, and as a Catholic, he had a certain rapport with Diem and the ruling clique. Nevertheless, being president was swiftly widening his horizons. "Why do we need to hold it?" he asked the head of policy planning at the State Department, Walt Whitman Rostow. "Why can't we get out of there?"

Unlike Truman and Acheson, Kennedy did not want to fight a war for the sake of prestige. "What is prestige?" he wanted to know after the Bay of Pigs, which had been mounted not because Cuba posed a military threat to the United States, but as an attempt to recover the prestige lost to Castro's infuriating survival. "Is it the shadow of power or the substance of power? We are going to work on the substance of power."[4]

Rostow, however, was, like most of Kennedy's advisers, an Achesonian prisoner to all of the unexamined Cold War assumptions about Communism and the Soviet Union. So, too, was Kennedy's national security adviser, McGeorge Bundy, formerly a Harvard dean and before that a protégé of Henry Stimson. Bundy's brother, William, had married Acheson's daughter. Bundy had absorbed Acheson's blinkered views of China, and he fell back on intellectually lazy references to "the Oriental mind," as if he could read it, unlike other people. Rostow had his own way of expressing what he thought, calling the Chinese "the goddamn Chinks."

This, then, was a national security elite that knew nothing much about China or Mao, not much more about the Soviet Union after Stalin, and nothing at all about Ho Chi Minh or the inner world of the Vietnamese. Diem's generals were much like Diem—Catholics from the North, born into upper-class French-speaking families and adept at the demands of a feudal society. There was hardly a democrat among them, and for most, their commitment was less to their country than to their careers and bank accounts in other countries.

The NLF leadership, by contrast, had its roots in the peasantry and was able to call upon nationalism rather than ideology, a nationalism that was as deeply rooted as American nationalism, and tempered, like its American counterpart, by having fought repeatedly for its survival. Acheson had dismissed Ho as a hard-line Marxist-Leninist, but Stalin and Mao had not. To them, he wasn't a Marxist-Leninist at all, but another troublemaking Vietnamese nationalist.[5]

This American national security elite sometimes glimpsed the obvious, but they were even better at missing it. None of them seemed to realize that it was China that had masterminded the French defeat at Dien Bien Phu and China that had capitalized on this success to make possible the Geneva Accords. Their attitude to the Chinese was so steeped in casual racism that it was part of public discourse. The Chinese Communists were the Chicoms, a belittling expression, much like beatnik. Nor were the Chinese Nationalists spared. After all, they too belonged to the ludicrous Chinks. Thus America's Chinese allies became the Chinats. In Western Europe, racism was not permitted. Not after the Holocaust. So there were West Germans and there were East Germans, but there were no Gernats and no Gercoms.

Presidents and their advisers since 1949 had not so much failed as refused to acknowledge that there were two Cold Wars, not one. There was a Cold War in Europe, sustained by the unity of NATO and a girdle of SAC bases, where the United States and the Soviet Union metaphorically butted heads. There was another Cold War in

Asia, where the underlying conflict was between China and the United States. To conflate the two had never made sense, although Truman and Acheson refused to see the Chinese Communists as anything but Soviet tools. After the Sino-Soviet split in 1959, refusing to recognize that the Cold War in Asia had indigenous roots and indigenous goals was a kind of intellectual defeat.

In Europe, a sclerotic if dangerous Soviet Union could cause trouble, but it had no hope of outlasting a continent that was becoming richer by the day. In Asia, the adversary was China, the country that played the longest game in history. Mao was also very different from the parochial Stalin and the volatile Khrushchev. Mao was prepared to sacrifice economic development for larger goals. A born romantic, and one of the most successful generals of modern times, he embraced war as a way of keeping the revolutionary spirit alive in a society that always seemed ready to slip back into the old feudal ways.

When JFK became president, there was a fierce ongoing debate within the CIA and the State Department over whether there really was such a thing as monolithic Communism. The China experts in both the CIA and State had their doubts. At the same time, the idea of having to confront China on its terms was simply too challenging, too complex—maybe even too scary—to their superiors. Eisenhower, John McCone, George Kennan, and Walt Rostow were in the majority that refused to believe it.[6]

The Asia experts, however, were moving toward a solid consensus, as Kennedy was aware. At a meeting in the State Department in January 1962, they concluded that China was a stand-alone proposition, not a Soviet tool. It would have to be taken seriously and on something approximating its own terms. Roger Hilsman, the assistant secretary of state for Far Eastern affairs, was thrilled as he took notes of the meeting. "You could hear the ice of 12 years begin to snap and crackle."[7]

Kennedy was ready to put the Chinese at the heart of the debate over Vietnam. "They are bound to get nuclear weapons at some time. From that moment, they will dominate Southeast Asia anyway," he told Arthur Krock. If any dominoes fell, the Chinese would be the ones picking them up, not the Russians. So why fight to save Diem?[8]

Not only had he inherited Phoumi Nosavan and Diem from Eisenhower but he had also been handed a poison pill in the form of a plan to topple Castro. In 1960 Eisenhower had broken diplomatic relations with Cuba and ordered a program of sabotage that would hurt Cuba's economy and undermine Castro's regime. The director of Central Intelligence, Allen Dulles, turned it into a plan for invasion, without bothering to tell Eisenhower.[9]

Kennedy went ahead with it rather than cancel the operation and have to live with the stories that the Chiefs and the CIA would leak to Congress and the press about how weak he was compared with the strong and decisive Eisenhower. On April 17, 1961, a force of twelve hundred undertrained, poorly equipped, and wholly misguided Cubans were landed without air cover or naval gunfire at the Bay of Pigs. Cuban pilots soon found and sank the ships that were bringing in ammunition, fighting vehicles, and communications equipment. Up to twenty thousand Cuban troops closed rapidly on the tiny beachhead and rounded up the invaders. This fiasco cast a shadow over Kennedy's presidency then and after.

Even so, Kennedy told Walt Rostow that there was no choice in the wake of this setback but to hang tough. "The British could have a nervous breakdown in the wake of Suez, and the French over Algeria," he said. "They each represent six to seven percent of the free world's power—and we could cover for them. But we can't afford a nervous breakdown. We're forty percent, and there's no one to cover for us."[10]

When he addressed the American Society of Newspaper Editors shortly after the Bay of Pigs, Kennedy declared, "Let me make it clear, as the President of the United States, that I am determined upon our system's survival and success, regardless of the cost and regardless of the peril." One of his White House assistants wondered if maybe that wasn't raising emotions too high and making promises that might not be met. "I did it to make us appear tough and powerful. Anyway, it's done. You may be right, but it's done."[11]

By this time, the place where he was expected to live up to his fighting talk had become Vietnam. Following a failed coup attempt against Diem in March 1961, Kennedy had sent his vice president, Lyndon B. Johnson, to Saigon to assure Diem that America remained his true friend. Johnson did not want to go, telling Kennedy, "I wouldn't want to embarrass you by getting my head blown off."

In his lighthearted, mocking way, Kennedy turned it into a joke: "Don't worry, Lyndon. If anything happens to you, we'll give you the biggest funeral they've ever seen in Austin." Johnson turned the trip into something resembling a political campaign on behalf of Diem, repeatedly extolling him as "the Winston Churchill of Southeast Asia."

Johnson even gave his approval to Diem's system for getting his rule approved in rigged referendums instead of democratic elections. When other Third World despots did the same, they were likely to be denounced. Not Diem. "Your people, Mr. President, returned you to office with 91 percent of the votes," said Johnson. A majority like that made Diem, in Johnson's opinion, "not only the George Washington, the Father of your country, but the Franklin Roosevelt as well." Away from the press, they got down to negotiating the details of future American assistance, and Johnson began to have second thoughts. All Diem was interested in was American money and weaponry. Whenever Johnson began to talk about economic and social reforms, Diem ostentatiously ignored him. Johnson asked him if he wanted combat troops. No, said Diem emphatically, not unless there was an invasion from the North, but a bigger military training program would help. On Johnson's return to the United States, a journalist asked him if he really believed that stuff about Diem being the Churchill of Southeast Asia. "Shit, he's the only boy we've got out there."[12]

Johnson's first official report on his trip phrased the issue slightly differently, but it amounted to the same thing. It came down to a single sentence: "We must decide whether to support Diem—or let Vietnam fall." But someone else—probably someone in the State Department—wrote another report that was issued in Johnson's name yet did not sound remotely Johnsonian. This report said that the South Vietnamese craved leadership at this perilous time and would respond to it were it offered them, "but it cannot be evoked by men in white linen suits [i.e., Ngo Dinh Diem] whose contact with the ordinary people is largely through the rolled-up windows of a Mercedes-Benz."[13]

Diem held on through the summer, but by the fall his hold on South Vietnam seemed more precarious than ever. The Joint Chiefs urged Kennedy to send forty thousand men to South Vietnam. Instead, he sent two: his military chief of staff, General Maxwell Taylor, and Rostow. Was the Joint Chiefs' plan the only way of preventing the collapse of the South Vietnam government?

Taylor and Rostow came back and told Kennedy it was essential to send troops to prop up South Vietnamese morale. Eight thousand ought to do the trick, provided they were combat engineers deployed to the South in the guise of flood-control specialists to help with recent heavy floods.

Kennedy wasn't convinced. "The troops will march in; the bands will play; the crowds will cheer; and in four days everyone will have forgotten. Then we will be told we have to send more troops. It's like taking a drink—the effect wears off and you have to take another."

Dean Rusk supported the Taylor-Rostow recommendations, but his deputy, Under Secretary of State George Ball, told Kennedy that Taylor and Rostow were pushing him into a trap. Ball was a highly regarded international lawyer, more sophisticated intellectually than Rusk, who leaned heavily on platitudes made slippery by excessive usage. "If we go down that road," said Ball, "we might have, within five years, 300,000 men in the rice paddies and jungles of Vietnam and never be able to find them." What the Tayor-Rostow report amounted to was "an open-ended commitment."

Kennedy dismissed Ball's pessimism in what came close to an insulting response: "George, you're just crazier than hell. I always thought you were one of the brightest guys in town, but you're crazy. That just isn't going to happen."[14]

Even so, Secretary of Defense Robert McNamara seemed to be thinking along similar lines, but without the pessimism. McNamara advised Kennedy that it was going to take years to turn South Vietnam around, but it could be done. All the president had to do was to commit up to 250,000 troops to the war. Bundy meanwhile was trying to have it both ways. Let's make a decision to put a lot of men in there, he advised Kennedy, and announce that's what we'll do. That kind of commitment will scare the Communists into holding back, and then we won't have to send the troops after all. Bundy could no more stop trying to be clever than he could stop being naive.[15]

Not only were the Joint Chiefs urging Kennedy to send tens of thousands of troops into South Vietnam, but they also advised him to invade Cuba. They were, in effect, pressuring him into putting combat troops into Vietnam because no one could seriously believe that he would also invade Cuba and risk starting a war with Castro's new patron, the Soviet Union.

Kennedy went for what he saw as the minimal response: raising the number of American advisers in South Vietnam from just under 1,000 to roughly 2,500, with another 2,500 to follow. He also recalled the present ambassador, the hawkish Elbridge Durbrow, who doubted that Diem could survive. Kennedy replaced Durbrow with Frederick Nolting, who doubted that South Vietnam could survive without him.

With the troop total rising, the military role was certain to change, with more advisers engaging in combat and more advisers being killed. The Military Assistance Advisory Group, Vietnam, became the Military Assistance Command, Vietnam (MACV), on February 8, 1962. It was like hauling down a beige flag and running up one in red, white, and blue. The commander of MACV would be Paul D. Harkins, a Maxwell Taylor protégé who sometimes approached common sense as yet another enemy to be defeated.

The government of North Vietnam protested that MACV's existence was an act of aggression, which was an exaggeration, and violated the Geneva Accords, which it definitely did. China expressed its full support of the North Vietnamese protest, and Chinese press and radio conveyed Mao's indignation to the people of China. This was no mere overheated fulmination. Mao had concluded that China's security was again under threat. Kennedy's advisers told him that the latest Maoist venture, the Great Leap Forward, had created such chaos that the country was virtually paralyzed. Mao had peasants trying to make steel in backyard furnaces instead of producing food.[16]

Kennedy was prepared at last to send large numbers of American troops into Vietnam with a mission to fight. Even so, his doubts about where he was heading grew stronger as the number of American troops in Vietnamese bars, brothels, and rice paddies mounted. Meeting with Averell Harriman and Michael Forrestal, son of James Forrestal and now a member of the NSC staff, Kennedy confessed that what he really wanted was for the number of American troops in Vietnam to go down, not up. Harriman and Forrestal were to be ready "at any favorable moment to reduce our involvement."[17]

Sometime in early 1962, McNamara too began to have second thoughts. He even began to think the unthinkable: a withdrawal would mean a defeat for the South Vietnamese, but the consequences of that defeat would be better than the consequences of an unwinnable American war. *That* would be incomparably worse.[18]

Kennedy was also being encouraged to get out by the one member of the Senate who was an authority on Vietnam, Mike Mansfield of Montana, and by John Kenneth Galbraith, normally at Harvard but now Kennedy's ambassador to India. Galbraith was scathing and prescient, telling him, "This could expand step by step into a major, long-drawn out military involvement [and] there is a consequent danger we shall replace the French . . . and bleed as the French did."[19]

By June, there were so many combat troops in the guise of advisers and helicopters in the guise of the future of war, that there was a diminution in the number of Vietcong attacks. Even McNamara began to wonder if the war might be won. For him, the truth was in the numbers, because numbers don't lie. "Every quantitative measure we have shows we're winning the war," McNamara informed the press that fall.[20]

Meanwhile, Kennedy had a marine general, Victor Krulak, and a career Foreign Service officer, Joseph Mendenhall, go to South Vietnam and make a civil-military analysis of the narrative behind McNamara's beloved statistics. It was like sending Oscar and Felix from *The Odd Couple* five years before the movie was released. Krulak (the macho Oscar) reported that victory was within reach, and Mendenhall (the more sensitive Felix) reported that Diem's government was unraveling. Kennedy was slightly incredulous. "You two did visit the same country, didn't you?"[21]

Unable still to fathom what the truth was and the prospects were, near the end of the year Kennedy asked Mike Mansfield to go and take a look at the situation in Saigon. Kennedy had managed to extract a pledge from Diem to implement democratic reforms, and there was a steady stream of optimistic reports coming out of MACV. Hope stirred.

Ten days later Mansfield returned and handed Kennedy a report that said corruption was rife and Diem was becoming more repressive than ever. Kennedy turned red in the face as he read the report, and tried to dismiss it. "Do you expect me to take this at face value?"[22]

All these fact-finding missions produced were more facts, when what he needed was a clear picture—but one was on its way. In January 1963, a force of 340 Vietcong deployed near the village of Ap Bac, only thirty miles from Saigon. They were soon confronted by 1,500 troops of the Army of the Republic of Vietnam (ARVN), who attempted to encircle them. Half the ARVN force consisted of paratroopers, Diem's best-trained soldiers. It also had the benefit of helicopters, close air support, tanks, and artillery.

The Vietcong stood their ground, shot down five helicopters and damaged six more, killed nearly a hundred ARVN soldiers, wounded an even larger number, drove them off the field, then retired in good order with modest losses. Paul Harkins offered a mendacious account of what had happened. American journalists who arrived on the scene swiftly contradicted him.[23]

At first Kennedy received carefully falsified accounts of the battle from MACV and the Joint Chiefs. Eventually he learned enough to convince him that the ARVN would never be able on its own to defend South Vietnam. He felt forced to put even more Americans into South Vietnam to keep the ARVN from falling apart. By the fall, there would be sixteen thousand "advisers" there. Many of the advisers were already combatants in all but name.

No matter how much training they received, the politics and the corruption of the Diem regime undermined the effectiveness of South Vietnamese soldiers. Talking to Mansfield, Kennedy acknowledged that the war was probably unwinnable on any terms that public opinion would accept.[24]

McNamara did not need persuading. Nor did Kennedy's military chief of staff, Maxwell Taylor. The United States Army was known as the Never Again Club after Korea: never again should an American army be sent to make war on the mainland of Asia. That army would never be able to secure victory and would be stymied at best, defeated at worst. If the question was "Do we send an army into South Vietnam?" Taylor's honest answer was going to be no, as Lyndon Johnson would one day discover.

Kennedy also told his appointments secretary, Kenneth O'Donnell, one of his oldest friends, that the war was hopeless, but "if I tried to pull out completely now from Vietnam we would have another Joe McCarthy Red scare on our hands. But I can do it after I'm reelected. So we had better make damn sure that I am re-elected."[25]

He also summoned Roger Hilsman to a meeting with no one else present. Kennedy could never have trusted Dean Rusk, his secretary of state, with the task he assigned to Hilsman. During World War II, Rusk had served in Burma as a staff officer under the colorful, Chinese-speaking, but militarily hapless "Vinegar Joe" Stilwell.[26]

Hilsman had been there too, but as a guerrilla commander fighting the Japanese in the jungle. While Rusk could not see beyond the dreary litany of Cold War debating points, Hilsman could not see how the United States Army—as it was currently organized, equipped, and led—could win a war in the jungles of Southeast Asia. The army was ready to fight tank battles in Germany, not skirmishes under jungles with a three-layer canopy—masses of trees rising to sixty feet, topped by trees rising to eighty feet, topped by trees that rose to more than one hundred feet.

Kennedy told Hilsman that his job was to make sure that the United States did not find itself fighting a major war in South Vietnam. The right policy was to neutralize South Vietnam or bring a coalition government into existence, preferably one that would ask the Americans to leave. Either way, the United States would have an exit strategy.[27]

Did Kennedy mean it? At the time he spoke, in early 1963, almost certainly. Roosevelt and Truman had the same habit of thinking out loud to their staff about doing bold things, saying something else publicly, all the while circling the subject, not yet ready to take the final, irrevocable step. And for the moment, he had to defend the war at press conferences, go on television and say the United States should not withdraw, tell journalists he believed in the domino theory. Otherwise he would only undermine the morale of the military and intelligence personnel in South Vietnam while wrecking his own chance of being reelected.

If reelected, Kennedy may not have succeeded in extricating the United States from Vietnam, but it is almost certain that he would have tried. He was more realistic than most of his advisers, as he had been during the Cuban missile crisis. Getting out of South Vietnam would save Americans from fighting a war that would benefit China while inflicting harm on themselves. Avoiding disaster is always worth taking risks.

Meanwhile, senior army commanders, such as Paul Harkins, were showing the president that they had learned nothing from Ap Bac. Harkins's ultimate response was to claim in MACV's first annual report in March 1963 that "the military phase of the war can be virtually won in 1963."[28]

Harkins probably believed it, and when he belittled the significance of Ap Bac, he was serious. Even so, this comparatively small engagement is taught nowadays at West Point as an example of how to lose a war by refusing to draw the right conclusions early in the fight. The Vietcong had been studying the changes the Americans had brought to the battlefield, mainly by introducing helicopters. In their response, the Vietcong displayed greater initiative, greater confidence, greater willingness to fight, and greater willingness to die than the ARVN. That ought to have been enough to inspire a serious reappraisal of the army's own way of fighting and the training it provided the South Vietnamese, but it didn't.[29]

With his brutal and ineffectual government losing the war, Diem turned increasingly to his brother, Ngo Dinh Nhu, the head of the paramilitary police. Nhu's police were raiding and looting Buddhist temples in a brutal attempt to terrify the government's critics into silence. American protestations that this would only drive people into the Vietcong were dismissed as unwanted advice.

Kennedy needed someone who would put pressure on Diem, something that Ambassador Frederick Nolting would never do. So he replaced Nolting with Henry Cabot Lodge, a Republican grandee whose Senate seat Kennedy had captured in 1952. Arriving in Saigon as a true believer in the rightness and winnability of the war, Lodge soon had serious doubts that it could be won so long as Diem remained president of South Vietnam.

A group of ARVN generals had already reached the same conclusion, and they indicated that they were prepared to mount a coup, provided the Americans had no serious objections. In late August, a cable drafted by Roger Hilsman went to Lodge. It declared that if Diem refused to stop the repression of ordinary Vietnamese, THEN WE MUST FACE THE POSSIBILITY THAT DIEM HIMSELF CANNOT BE PRESERVED.[30]

At a meeting the next day, Kennedy said there was a clear choice: either go with the coup and keep Diem in the dark; tell Diem he had to reform; or simply revoke the cable. The issue was debated over the next three days, and eventually, everyone voted for choice one—go with the coup and tell Diem nothing. From Saigon, Lodge sent his agreement: WE ARE LAUNCHED ON A COURSE FROM WHICH THERE IS NO TURNING BACK: THE OVERTHROW OF THE DIEM GOVERNMENT. The result of all this cabling and conferring was . . . nothing. The generals balked, but they now knew the way the wind was blowing from Washington.[31]

By this time Kennedy and McNamara seemed determined to put a lid on the number of troops in South Vietnam. It could not continue rising without turning into a major war, not just a counterinsurgency, and a war that could not be won. Kennedy had McNamara and Taylor make yet another fact-finding trip. On his return, McNamara solemnly asserted, "The military campaign has made great progress and continues to progress." Taylor, on the other hand, advised cutting aid to Diem to make him stop his idiotic brother from making war on the Buddhists, who were no friends of the Vietcong.

McNamara's optimism was of the strategic variety: it allowed him to suggest beginning a withdrawal. The idea began some months earlier with Maxwell Taylor, who thought it would force Diem to reform. But it was McNamara who was pushing it now. He urged Kennedy to bring out a thousand soldiers before the end of the year and to announce the government's intention of having all of them out by 1965.

The NSC debated the withdrawal issue, fiercely, on October 2, and Kennedy accepted McNamara's recommendation, something he was probably going to do anyway. He had already taken a major step toward educating the country on the basic question. Fighting a major war in Vietnam probably meant war with China. Was the country prepared to support that?

Kennedy had raised the question in a television interview on September 9. "China is so large, looms so high just beyond the frontiers, that if South Vietnam went, it would not only give them an improved geographic position for a guerrilla assault on Malaya but would also give the impression that the wave of the future in Southeast Asia was China and the Communists."

Kennedy had already come to the conclusion that within a few years China would eventually dominate Southeast Asia whatever the United States did. He sought an honest public debate, without any of the picture cards being hidden under the table. All Americans, including those on the NSC, needed to start asking themselves if South Vietnam was worth a war with China. He did not think it was. Neither did McNamara or Rusk, but the Joint Chiefs had managed to reach a different conclusion.

The initial step out of Vietnam would be only a token withdrawal.

It would have no discernible impact on operations, but once American troop strength in Vietnam began to fall, it would be harder for anyone to persuade the president to push it up again. In the meantime, the Vietnam question might move to page 17 of *The New York Times* and not become an issue in the 1964 election. But whenever the question was raised, those who argued for an increased commitment would need to address how big it would have to be if it meant war with China. Besides, Kennedy liked to remind people of a Chinese apothegm: "A journey of a thousand miles begins with a single step."[32]

These were anxious days for the true believers. Not only was Kennedy enlarging the debate while reducing the commitment, but credible rumors were circulating in Saigon that Diem was trying to sound out the North Vietnamese on negotiating an end to the war. He may well have heard that the Americans were preparing to pull the plug on him. What a coup it would be if he pulled the plug on them first! When these rumors reached Lodge, the State Department, and the CIA, there was outrage that the South Vietnamese might try to settle what had repeatedly been billed as "their war, not ours" by talking to the Vietcong.[33]

But there was hope. On October 5, an ARVN general, Duong Van Minh, hinted to a CIA officer that a coup was coming. What would the Americans do? John McCone, the director of Central Intelligence, did not think Kennedy ought to encourage the plotters. "Mr. President, if I was manager of a baseball team, and I had one pitcher, I'd keep him in the box whether he was a good pitcher or not." Kennedy ignored McCone's advice, telling Lodge, "While we do not wish to stimulate a coup, we also do not wish to leave the impression that the U.S. would thwart a change." The thought may well have occurred to him that he might soon be dealing with a government that was neutralist or one so fiercely nationalistic that it told the Americans to leave.[34]

This time, the disaffected generals struck. The coup was launched on November 1. Diem and his brother were arrested and killed in the back of an armored personnel carrier. When Kennedy was informed that they might well be dead—"murdered or suicides"—he burst into tears. He could not believe fellow Catholics would kill themselves; it had to be murder.[35]

Before JFK, presidential election campaigns began with the party convention. Kennedy turned them into yearlong marathons, and he was scheduled to go to Texas on November 21 to begin his reelection campaign and raise $4 million to pay off the debts of the Democratic National Committee.[36]

As he got ready to leave Washington, Kennedy discussed Cambodia with Michael Forrestal. He told Forrestal to assure the Cambodian ruler, Prince Norodom Sihanouk, that the United States would not undermine Cambodia's neutrality. And, he went on, "when you come back, I want you to come and see me . . . I want to start a complete and very profound review of how we ever got into this country [Vietnam] . . . I even want to think about whether or not we should be there." Then he headed for Marine One, squatting on the South Lawn, ready to take him to Andrews.[37]

Chapter 15
Hard Choices

WHEN AIR FORCE ONE LANDED BACK AT ANDREWS, THE NEWLY sworn president, Lyndon Johnson, stood in front of blinding floodlights. There was something he wanted to say, and he had to shout it over the noise of the engines as they wound down to silence. "This is a sad time for all people. We have suffered a loss that cannot be weighed. For me, it is a deep personal tragedy. I know that the world shares the sorrow that Mrs. Kennedy and her family bear. I will do my best. That is all I can do. I ask for your help—and God's."

Marine One deposited him on the South Lawn, and the lights in the Oval Office were on as he walked through the Rose Garden, but he strode on, heading for the Executive Office Building. He wasn't yet ready to sit at the antique keyhole desk. From his own familiar desk, he called Eisenhower and Truman, saying he needed their help and advice. They said they would be there in the morning.

Dawn brought weather to match people's mood—gray, wet, miserable. The pillars on the front porch of the White House were draped in black. The rain was heavy, falling with a steady cadence, as if it never intended to stop.

Over breakfast, Johnson met with the congressional leadership. Afterward, during a short meeting with the cabinet, he said his first priority was to show the world that John Kennedy's program and policies had not died in Dallas. They would be continued. America, even in grief, remained the country the world knew—confident, united, resolute. He wanted everyone to recognize that.[1]

The next day, Sunday, November 24, Johnson met with Henry Cabot Lodge, who had been on his way to Washington to confer with Kennedy when Kennedy was murdered. Johnson arrived for their meeting having just returned from the rotunda at the Capitol, where a eulogy to the dead president had been delivered. His face streaked with dried tears, Johnson shook hands with the ambassador.

The Vietcong had taken advantage of the political vacuum created by the murder of Diem and his brother, said Lodge. The military junta now in power in South Vietnam lacked competence and legitimacy. Some hard decisions would have to be made if the country was not to be lost to the Vietcong and their masters in Hanoi. "Unfortunately, Mr. President, you will have to make them."

"This is the only war we have," said Johnson. "I am not going to lose Vietnam. I am not going to be the President who saw Southeast Asia go the way China went." There was something he wanted Lodge to tell Duong Van Minh, the general in charge of the new government. Nearly six feet tall and weighing roughly two hundred pounds, the general was huge for a Vietnamese and was known as "Big" Minh, to distinguish him from any number of other generals named Minh. The message for Big Minh was, "He can count on us."[2]

The next day, Johnson approved a National Security Action Memorandum confirming the existing policy: "It remains the central object of the United States in South Vietnam to assist the people and Government of that country to win their contest against the externally directed and supported Communist conspiracy."[3]

And the day after that, there was a message to the armed forces from their new commander in chief. He underlined the seamless transition from one president to another, however great the national tragedy, and he assured the military "that the policies and purposes of your country are unchanged and unchangeable."[4]

He felt the breath of the world on his neck even as he sought to steady the nerves of the American people. "The whole world is looking at us," he told a Senate staffer. "Our ambassadors are warning us that they're wondering whether a strong man or a weak man is leading this country."[5]

Here was someone steeling himself to make hard decisions on far-away places—the kind of decisions that John Kennedy had been training himself to make almost since childhood. It was part of the cruelty of the moment. Yet as every president does, Johnson brought something to being commander in chief, starting with his decision to look like a war hero. In his buttonhole, day in and day out, he wore the miniature ribbon of the Silver Star, the nation's third-highest decoration for gallantry. Johnson was proud to remind people that only a week after the attack on Pearl Harbor he had been commissioned in the navy reserve, making him the first member of the House to get into uniform.

Certainly he had a promising future to protect back in December 1941. Johnson was blessed with two powerful patrons, Franklin D. Roosevelt and Sam Rayburn. He and they recognized that if the ascension of Lyndon B. Johnson was to continue unabated after the war, he needed to boast at least one wartime mission in the combat zone. In May 1942, Roosevelt found one for him.

After the Japanese captured Bataan in early 1942, Douglas MacArthur had been ordered to leave. He made his way by PT boat and airplane through the Japanese cordon. It was a defeated and depressed MacArthur who arrived in Australia. The news from the Pacific was grim in those early months, with the Japanese advancing everywhere, the Allies going nowhere.

George Marshall, then the army chief of staff, decided to send two bright young colonels, Samuel Anderson and Francis Stevens, out to New Guinea to find out why the war was going so badly and what could be done about it. The Japanese had just landed in New Guinea, and MacArthur, from his headquarters four hundred miles away in Melbourne, was trying to stop them from mounting an invasion of northern Australia.

Roosevelt had Johnson assigned to the fact-finding trip, not so much to report on the war—Johnson knew nothing about military operations—but to size up MacArthur. After a theatrical briefing by

MacArthur, Anderson and Stevens headed for New Guinea. Johnson insisted that he had to go with them. Anderson and Stevens were not thrilled. On the long journey to the other side of the world they had found Johnson to be not simply ignorant of military matters, which was only to be expected, but vain, arrogant, and completely self-absorbed, which was not.[6]

After several days traveling around grass airfields in New Guinea, Anderson and Stevens were assigned to fly on a mission by a B-26 unit to attack Japanese shipping. Johnson, repeatedly invoking the mighty name of Roosevelt, said he was coming along too. Just what he had to contribute to a low-level anti-shipping attack he could not say; nor could anyone else.

A dozen Japanese fighters were waiting high above as the bombers made their attack on the ships. And then the Zeros descended like carrion on the B-26s when they were at their most vulnerable, coming off the target. The bomber that carried Stevens was shot down; he and the entire crew perished. Fortunately, eight pilots of an exhausted P-39 group had volunteered to fly out and provide fighter escort for the withdrawal. They plunged into the Japanese fighters, and in the ensuing melee, the remaining bombers broke free.[7]

Back in Melbourne, MacArthur told Johnson and Anderson that he was awarding each of them the Silver Star. Stevens would receive a posthumous Distinguished Service Cross. One thing puzzled him, though, he told Johnson: "I still don't understand why you went on that mission." Stevens had manned a machine gun during the fighting. Johnson had, at most, looked out of a window. But MacArthur was not going to send Johnson, a presidential protégé, home empty-handed.

Back in Washington, Johnson told Harold Ickes, the secretary of the interior, his story: the bomber pilots were more or less hopeless, and the P-39 pilots weren't any better. The implication was that it had not been merely a dangerous mission; it had been almost suicidal. Only a truly brave man and a great patriot would have trusted his life to such rank amateurs. Somehow, by some kind of miracle, though, he had survived. Fortune favors the brave.[8]

As he tried to write a report on what he had seen and the conclusions he drew, Johnson ran up against an old problem: he could not organize his thoughts well enough to produce a coherent piece of prose. Even a one-page letter was a struggle for him. Desperate to appear knowledgeable and analytical, he persuaded Robert Sherrod, a noted war correspondent, to write his report. Sherrod loathed MacArthur and produced a blistering attack on the general, the general's staff, and the general's conduct of the war. The Silver Star that MacArthur hoped might generate some goodwill and a favorable report proved a wasted gesture. But for Johnson, that same Silver Star was a talisman, his impenetrable shield against any bemedaled veteran with political ambitions who wanted to make an issue of what Congressman Johnson had done to defeat the Axis.[9]

Nor did Johnson come to the presidency as a blank slate. His heart was in domestic politics, as was natural for someone steeped in the New Deal and forever true to the memory of Roosevelt. Yet he was not completely unprepared for the problems of war and peace that were thrust upon him beginning with Lodge and Vietnam. His mind was already made up on the fundamental question: What was his attitude toward Communism? By 1963 anti-Communism had become a secular religion. Not all Americans were believers, of course, but the majority were; yet, even among the believers there were degrees of devotion. Johnson stood with the stalwarts, and at times flirted with the fringe.

He had served on House and Senate committees that oversaw the president's handling of national security and foreign policy and could be as stridently anti-Soviet as almost anyone in Congress. Not only had Johnson supported Truman's intervention in Korea, but in 1951 he told his constituents, "We should announce, I believe, that any act of aggression anywhere, by any Communist forces, will be regarded as an act of aggression by the Soviet Union [and] we should unleash all the power at our command upon the vitals of the Soviet Union." Nuclear war evidently held no terrors for him.[10]

For all the value he placed on his Silver Star, Johnson's attitude to the professional military was much like Truman's and Kennedy's: disdain for the brass, but respect and affection for those who did the fighting. One of his earliest actions on becoming president was to dismiss three of his four military aides. As far as he was concerned, they were the Joint Chiefs' spies—and sometimes their lobbyists—in the White House. He would probably have got rid of all four, but a military aide was a vital ornament for formal occasions.

The Chiefs were outraged. Johnson proceeded to put them in their place. "Tell the admiral and tell the general that if their little men like to believe they can pressure their Commander in Chief on what his strategy ought to be in war or what his decision ought to be in peace, they don't know their Commander in Chief."[11]

Throughout Johnson's time as vice president, Dean Rusk, another marginal player in the Kennedy administration, had briefed him on what was going on in the world, as portrayed in secret telegrams. Rusk was another poor boy from the South who had made good within the Eastern Establishment, making it easy for Johnson to like and trust him. Johnson had also made extensive trips to the most volatile parts of the world—Southeast Asia and the Middle East.

During his 1961 trip to Vietnam, Johnson had hoped to demonstrate his defiance of Communism. His journey to Saigon took him through Taiwan, where he was introduced to the CIA station chief, Ray Cline. Only two years earlier Eisenhower had also visited Taiwan. "You know, on that occasion it was rather exciting," said Cline. "The Chinese Communists announced that they resented the presence of the American President on Chinese soil and fired a hundred and forty thousand artillery rounds against Quemoy."

Johnson was intrigued. "You mean they just did that to show their contempt and disapproval of our President?"

"Yes. I don't know whether they'll do the same for you, but I thought perhaps you should be warned."

"That's marvelous," said Johnson. "If they fire at Quemoy I want to know it immediately."

Each day he was there, however, it was Johnson who called Cline at least once, sometimes more: "What are they doing out on Quemoy?" The answer, invariably, was, "Nothing." Johnson did not consider his trip to Vietnam a success. The injured pride of a man who hoped, and failed, to trigger a denunciation from China was to be expected, but what hurt was the missing artillery barrage. He needed to be noticed.[12]

The bright spot was meeting politicians from Thailand. They were as vehemently anti-Communist as anyone in Texas and alarmed at the inroads the Vietcong were making in South Vietnam and the inroads the North Vietnamese were making in Laos. The Thais, unlike many Vietnamese, were primed to fight Communist encroachment.

Johnson's official report to Kennedy on his trip stated, "The battle against Communism must be joined in Southeast Asia." What was at stake was not Southeast Asia alone, but the future of Japan, the Philippines, and Taiwan. Yet without the United States to protect them, "they have no security and the vast Pacific becomes a Red Sea." No domino theorist could have expressed it more graphically. Nor was Johnson under any illusion about the possible cost of defending Southeast Asia or about the risk of failure. "At some point we may be faced with the further decision whether we commit major United States forces to the area or cut our losses and withdraw . . ." It would be fanciful to think that Johnson actually wrote this. Someone from the State Department almost certainly wrote it for him. Yet there is no reason to believe that he disagreed with a word of the report and every reason to believe he agreed with it.[13]

Over the first few weeks as president, Johnson suffered no shortage of advice on what to do about Vietnam. His predecessor as the Democratic leader in the Senate, Richard Russell of Georgia, had been yet another powerful mentor to the rising LBJ. One day in December, Russell reminded him of a discussion the congressional leadership had had with Eisenhower at the time of the Dien Bien Phu crisis. "I tried my best to keep them from going into Laos and Vietnam—you were there, of course—last meeting we had under Eisenhower before we went in there. Said we'd never get out, be in there fifty years from now."

Eisenhower had finally drawn back from direct intervention, but when the 900 French advisers to the South Vietnamese military departed shortly after the Geneva Accords went into effect, Eisenhower had sent 900 American advisers to replace them. Russell, wise in the way of presidential behavior, saw that today's adviser can be transformed into tomorrow's warrior, if the president wishes it. He urged Johnson to start looking for a way to get out, right now. He had to admit, though, that he had no ideas of his own on how to do it.[14]

Russell did not give up. Shortly after this conversation he did have an idea, and he offered it to Johnson. "I'd spend whatever it takes to bring to power a government that would ask us to go home." Johnson ignored it.[15]

There was another Senate skeptic Johnson felt compelled to listen to: his successor as Senate majority leader, Mike Mansfield of Montana. Over the past decade Mansfield had become the Senate's leading authority on Southeast Asia. Two weeks into Johnson's presidency, Mansfield came to the White House with a memorandum he wanted Johnson to read. Charles de Gaulle had recently offered French help in bringing the signatories of the Geneva Accords together to oversee the neutralization of Vietnam, including the withdrawal of all American troops. This would provide a forum where Vietnam, North and South, could explore mechanisms such as forming a coalition government or holding a nationwide election to resolve their differences. Look for a way to neutralize South Vietnam, wrote Mansfield. He pointedly remarked, "Eisenhower's response was not to pursue the war to victory but to go to Korea and make peace, in reality, a truce."[16]

McGeorge Bundy told Johnson the situation was so bad that the United States could not risk any kind of negotiation. "*When* we are stronger, *then* we can face negotiation." This "position of strength first" reasoning was illogical, but the seed was planted early. For now, though, Johnson had to do something, and what he chose to do was send McNamara back to Saigon.

McNamara had been there shortly before the assassination of Diem. Johnson asked him to go back and take another look. On his previous visit, McNamara had concluded that all the statistics were looking good. No football coach ever placed such emphasis on statistics as a way of telling how the game was going as McNamara did. But this time he returned to report that the stats were not as good as he'd believed earlier. The figures that had been bad under Diem—weapons lost to the enemy, the number of villages overrun, and so on—were getting worse. However you measured it, the Army of the Republic of Vietnam, a.k.a. the ARVN, was losing the war. Yet as bad as the figures were, said McNamara, "The stakes in preserving an anti-Communist South Vietnam are so high that, in our judgment, we must go on bending every effort to win."[17]

There was also something fundamentally wrong with the American effort, and that flaw had a name—Henry Cabot Lodge. The president needed to be able to put his full confidence in the head of the "country team" in South Vietnam. Even so, the unhappy truth was that the blue-blooded and French-speaking Lodge was failing as badly as the ARVN. The country team "lacks leadership and is not working to a common plan," McNamara told Johnson. LBJ had decided even before this that Lodge's judgment was poor. The proof was Lodge's eagerness to promote a coup to overthrow Diem without any insight into the likely consequences. Johnson told an old friend, Donald Cook, how he yearned to be rid of Lodge. "We need the ablest man we've got, the toughest Chief of Mission you can have." But Lodge was hopeless: "Just leaks to the press and keeps everybody fighting each other." Even so, Johnson did nothing. Lodge remained where he was. For all the tough talk, Johnson did not dare remove the ambassador. He'd been Jack Kennedy's choice. Supposedly the most powerful man in the world, and he lacked the firmness to remove an ambassador. The commander in chief was already discovering what it was like to be chained and pegged by forces bigger than he was.[18]

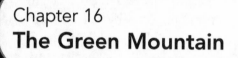

Chapter 16
The Green Mountain

DEAN RUSK CAME INTO JOHN KENNEDY'S CABINET WITH INTERNA-
tional cachet. He was, after all, a Rhodes scholar. Many people took
that as a sign of intellectual brilliance, much as they take a Medal of
Honor as an irrefutable sign of great courage. They are right about the
medal, but wrong about the scholarship.

Until the 1990s, Rhodes scholars were chosen as much for athletic
ability as brains. Rusk was the son of an impoverished clergyman in
rural Georgia. Intelligent and hardworking, he had little difficulty being an academic success at Davidson College, in North Carolina. The
college had been created to train Presbyterian ministers, not original
thinkers. As well as being Phi Beta Kappa, the six-foot-one-inch Rusk
was a star basketball player at a time when the seven-foot slam-
dunking center was only a fantasy that tormented Coach.

Oxford students in the age of *Brideshead Revisited* were sorted into
"hearties"—i.e., jocks—and "aesthetes," those with artistic sensibilities or intellectual talents. Rusk was a hearty, more likely to be found
on the tennis court than in the library or engaged in ratiocination.

Rusk distinguished himself at Oxford by winning a place on the university tennis team, thereby securing a coveted "blue." He did not stand out intellectually.

After serving in Burma during World War II, Rusk became by turns an assistant secretary of state, a college professor who never published anything, and president of the Rockefeller Foundation. Then he became Kennedy's secretary of state, which, he soon discovered, meant swallowing the humiliation of being ignored in favor of McGeorge Bundy, Kennedy's national security adviser.

Alas, poor Rusk. How he yearned to be a real secretary of state, the man who stood literally shoulder to shoulder with the president, guiding him through the snares and swamps of foreign policy the way Acheson had guided Truman. But John Kennedy had always intended to be his own secretary of state, much as Roosevelt had been. The approach in both cases was the same—pick a lightweight. In effect, Rusk sat at his imposing desk in his imposing office on the fifth floor of the stylish new State Department building, waiting for the phone to ring. Come over at once! The president needs you!

It did not happen. Even during the Cuban missile crisis Rusk played a minor role, overshadowed by Bundy, Robert McNamara, and the attorney general, Robert Kennedy. There was much speculation in 1963 that Rusk, being dispensable, would be dispensed with, but why bother to replace one cipher with another? Rusk would have been asked to stay on. Meanwhile, he waited for the phone to ring, and he did not even try to manage his sprawling department. State seemed less able than ever to cope with a dangerous world, where independence movements and liberation struggles were overthrowing old certainties and new U.S. embassies were sprouting in some of the most remote places on Earth. Then, in the most tragic way imaginable, everything changed, and Dean Rusk at a single bound found he had the president's ear, only now the president was Johnson.

Bundy was too much the product of the Eastern Establishment for Johnson ever to feel close to him. Bundy fawned and groveled to an Olympic standard in trying to win Johnson's confidence, and got nowhere. Johnson already knew, liked, and trusted Rusk, who came into his own at last, at a price.

LBJ was a master at breaking people down. He demanded that they come and talk to him while the presidential bowels were being moved, noisily. He also had an unpleasant habit of pulling out his penis—nickname, Jumbo—to convince doubters and critics that he was more of a man, and a bigger man too, than any of them. Once, becoming irritated at journalists who kept asking just why the United States was sending men to fight in Vietnam, he waved Jumbo at them and barked, "This is why!"[1]

It wasn't only the scribblers who got a good look at the presidential member. One of his Secret Service detail was shocked to discover that his leg was getting wet as he stood next to the president. "You're pissing on my leg, Mr. President!"

Johnson smiled at him. "I know I am. That's my prerogative."[2]

At other times he used his height, six feet four, and his huge body to crush them figuratively by pushing his face up to theirs. Johnson's substantial paunch, camouflaged by superb tailoring, was thrust against them. No one but himself was entitled to personal space.

The vulgarian Johnson disgusted even Robert Kennedy, and Bobby had not only worked for but socialized with one of the most repulsive creatures of the age, the drunken, knuckle-dragging Joe McCarthy. Bobby Kennedy could hardly credit how easily Johnson reduced able and otherwise intelligent men into cronies and toadies. "He is able to eat people up, and even people who are considered rather strong figures—I mean Mac Bundy and Robert McNamara," Kennedy remarked in an interview shortly before his death. "There's nothing left of them . . . He's mean, bitter, vicious—an animal in many ways."[3]

Dean Rusk presented no challenge at all. That was one reason why in the five-year hagride that was LBJ's Vietnam, Rusk was the cabinet member he turned to first for advice and, just as important, reassurance.

The foreign policy challenge in which Rusk had the longest and deepest interest was China. In 1949, as assistant secretary of state for Far Eastern affairs, he had encouraged Truman to fight China. In 1950, he got his wish. That fall, the Chinese inflicted the biggest battlefield defeat the U.S. Army has ever suffered, and the biggest the Marine Corps has suffered too. Rusk's enthusiasm for a war with China vanished more or less overnight. Yet throughout Johnson's presidency the Chinese conundrum was never far from his thoughts: How do we defeat North Vietnam without fighting China? Mao had addressed the same question by reminding Ho Chi Minh, "So long as the green mountain is there, you will never lack firewood."

In January 1964 Johnson was informed that de Gaulle was courting the Chinese. "De Gaulle's going to recognize China and the question comes whether *I* ought to protest it rather strongly or whether I ought to just let the government protest it," Johnson told Richard Russell.[4]

De Gaulle was also urging the United States and South Vietnam's new, untested government to move toward neutralization, and there were generals around Big Minh who seemed receptive to the idea. A frisson of alarm ran through the White House, the Pentagon, and the State Department. What do we do if the neutralists take over?

The threat of neutralism had barely registered before it was lifted. Big Minh's government was overthrown in a coup led by yet another general, who felt he had been cheated of his fair share of the spoils following Diem's murder. The new man's name was Nguyen Khanh, and Johnson was exultant. "This Khanh is the toughest one they got and the ablest one they got. And he said, 'Screw this neutrality, we ain't going to do business with the goddamned Communists, and get the hell out of here. I'm pro-American and I'm going to take over . . . It's De Gaulle's loss, and the neutralists' loss, not the Americans' loss . . .'"

Soon, though, Lodge was reporting to the president that Khanh's problems were the fault of de Gaulle, not Khanh. FRENCH AGENTS HAVE CONSPIRED WITH THE VIET CONG TERRORISTS DURING THE LAST WEEK, Lodge cabled from Saigon. He offered no evidence for this assertion. The story came, he said, from Khanh, who offered no evidence either. Nevertheless, Lodge fulminated against de Gaulle. HOW CAN ONE AVOID THE CONCLUSION THAT A CHIEF OF STATE WHO TALKS ABOUT NEUTRALITY IS LESSENING THE WILL TO WIN OF THE VIETNAM ARMY?[5]

Indignation at de Gaulle's neutralization proposal continued to inflame White House sensibilities. It was undermining confidence in Khanh, McNamara told the president more than a month after Khanh came to power. And Khanh DOES NOT YET HAVE WIDE POLITICAL APPEAL AND HIS CONTROL OF THE ARMY IS ITSELF UNCERTAIN . . . THERE IS A CONSTANT THREAT OF ASSASSINATION OR OF ANOTHER COUP.[6]

CIA director John McCone cranked up the distemper in the Oval Office by informing Johnson, "De Gaulle is reported as saying that France is violently opposed to the blatant American imperialism now rampant in the world."

Rusk had the ambassador to France, Charles Bohlen, go and talk to the general to probe his true views and intentions. Bohlen was widely regarded as one of the outstanding diplomats of his generation—worldly-wise, multilingual, accustomed to dealing with heads of state. De Gaulle told Bohlen that the United States faced a clear choice: either allow a neutralist government to come to power in Saigon or carry the war into North Vietnam and, very likely, into China.

Bohlen dismissed both ideas as being ridiculous, but nothing could have been more obvious to *le grand Charles*. If Indochina was ever stabilized politically, he said, "it will only come about with Chinese consent and with Chinese consent there can be genuine neutrality." Once that happened, it would open the way to Vietnamese unification.

The ambassador remained incredulous. Was the general seriously suggesting that the United States declare war on China? De Gaulle said he was not recommending it, but that would at least address the basic challenge in Vietnam. So long as the Chinese supported the North, the United States could never win. Behind de Gaulle's words was a peninsula-shaped question—Korea. The United States had found it impossible to win there because of China. Why should Vietnam be any different?

Instead of addressing the implications of what de Gaulle was saying, Bohlen ended the conversation abruptly. In reporting back to Rusk, Bohlen made light of the China question, as if it were hardly worth a serious diplomat's time. Instead, he preferred to portray de Gaulle's views as reflecting little more than French pique at the possibility of the Americans succeeding in Vietnam where the French had failed: "His firm belief is that the course we are on is one that will only end in failure . . . [But] it was not clear to me to what extent de Gaulle was operating on genuine conviction or whether past failure and humiliation played a large part in determining his current attitude." It was inconceivable to Bohlen that de Gaulle might be not merely convinced of what he was saying but, just possibly, right.[7]

When, shortly after this, Bundy drew up a list of "adversaries of major importance," along with North Vietnam, China, and the Soviet Union, he included France.[8]

As diplomats exchanged cables, the president was becoming impatient for action. He had recently approved a proposal called Operations Plan 34A, for launching sabotage raids into North Vietnam.

Small boats would put saboteurs ashore, and nighttime parachute drops would insert potential guerrilla leaders who would recruit disaffected North Vietnamese. Nothing had happened since Johnson okayed the plan, because Lodge doubted that small raids would discourage the North Vietnamese. Op Plan 34A was more likely to provoke them into pushing their soldiers into the South. Big Minh had agreed with Lodge. But now, with Khanh in charge, things were looking up for pinprick attacks against the aggressor.[9]

Seized by hope, Johnson thought the struggle was coming right at last. John Kennedy had said time and again, "It's their war," and it was. To beat the Indians, you use the Indians; that was how the West was won. The thing to do was to train the South Vietnamese up to something like American standards, give them the firepower and mobility, then let them take the fight to the insurgents.

That had always been the idea behind sending advisers to South Vietnam, but Johnson needed results soon if he was to keep public opinion behind him during an election year. What he wanted would later become famous as "Vietnamization." In February 1964 he ordered McNamara to develop a three-year plan to train enough South Vietnamese troops to defend the country so he could start bringing the advisers home. "It's their war and their men. And we're willing to train them. And we have found that over a period of time that we kept the Communists from spreading . . . We did it in Greece and Turkey . . . We haven't done it by going out and sending men to fight. And we have no such commitment there. But we do have a commitment to help Vietnamese defend themselves. And we're there for the training and that's what we're doing."

McNamara replied, "All right, sir. I'll get right onto it."[10]

As Johnson and Rusk, McNamara and Bundy studied huge maps of Southeast Asia in those early months of the new administration, the most telling thing their eyes passed over wasn't the terrain symbols or the location of cities. It was a single word: "Indochina." Its four syllables conjure up one of history's oldest narratives. Southeast Asia is where two great civilizations meet. China had dominated the eastern half for more than two thousand years, while the civilization of the Indus valley was dominant in the west. In countries such as Thailand and Malaya there was a blending of influences, but across Southeast Asia the largest part of the merchant class was likely to be

Chinese; the food was a form of Chinese cuisine; languages such as Vietnamese were tonal, just like Chinese; and much of the culture, from art to music, was strongly influenced by Chinese models. The Chinese were hardly intruders in the region.

Despite this, Johnson and his principal advisers denounced them as outsiders, aggressively trying to muscle their way in. Even as Bundy—a self-styled "ex-historian"—acknowledged China's historic role, he dismissed it as irrelevant because "we mean to keep at it out there." Besides, Bundy told Johnson, China's importance was much overrated: "India is in fact the great prize in Asia."[11]

The president would have loved to ignore China, but unlike Bundy, he knew that was impossible. China posed an intractable challenge at home as well as abroad. Talking to John S. Knight, a newspaper publisher, Johnson said that he couldn't get out of Vietnam because "God Almighty, what they said about us leaving China would just be warming up, compared to what they'd say now."[12]

There was another parallel, too, between the failed efforts of the 1940s to save the Guo Min Dang regime of Jiang Jieshi and the costly attempt to prop up Diem and his successors, a parallel that Johnson did not seem to appreciate. So long as the United States provided billions of dollars, Jiang had never had any incentive to reform. Nor did Diem. Both Jiang and Diem were at liberty to reject anything resembling fundamental reform. Nationalist China and South Vietnam were in a privileged position, comparable to that of Third World petro-states, without having to go to the trouble of pumping oil. The money flowed in whatever the government did or failed to do. There was no need for good governance or even mere competence. Just keep the Americans on the hook. Jiang had been good at that. So was Diem, and Khanh was now trying to acquire the same skills set.

A mountain of money, almost no accountability—that was bound to excite thoughts that could bring on a sweat and get people thinking. In early 1964 coup rumors were swirling around Saigon even as the Vietcong took over district capitals and seized the weapons the United States had sent to arm the ARVN. Fearing that South Vietnam might collapse, Johnson wondered what he should tell Congress and the country. McNamara told him to sit tight: "It would be wise for you to say as little as possible, Mr. President."[13]

Bundy too feared something terrible was about to happen. "The only thing that scares me," he told Johnson, "is that the government would up and quit on us, or that there would be a coup and we get invited out."

In April, with the CIA warning that unless something happened soon, the Saigon government would probably collapse and Khanh would be overthrown, Lodge proposed a solution. If Khanh goes, Lodge told McNamara, "The U.S. should be prepared to run the country."[14]

Rusk went to see General Khanh, to assure him that the United States was behind him. Khanh said he was glad to hear that, but South Vietnam was on the verge of going under. It could fall to the Vietcong at any moment. The only way to save the situation was to invade the North.

Rusk said that might trigger a war with China, a war that would probably go nuclear. He did not spell it out for General Khanh, but despite the Sino-Soviet split, the thirty-year mutual protection treaty between the Soviet Union and China, signed in 1950, was still operable as far as anyone knew. If the United States used nuclear weapons against China, that might push the Soviets into using nuclear weapons against South Vietnam, or into giving the Chinese nuclear weapons. Khanh wasn't worried. A nuclear war with China was the only strategy that would work, he said. As long as there was a Communist China, he told Rusk, the United States would never be secure.[15]

In May, McGeorge Bundy informed the president that the time was coming when he might have to sanction a "resolute and extensive deployment" to South Vietnam. In other words, send an American army. Bundy acknowledged the risks: "the risk of escalation toward a major land war or the use of nuclear weapons." Rusk, McNamara, and the Joint Chiefs were prepared for these risks, Bundy assured the president. There was also the risk of a revolt by the South Vietnamese, who would presumably object to seeing their country occupied by an American army.

For now, though, "the best estimate of your advisers [is] that a decision of this kind can be executed without bringing a major military reply from Red China, and still less from the Soviet Union." But, added Bundy in an attempt to firm up presidential resolve, "we repeat our view that a pound of threat is worth an ounce of action—as long as we are not bluffing." At times like this, Bundy demonstrated a trait for which intellectuals are notorious. The desire to display his cleverness was stronger than any urge to embrace common sense.

If they were not bluffing, Bundy and the others were pushing Johnson toward a nuclear attack on North Vietnam. Bundy seemed blithely confident that the Chinese and Russians would remain calm even as radioactive clouds passed over their territory, killing their people. The more likely result would be a nuclear war.[16]

With bad news and even worse advice pouring in, Johnson became desperate to create some good news, something that would make him feel that things weren't spinning out of control. "This war," he told McNamara, "I'm not doing much about fighting it. I'm not doing much about winning it. I just read about it . . . We're not getting it done. We're losing. So we need something new . . . What I want is somebody that can lay up some plans to trap those guys and whup hell out of them, and kill some of them. That's what I want to do."[17]

In the weeks that followed, the Pentagon sought to give him what he wanted. Op Plan 34A raids were made against coastal targets in North Vietnam, sabotage teams were dropped in, navy destroyers went into the Tonkin Gulf at night to pick up coded radio signals and track North Vietnamese radar sites, and in Laos the air force was flying bombing missions, something the administration denied even after two planes were shot down. And although American soldiers were increasingly being used in combat roles in South Vietnam, that too was strenuously denied. They were still training, not fighting, McNamara insisted.

Even this pickup in activity failed to satisfy Johnson. Near the end of May he freely expressed his fears to Bundy. "It looks to me like we're getting into another Korea. It just worries the hell out of me . . . I believe the Chinese Communists are coming into it. I don't think we can fight them ten thousand miles from home [and] what the hell is Vietnam worth to me? What is Laos worth to me? What is it worth to our country?"[18]

Meanwhile, Robert McNamara had devised a succinct formula for what the war was about: "We seek an independent non-Communist South Vietnam." Johnson endorsed it, and when McNamara later tried to rewrite it to allow some room for the wishes of the South Vietnamese, Johnson told him to leave the formula alone.

The United States thus barred the South Vietnamese from electing a government that included the Vietcong. Nor would a South Vietnamese government be allowed to unite with North Vietnam. Would this new South Vietnam be able to have normal relations with China or any other Communist country? Would it even be allowed to recognize China? Given the current hostility to China, including an adamantine refusal by the United States even to recognize it, the answer was "Certainly not." What the people of South Vietnam could look forward to was life as they presently knew it—as the inhabitants of an American protectorate.

The country was a pluperfect example of dictionary definitions. The Random House dictionary defines a protectorate as "the relation of a strong state toward a weaker state or territory that it protects and partly controls." The *Oxford English Dictionary* has "a state or territory placed or taken under the protection of a superior power." Protectorates had been commonplace since the days of the Roman Empire, allowing considerable autonomy on routine administration but leaving the big decisions to the protecting power.[19]

The Joint Chiefs pointed out that the political goal of a non-Communist South Vietnam did not give them "a militarily valid objective for Southeast Asia." They tried to help Johnson formulate one by offering a clear choice: order us to destroy North Vietnam, which we can do through bombing, or order us to crush the insurgency in the South, which we can also achieve by bombing. Their preference was for the first choice—the obliteration of North Vietnam, even if that meant war with China. McNamara declined to sanction either.[20]

Johnson, McNamara, Bundy, and Maxwell Taylor, the chairman of the JCS, departed at the end of May for Honolulu, where they would meet up with Lodge and other major advisers based in Saigon. The question before them was McNamara's recommendation of turning what was still a small war into a big one. The point of the meeting was whether or not Johnson should approve in principle McNamara's recommendation to deploy large numbers of American troops to fight in South Vietnam. The result was enough of a yes to allow planning for a major air offensive and a major ground troop deployment. South Vietnam lacked the infrastructure to support either an American army or a major bombing offensive. It would take some months to improve the roads, the airfields, the ports, and other logistical facilities, and the president would not have to make the final decision until after the election. Meanwhile, there was one new objective that almost everyone at the Honolulu conference could agree on: "Obtain joint resolution approving past actions and authorizing whatever is necessary with respect to Vietnam."[21]

Lodge, horrified at what the president was going to do, was suddenly seized with doubt. "Clearly a very strong, if not impregnable, argument can be made for the proposition that Southeast Asia is of vital concern to the United States," he informed Johnson in a hand-wringing letter from Saigon. Lodge would have had no trouble concluding that Western Europe was of vital concern, or Japan or Latin America. In those areas, the national security argument *was* impregnable. Lodge had just glimpsed daylight. McNamara's proposal, he concluded, "is largely a U.S. venture of unlimited possibilities which could put us on a slope along which we slide into a bottomless pit."[22]

After reading this, Johnson could not wait to get rid of Lodge, and a week later, the ambassador to South Vietnam submitted his resignation. The upcoming Republican convention provided cover for his departure: Lodge was going to attend the convention and give his support to the leading moderate candidate for the Republican nomination, Governor William Scranton of Pennsylvania.

Johnson chose Maxwell Taylor to replace Lodge. Khanh was a general. So was Taylor. "I want the military to work with Khanh, 'cause they've got a military President—and try to get his cooperation. If he falls over, as he may any day, and we have another coup, we're through in Asia. And I'm trying to get a man that can lead him and give him advice," Johnson told the speaker of the House, John McCormack.[23]

Whichever way he turned, Johnson felt trapped. "Eisenhower got us into Vietnam," Johnson said time and again, in what was becoming a threnody against the cruelty of fate. "I inherited it," he lamented. That wasn't true. Eisenhower's offer of assistance to Diem in October 1954 came larded with conditions.

He had said there would be American money and expertise only, "provided that your Government is prepared to give assurances as to the standard of performance it would be able to maintain in the event such aid were supplied." Eisenhower spelled out what he meant: Diem had to "undertake needed reforms" and provide governance "so enlightened in purpose and effective in performance that it will be respected both at home and abroad." The first reform that Diem should have tackled was land reform. Apart from a token effort, it never happened. Nor had the government of South Vietnam ever conducted a free and fair election. Diem was never elected to anything.

Like despots across the Third World, he staged referendums, which were easy to rig, on whether his rule should continue, and he could summon up whatever percentage he desired. He had modestly settled for 91 percent on his last referendum. Nor did Diem legitimize his rule by sharing power with a representative elected body. He ruled by presidential decree. Diem, whom Johnson compared with Churchill, was just as much a small-time tyrant as "Papa Doc" Duvalier in Haiti or Kim Il Sung in North Korea.

None of the conditions that Eisenhower imposed had been met, nor had any attempt ever been made to meet them. Diem had refused to be bound by Eisenhower's letter, and far from commanding international respect, South Vietnam was widely and rightly considered brutal and repressive, not substantially different from the regime in the North.

Neither Kennedy nor Johnson was bound by the terms of Eisenhower's letter. It was Kennedy's choice to raise the number of "advisers" to sixteen thousand; it would be Johnson's choice to send an army.

Even as Johnson was blaming Eisenhower for his troubles, he courted the general assiduously. Johnson wooed Eisenhower by telling him that his advice was essential, regularly sending a helicopter to bring him to Washington. Gifts of deer sausage were delivered from the Johnson ranch to the Eisenhower farm at Gettysburg with thank-you notes attached. LBJ strove to make an old soldier feel that he was still on duty, still protecting the nation.

Eisenhower was ready to back Johnson as commander in chief, and urged him, now that he had a war on his hands, to win it. But Ike rejected any and every suggestion that he had made a binding commitment to Diem, and he resented Johnson's insistence that it all began with him. In June, with the presidential campaigns gaining speed, Ike told the press what he thought of Johnson's handling of Vietnam: "There is little hope for what we're doing now."[24]

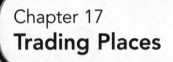

Chapter 17
Trading Places

ON HIS RETURN FROM HONOLULU, JOHNSON HAD A LONG TALK with James "Scotty" Reston of *The New York Times*, one of the nation's most influential political commentators. "Tell me," said Johnson, "what is your feeling about Vietnam."

"Oh, I'd just depress you," said Reston. "Nothing big can be done there without the acquiescence of China. We can't get out, and we can't go smashing into China."

"All right, now that's exactly the way I look at it," said Johnson. He proceeded once again to put the blame on Eisenhower's 1954 original letter to Diem. And now "our national honor is at stake. We've got a treaty and, second, we like to see people free." Not only had Ike written that letter, he had also stuck his successors with the Southeast Asia Treaty Organization (SEATO). The way LBJ told the story, Eisenhower was to blame twice over for Johnson's predicament.

Despite all his experience in government, LBJ at times seemed an innocent when it came to national security and state sovereignty. No government can hog-tie its successors to the end of time, whether through national or international law, to say nothing of a letter that was so open to interpretation. Roswell Gilpatric, the deputy secretary of defense, had been a senior partner at Wall Street's most famous law firm, Cravath, Swain, a former secretary of the air force, and a highly paid international lawyer, much like George Ball. Gilpatric read Ike's letter, and it was obvious to him that it contained no binding commitment, legal or political.

Nor was SEATO what Johnson believed. Treaties are incorporated into national law once they have been ratified, but they are not like the Ten Commandments, beyond revocation. Prohibition was incorporated into national law by amending the Constitution. Nothing could seem more fundamental. Yet twelve years later Prohibition was repealed, by another constitutional amendment. In politics, today is not yesterday, and forever does not exist.

As with Prohibition, treaties that create problems are going to be ignored, rejected, or renegotiated. Theodore Roosevelt had broken a treaty with Colombia dating back to 1846 in order to foment a revolt in its most northerly province, Panama, send in the marines, and take the province away from Colombia. The result—the Panama Canal. Roosevelt was said to have joked about Panama, "We stole it fair and square."

At Yalta, Roosevelt revoked America's 1942 pledge to support the Polish government in exile. He also encouraged the Soviet Union to abrogate its neutrality pact with Japan. Stalin delivered six months later.

In training and arming the Cuban exiles that were put ashore at the Bay of Pigs in April 1961, John Kennedy had flouted the UN Charter, abrogated a 1934 treaty with Cuba, and ignored various other treaties that committed the United States not to overthrow the government of a fellow member of the Organization of American States. But, as one leading authority acknowledges, "whenever national interest walked in the door, the treaty was pitched out of the window." 'Twas ever thus; remains thus.[1]

In 2001 the United States flouted the United Nations Convention Against Torture, to which it was a signatory, and it continues to do so. That same year, it also abrogated the Anti-Ballistic Missile Treaty, over the objections of Russia, the other signatory. And in 2003, during the invasion and occupation of Iraq, the United States rejected the

Geneva Conventions' standards on the treatment of prisoners and the provision of governance in occupied countries. The conventions were ridiculed as "quaint" relics from a bygone age.

It was entirely Johnson's choice—strongly supported by Rusk—to flash what he liked to present as a pair of handcuffs stamped SEATO. It would have been more accurate had they been stamped MADE IN THE USA. When the Geneva Conference of 1954 drew to a close, the French were about to withdraw from Vietnam, and Eisenhower did not want to replace them. All he wanted was to stop the Vietminh from taking over all of the country. The solution was SEATO. "We must get that pact!" the deputy secretary of state, Walter Bedell Smith, told his staff. Smith had been Ike's wartime chief of staff, sometime ambassador to Moscow, and, more recently, director of the CIA. And so it was done.[2]

The entire purpose of the treaty was to provide the United States with a justification to intervene militarily in Indochina if it chose to do so at some future point. Yet it was also crafted to provide the United States with a justification for not intervening if it so chose.

Johnson spoke of SEATO as if it were the Southeast Asian equivalent of NATO. Anyone reading the text of both will see at a glance that he was trying to compare a mouse with a rhinoceros. The NATO treaty opens on a martial note, breathing defiance and resolution in equal measure: "An armed attack against one shall be considered an attack against all."

Much of the language of the NATO treaty was echoed, and some was a verbatim copy, in the SEATO text, but its opening declaration is all rose water and petals: "Each Party recognizes that aggression by means of armed attack against any of the Parties would endanger its own peace and safety [and] the Parties shall consult immediately in order to agree on the measures which should be taken for the common defense."

Of the treaty's eight signatories—Australia, Britain, France, New Zealand, Pakistan, the Philippines, Thailand, and the United States—only three are in Southeast Asia. The United States added Cambodia, Laos, and Vietnam to the list of the countries the treaty would cover, but the other signatories did not put their names to this addendum. What SEATO unmistakably called for was a conference, not a fight to the death. Fighting was optional.

While Johnson grimaced and groaned in his paper handcuffs, others slipped away with a smile. The president of Pakistan, Field Marshal Ayub Khan, would not send troops to fight in Vietnam; Britain offered free advice, but not a single soldier; and France was never going to wage war in Vietnam again. Once was enough. Australia, which had sent thousands of troops to Korea, sent only six hundred to Vietnam. New Zealand also sent a token force. The Philippines, one of the Southeast Asian signatories, did not send troops, and even the Thais, as fearful as anyone of North Vietnam, sent only a few thousand.

John Kennedy had no illusions about SEATO. In February 1962 Kennedy had asked George Ball, the deputy secretary of state and one of the country's leading international lawyers, whether SEATO obliged the United States to the defense of South Vietnam. Ball's answer was brief: there was no binding commitment there, no obligation to fight.[3]

Johnson and Rusk nevertheless insisted that if the United States did not abide by its SEATO commitments, its NATO allies would lose faith and the whole apparatus of collective security on which the free world depended would fray and, eventually, collapse. Strangely, none of those NATO allies was willing to provide troops, not even countries such as Britain and Turkey, which had sent thousands of men to fight in Korea. Not one liberal democracy accepted the argument that Johnson and Rusk were making.

Johnson was not about to trust the Ike letter or the SEATO treaty to bear the weight of sending two hundred thousand Americans to South Vietnam in order to fight what had until now been billed as "their war." He wanted the sturdy pillar of a congressional resolution. Truman had refused to seek one in June 1950. Congress had supported him for a while, but once the Chinese entered the war, both public and congressional support had taken a dive, from which Truman's standing as a commander in chief never recovered, crippling his presidency. When Johnson returned from Honolulu, White House and State Department staffers began drawing up potential drafts for a congressional resolution.

Even as he braced himself to turn "their war" into "our war," Johnson needed to cast himself as the peace candidate for the November election. He got the Canadian prime minister, Lester Pearson, to ask the Canadian diplomat on the International Control Commission to pass a message to Ho Chi Minh: the United States was not trying to bring down the government of North Vietnam. It had no desire for permanent bases in South Vietnam. All it wanted was for the North to stop supporting the insurgency in the South and to stop taking advantage of the neutralization of Laos. If Ho was willing to act as a partner for peace, the United States would assist the economic development of North Vietnam.

This message had hardly been delivered before Johnson became apprehensive. Maybe he seemed too eager; maybe they'd think he wasn't tough enough for this game. So he had yet another message for Pearson to pass on to the diplomat to pass on to Ho: the president of the United States wanted him to know that if the North did not cease its aid to the insurgency in the South, it would pay a very heavy price. "We will not be pushed out of Vietnam."[4]

The night of July 31, 1964, an American force raided two small islands in the Tonkin Gulf, off the coast of North Vietnam. The boats that put them ashore bombarded the island's unimposing defenses while a U.S. Navy destroyer, the *Maddox*, sailed close by to intercept North Vietnamese radio transmissions so that cryptanalysts aboard ship could try breaking their codes.[5]

North Vietnam lodged a protest with the International Control Commission asserting that the *Maddox* had intruded on its territorial waters, which extended twelve miles out to sea. Three nights later, on August 2, the *Maddox* returned, not only to intercept radio transmissions but to try to provoke the North Vietnamese to turn on their radar sets. That would make it possible to pinpoint their locations for potential air strikes.

The *Maddox* was eleven miles off the coast when three obsolescent Soviet-made torpedo boats sailed out to challenge her. The destroyer turned about but was followed by the PT boats into international waters. Her captain, John J. Herrick, was meanwhile receiving decoded messages from the cryptanalysts aboard that the PT boats had been ordered to get ready for "military operations." He gave orders to open fire on them if they came within ten thousand yards, which was nearly six miles, well beyond the range of any of the weapons on the PT boats.

The "military operations" decryption was ambiguous, and the *Mad-*

dox had blinker lights on her bridge wings. The standard procedure where intentions are unclear and two warships are in international or territorial waters is to use the International Code of Signals to clarify each other's intentions. The right course for the *Maddox*'s commander was to send at least one blinker light message, telling the PT-boat skippers not to come any closer. Instead, when the nearest boat was 9,800 yards distant and the *Maddox* was 28 miles out to sea, she opened fire with one of her five-inch guns.[6]

Not surprisingly, the three North Vietnamese warships spread out for a torpedo attack and went to flank speed. The *Maddox* blazed away, firing 283 rounds. The torpedo boats launched their torpedoes earlier than their captains wanted, but the hail of shells they were heading into left them little choice.

None of the torpedoes hit anything. However, a heavy-machine-gun bullet from one of the boats struck the *Maddox*, doing little more than chipping the paint. Aircraft from the carrier *Ticonderoga* were summoned to attack and sink the enemy boats. The pilots reported at least one boat sunk and the other two crippled. All three boats returned to base, and only one had suffered serious damage.[7]

No American sailor had been killed or wounded, and it was open to question whether the North Vietnamese government had authorized the attack. Johnson chose not to retaliate. He was going to continue running as the peace candidate against Senator Barry Goldwater, whom he was portraying—with considerable help from the senator—as a man so entranced by war as the solution to America's problems that the whole planet and everyone on it might be turned to radioactive ash if the senator got his heavy hand anywhere near the button, codebook, telephone, or whatever it was that would launch a nuclear attack on the Russians and Chinese.

The only actions the president authorized in response to the encounter in the Gulf of Tonkin were to add a second destroyer to the patrol, to have combat air patrols flown over the destroyers by navy fighters at all times, and to sink any North Vietnamese craft that mounted an attack. Johnson publicly asserted that the United States would continue exercising its rights to peaceful passage in international waters. Most people were satisfied with that, although Goldwater inevitably wasn't.

McNamara meanwhile gave the Senate Foreign Relations Committee an account of what had happened. In reference to the July 31 raid on the two islands, he said, "Our navy played absolutely no part in, was not associated with, was not aware of, any South Vietnamese actions, if there were any." As for the *Maddox*, she was "operating in international waters, was carrying out a routine patrol of the type we carry out all over the world at all times." The PT boats fired first, and no attempt was made to sink them, only to drive them off.

Almost none of what he said was true, including the comment about a routine patrol. In the 1960s American and Soviet warships played chicken in nearly every ocean, every sea in the world. Ships not only closed on one another at high speed but minor collisions weren't unusual, and paint got scraped. Fortunately, no one on either side was so nervous that they opened fire. McNamara's account was false in virtually every detail, but putting questions of integrity to one side, there is always a price to be paid for such dishonesty: people who lie to others invariably lie to themselves. The capacity to think clearly takes a beating whenever powerful people flee for the leaky shelter of dishonesty. And by this time, McNamara was unable to distinguish the true from the false, becoming the living embodiment of an old southern expression: "One of those fellas that will lie on credit when he could tell the truth for cold cash."

Dean Rusk was not in the same league, but he was susceptible to the same pathology. In his account of what happened, he informed the Senate that although the government was aware of South Vietnamese raids on small islands in the Gulf of Tonkin, it had no direct involvement or detailed knowledge. He chose not to reveal that the raids had to be approved by a committee in Washington that included the deputy secretaries of both Defense and State, as well as McGeorge Bundy.

When the PT boats came out, the *Maddox* had been within what North Vietnam claimed as its territorial waters, which extended twelve miles out to sea. McNamara ridiculed that, telling Johnson that the only limit the United States recognized was three miles, which was an interesting idea. It was the United States that had first proposed the three-mile limit as an international standard back in 1793. Within a decade or so, nearly every country in the world had accepted that. There were a few exceptions, but until September 1945 none of the major maritime nations had challenged the three-mile limit. And then Harry S. Truman issued a proclamation saying that the territorial waters of the United States extended to the limits of the continental shelf; in the Gulf of Mexico that meant 10.5 miles. The law of the sea was suddenly up for grabs. It took until the 1980s for a committee working under the auspices of the UN to formulate a new set of standards.

Meanwhile, countries around the world began moving toward something approximating the limit that Truman claimed for the United States—twelve miles. By 1964, dozens of countries had adopted it, including all the Communist nations, and in 1963 the director of naval intelligence had warned that North Vietnam considered itself entitled to a twelve-mile limit. If there was a scintilla of doubt, the protest lodged with the International Control Commission on August 1 removed it.

The message evidently got through, because on August 4, the *Maddox* and the *Turner Joy* sailed into the Gulf of Tonkin with instructions not to go closer to the coast than eleven miles—quite a change from the earlier penetration to within four miles. And at eleven miles, a one-mile difference might be plausibly passed off as a navigational mistake.

Hardly had the two destroyers moved within the twelve-mile limit than the *Maddox* began reporting it was under a ferocious attack by enemy boats firing dozens of torpedoes. When McNamara called the president to inform him, Johnson was having breakfast with the congressional leadership. As he passed on what McNamara had just said, the mood in the room turned angry. The president had to retaliate. Johnson agreed.

He was worried now not so much about what the North Vietnamese might do, but about what Congress might do and what Goldwater might do. "What I was thinking about when I was eating breakfast," he told McNamara, "I was thinking that it looks to me like the weakness of our position is that we respond only to an action and we don't have any of our own, but when they move on us and shoot at us. I think we ought not only to shoot at them, but almost simultaneously pull one of these things you've been doing, on one of their bridges or something."

"Exactly. I quite agree with you," said McNamara.[8]

Johnson hurried down to the White House basement, where

Bundy had his office. He intended to make an address to the nation on the latest attack and explain why he was hitting back. Bundy, who knew how fragmentary and confused the reports were, said, "Maybe we should think it over."

Johnson responded, "I didn't ask you that. I told you to help me get organized."[9]

Meanwhile, over at the Pentagon, McNamara was still grabbing the raw intelligence on intercepted North Vietnamese radio signals, which had been hastily decoded. He then tried to put them together with the accounts from the *Maddox* to figure out just what was happening. But there was no clear picture. There was, however, a message from John Herrick, aboard the *Maddox*. Herrick said there were no visual sightings. The earlier reports could be exaggerated readings by overly eager sonar men or possibly false readings produced by freak weather effects.[10]

By this time, the snowball had moved so far and so fast down the mountain that nothing could stop the avalanche. Johnson ordered retaliation air strikes and went on television close to midnight to announce them as the pilots were on their way toward their targets.

The next day, a joint resolution was introduced in Congress. The key passage read:

> Congress approves and supports the determination of the President, as Commander in Chief, to take all necessary measures to repel armed attack against the forces of the United States and to prevent further aggression . . . The United States is . . . prepared, as the President determines, to take all necessary steps, including the use of armed force, to assist any member or protocol state of the Southeast Asia Collective Defense Treaty requesting assistance in defense of its freedom.

The resolution passed with only two dissenting votes in the Senate and none in the House. The senator who steered the resolution through Congress was J. William Fulbright of Arkansas, another Rhodes scholar and probably the most urbane racist of his generation, always ready to justify segregation of and humiliation for black Americans. Johnson despised him, but Fulbright had his uses, much like Rusk.

Instead of picking Johnson up, the Tonkin Gulf Resolution plunged him into depression. The war was still rumbling on, still going badly, and the pressure for escalation would become irresistible now. Congress had given him what he asked for—the latitude to make the truly momentous decisions, the kind there was no way of undoing. Given that power, he'd be expected to use it, and it scared him. "I don't want the power of the Bomb," he told his press secretary, George Reedy, on August 25, the day the Democratic convention opened in Atlantic City. "I just don't want these decisions that I'm being required to make." He was not going to accept the nomination, he said. The next day, depressed and tormented, Johnson reached for the only way out: he told Reedy to draft a statement to the Democratic National Committee: he would not accept the presidential nomination.[11]

He had witnessed his grandmother's agony in her last years, struck down by a crippling stroke, hardly able to speak, so paralyzed she could not even move her hands. Near the Oval Office was a large painting of Woodrow Wilson, who had spent the last two years of his presidency almost as helpless as Grandma. Dying by inches; what a fate. And he had already been warned. In 1955, at the age of forty-seven, he had suffered a near-fatal heart attack. Johnson did not expect to live to a ripe old age. None of the men in his immediate family seemed to have reached their three score years and ten. There was no reason to believe he'd be the exception. Vietnam might kill him or, worse yet, condemn him to the same fate as Grandma or Wilson. If he wanted to live out his last years in peace, he needed to get out of this place.[12]

There was only one person who could make him change his mind—Lady Bird. And that's just what she did. Lady Bird could reach parts of his psyche that other people did not even know existed. What exactly did she say? We don't know. But it seems that this was one of the hardest selling assignments she ever attempted. In the end, LBJ relented, and the supposition has to be that he did it to placate her, not that he was persuaded.[13]

The statement Reedy had written declared, "After 33 years in political life most men acquire enemies, as ships accumulate barnacles. The times require leadership about which there is no doubt and a voice that men of all parties, sections and color can follow. I have learned after trying very hard that I am not that voice or that leader." Reedy was told it would not be needed after all.

Instead, Johnson flew to Atlantic City. In his acceptance speech he referred only obliquely to Vietnam, but in terms that made victory seem inevitable: "I report tonight as President of the United States and as Commander in Chief on the strength of your country, and I tell you that it is greater than any adversary. I assure you that it is greater than the combined might of all nations in all the wars, in all the history of the planet. And I report that it is growing." Rapturous applause.[14]

The North Vietnamese knew that there had been no unprovoked attack on the *Maddox* on either August 2 or 4. When the Canadian diplomat, Glenn Seaborn, delivered Johnson's message for Ho Chi Minh, Ho refused to see him. Seaborn had to deliver it to the number two figure in the North Vietnamese government, Pham Van Dong. To Seaborn's alarm, Pham Van Dong was fizzing with anger, but he contained himself long enough for Seaborn to say what he had come to say, then bid him a frosty goodbye.[15]

Ho and Pham had already concluded that the Tonkin Gulf Resolution was passed on the basis of an edifice of lies so that Lyndon Johnson could begin a bombing offensive against North Vietnam. The lies were also designed to rally public opinion behind the president. And it was working. Opinion polls showed that 85 percent of Americans supported the Tonkin Gulf Resolution and a clear majority supported a bigger war.

The North Vietnamese ordered the Vietcong to start mounting attacks that would kill Americans, and one of its regular army regiments was sent down the Ho Chi Minh Trail—the first regiment of North Vietnamese troops to join the war in the South. There were at least another hundred regiments in the People's Army of North Vietnam (PAVN) that could go down the same trail. And then there was China.[16]

Following the 1954 Geneva Conference that had eased the French out of Southeast Asia, Mao turned his attention to industrializing China's economy. He sought to avoid doing anything provocative, anything that might lead to an American military intervention in Vietnam. An American army in Vietnam would inevitably drag China into yet another war. The North Vietnamese too wanted to keep their troops out of the South.

By 1962, however, that was becoming impossible for both Ho and

Mao. At a meeting of the Chinese Communist Party Central Committee in September, Zhou Enlai declared, "The center of the world revolution has moved from Moscow to Beijing. We must be brave and not shrink from our responsibilities." With that declaration, eight years of Chinese hesitation came to a close, but the North Vietnamese at that time had neither needed nor wanted anything but political and verbal support.

The Tonkin Gulf fabrications changed that. The day the resolution was passed, *The New York Times* carried the Chinese government's response: "The Democratic Republic of Vietnam and China are neighbors closely related to each other like the lips and the teeth . . . Aggression by the United States against the Democratic Republic of Vietnam is aggression against China. The Chinese people will not sit idly by . . ."[17]

They were not bluffing. Within weeks, they gave the North dozens of MiG fighters to help defend against the major bombing offensive they expected to be unleashed. They began sending in thousands of engineer troops to improve and keep the railroads running under air attack, and they began moving thousands of tons of military supplies across the border. That October, there were two other important developments: the Chinese set off their first nuclear explosion, several years before the CIA had forecast; and in Russia, Nikita Khrushchev was ousted. The two men who replaced him, Aleksey Kosygin and Leonid Brezhnev, swiftly junked Khrushchev's post–missile crisis policy of cooperation with the United States. They began offering weapons to Hanoi. They did not believe in wars of national liberation, but they did believe in persuading Ho not to move ever closer to Mao.

The world had just turned upside down. Before August 1964, the North Vietnamese were deeply apprehensive about being confronted by American power. The Americans meanwhile had been confident that they would eventually prevail in South Vietnam. Now it was the North Vietnamese leaders who were confident and an American president who writhed in the night, tormented by doubt.

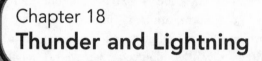

Chapter 18
Thunder and Lightning

LYNDON JOHNSON WAS A POLITICIAN, AND CAMPAIGNING ENER-
gized him. His mood revived. One day early in the campaign, holding
court aboard Air Force One, he remarked, "Look around the world.
Khrushchev's gone. Macmillan's gone. Adenauer's gone. Nehru's
gone." He paused, reluctant to drag the detested de Gaulle into the
proceedings. "Who's left—de Gaulle?" he said at last, in a tone that
dripped contempt. Johnson then thumped his chest, defiant: "I am
the king!" It was vintage LBJ. Lyndon was back.[1]

The theme of the campaign almost wrote itself. He would offer
himself to the country as the peace candidate. To the voters, Johnson
gave this pledge: "We seek no wider war." In the meantime, he told
McNamara to deny that any American soldiers were engaging in combat in South Vietnam, even though "advisers" were being killed and
wounded every month.[2]

As he portrayed himself as Washington's staunchest believer in
peace, Johnson was reconciling himself to the near certainty of a big-

ger war. At times, he indirectly revealed what was going through his mind. Addressing a crowd in New Hampshire at the end of September, he offered this equivocal assurance: *"For the moment,* I have not thought that we were ready to do the fighting for Asian boys . . . So we are not going north to drop bombs *at this stage of the game . . ."*[3] (emphasis added).

That kind of temporizing passed almost unnoticed. It was the gestures of restraint that grabbed the headlines. The president had ordered destroyers back into the Gulf of Tonkin on September 12, but when North Vietnamese patrol boats challenged them six days later, the destroyers quickly pulled back, and Johnson ordered them to stay out of the gulf indefinitely. On November 1, two days before the election, the Vietcong launched a mortar attack against the Bien Hoa air base, twelve miles north of Saigon. Their target was a squadron of obsolescent B-57 bombers recently deployed there as a signal to Hanoi that the United States would bomb the North if the Vietcong insurgency continued. Six B-57s were destroyed and five American servicemen were killed. No one in the White House or the Pentagon doubted—wrongly, as it turned out—that this was Hanoi's implicit reply to Johnson's implicit threat. Even so, he held back.[4]

Such circumspection would normally have cost a president heavily at the polls, but he had a dream opponent—Barry Goldwater, senator from Arizona, two-star general in the air force reserve, a man who was likely to show up in the Oval Office with his flight helmet tucked under his arm, fresh from flying something deadly and ready to talk tougher than thou. Goldwater's solution to the Vietnam problem was simple—bomb North Vietnam into submission, even if it meant using nuclear weapons. Goldwater subscribed to the myth that Eisenhower had secured an armistice in Korea by threatening to use nukes and by being ready, if the threat failed, to go ahead.

Taken all in all, Goldwater was almost self-destructive. No one had to teach Johnson about the art of grabbing an aggressive opponent as he rushed at you, upsetting his balance, then using the energy his charge had generated to throw the poor sap to the floor.

In his acceptance speech at the Republican convention, Goldwater had hurled himself at the Democratic opposition by proclaiming, "Extremism in the defense of liberty is no vice!" That set him up perfectly for Johnson and the liberal press, which wondered aloud if anyone with such extreme views could or should be trusted with the legendary "button" that would unleash America's nuclear might.

Near the end of the election campaign, a new kind of commercial appeared in major television markets. It showed a winsome blond moppet standing in a field. She holds a daisy and begins, as children will, to pluck the petals from it one by one, as if silently reciting to herself "He loves me . . . he loves me not . . ." And then the voice-over begins: "Ten . . . nine . . . eight . . ." As the last petal is plucked, the sky brightens, that innocent little face looks up, startled, and a mushroom cloud appears for an instant before the screen goes black.

Then the unmistakable voice of Lyndon B. Johnson intones with melodramatic solemnity, "These are the stakes! To make a world in which all of God's children can live, or go into the dark." He concluded by mangling some Auden, a poet he would never have read but one of his speechwriters had: "We must either love each other or die!" The commercial was shown only twice, but that was more than enough. It became the most famous commercial of 1964, and it ushered in the modern political attack ad.

Goldwater secured only 38 percent of the vote on November 3, the smallest ever racked up by any major party's presidential candidate. Late in life, Goldwater, like many another Cold War stalwart reaching the end of the line, renounced the half-baked belligerency of his salad days. Moving briskly away from the bellicose Republican right wing he had done so much to create, Goldwater in old age became a gay rights activist.

As Washington and the country congratulated Johnson on his election, the commander of the People's Army of North Vietnam, Vo Nguyen Giap, had already divined what Johnson's mandate would bring. Giap saw that the war would quickly move from the insurgency stage to become one of the biggest wars of the century. Bigger even than the struggle against the French.

Giap guessed that Johnson would put 600,000 men into South Vietnam and the ARVN would reach a strength of 500,000. The largest number of troops that the Vietcong and the PAVN could support in the South would total 300,000. They would therefore be outnumbered by roughly four to one. Given that ratio of forces on the battlefield, Giap concluded, North Vietnam and the Vietcong were certain to win the war.[5]

Why would anyone be so optimistic, knowing they would be out-numbered four to one? Because of China.

In 1958, looking for a shortcut to industrialization, Mao had pushed hundreds of millions of Chinese peasants into communes, where they could be controlled from Beijing. The communes were ex-pected to be self-sufficient, feeding themselves and becoming sites of industrial production. Mao's Great Leap Forward saw backyard blast furnaces in the deep countryside in a bizarre attempt to make China a major steel producer. By 1962 this harebrained venture had gener-ated a little steel and a lot of famine. Mao's experiment had failed, and China remained almost as far from being industrialized as it had been in 1949.

The failure of the Great Leap Forward had turned much of the Communist Party leadership against Mao, and if he was to remain in control, he needed a war. As John Kennedy was pushing "advisers" into South Vietnam in 1963, the Chinese and North Vietnamese leadership were holding meetings to discuss strategy and tactics. Mao assured the North Vietnamese that they had nothing to fear from aid-ing the insurgency in the South. If American troops crossed into the North, China would send an army into North Vietnam to drive them out. And this, he assured them, was an unconditional offer. China would fight with everything it had.

In December 1964 an agreement was signed to formalize that pledge: three hundred thousand Chinese troops would be deployed to North Vietnam. Mao also began moving hundreds of thousands more to the border, in case they too were needed. Any American invasion would be met by a North Vietnamese counteroffensive. If the PAVN counteroffensive failed to drive the Americans out, the Chinese would mount an even bigger counteroffensive of their own, with up to eight hundred thousand troops. And if that was not enough, there was a reserve force of three and a half million men available.[6]

Meanwhile, following the ouster of Nikita Khrushchev, in Octo-ber 1964, the new Soviet leadership of Leonid Brezhnev and Aleksey Kosygin rapidly abandoned Khrushchev's ultracautious policy toward the war in Vietnam. They promised to provide the North Vietnamese with heavy weapons such as tanks and surface-to-air missiles. Much of this matériel would be shipped by road and rail through China. The rest would come by sea to Sihanoukville in Cambodia and the North Vietnamese port of Haiphong. If the ports were shut down, the flow of arms and ammunition would continue by the overland routes. North Vietnam would not run out of arms or men so long as it had the will to endure. By 1965, Giap was sure he could see far into the future—and victory for his outnumbered forces.[7]

For Johnson, the future looked less promising. On January 2, 1965, a force of roughly a thousand Vietcong deployed near Binh Gia, forty miles southeast of Saigon. Here was a chance for some of the ARVN's best units to show what they had learned from their American advisers since the disastrous battle of Ap Bac two years earlier. As at Ap Bac, they had the advantages of heavy artillery support, tanks, armored personnel carriers, and helicopter gunships. They were virtually routed in the fight for Binh Gia. The Vietcong killed nearly two hundred South Vietnamese soldiers and wounded more than three hundred, and when the fighting ended, the Vietcong melted away, barely scathed. A few more battles like this one and the ARVN might simply collapse.

The Vietcong were not only growing in strength; they were turning into formidable infantry. The implications were obvious: if anyone was going to defeat them, it would have to be Americans. Yet McNamara, like Maxwell Taylor, remained reluctant to put an American army into South Vietnam. The only alternative, though, was a bombing campaign, and he had doubts about that too.

McNamara had already obtained from the Joint Chiefs a list of potential bombing targets in North Vietnam. There were only ninety-four in all, ranging from ammunition depots to airfields. The Chiefs wanted a campaign that would hit all ninety-four at once, thinking that would shake the North Vietnamese leadership. But as Johnson could see, once all ninety-four had been hit, what then? An invasion? Nukes? A bombing campaign could easily turn into a trap, not for the North Vietnamese, but for Lyndon Johnson.

"What is much more needed and would be more effective is . . . military strength on the ground," Johnson told Taylor midway between election and inauguration, "and I myself am ready to substantially increase the number of Americans in Vietnam."[8]

Whether it was to be bombing the North or putting troops in the

South, time was running out. Bundy and McNamara were advising him, "Our current policy can lead only to a disastrous defeat." Rusk agreed with them.[9]

Although McGeorge Bundy was never short of an opinion of South Vietnam—its people, its politics, its war, the workings of "the Oriental mind"—he had never set foot there. To improve his credentials and to judge the true situation, Bundy departed for Saigon in early February. On February 7 the Vietcong attacked an American helicopter and Special Forces base near Pleiku, in the Central Highlands. Eight American soldiers were killed; ten helicopters and small planes were destroyed.

As Johnson convened a meeting at the White House, Bundy was wiring reports from the field. THE STAKES IN VIETNAM ARE EXTREMELY HIGH . . . AND ANY NEGOTIATED U.S. WITHDRAWAL TODAY WOULD MEAN SURRENDER ON THE INSTALLMENT PLAN . . . THE SITUATION MAY BE AT A TURNING POINT . . . Bundy cabled. What was needed now was A POLICY OF SUSTAINED REPRISAL AGAINST NORTH VIETNAM . . . JUSTIFIED BY AND RELATED TO THE WHOLE VIET CONG CAMPAIGN OF VIOLENCE AND TERROR IN THE SOUTH . . . AND EVEN IF IT FAILS TO TURN THE TIDE—AS IT MAY—THE VALUE OF THE EFFORT SEEMS TO US TO EXCEED ITS COST.

What was the value of this effort? THERE WILL BE A SHARP AND IMMEDIATE INCREASE OF OPTIMISM IN THE SOUTH [AND] A SUBSTANTIAL DEPRESSING EFFECT UPON THE MORALE OF VIET CONG CADRES IN SOUTH VIETNAM.[10]

Johnson responded swiftly, authorizing air attacks against military targets in North Vietnam even though Aleksey Kosygin was on a visit there. It was a rash and impolitic act. Even if Kosygin was not killed or injured, bombing while he was in North Vietnam would be seen as a slight and was almost certain to make the Soviets align themselves ever more closely with the North Vietnamese.

The policy of sustained reprisals merged seamlessly with the theory of sustained graduated pressure. In mid-February, Johnson authorized a bombing campaign against North Vietnam called Rolling Thunder. Starting March 2, the air force and navy began working their way through the list of ninety-four targets.

Johnson liked to think that his gradual approach to the bombing was sure to concentrate enemy minds. He told Senator George

McGovern, "I'm going up old Ho Chi Minh's leg an inch at a time." Only a matter of time, then, before he had Ho by the balls.[11]

Meanwhile, the Canadian representative on the International Control Commission established to monitor the Geneva Accords was in Hanoi. He offered a different perspective, reporting to his government that the bombing had changed nothing and wasn't likely to achieve anything. The North Vietnamese government, he wrote, "considers it holds all the trump cards, will never negotiate under duress, and could in any event absorb all attacks. World opinion is sympathetic. Effectiveness of United States retaliation is limited. Order in South Vietnam is steadily crumbling."[12]

Mao's emissary to North Vietnam was quick to assure Ho that even if the bombing proved to be the prelude to an invasion, "We will do our best to provide you with whatever you need [and] we will send whatever troops that you request." Shortly after this, Ho went to see Mao: Would China be prepared to build and repair major roads between Hanoi and the Chinese border? Better infrastructure would ensure a steady flow of military supplies. The roads in need of repair were repaired; the roads that needed building were built.[13]

What the Chinese provided for the North Vietnamese army during the war covered a list of nearly seven hundred items, from arms and ammunition down to uniforms, toothpaste, rations, harmonicas, sewing kits, table-tennis balls, lard, mosquito nets, hammocks, and ink for fountain pens. Huge truck convoys carried Chinese products across the border. The Chinese also shipped weapons destined for the Vietcong through Cambodia.

Rolling Thunder was a strategic blunder on a par with the decision to try to send MacArthur across the 38th parallel in October 1950. Before Rolling Thunder, some Chinese leaders remained doubtful about getting directly involved in Vietnam. Mao had yet to convince them. In January 1965 the Chinese Military Commission had issued an order that any American aircraft intruding into Chinese airspace would not be attacked. When Johnson launched Rolling Thunder, Mao revoked the order: any American aircraft entering Chinese airspace would be shot down.

As American fighter-bombers worked over small, easily repaired targets across the North, the Chinese ambassador to Poland, Wang

Guoquan, informed the American ambassador to Poland, John M. Cabot, that the United States was certain to lose the war in Vietnam. In the meantime, he added, "The Chinese people will not sit idly by."

Giving point to Wang's assertions, more than a hundred thousand Chinese troops were deployed to North Vietnam, and Mao wanted the Americans to know it. They wore their uniforms and deliberately transmitted radio signals that not only revealed their presence but were certain to be intercepted by the American signals intelligence.[14]

In May, China's collective leadership endorsed publication of an article titled "Long Live the People's War." It called on the underdeveloped world to embrace protracted wars and insurgencies as a strategy for containing the United States and its allies. The revolution would take root in the countryside on a global scale, and one day the rich cities of America's allies would be isolated and eventually they would fall. That was the promise, anyway.

Johnson and his advisers were alarmed when they read "Long Live the People's War." This was a bellicose and expansionist China, they told one another, denouncing it as an Oriental *Mein Kampf*. They remained in a box labeled MUNICH, from which none of them ever managed to escape.

The point of the article was to persuade Third World leaders that the new Soviet leadership of Kosygin and Brezhnev were capitalist lackeys, a couple of dreary apparatchiks who had wasted no time selling out to the West. What the Chinese were offering was a call to all those nations oppressed and humiliated by colonialism and racism not to be seduced by the Russians, not to reach for the poisoned cup of peaceful coexistence. It was designed, too, to bind North Vietnam ever more tightly to China. By reasserting Mao's romantic belief in people's war, it meant that China's offer of support was genuine, unlike help from the treacherous Russians, white imperialists at heart.

At the end of May, the Chinese foreign minister, Chen Yi, held a lengthy conversation with the British chargé d'affaires in Beijing, Charles Richards. "He was courteous throughout and in good humor," Richards reported, although what Chen Yi had to say could not have been more serious. As one of Mao's oldest comrades, a veteran of the Long March, and one of the ablest generals on the Communist side during the civil war with the Guo Min Dang, he commanded respect.

The Americans needed to understand China's position on Vietnam, said Chen Yi.

First, China did not intend to provoke a war with the United States. Second, the Americans had to take what China said seriously. Third, if war did occur, China was ready to fight. And finally, unlike in Korea, the United States would not be allowed to fight a limited war this time. If China entered the war, it would become a war without limits. Anyone with a map could grasp the implications—a war across a two-thousand-mile front, from North Korea to northern India.

"Let the Americans, Japanese and Indians all come. China will suffer greatly. It might mean the destruction of China's industries but the sacrifice will be worth it to hold down and defeat the United States. China is not afraid of the American expansion of the war." If it turned into a huge fight to the death, "This would in fact provide the solution. The present situation can only be resolved in a major struggle. We are prepared. Let Johnson escalate if he wants. When he escalates to the level of China, then we'll take part . . . Peace will prevail in the end. In China's five thousand years there have been only some hundreds of years of war."

Behind Chen Yi's words stood a huge shadowy presence: the 4.5 million soldiers of the People's Liberation Army and a growing nuclear arsenal. He did not say so, but the Chinese government had just committed itself to developing thermonuclear weapons and long-range missiles that could reach the United States.

Even if a world war was avoided, said Chen Yi, the Americans still did not seem to realize what they faced in Vietnam. In 1962–63 the North Vietnamese had been of two minds about confronting the Americans in a major war. But being poor, they decided they had nothing to lose. Now they had fought them hard enough and often enough to learn the most important lesson of all: the Americans could be defeated.

The Vietnamese leadership had no illusions about the cost. Millions of Vietnamese would die in this war. Victory might not be achieved in this generation, but they expected to win it in the next one. The Americans were turning Vietnam into "a bottomless pit," and one day they would crawl out, exhausted and humbled, and go home.

China was not pushing the Vietnamese into this fight, Chen Yi added. If the Vietnamese wanted to resist the Americans, China felt that as a people who had themselves suffered from American aggression, they had a duty to help. "Aggression against Vietnam is aggression against China. China supports Vietnam unconditionally." It would be like the war in Korea. In 1950, less than a year after taking power, China's government had gone to the aid of the Koreans and saved North Korea. It was ready to fight the Americans again in defense of the Vietnamese.

Chen Yi mocked the idea that American ambassadors were pushing—over catered canapés and two-olive martinis at diplomatic receptions—that without the Soviets to back them, China would shrink from intervening in Vietnam. In Korea, he reminded the British chargé, it was Stalin who refused to send his armies into the peninsula to save North Korea. It was the Chinese who committed their troops. "China is still ready to fight fifteen years later." Chen Yi also referred indirectly to Mao's promise to the North Vietnamese to provide whatever military assistance was in China's gift. It was going to be a very long war.[15]

On June 4, Lyndon Johnson read the full account of Chen Yi's conversation with the British chargé. For Johnson and Rusk, McNamara and Bundy, the implications of what Mao had pledged to Ho could mean only one thing—defeat. The one thing China had in abundance was manpower. With China offering a secure base in its rear and a Chinese army ready to intervene, the North could never lose in a conventional war. For every soldier it lost, the North could have two more if Ho wanted, or even five. He only need ask.[16]

Several days later, Ambassador Cabot called on Ambassador Wangquan with a message from the president of the United States: Chen Yi's message had been received and understood. Cabot wanted to assure the government of China that the United States was not trying to destroy North Vietnam and had no intention of doing so at any time in the future. And it was definitely not going to attack China.[17]

What had begun as an attempt to contain China was suddenly a different war, one in which China would contain the United States. As with Korea, the war would last until the Chinese wanted it to end. By threatening to intervene and by making clear its backing for North Vietnam, China was imposing limits on what the United States could and could not do. The war would continue, certainly for years, probably for decades, possibly for generations until, ultimately, the United

States accepted defeat and withdrew from Southeast Asia. Or it might evolve into a world war. Your choice, said Mao, through Chen Yi.

Johnson was always demanding that his advisers bring him options regarding Vietnam. Bundy and McNamara had developed a way of satisfying that demand. They sent him a stream of memos that offered three options: get out with as much grace as we can manage; continue on the present course and fail; or bomb more heavily and send in more troops. They nearly always said they favored option three.

There was, however, something they kept out of their memos. It was option four, the choice of the Chiefs: nuke China. The question now was, how could Johnson avoid it?

Chapter 19
All-Out Limited War

DURING THE CUBAN MISSILE CRISIS, JOHN KENNEDY HAD FOUND himself under pressure from the Joint Chiefs that was almost equal to the pressure of dealing with Khrushchev. In the early 1960s the United States alone had the technology to launch an intercontinental ballistic missile carrying a nuclear warhead and remain confident that it would reach its target, up to five thousand miles distant, and detonate as planned. During the missile crisis, the Soviet Union had no more than four ICBMs, all of them unreliable. It took twenty-four hours to fuel them, and they had a habit of blowing up during the process. The United States also had several Polaris submarines on station at all times, able to strike targets fifteen hundred miles away, and the Soviets had no ability to track American nuclear submarines.

That was the main reason for putting Soviet missiles into Cuba—to achieve at a stroke something approximating equivalence in nuclear striking power. Khrushchev seems to have been motivated, too, by a romantic vision that drew upon his fast-retreating youth—a vision of Communist pioneers, heroic Cubans, and the charismatic Fidel.

The Joint Chiefs were a lot less romantic. They demanded that the missiles be removed. Had a deal not been struck at virtually the last moment, the Chiefs would have had their way: the United States would have invaded Cuba.

The confidence the military had in America's military supremacy was sky-high during the Kennedy administration. Under Eisenhower, they had created a force of land-based missiles, sea-based missiles, and long-range bombers capable of destroying the Soviet Union and China in a single, overwhelming preemptive strike, hitting 1,060 targets with 3,200 atomic and hydrogen bombs. That was Eisenhower's policy—"SAC must not allow the enemy to strike the first blow"—but he could hardly say so. Instead, he had Dulles tell the world that American nuclear policy was "massive retaliation," a better political stance than "first strike," and with any luck the true policy would never have to be implemented anyway.[1]

The bellicosity of the Chiefs during the Cuban missile crisis had a lasting effect on both Kennedy and McNamara. The estimated number of deaths from the planned preemptive strike was 275 million in the Soviet Union, China, and Eastern Europe. Millions more would die in countries that bordered the Soviet Union, China, and Eastern Europe. Virtually the entire population of friendly countries such as Finland and Austria would perish, while densely populated countries such as Japan and India would suffer grievous losses. The death toll in the nontarget countries would be at least 300 million people— including Americans—killed by high levels of radiation borne on the wind.[2]

Kennedy and McNamara gave a lot of thought and not a little effort to keeping the Chiefs on a tight rein. The attitude of the Chiefs infuriated Kennedy at times. They seemed to look down on, not up to, their commander in chief, as if to say, Another here today, gone tomorrow politician, while we remain. McNamara, absorbing much of Kennedy's suspicion of the JCS, carried it intact into the Johnson presidency.

First, though, McNamara had to convince Johnson to trust him. Johnson had lingering doubts about the loyalty of Kennedy's appointees. Each had to show that he was loyal to a living man, not a dead one. McNamara won over Johnson by abasing himself. To keep Congress and the country from realizing that expenditures on the war were going to rise dramatically in 1964, McNamara offered to issue a fictitious low estimate of what the Pentagon budget would be. Then, when the true figures became known nearly a year later, he would express astonishment and mystification. "He's a can-do fellow," declared Johnson.[3]

McNamara had also blunted one of the Chiefs' favorite weapons—the congressional appearance, featuring glittering stars, row upon row of silk ribbons, and some impressively jutting jaws. Each of the military services had its own powerful following on Capitol Hill. The Chiefs were practiced performers, and over the years they had embarrassed presidents and defense secretaries by providing testimony in which they overtly supported government policy as a theory, while undermining it as a practical reality. Under McNamara, none of the Chiefs could testify without his permission.

Kennedy had also installed Maxwell Taylor, the retired former chairman of the Joint Chiefs, as his military adviser. Johnson found him useful in the same way that Kennedy had: wily shepherd to a troublesome flock. With Taylor standing between the Chiefs and the president, their influence was diminished, and Taylor installed one of his protégés, Earle "Bus" Wheeler, to be the chairman of the JCS, and yet another protégé, Harold K. Johnson, to be the new army chief of staff.

The Chiefs also contributed to their increasing irrelevance with parochial squabbles over what was needed in Vietnam. The navy recommended more riverine patrols, more aircraft carriers offshore, more naval aviation overhead. The marine commandant, Wallace Greene, said no, the key to success was to get a lot of marines in there. Curtis LeMay, a World War II legend and the creator of Strategic Air Command (SAC), dismissed the navy and the Marine Corps arguments and said that bombing the North was the key to success. Only Harold Johnson held back. Like his mentor, Maxwell Taylor, Johnson was reluctant to see an American army pushed into Vietnam.

The one point the Chiefs agreed on was that graduated pressure was no way to fight a war, but a good way to lose one. In December 1964, with the president elected and major decisions sure to come following the inauguration, they leaked their idea of how the war should be fought to Hanson W. Baldwin, esteemed military correspondent of *The New York Times*.

The United States should either get in to win or get out of Vietnam, they argued, and the only way to win a war was to use every weapon at the nation's disposal. That meant a massive bombing campaign, one that might mean destruction of the dikes and the death by drowning of hundreds of thousands of North Vietnamese peasants. At some point, there would probably be an invasion of the North. And if the Chinese dared to intervene, there would be mushroom clouds on the horizon. One way or another, the United States had to break the will of the enemy and force him to his knees.[4]

What they got instead was Rolling Thunder, and LBJ no more expected it to stop the North Vietnamese after it started than he did before it began. He felt trapped. Maybe a ground war, a big one, was the answer? Johnson had Harold Johnson come to the White House. "You generals have all been educated at taxpayers' expense, and you're not giving me any solutions for this damn little pissant country. Now I don't need ten generals to come in here ten times and tell me to bomb." The general was to go to Vietnam and find a better way to fight the war. He pointed at Harold Johnson's beribboned chest: "You get things bubbling, General."[5]

It all seemed so hopeless. While General Johnson was out looking for answers in the jungles and mountains of South Vietnam, the president was close to despair. "I can't get out. I can't finish with what I've got. So what the hell do I do?" he asked Lady Bird. She didn't know either.[6]

If he had so little faith in Rolling Thunder, why then had he approved it? Johnson blamed it on Curtis LeMay. "That damn cigar-smoking Curtis LeMay is pushing me and I gotta let him know that I'm as tough as he is," Johnson told his staff. LeMay was coming up for retirement in February 1965, but Johnson took no comfort from that. He could easily imagine LeMay capitalizing on his fame to denounce the president and demand an all-out, unlimited war. In an attempt to get him out of the country, LBJ offered to make LeMay an ambassador to somewhere pleasant. LeMay wasn't interested. He was going to write his memoirs and promote his own strategy.[7]

While LeMay labored on the memoirs, Jiang Jieshi advised Johnson that the United States could never win in Vietnam. That was the wrong war, said Jiang. The real enemy was China, and the United States should bomb its nuclear plants. Madame Jiang came to the United States that summer to make the same argument publicly.[8]

And L. Mendel Rivers, the chairman of the House Armed Services Committee, gave a press conference in order to wonder aloud, "Should we use our atomic power to wipe out Red China's atomic capability? We must get ready to do this very thing." On the floor of the House, Rivers offered no word of comfort to an embattled commander in chief. "Even if we win the war in South Vietnam, I cannot help thinking that we are merely postponing the final victory of Red China—unless the Nation is prepared to risk the possible consequences of destroying her nuclear capability."[9]

LeMay probably inspired the interventions of the Gitmo (the generalissimo, Jiang), the Dragon Lady (Madame Jiang), and Rivers, the navy's favorite congressman (one day to have an aircraft carrier named in his honor), and when LeMay's memoirs were published later that year, in November 1965, they offered a plan for victory in Vietnam, one he had presumably offered to LBJ before retiring. The president should give the North Vietnamese a simple choice: "Stop the aggression or we're going to bomb you into the Stone Age." He also had a clear idea of how to deal with China, the root of the problem. "China has the bomb," said LeMay, "and some schools of thinking don't rule out the destruction of Chinese military potential before the situation grows worse than it is today. It's bad enough now."[10]

By this time, Johnson had the military so firmly under control that he had little difficulty rejecting demands for taking the war into China. Even so, that did not mean he was a good commander in chief, or even an effective one. He was too impulsive and too emotional. Worse yet, he was fighting a war as if he were still the Senate majority leader. Discussions of strategy and tactics, of force levels and operational planning, were approached as if they were difficult pieces of new legislation facing a rough passage through a Senate committee and then on the Senate floor. Johnson paid more attention to getting support for his war policy than to whether it made sense.

Nor was there any structure that would pull all the pieces together. There was no unified command in South Vietnam. The air force fought a bombing and close air support war; the navy fought a war upon and from the waters; the army fought a ground war; the CIA fought an intelligence war. There was also what was known as "the other war," the struggle to win for Saigon the hearts and minds of the peasants who made up at least 80 percent of South Vietnam's population. No individual or agency was created to pull the various military and political efforts into a coherent design. The ultimate expression of the lack of central direction was the commander in chief's staying up late at night to pick a small bridge ten thousand miles away to be bombed.

Neither Johnson nor the bombing enthusiasts, such as McGeorge Bundy, expected Rolling Thunder to save South Vietnam. Only heavy bombing of the North combined with large numbers of troops deployed to the South would make any difference, they believed. In April there were 33,000 American soldiers in South Vietnam, with 18,000 more on their way.

How much advice can 51,000 people give? Questions from Congress and the press were becoming sharper, and campuses were becoming restive. To stem the rising tide of doubt, Johnson delivered a speech at Johns Hopkins that month. In it, he held out the prospect of American help with a rural electrification project on the Mekong River that would dwarf the Tennessee Valley Authority, bringing prosperity to the people of Southeast Asia. He also declared that he was ready for "unconditional discussions" with North Vietnam. As Marine One took him back to the South Lawn, Johnson was in an expansive mood. "Old Ho can't turn me down," he said.[11]

The hawks out of uniform—led by Bundy and Rusk—feared that whatever cheering effect the bombing might have had in South Vietnam, that had already passed. South Vietnam was once again close to collapse. Negotiating now would be negotiating from weakness, they told one another, and Johnson. "Unconditional discussions" were out of the question.

Meanwhile, the secretary general of the UN, U Thant, kept trying to get negotiations started. Every peace initiative that U Thant offered was welcomed publicly by his old acquaintance Ho Chi Minh. And all of these efforts were spurned privately by Lyndon Johnson. He would negotiate only when the United States held the upper hand. Meanwhile, whatever peace initiatives the administration mounted would be crafted not to shape what the Commies were thinking in Hanoi, but what people were thinking in Congress, in the American press, and in American living rooms.[12]

Rolling Thunder was originally intended to last sixty days. It was to be an experiment in pain. On May 10 Johnson announced a temporary halt to the bombing. Would the North Vietnamese see sense now? Did they want to be hurt some more? Johnson was unwittingly revealing his entire hand: bomb, pause, bomb, pause, bomb, pause, ad infinitum until the North quit. If that was the strategy, North Vietnam could defeat it simply by holding fast. They knew it, the Russians knew it, and the Chinese knew it. Yet no one in the White House, the State Department, or the Pentagon seemed to know it.

Hanoi derided the pause as "a worn-out trick of deceit and threats." The bombing resumed after eight days, and this time, Johnson was resolved, it would not be limited to sixty days. If Ho was interested in another pause, he'd have to offer something in return.

It was shortly after the bombing resumed that Chen Yi had his long, frank conversation with the British chargé in Beijing, setting limits on what Johnson could do in Vietnam. There had been roughly two schools of thought up to now: those who argued, as Rusk and McNamara did, that the war in the South could be won only in the South, and those, like Bundy and LeMay, who said it could be won only by attacking the North.

It hardly mattered now which argument was right. Johnson was going to have to seek victory in the South. There could be no invasion of the North and no attempt to bomb it into the Stone Age. By early July, Johnson was committed to raising the total number of troops to 179,000, including the 1st Cavalry, the "air-mobile division." In April the proclaimed mission had moved from advice to base security. It now gravitated upward to search and destroy.

On July 20, 1965, McNamara sent a long memorandum to Johnson on the need to call up 235,000 members of the reserve and the National Guard and an increase in the regular forces of 375,000 men. These extra troops would help to restore the army's strategic reserve while providing General William Westmoreland, the army commander in Vietnam, with the large infusion of troops he was requesting. The purpose was to persuade the North Vietnamese and the Vietcong that "the odds are against their winning . . . if possible without causing the war to expand into one with China."

McNamara also advised Johnson to tell the country what was happening, but Johnson chose not to do so. He did not have to level with

Congress, he told Rusk—not while he was commander in chief and not while he had the Tonkin Gulf Resolution. Dramatic as the planned buildup in troops was going to be, it still would not be enough. The limited war was becoming what William Bundy wryly termed "all-out, limited war."[13]

After reading the warning from Chen Yi only six or seven weeks earlier, McNamara could have been under no illusion that the North Vietnamese were expecting to win the war that year, or even in that decade. The Chinese and the North Vietnamese would know that every soldier sent to Vietnam in 1965 would be long gone by 1975, so why would they be impressed by this show of resolution? Johnson would have retired to Texas by then, and McNamara might be back in Detroit extolling the merits of new model Fords.

A sensible person might also have thought that risking war with China was something to be avoided, not accepted. McNamara was evidently prepared to go to war with China, although he must have realized that such a war was likely to drag in the Russians and at some point would probably go nuclear. He did not even want Johnson to talk to the Chinese, advising him to open a dialogue with Moscow and "perhaps the VC," but not China.

McNamara had a chart in his office that showed a line for American and ARVN troops deployed and another line for enemy dead, weapons captured, and prisoners taken. When the two lines crossed, he confidently told visitors, the war would have reached the "crossover point." That was the moment when the United States would start to win.

McNamara's resistance to common sense amounted to denial, but there was a lot of that during the Vietnam War. China was as important to North Vietnam as the Soviet Union was, in some respects even more so. Why did McNamara and others refuse to face up to that not insignificant fact? Probably because admitting the truth about China meant admitting eventual defeat.[14]

All the same, Johnson could not permanently avoid the fact that South Vietnam was only a pawn in a much bigger struggle, the kind of titanic clash on which the fate of humanity turns. There was only one logical strategy, and that was to attack China. Johnson and Rusk, McNamara and Bundy did not so much flee from this conclusion as run around in ever-diminishing circles. Anything, rather than acknowledge that if they did not get the China part of the equation right, they would get none of it right.

Clark Clifford tried to counter the torrent of hit-'em-again-harder advice that Johnson was getting from McNamara, Bundy, and Rusk. Clifford sent a memorandum that said that the problem in Vietnam was "guerrilla rather than positional warfare. The fact that this may mean the VC cannot achieve a military victory offers small comfort; neither we nor the VC have yet demonstrated that we can win this kind of war." The only way to win was by applying military pressure in tandem with a political program, and of the two, the political side of the war was probably the more important.

Clifford was right, in a broad sense, but he still could not bring himself to acknowledge that the social revolution currently under way within South Vietnam was for the Vietnamese and only the Vietnamese to resolve. It was not for Americans to determine, any more than the social revolution taking place across the Confederacy during the Civil War had been for the British or French to resolve.

Had Clifford taken a close look at the various struggles currently under way in South Vietnam—the civil war, the national liberation war, the social revolutionary war, the proxy war spawned from the Cold War—he might have seen that the United States could not win any of them. The only choice was between leaving and being kicked out.[15]

As Johnson began pouring troops into South Vietnam, Mao's anger was rising in proportion. He had no doubt that the Americans were determined to contain China by maintaining their protectorate in South Vietnam at almost any cost. If the current efforts failed, what then—an air offensive against China's fragile and rudimentary industrial base?

It was these fears of an American air offensive that finally put China on the road to industrialization. In July 1965 Mao ordered the opening of what he called the "Third Front" in the struggle against the United States. He planned to spread major industrial plants away from the coastal cities where most of them were concentrated. Each factory had to create a twin, deep in the interior. At the province level, small plants had to create a twin somewhere else in the same province. Every province would also be expected to develop its own arms industry, turning out assault rifles, machine guns, mortars and small artillery pieces, bullets, and shells. China's military industrialization would be both wide and deep, and it helps to explain why many Chinese factories are operated to this day by the People's Liberation Army.[16]

The results of the Third Front are to be seen now in every town and city across the broad republic. Take a typical Saturday for the Jones family of Anytown, U.S.A. They set off early for their nearest IKEA, in a city eighty miles away. When they finally reach the store, they buy Bleppo lamps for their teenage daughter's bedroom, a Sörprid computer table for Mr. Jones's home office, a Kragskadik bunk bed for their twin sons aged nine, and a set of fashionable glass plates that look as if they are melting. Mrs. Jones can hardly wait to use them, anticipating praise from the design-conscious friends she is thinking of having for dinner. Everything that she and Mr. Jones have bought has a small sticker on it that reads MADE IN CHINA.

They stop at Sears on the way home to buy some "Made in China" underwear for the twins and a weed whacker for Mr. Jones. It too was made in China. And when they finally get home, Mr. Jones has his first chance of the day to read the newspaper. "Gee, Marge," he says, looking up, "it says here the Chinese are going to start making automobiles for export to the U.S. Do you think we should get our names down for one? You just know there's going to be a feeding frenzy from the get-go." Vietnam was only one triumph of Mao's Third Front. The other is the conquest of American homes, businesses, and T-bills.

Johnson, meanwhile, continued to escalate, but in graduated steps, mindful that he might stumble over a trip wire that could bring the Chinese into the war as combatants. With an army of four and a half million men available to Mao and the example of the Korean War to consider, Johnson had little choice. There was a positive side, though: by making war piecemeal, it was easier to disguise what he was doing from Congress and the public.

For the North Vietnamese, Johnson's gradualism was as good as being given an extra army. It made it easier for them to absorb the bombing. No matter how heavy it became, there were opportunities to manage the consequences. There was also a growing corps of Western and non-Western journalists in North Vietnam. They wrote about the civilians being killed by the bombing; their television cameras recorded the shattered homes, the weeping mothers, the dead children. These accounts rarely appeared in the American press or on American television, yet the rest of the world saw them. Every plea Johnson made to other countries to send troops to South Vietnam bumped up against the inevitable anger of the civilized world at the sight of the strongest citizen on the planet wreaking death and destruction on one of the weakest.

By December 1965, Johnson and McNamara were poised for yet another major escalation of the war. It might be a good idea, McNamara reasoned, to have a bombing pause first. A pause that would "lay a foundation in the minds of the American public and world opinion . . . for an enlarged phase of the war." It was, that is, a ploy, or—as they might say in Hanoi—"deceit and threats" all over again.[17]

In his bigger-is-better way, Johnson decided to magnify McNamara's proposal. He turned it into a global theater of peace seeking. Hubert Humphrey, Averell Harriman, and other well-known reasonable people were dispatched to thirty-four world capitals to announce that the president was a man of peace, looking eagerly for a sign of some kind from Ho Chi Minh that serious negotiations could finally begin.

Ho had already laid down four conditions for talks. Now Johnson laid down fourteen conditions of his own. With a total of eighteen conditions to be resolved before talks could begin, it could hardly be said that the two parties were seriously interested in peace. Both were grandstanding, and both knew it.

The North Vietnamese, however, had a good idea of where all this bombing and pausing, escalating and menacing would eventually lead. The Chinese Communists had developed a strategy during their war with the Nationalists of "fighting while talking, talking while fighting." They had carried that into Korea, hence the two years of talks and continued fighting up to the moment the armistice was signed, ignoring the fulmination from American generals and politicians at the time, who denounced the continuing fighting as a proof of insincerity. Whenever the talking stage was reached, the North Vietnamese intended to follow the same script, fighting while talking.

Johnson and McNamara had their own idea of the endgame: it would be reached by force, by inflicting pain, at a high political cost. The North Vietnamese knew it would be reached by politics, by absorbing pain, at a high military cost.

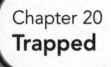

Chapter 20
Trapped

LYNDON JOHNSON FELT ALMOST FROM HIS FIRST DAY AS PRESIDENT
that John Kennedy had left him with a poisoned chalice, and there
were reminders of the dead president almost wherever he looked—in
half the faces around the cabinet table, in the bronze bust of JFK presiding over the Cabinet Room, in the Harvard and Boston accents of
the presidential staff, and in the inscription that Jacqueline Kennedy
had ordered cut into the marble of the mantel in the president's bedroom: "Occupied by John Fitzgerald Kennedy during his Two Years,
Ten Months and Two days as President of the United States. Jan. 20,
1961–Nov. 22, 1963." And there was more, much more.

Johnson was doubly oppressed, with Jack Kennedy being both absent and present, dead and alive. There may have been moments
when Johnson felt as if he were living in the Kennedy White House,
with Jack not across the river in Arlington Cemetery, but up at Hyan-
nis on vacation with his lively family and about to arrive back anytime
and ask him what he thought he was doing sitting at Benjamin Harri-
son's oak desk in the Oval Office.[1]

The bitter cup Johnson drank from could kill him, literally, he sometimes feared. It was already destroying the highest ambition he had ever cultivated during a lifetime in politics—to build a new society, as Roosevelt had done, and this one would be a truly great society, where poverty would be abolished, racism defeated, and justice truly available to all. Instead, after two years he had his hands full with what he called "that bitch of a war."

Part of the unfairness in Johnson's life was that Kennedy could charm the nation on television, while he looked like the jowly embodiment of the adage that says politics is showbiz for the ugly. His heavy Texas accent screamed "redneck," although he was anything but. He could tell dirty jokes by the hour, yet he lacked the spontaneous wit of a JFK, someone with a mind as sharp as broken glass. Compared with JFK, Johnson walked, dressed, looked, and sounded like Jubilation T. Cornpone. As the war dragged on, he aged rapidly, making him more than ever yesterday's man. What loyalty he commanded was more for the office than it would ever be for himself.

Although Johnson had above-average intelligence, he possessed limited intellectual skills, much like Truman. He was not well-read or knowledgeable about anything outside cattle and politics. Unlike Truman, Johnson read few books. His reading was limited to newspapers and government documents. Well aware of his limitations, both physical and intellectual, he could never forget that he would always excite pity and scorn among what he called "the Harvards"—people he dreaded, because the Harvards write history. And although the presidency had been the driving ambition of his life, once there, he fell prey to the imposter syndrome, which rises like vapor from tall, greasy poles.

Johnson told himself, told his advisers, told his critics—maybe even told Lady Bird—that he was not really to blame for the huge, suppurating wound that was Vietnam. This wasn't Johnson's war, he insisted, it was Jack's. He was only doing what Jack Kennedy would have done.

In truth, though, LBJ did not know what Kennedy would have done. Johnson did not even know what Kennedy was thinking. McNamara, who did have access to Kennedy's mind, never defended Johnson's actions as being what Kennedy would have done. And many years later, in a documentary film about his time as secretary of defense, McNamara would say exactly the opposite: a different president would have meant a different war. He said this in a tone that implied a smaller war and maybe, at some point, no war at all.[2]

Like Truman and Lincoln and most war presidents, Johnson sought solace and support wherever he might find it, and he tried to off-load as much of the burden as he could onto the Almighty. He went to church, almost any church would do, every Sunday without being prodded. "I would estimate that I say a prayer about a dozen times a day," he told Jim Bishop, who was writing a flattering account of the president.[3]

And he did not simply speak to God. Johnson assured the Austrian ambassador, Ernst Lemberger, that in his most troubled moments he received visits from the Holy Ghost. "He comes and speaks to me about two in the morning," he assured the startled Lemberger, "when I have to give the word to the boys, and I get the word from God whether to bomb or not."[4]

Like JFK, Johnson had come to accept that the primary objective of the war was containing China. Blocking the unification of Vietnam by the VC and the People's Army of North Vietnam was the secondary objective. He couldn't go to war with China, any more than Kennedy could have done, but he had to do something. "There is nothing on the Asian mainland except United States forces, to stop the Chinese from overwhelming all of it," he told Bishop and others. Yet even as he waged a war, he wasn't sure it could ever be won.[5]

That realization was part of his near-physical agony. Johnson took casualty figures personally. Both of his sons-in-law served in Vietnam, and one of them, Charles Robb, was wounded. Casualty figures usually came in from Saigon in the early hours. Johnson would call down to the Situation Room and ask for them. If they were unusually bad, his staff could read it in his face in the morning.[6]

What probably made them seem unbearable at times was the feeling that these deaths, lost limbs, shattered bodies, and ruined lives were all for nothing. The burden of guilt must have been crushing. No wonder he was depressed much of the time. And how does any commander in chief convince his countrymen to fight a war that in his heart he suspects is unwinnable? Truman was the first to face this question. Johnson would not be the last.

The formula Truman had devised for ending the Korean War after the Chinese came in was to assure the country, and the Chinese, that victory was not his aim. All he wanted was a truce. Johnson went for something that he thought was similar, and Rusk only encouraged him. Rusk had persuaded himself early on that Vietnam was just a replay of Korea and would end the same way. However, Rusk had never understood the Korean War or the Chinese challenge, although he considered himself an authority on both. Nor did he understand Vietnam.

For Mao, the establishment of a Communist government in a unified Vietnam was only the means to a larger end. Mao was a nationalist as well as a Communist. That was why Stalin had never trusted him and one reason why the Sino-Soviet split was inevitable. The larger goal was to restore China to its historic position as the richest and most advanced country on Earth. By talking and thinking in nothing but Cold War clichés, Rusk et al. could only get China wrong. Mao was probably thrilled at American incomprehension, close student that he was of Suntzu's *The Art of War*, which offers this advice: "He who knows himself and knows his enemy, will win every battle. He who knows himself but not his enemy will lose as many battles as he wins. And he who knows neither himself nor his enemy will lose every battle."[7]

That was why, as long as Johnson was in the White House, the Chinese invariably refused to countenance peace talks between Washington and Hanoi. They also ruled out a Russian attempt to organize an international conference. The British suggested a conference on Cambodia, but the real intention was to bring American and North Vietnamese diplomats into direct, personal contact. The Chinese blocked it. The Indian government proposed organizing a ceasefire along the 17th parallel, which would be monitored by a military force from nonaligned Third World nations. When the French pushed for neutralization as the solution, the Chinese ruled that out too. Ghana, Poland, and other countries attempted in one way or another to get talks started, and the Chinese shot down every one. Only one outcome was acceptable to Mao—victory. The victory of People's War.

Meanwhile, Johnson clung to the belief that by not demanding a North Vietnamese surrender, he could be another Truman. Like Harry, he just wanted the bastards to stop what they were doing. To him, as to Rusk and Bundy, this was as reasonable a demand as any country at war could make. It did not occur to him or to them that it was tantamount to demanding an admission of defeat by the North Vietnamese and the Chinese. This was not Korea, where the North Korean state was brought to the brink of extinction. In Vietnam, the North was sure to survive, and the South was not.

The failure of LBJ and his principal advisers to think themselves into the mind of the enemy was probably inevitable, given what they brought to the war. They were ideologues in an ideological age. Descriptions of the West by Communist ideologues during the Cold War contained diatribes that were so naive and absurd they could make a person feel sorry for anyone who really believed such guff. Denunciations of Western people as "lackeys of monopoly capitalism" and "the running dogs of American imperialism," and of Western countries as "paper tigers" could raise a smile: no one took them seriously. It worked the other way too. Ignorance about the Communist world among American cold warriors made a mockery of the presumed sophistication conferred by an Ivy League education and frequent-flier miles.

There was also the mental universe created by too much time attacking the problem and not enough time thinking about it: the sixteen-hour days that revolved around writing memos on Vietnam, telephone conversations about Vietnam, meetings about Vietnam, phone calls and telegrams to and from Vietnam, interviews with journalists about Vietnam, meals where Vietnam was the main if not the only topic of conversation, and on and on and on, seven days a week. In the first eighteen months of Johnson's presidency, Vietnam was almost a side issue, but after Rolling Thunder began, it drove Johnson and his principal advisers into increasingly subjective states. The objective world faded away. People in subjective states are prey to hallucinations. However much they might know, their contact with reality grows weaker.

By 1966, Johnson felt well and truly trapped, telling Rusk and McNamara in January that year, "I am not happy about Vietnam, but we cannot run out. We have to resume the bombing." He could not stop the bombing, because doing so might make him look weak. But the fact that Johnson had got himself into a position where he could not stop the bombing meant that he *was* weak. The North Vietnamese and the Chinese had probably figured that out.[8]

Johnson would have felt even unhappier had he known McNamara's true state of mind these days. The secretary of defense despaired that escalation had become the president's preferred response to the Vietnam challenge, and at a Georgetown dinner party he had spelled out what he thought Johnson should be aiming for: "withdrawal with honor." Even so, he did not tell the president that. Nor could McNamara bring himself to see that the real choices were not between bombing and withdrawal, but between staying and having a disaster, or leaving and having a disaster. There was no budget ticket out of Vietnam, and talking up honor wouldn't provide one.[9]

Meanwhile, Rolling Thunder was moving toward its first anniversary with no agreed military objective that the air force was expected to deliver. Johnson left the Joint Chiefs to decide what the objective should be. The principal object became interdiction of supply routes, to reduce the flow of men and supplies from North to South. The bombing had an impact on the flow, but more than enough got through for the war in the South to continue. Flow reduction was not even attrition. It amounted to an implied confession of bewilderment. Dropping millions of tons of bombs would not change that.[10]

Curtis LeMay had wanted to bomb the North Vietnamese "back into the Stone Age," but that would have meant bombing major population centers. His successor, John P. McConnell, was LeMay's protégé. LeMay gone, his thinking lingered. "I seem to be the only one that's afraid they'll hit a hospital or a school or something," Johnson complained.[11]

As a result, he was slow to sanction bombing of Hanoi and Haiphong, but that would come in time. For now, he created a bombing-free zone twenty miles deep along the Chinese border. Yet he allowed the CIA and the air force to organize overflights by U-2s flown by Chinese Nationalist pilots. After four were shot down, the U-2 flights stopped.[12]

In an anachronistic reprise of its history, the air force revisited an old obsession: let's bomb their oil. In February 1966 Walt Rostow succeeded McGeorge Bundy, who had never secured Johnson's trust, despite being truly, deeply, and madly obsequious. Bundy not only wanted to *be* a powerful figure—it mattered that he be *seen* as a powerful figure. Craving attention, he drew four aces in June 1965 with a

Time magazine cover story that enthused over his pedigree, his brilliance, and his closeness to John Kennedy. Little wonder that the cover portrait showed Bundy looking highly pleased with himself. That kind of national publicity for a member of his staff was sure to annoy the pathologically insecure Johnson.

It was about this same time that Bundy had second thoughts about Rolling Thunder. With Chen Yi threatening Chinese intervention, and escalation virtually built into Rolling Thunder, Bundy now decided that the bombing campaign was "rash to the point of folly." Yet he also urged Johnson to make big threats and not shrink from the consequences, even if that meant war with China. What kind of national security adviser was this? A confused one, evidently.[13]

The rupture came when Bundy went on television to debate the war with Hans Morgenthau, a professor of international relations at the University of Chicago. Morgenthau was probably the most renowned American exponent of realpolitik. When it came to Vietnam, though, he turned out to be squishy. The war is all wrong and cannot be won, Morgenthau argued. Even so, he could not bring himself to call for a withdrawal. Fear of seeming unpatriotic in fact proved more powerful than realpolitik in theory. Bundy butchered him kosher-style—cut his throat, then watched him bleed to death.

Johnson couldn't care less. He did not want anybody debating Vietnam. He wanted total, unquestioning support from his advisers. What was a debate going to do, apart from announcing that there were people who disagreed with the policy? Having risked the presidential ire, Bundy got it in spades. What LBJ needed, what the war needed, Johnson had no doubt, were true believers.

Johnson chose Walt Whitman Rostow, Bundy's deputy, to succeed him. "I'm getting Walt Rostow as my intellectual," Johnson told Robert Kennedy. "He's not your intellectual. He's not Bundy's intellectual. He's going to be my goddamned intellectual and I'm going to have him by the short hairs. We're not going to have another Bundy around here."[14]

Rostow was another Rhodes scholar, one whose scholarly field was economic history. His best-known work, *The Stages of Economic Growth*, had a subtitle that indicated where Rostow saw himself in the pantheon of major economic and social thinkers. It was *A Non-*

Communist Manifesto. A collection of development truisms and un-examined assumptions, his work is now only a curiosity, but the *Communist Manifesto* still manages to attract deluded adherents.

When Rostow took over from Bundy, the Joint Chiefs were pressing Johnson and McNamara to devise a policy that was flexible enough to allow airpower to "deter Communist China from direct intervention" while unleashing Rolling Thunder attacks across nearly all of North Vietnam. With the Chinese warning that they were prepared to enter the war, the old appetite for attacking China had faded. The Chiefs finally accepted containment as enough in itself, much as they had grudgingly accepted containment of Russia.[15]

In Rostow, they had one of their own, a national security adviser whose faith in bombing never wavered. During World War II he was one of the civilians who advised on target selection for the Eighth Air Force, which was trying to bring the German war economy to its knees. Guided by Rostow and others, Carl "Toohy" Spaatz, the general commanding American air operations in Europe, became convinced he could do it by attacking oil refineries and storage facilities.

Neither Rostow nor Spaatz seemed to notice that the anti-oil offensive failed not once, but twice. The heart of the German war economy wasn't oil. It was brown coal from Silesia. Bombing German oil had no impact on the production of tanks or planes, artillery or ammunition. The output of war matériel increased remorselessly until December 1944, when bombing was switched to the canals and railroads that moved the brown coal.[16]

In *The Stages of Economic Growth*, Rostow asserted that despite Soviet military power, "nationalism in Eastern Europe cannot be defeated." Yet he advised Johnson that nationalism could be defeated in Vietnam by bombing.[17]

In January 1966, oil became *the* target. For eight months, small refineries and storage areas were pounded unmercifully. Meanwhile, Soviet oil was moved across the Chinese border by rail and at night, off-loaded in the darkness, and hidden in small, camouflaged storage sites all over the country.

Meanwhile, dissent was growing in the Senate. Vance Hartke, a Democratic senator from Indiana, wrote the president a letter asking him to stop the bombing and seek a peaceful end to the war. Fourteen other senators signed Hartke's letter. Johnson called Hartke "prick," and had people holding federal jobs on the senator's recommendation fired. If the intent was to cow other senators, it didn't work.[18]

By the spring of 1966 there were at least twenty-two antiwar senators, drawn from both parties. They pushed for and got televised hearings into the conduct of the war. Shortly before the first hearings opened, Johnson called Rusk. "I don't want any other human to know this," he said, "but I fairly think I would like to go out to Honolulu." His trip was ostensibly to spend three days conferring with the senior figures fighting the war, but the conference was scheduled to begin only hours before the hearings began and to overshadow them.[19]

It also gave Johnson the chance to meet with Nguyen Cao Ky, one of the two generals currently in power in Saigon. The other was Nguyen Van Thieu. Ky was a youthful, flamboyant airman, with a huge black mustache and a lavender silk scarf. He had been trained to fly by the French, and trained to fly Skyhawk fighter-bombers by the Americans. In his brashness, he was more Western than Vietnamese, and the Thieu-Ky partnership had a slightly comic, slightly tragic character, something to both laugh at and fear. A Vietnamese Odd Couple in command of a country at war. Still, Ky assured journalists that he had a well-known political hero to guide him in his new role—Adolf Hitler.[20]

With his military options limited, Johnson more than ever wanted to prosecute "the other war"—the pacification program. "Pacification" sounded good. Who could be opposed to pacification? Although it meant sinking wells and building schools and organizing villagers to defend their villages, the program was also cynically manipulated by the Saigon government to make millions of peasants little more than prisoners in their own homes. After the conference ended, Johnson was able to reassure his countrymen, "We shall fight the battle against aggression in Vietnam and we shall prevail."

The up escalator continued to push troops into South Vietnam. In April, Westmoreland called for another two hundred thousand men, and the Chiefs pressed Johnson to make the war bigger: invade Laos and Cambodia, they told him, and we might still be able to win this one. They also wanted him to let them mine North Vietnam's ports and accept the risk of sinking Russian ships and killing Russian seamen. Johnson refused the mining, but he agreed to the extra two hundred thousand men for Westmoreland.

He also finally allowed air attacks on fighter airfields in the North, even though there was a risk of dogfights that would see North Vietnamese MiGs being pursued by American fighter pilots into China. On August 21, two fighters strafing a railroad line crossed the border and were shot down. Another incident like this, Johnson told his advisers, and the Chinese might join the war.

With the oil bombing campaign failing to achieve anything significant, McNamara told Johnson, "I myself am more and more convinced that we ought to definitely plan on termination of bombing in the North." Almost as an afterthought, he said a limit ought to be placed on the number of troops committed to fighting the war.[21]

While McNamara was beginning to think escalation had been a ghastly mistake, John McNaughton, the assistant secretary of defense, offered him a different air strategy: let's starve them to death. McNaughton proposed bombing the locks and dams on which the North Vietnamese depended to irrigate their rice paddies. Destroying the rice crop wasn't the same as targeting the civilian population, he argued, but this was specious. The intended result was what mattered, and the intended result was starvation. That might force Ho Chi Minh to negotiate, said McNaughton.

Had McNaughton's proposal worked, he anticipated a death toll of at least a million. General John McConnell thought mass deaths by starvation—a tactic favored by Stalin and Mao to destroy masses of peasants—was a good idea.

Little wonder, then, that the air force had LBJ worried. Fear of what it might do if he did not keep a close watch on the bombing provided a powerful reason for the commander in chief to stay up late, micromanaging the air war.[22]

Although starvation was ruled out, a new air strategy was launched in October 1966. The air force would bomb electric power plants and the handful of industrial sites that North Vietnam possessed. Although there were some large power plants in the North, demolishing them would make no difference. Thousands of small generators could provide enough electricity for a country where most homes and many businesses had never depended on electricity. As for bombing steel plants and cement producers, China would make good whatever cement and steel was lost in the bombing. The American pilots who lost their lives attacking these facilities amounted to human sacrifices offered up by Walt Rostow to an aerial offensive that was certain to fail.

It would fail as a morale breaker too, because it had made life into an existential challenge for the North Vietnamese and the Vietcong, as it had done to the British when they were bombed by the Germans: Who are we? What is this life? What justifies our existence? The answers were determined by the core narrative of Vietnamese history, a narrative of resistance to domination: first the Chinese, then the French, now the Americans. Fighting the Americans became central to people's sense of themselves, and it justified both the living and the dead. Rostow could not have been more mistaken when he assured Johnson that bombing would make the North come to the table.

All the same, when Rostow stopped trying to show what a tough guy he was beneath that Caspar Milquetoast professorial mien, he at least recognized what Bundy never grasped: there could be no military success without a political success. We must get the South Vietnamese to lay the foundations of political stability, he told LBJ. How? Get them to write a constitution. If they can do that, he assured Johnson, "we will have passed a great turning point." Nothing would hit the Vietcong harder, and they could be brought into the process by giving them a place at the table, alongside the North Vietnamese, at a conference to end the war. Carrot and stick—that ought to work.[23]

What Rostow failed to recognize was that in a war as politically complex as Vietnam, there were at least four wars (civil, revolutionary, liberation, proxy), not just one. That made politics primary. Politics should have guided every military action for the United States the way it was guiding every military action of the Vietcong and the North Vietnamese. Rostow had the core issue wrong, as all of Johnson's main advisers had it wrong: hit the enemy hard enough, Rostow argued, and they will have to talk. Bombing, however, was making the North stronger politically, not weaker.

Johnson ignored countless pleas to take the Vietnam problem to the United Nations. He feared that a UN debate would lead to at least half the world's ganging up on America. Besides, the American ambassador to the UN, Adlai Stevenson, believed that the war was a terrible mistake. "No white army will ever win another war in Asia or Africa," Stevenson told Rusk.[24]

Instead, Johnson looked to SEATO to provide international sanction for what the United States was doing. A meeting was arranged for Manila in October. While Johnson was on his way to the conference, a highly respected Republican senator, George Aiken of Vermont, made a speech in the Senate that offered a way out: "The United States could well declare unilaterally that this stage of the war in Vietnam is over—that we have 'won' in the sense that our Armed Forces are in control of most of the field and no potential enemy is in a position to establish its authority over South Vietnam," said Aiken. "This unilateral declaration of military victory would herald the resumption of political warfare as the dominant theme in Vietnam. Until such a declaration is made, there is no real prospect of political negotiations." Contrary to one of the great modern myths, Aiken did not call for withdrawal from South Vietnam. He wanted a smaller ground war and a bigger air and naval war. Adoption of his resolution "would not mean the quick withdrawal of our forces in Southeast Asia."[25]

In Australia and New Zealand, Johnson made the initial distribution of the gifts he had brought: two hundred busts of LBJ. When he met up with Ky in Manila, he gave Ky both a bust and some advice: carry a Bible and "be a man of good will. Love your neighbor; but indicate, of course, that you will not take steps which tie your hands behind your back when they are still shooting."[26]

The Big Idea that Johnson brought to the conference was that the United States would withdraw from South Vietnam six months after Hanoi pulled its troops out and pledged to stop attacking its neighbors.

This formula had echoes of how the British had managed to defeat an insurgency in Malaya. For twelve years they had fought an insurgency supported by the small Chinese population of Malaya. The goal of the eight thousand insurgents was to drive the British out. After that, they might be able to seize control of the government. The two much larger populations, the Malays and the Indians, had shunned the insurgency. That made it possible for the British to isolate the Chinese and check them militarily, but only by outnumbering the insurgents by more than twenty to one. Even then the killer blow was political: a pledge to grant independence once the insurgency ended. After that, the insurgency withered. Something similar happened in Kenya, but it was never going to happen in Vietnam. The Americans might remove their troops, but they would continue the war by using their air and naval power in support of the ARVN. The bombing of North Vietnam could, and probably would, continue.

The main result of the SEATO conference was bleak. There was no commitment to provide anything that might significantly ease the American burden. SEATO was a dead letter from that moment: if it became irrelevant to the United States, it was irrelevant to everyone else.

From Manila, Johnson made a short announced visit to South Vietnam. Arriving at Cam Ranh Bay, he pinned medals on chests and gave an emotive speech in the officers' club. "I thank you, I salute you," said an obviously moved commander in chief. "May the good Lord look over you and keep you until you come home with the coonskin nailed to the wall."[27]

The general flow of reports out of Vietnam that fall was positive, and Westy had a plan. According to the general, 1967 was going to be the Year of the Offensive. In January, Westmoreland launched the first big search-and-destroy operations of the war. The VC and their North Vietnamese allies had the strategic initiative. Nearly every battle occurred when and where they chose to fight. By launching these big offensives, Westmoreland was trying to take the strategic initiative back, making them fight where and when he dictated.[28]

His first offensive, Cedar Falls, was launched in January to seize control of an area called the Iron Triangle, only twelve miles from Saigon. The army considered it a great success because 750 Vietcong were confirmed killed and more than 3,700 tons of rice were seized, as were more than half a million pages of documents from a VC headquarters. The follow-up operation, Junction City, also yielded a pile of statistics.

This was war as McNamara liked it, but McNamara did not have the mind of a great war minister. He had the mind of a management consultant. His approach to fighting the war seemed to come straight from McKinsey and Co., the world's most successful management consultancy. The company motto was "Everything can be measured and whatever gets measured gets managed." The commonsense dissent of Albert Einstein—"Not everything that can be counted counts and not everything that counts can be counted"—never seemed to make an impression on McNamara, or on McKinsey. But by this point in the war, Westy too was as big on statistics as the secretary of defense.

Even as the war seemed finally to be going Johnson's way, public support was dropping and massive antiwar demonstrations were spreading from college campuses onto the streets. They would even reach the Pentagon parking lot, where one protestor would burn himself alive.

Johnson liked to think that he, the graduate of an obscure teachers' college and a former schoolteacher, was a natural friend to college students. But when they chanted, "Hey! Hey! LBJ! How many kids did you kill today?" they became "those little shits on the campuses."[29]

He was never going to read the semiotics of street theater. Instead of trying to understand the protests, he railed at them as nothing more than Communist conspiracies and blatant acts of treason. Johnson told the CIA director, Richard Helms, to prove that these protests were being organized and manipulated by the Soviets and other Communists.

Helms reported the conclusions of his investigation to the cabinet: "On the basis of what we know, we see no significant evidence that would prove Communist control of the peace movement or its leaders." Johnson told him he was wrong, and Dean Rusk rejected the report out of hand. A second report arrived at the same conclusion. It too was rejected by Johnson and Rusk.[30]

By this time, McNamara's belief in the rightness of the war was dying. He was beginning to see at last what it was doing to the United States: degrading the nation's idea of itself. "There may be a limit beyond which Americans and much of the world will not permit the United States to go," he told Johnson. "The picture of the world's greatest superpower killing or seriously injuring 1000 non-combatants a week while trying to pound a tiny backward nation into submission . . . could conceivably produce a costly distortion in the American national consciousness and in the world image of the United States."[31]

Having cranked out a constitution to keep the Americans happy, Thieu and Ky had gone on to crank out an election to make them even happier. Thieu would run for president, Ky for prime minister. On September 3, *The New York Times* reported the results:

United States officials were surprised and heartened today at the size of the turnout in South Vietnam's presidential election despite a Vietcong terrorist campaign to disrupt the voting.

According to reports from Saigon, 83 percent of the 5.85 million registered voters cast their ballots yesterday. Many of them risked reprisals threatened by the Vietcong . . . The fact that the backing of the electorate has gone to the generals who have been ruling South Vietnam for the last two years does not, in the Administration's view, diminish the significance of the constitutional step that has been taken.[32]

With this political triumph in the bag, the director of the U.S. Information Agency, Leonard Marks, came to the private quarters and reminded Johnson of George Aiken's idea that the president should declare that military successes now allowed him to shift the focus away from fighting and onto politics. "The Vietnamese have just held a national election. Democracy seems to be thriving there. Why don't we say we've achieved that objective, provide equipment and take our troops out?" said Marks.

Johnson screamed at him. "Get out of here!"[33]

That was probably a scream of pain rather than rage. At a meeting in the White House shortly after this outburst, Johnson blurted out, "History may make us look silly on this whole thing." Nor did he think the bombing made any sense: "They have no more intention of talking than we have of surrendering." McNamara and Johnson had arrived at virtually the same conclusion at virtually the same time: this was an unwinnable war, but they did not have to stick with it. They could just walk away.[34]

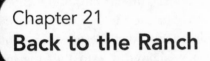

Chapter 21
Back to the Ranch

IN THE AFTERGLOW OF THE SOUTH VIETNAMESE ELECTION, RICHARD
Helms came to the White House with a document stamped EYES
ONLY and handed it to the president. It would be for him alone to decide who else would see it. The CIA had looked at withdrawal and
concluded there would be unavoidable costs and damaging consequences. "The risks are probably more limited and more controllable
than most previous arguments have indicated." It wasn't only the
words, couched in this dry bureaucratic language, that hit LBJ hard.
It was the tenor of the piece, a siren song that said, "Get out . . . get
out." Johnson showed the report to no one, not even McNamara and
Rusk.[1]

The CIA was saying the war had been a terrible mistake. There
weren't going to be dominoes falling from Saigon to Sydney; NATO
would not collapse; Americans would not find the Red Army on the
front porch or the People's Liberation Army landing on the beaches of
California. Life would go on much as it had done before the Vietnam
War. All of the dire predictions the president had made about what

would happen if the United States pulled out its troops had just been rebuffed, not by a bunch of newspaper columnists, but by people in government who were supposed to know about these things. If they were right, he, Lyndon Baines Johnson, child of his times—ardent patriot, archfoe of Communism and all its works, a president baffled by China—had destroyed himself.

He had felt the tug of the riptide that was sweeping him toward historic disaster from the moment Jack Kennedy was shot. Yet despite that feeling in the gut and despite all his political skills and good intentions, LBJ lacked the depth of character and strength of mind to stand against the force of events. His first line of defense was Ike and Jack: their fault, not his. The second line was, "All of my advisers told me what I was doing was right." He could never admit he had been wrong on the most important decision he was ever called on to make, but it's a rare politician who can.

Johnson certainly never lacked for advice, and he liked to say, "A man's judgment is no better than his information." Even so, he clung, almost pathetically, to memos, meetings, and official reports. Unlike Ike and JFK, Johnson brought no relevant knowledge on Vietnam, China, or modern war with him. That made him feel comfortable only with advisers who did not know much more than he did—Rusk, a man with a history of getting China wrong; McNamara, whose world was numbers, not people; Bundy, the academic dean who never seemed to read anything; Rostow, so eager to please it suggested arrested development; and Abe Fortas, the Johnson family's lawyer, whom Johnson had placed on the Supreme Court.

The diminutive, sharply tailored, and "what's in it for me?" justice took part in discussions on Vietnam and invariably recommended the same thing: no halt in the bombing, no second thoughts, no turning back. Fortas had rejected McNamara's recommendation of an indefinite bombing halt as "an invitation to slaughter [and] a powerful tonic to Chinese Communist effectiveness in the world." Worse, it would probably lead to withdrawal, which he seemed to think was the equivalent of general nuclear war.[2]

Johnson's attempts to elevate the intellectually undistinguished Fortas to chief justice in the waning days of his presidency failed because Fortas's primary interest proved to be moneygrubbing, not justice. A year later, Fortas's involvement with a big-time swindler, Louis

Wolfson, brought his long-overdue resignation from the Supreme Court. Fortas, like the other people Johnson actually listened to, routinely intoned the dull thud of "Stay the course," which was what he wanted to hear.

When LBJ became president, there was only one person on the National Security Council who could claim expert knowledge of Southeast Asia. That was Paul Kattenburg, a career Foreign Service officer. Kattenburg had been stationed at the Saigon embassy for most of the 1950s. He told Johnson from the start that the Vietnam War could never be won. Johnson's answer to that was to get Kattenburg off the NSC.[3]

There was no shortage of people who urged Johnson not to turn Vietnam into an American war—people who possessed a range of knowledge and experience as great as, if not greater than, anything Rusk, McNamara, and Bundy could bring to bear. These included Mike Mansfield, Richard Russell, George Ball, Adlai Stevenson, Charles de Gaulle, John Kenneth Galbraith, Averell Harriman, and David Shoup, a Medal of Honor winner chosen by John Kennedy to be the first Marine Corps commandant to sit on the Joint Chiefs. Impressed by Shoup's courage, Kennedy was even more impressed by his brains.

When a commander in chief picks an adviser, he is picking his advice, but for the sake of ritual fairness and to make it appear that he was consulting widely, Johnson allowed those who disagreed on Vietnam to make their case. He actively encouraged Rusk's deputy, George Ball, to compose long and detailed memos of dissent. But that was just another way of keeping Ball's pecker in the presidential pocket. Ball gladly labored over his memos, in the flattering belief that this was a way of retaining influence. He was simply being used.

The CIA report continued to weigh on LBJ, and on October 3, at a meeting with Rusk, McNamara, Helms, and Rostow, he spoke his heart aloud: "I don't want any of the information that I'm about to discuss to go outside this room," said Johnson. "What effect would it have on the war if I announced I was not going to run for another term?"

McNamara seemed almost unconcerned, but Rusk became agitated. "You must not go down," he told Johnson. "You are the Commander in Chief, and we are in a war . . . Hanoi would think they've got it made."

Recent polls showed that trust in the president and support for the war were falling sharply. For a year or so, polls had consistently shown that support for the war was greater than support for the president, but with both falling together, staying the course meant staying on course for withdrawal. "Our people will not hold out four more years . . . and I just don't know that I want four more years of this," said Johnson, sounding weary.[4]

As his spirits sank, Johnson reached out to the Wise Old Men, or WOMs, as White House staffers had it. The core of the group consisted of the advisers who had guided Truman through the early years of the Cold War and created America's frame of reference for waging it. There were eleven WOMs in all, including Dean Acheson, Clark Clifford, Omar Bradley, and Averell Harriman. They looked almost like the parents of some of the younger people there, such as McGeorge Bundy and Henry Cabot Lodge.

Less than twenty-four hours before the WOMs met, McNamara handed Johnson a memorandum. Like the CIA report, the way it parsed the case for the war made it seem hopeless and endless. And if that happened to be true, withdrawal was inevitable at some point.[5]

The gathering of the Wise Old Men the next day gave Dean Acheson a chance to remind people of his heroics after the Chinese entered the Korean War. He had shaken up the cookie-pushers at the State Department, he recalled, with this rallying cry: "We want less goddamn analysis and more fighting spirit!" Although he sometimes acknowledged the risks of frequent worldwide armed intervention, Acheson had backed every one, including Vietnam.[6]

General Wheeler gave the WOMs an assessment of the way the war was going: more VC killed than ever, more prisoners taken, more weapons seized, more bombs dropped, more targets hit, South Vietnamese morale rising, VC morale falling, more troops in-country, more big operations planned. But there was one serious problem, Wheeler conceded. Negative newspaper and television coverage was undermining support for this very successful war.

All of the Wise Old Men but one accepted Wheeler's presentation without demur. Averell Harriman said, "Negotiation is inevitable and necessary." This anodyne statement gave George Ball a chance to ingratiate himself with the president. "No one in this group thinks we should get out of the war," said Ball. Clifford endorsed that. "No matter what we do, this will never be a popular war," said Clifford. "But we must go on because what we are doing is right."[7]

None of them—not even Harriman—asked, If the war is well on the way to being won, why are we having this meeting? The WOMs thus provided the commander in chief with just what he needed, just when he needed it most. He hadn't been looking for advice: he was looking for reassurance from the foreign policy establishment. They almost buried him in it.

In these depressing days, Johnson had Westmoreland return, to get the country behind the war. Looking like the chief of staff from central casting, Westy solemnly told television audiences, the National Press Club, and a gathering of congressmen that victory was some way off, but the army would be able to start coming home "in two years or less." To do that, though, the bombing had to continue. "The best way I know of prolonging the war is to stop the bombing."[8]

Westmoreland had gone to Vietnam three years before believing there was an answer waiting to be found somewhere in the jungle. That wasn't just Westy's idea of the war—it was the "can-do" attitude of the career soldier when duty calls. In those early months, Westmoreland recognized that if the political side of the war was lost, the entire enterprise was doomed. But as American troops and helicopters flowed into the country, he forgot about the politics and set out to defeat the Wehrmacht all over again, something he had helped achieve as a young artillery officer twenty years earlier.

The big search-and-destroy operations of 1967 had not resulted in the much-hoped-for tens of thousands of enemy dead and the subsequent cracks in the enemy's fighting spirit. The only strategy that might achieve that, Westmoreland had come to realize, was to invade and conquer North Vietnam and call China's bluff. And if it wasn't a bluff, what was the answer then? Big, brave Westy hadn't a clue. But it infuriated the military, from the Joint Chiefs down to two-stripe riflemen, that the enemy held the strategic initiative and set the tempo of the war. All the Americans could do was make tactical moves, usually in response to a Vietcong action.

Unable to invade the North, Westmoreland had a new plan for

1968: there was a Special Forces camp close to the North Vietnamese border, at a place called Khe Sanh. The North Vietnamese were preparing a major attack. Westmoreland proposed to turn Khe Sanh into a massive killing ground. Before returning to Saigon, the general hinted to a journalist who interviewed him that something big was in the works. He wanted the Communists to make a big attack. "I hope they try something, because we are looking for a fight."⁹

Westmoreland calculated that there were nearly 500,000 Vietcong guerrillas and North Vietnamese regulars fighting in South Vietnam in December 1967. American and South Vietnamese forces numbered approximately 1.5 million. That gave him an advantage of three to one in troop strength. A margin like this, combined with superior fire-power and mobility, had been enough to win conventional wars. The coming year would thus bring a rising tide of remorseless success. South Vietnamese troops would take on more and more of the fighting in 1968, paving the way for the American withdrawal to begin in 1969.¹⁰

The president could not have asked for more, but by this time he had given up all expectation of winning anything in Vietnam. It was hopeless, and he knew it. Johnson was preparing for his own with-drawal—from the White House. Let somebody else take the blame for defeat and retreat when the moment came.

During Westmoreland's brief trip stateside, Johnson asked him, "What would my men in Vietnam think if I failed to run for reelection in 1968? Would they consider that their commander in chief had let them down?" Westmoreland equivocated, unable to grasp what an-swer he was expected to give.¹¹

As Christmas drew nigh, Walt Whitman Rostow had a revelation, one he shared with the press: the crossover point had been reached in Vietnam. "Their casualties are going up at a rate they cannot sustain," said Rostow. "I see light at the end of the tunnel." The glad news spread swiftly to Saigon, in time for the U.S. embassy's invitations to a New Year's Eve party. The invitations read, "Come see the light at the end of the tunnel."¹²

In handing him that gloomy, almost doom-laden memo just before the Wise Old Men met, McNamara had virtually asked Johnson to re-place him. He was not going to quit. McNamara had too much pride for that. Besides, resignation would only make Johnson's agony worse.

Johnson rose to the occasion by kicking McNamara up and out, making him president of the World Bank. The first McNamara heard of it was from reading the newspapers, but he can't have been surprised.

At the World Bank, the former secretary of defense would once again demonstrate his talent for thinking on a vast scale, badly. McNamara's big idea was to bring clean water to every village in the Third World. That part of the plan worked. Tens of thousands of villages got new wells and shiny pumps. Yet nothing had been done to ensure routine maintenance and easy access to spare parts. Across the global south these days there is hardly a village so remote it does not have its own rusty, broken pump.

Johnson replaced McNamara with the overly slick Clark Clifford, a man whose reputation as a well-connected Washington lawyer was as well deserved as that of Abe Fortas. Late in life, Clifford's renown as a friend of presidents and a great lawyer was probably crucial to keeping him out of a federal penitentiary. Like Fortas, Clifford practiced ethical relativism. The sweeter the deal, the more relative the ethics became. He was, as Congressman F. Edward Hebert expressed it, "a real con artist." Hebert intended this as a compliment; but then, he was from Louisiana, where such artistry was much admired in political circles.[13]

Clifford had been all over the map on the war. During Kennedy's thousand days and in the early months of the Johnson presidency, Clifford had told Johnson that the war was a mistake. Courtier that he was, though, Clifford soon realized that he was heading for dissidents' corner, where protests could be made without any danger of being heard and George Ball already held the post of dissident in chief. For a man determined always to be in the know, on the inside, have pull where it mattered, being that far from the fire was unthinkable.

Johnson surely thought that in replacing McNamara with Clifford, he would be getting rid of a doubter and installing a believer. Clifford had recently given a speech at a Washington school in which he lambasted congressional attempts to pass a resolution calling for withdrawal. Those congressmen, said Clifford, were being "unrealistic and impractical." The result would be a bloodbath in South Vietnam, and the United States had a moral obligation to see the war through to victory. The only honorable course now was Vietnamization. Once the

Vietnamese could fight the war on their own, the American army could return home with honor.[14]

When offered a cabinet post, Clifford grabbed it with both hands. This was what he had wanted from Harry Truman, but Truman only offered him the post of under secretary of state. Clifford had then departed to make money. Now, though, he had what he longed for, a major place in the cabinet. And yet, as he listened to the briefings and read through the documents, he began asking himself—as the WOMs hadn't—If the war's being won, why does the Pentagon have an atmosphere of unending, unrelenting crisis? Clifford's old doubts returned, full bore.[15]

The new year found Johnson obsessed with Khe Sanh; he dreaded that it would prove to be a Dien Bien Phu for the marines who were holding it, rather than a trap for the North Vietnamese who were attacking it. Before he approved the operation, he made the Joint Chiefs sign a letter saying that it would not fall. Before long, there were at least 25,000 PAVN troops investing Khe Sanh and its garrison of 6,000 marines.

As the Khe Sanh drama unfolded, the North Koreans delivered an electrifying jolt to the system. So far as they were concerned, they were (and still are) at war with the United States. A truce is a long way short of peace. On January 23, 1968, they seized the USS *Pueblo*, a squat gray tub that was harvesting electronic emissions off the coast of North Korea.

Johnson was more flummoxed by the seizure of the *Pueblo*, and the death of one of its crew, than people would want their commander in chief to be. He mobilized 14,500 army reservists, but that was a gesture, a sign that he was responding, when in fact he had no idea what to do. With the world closing in on him, Johnson was convinced the *Pueblo* humiliation was yet another démarche in the worldwide Communist plot to ruin him. The North Vietnamese were applying intense pressure at Khe Sanh, and now the North Koreans might be getting ready to march on Seoul again. And there were the Soviets: they were going to start trouble in Berlin, he was sure of it. In Johnson's mind, the world trembled on the brink of World War III. These days, he had a disconcerting habit of bursting into tears and weeping uncontrollably.[16]

Westmoreland and Wheeler were also warning that the VC might mount a fresh wave of terrorist attacks during the three-day lunar new year celebration in Vietnam, a holiday called Tet. But there was nothing to worry about, Westmoreland assured Wheeler: "Friendly forces have seized the military initiative from the enemy."[17]

And now the reason for the PAVN investment of Khe Sanh was revealed. B-52 strikes and heavy artillery were inflicting fearsome losses on the North Vietnamese, and it was evident that they stood no chance of overrunning the garrison. This was not going to be what Johnson feared, another Dien Bien Phu. It was a diversion, and Westy and Wheeler raced after it, eyes wide shut.

The political and military elite in Hanoi had for years been developing a theory of how to fight and win a people's war. The final stage was to be "the general offensive and uprising." Here was a romantic notion that had nothing to do with firepower, or the Chinese. Ho's contribution was to argue that the best time would be an American presidential election year. On January 30, the Vietcong launched the offensive that they expected to spark a revolt by millions of ordinary Vietnamese. This uprising would drive the occupiers from their land. As it turned out, the theory was half-baked, but Ho's timing was perfect. This was the right year.[18]

The VC had been fighting almost entirely in the countryside, rarely battling in the larger towns and cities. With American forces in the cities being thinned to bolster the defenses of Khe Sanh and the area around it, the VC and the North Vietnamese moved into urban areas and launched their offensive against five of the six largest cities, forty-four provincial capitals, and sixty-four district capitals. In Saigon, they attacked Westmoreland's headquarters and shot their way into the U.S. embassy.

There was no general uprising. The urban population of South Vietnam for the most part shunned the hicks from the sticks in their black pajamas and flip-flops. Of the eighty-four thousand VC and North Vietnamese who launched the Tet Offensive, the vast majority were killed, wounded, or captured. Westmoreland and Wheeler proclaimed a great victory.

Nevertheless, they had prepared the ground for their defeat. Naive to the point of recklessness, they never answered the critics of the war by sticking to the truth. Instead, they lied, twisted, exaggerated, fooled themselves in their attempt to fool others, and reaped the results. In the end, they did not serve the best interests of their country or their troops. The majority of Americans who supported the war were shocked and horrified at what television brought them during the three days of Tet. This was not the war that Johnson or the generals had described to them. It was bigger than anything they had imagined, and winning it would take more than a deeply divided nation would ever be willing to give.

The most trusted commentator on television, Walter Cronkite, went to take a look at it for himself. Cronkite had seen a lot of war, especially in Europe. He knew and liked soldiers. He had never been critical of the war, until now. "To say we are closer to victory today is to believe, in the face of the evidence, the optimists who have been wrong in the past," Cronkite reported in measured tones. "To suggest we are on the edge of defeat is to yield to unreasonable pessimism. To say that we are mired in a stalemate seems the only realistic, yet unsatisfactory, conclusion." Here, at last, was the truth. Vietnam was an unwinnable war.

It always had been, and Johnson had known that all along. China was never going to allow the Americans to win there, but how could he go on television and say that? Congress and the country would demand that he either attack China or pull out of Vietnam, start a world war or retreat.

Instead, he stalled, sending Wheeler to South Vietnam on a Cronkite-like fact-finding mission. The owlish-looking but not very wise Wheeler came back with a Cronkite-like conclusion: neither side was winning the war. It was deadlocked. Wheeler and Westmoreland thought it might still be possible to turn things around, if only the president would give them another 206,000 troops. They did not offer an estimate of how many Chinese troops Mao would provide North Vietnam in response.

Even after Tet and Cronkite, a clear majority of Americans continued to support the war in public-opinion polls, but that was mainly an expression of moral support for the troops. There was no political capital attached. Had Johnson announced that he was going to send another 206,000 men to Vietnam after Tet, the streets would have been filled with millions of protestors and Congress might have refused to provide the money.

The country was not simply turning away from LBJ—it was turning hostile. Even the people who claimed to support the war drew the line at supporting him. He would drag the party to a crushing defeat in November if he ran. Meanwhile, as Clark Clifford discussed the request for another 206,000 men with the president, he cast doubt on Westmoreland's seek-and-destroy strategy and told Johnson that the war could not be won. He did not call for a withdrawal but "we seem to have a sinkhole," he said. "We put in more, they match it . . . and [there is] no end in sight."[19]

On March 12, the voters of New Hampshire went to the polls. Senator Eugene McCarthy of Minnesota was running for the Democratic nomination as the presidential candidate who would seek a negotiated end to the war. McCarthy won 42 percent of the vote, to Johnson's 49 percent. But McCarthy also picked up twenty of New Hampshire's convention delegates. With McCarthy having taken the temperature of the water, another antiwar senator, Robert F. Kennedy, jumped in. Johnson set his speechwriters to work on a "peace speech."

Clifford advised him to convene another meeting of the WOMs. They came together the morning of March 25, at the State Department, for a highly detailed briefing on Vietnam. Then they were driven to the White House, where McGeorge Bundy spoke for the group. Of the eleven Wise Old Men, said Bundy, only three— Maxwell Taylor, Omar Bradley, and Associate Justice Fortas—wanted to continue with the war. The other eight, including Dean Acheson, the pluperfect cold warrior, had arrived at the opposite conclusion: "We must begin to take steps to disengage."[20]

Johnson had had one of his speechwriters, Horace Busby, working on a resignation speech for several months, but it was still formless, an expression of desire rather than a statement of intent. The speech at last took shape, and he prepared to deliver it on national television the evening of March 31.

When the day arrived, he felt sorry for himself. Self-pity was the other side of the overbearing LBJ, and it ran just as deep. Hubert Humphrey came to see him, to offer some words of encouragement in the wake of recent poll results. Johnson dismissed Humphrey's reassurances. "Hubert, maybe the people just don't like my face." And then he became emotional and agitated, feeling the burden of a people's contempt. He was close to tears, and Humphrey left before Johnson dissolved.[21]

By the afternoon he had regained his composure. He rehearsed the speech for the benefit of Lady Bird, daughter Luci, son-in-law Patrick Nugent, and a couple of old friends, Mathilde and Arthur Krim. As Johnson reached the final paragraph, Luci burst into tears.[22]

With a few minor changes and corrections, this was the speech that he delivered that evening on television. "Tonight I want to speak to you of peace in Vietnam and Southeast Asia," Johnson began. He was stopping the bombing of North Vietnam, except in the demilitarized zone, a strip of land ten kilometers wide bisected by the Dong Nai River at Bien Hoa. Westmoreland would get another 13,500 men instead of 206,000. Johnson called on Ho Chi Minh to take advantage of "this new step of peace." And the president did not want partisan politics to impede progress on ending the war. "Accordingly, I shall not seek, and will not accept, the nomination of my party for another term as your President."[23]

Three days after Johnson's speech, Hanoi said it was ready to negotiate, but Ho was only testing the waters. Johnson had personalized the war, turning it into a global smackdown between LBJ and Ho Chi Minh. Personalizing the war and publicly belittling Ho made it harder, if not impossible, for the North Vietnamese to talk to him, even if the Chinese were out of the equation. And making a negotiated end harder to reach, when it was already hard enough, was a commander in chief failure. Johnson, however, personalized everything. All that Ho was interested in now was a pledge of American withdrawal. Talks began, in Paris, but the Chinese did not think the time was right to negotiate: the Americans would not be willing to discuss withdrawal for at least two or three years, Zhou told Pham Van Dong. The North Vietnamese agreed. Negotiations moved with glacial slowness, but the 1968 election seemed to be arriving on skates.

Even with peace talks under way, Johnson refused to give an inch. Back when he was only thinking of quitting, he had told "Bus" Wheeler, "As long as I am Commander in Chief, I am going to control [the war] from Washington!" And that was what he did.[24]

He continued bombing almost all the way to the Chinese border, although Americans were never told that. The number of American troops in Vietnam continued to rise. And when the Democratic convention rolled around in August, he began to have second thoughts about quitting. His greatest rival for the nomination, Robert F. Kennedy, was dead, killed by Sirhan Sirhan, a Palestinian immigrant outraged by the dispossession of his people. The Kennedys had always been strongly pro-Israel. With RFK's death, Johnson began to encourage a "Draft LBJ" movement.[25]

With his support dropping to 35 percent of registered voters, that effort went nowhere. Even so, Johnson held an iron grip on the convention, which met amid tumultuous scenes in Chicago. There was so much boiling anger among the delegates that if he had appeared at the convention, Johnson might have split the Democratic Party and given the election to Richard Nixon. He stayed away, but nothing important would be decided without his approval.[26]

Humphrey was chosen as the presidential candidate, but Johnson was never going to support him, because Humphrey wanted to run as the candidate who would bring an end to the war. He had long had doubts about the wisdom of fighting a war in Vietnam, and during his first year as Johnson's vice president he had opposed escalation. That meant being frozen out from nearly all the important meetings on Vietnam and rarely being asked for his advice. The humiliation of the vice president was an open secret in Washington.

A thoroughly decent and intelligent man, Humphrey had found his limits, and so had Johnson. Humphrey came close to being a living, breathing, and slightly sad example of the stereotypical Farmer-Labor Party liberal from far-off Minnesota: plenty of principle, not enough spine.

Johnson could smell weakness as sharks can smell blood—in small traces, over long distances. Having humiliated and bullied Humphrey for more than three years, Johnson was a cobra to a mongoose during Humphrey's campaign. Every hint of independent thinking on Vietnam brought a threat from above.

It began during the convention, when Johnson warned Humphrey, "The Vietnam plank will be mine—not yours." Sure enough, the platform supported LBJ's negotiating position: no end to the fighting and bombing until the North agrees to stop attacking the South.[27]

A month or so after the convention, Johnson heard that Humphrey was working on a speech that would offer to stop the bombing indefinitely if the North promised to reduce—not stop, only limit—the flow of troops and weapons into South Vietnam. LBJ called Hubert to heel. Give that speech, he told Humphrey, and I will personally see to it that you lose Texas. At other times, he told Humphrey that he would make sure that the Democratic National Committee and the big party donors stopped financing Humphrey's campaign. A large amount of money that ought to have gone to Humphrey's campaign was withheld to the end.[28]

With only a week to go, Humphrey finally put some distance between LBJ and himself over Vietnam. Humphrey's poll numbers rose dramatically. Had he shown a little more independence only a week earlier, he would probably have won the 1968 election. He lost to Richard Nixon by half a million votes out of more than seventy-three million cast.

In that final week of campaigning, Nixon was holding a trump card. Anna Chennault, widow of a famous World War II airman, acted as Nixon's intermediary. She assured Nguyen Van Thieu that if Nixon was elected president, he would provide the kind of unequivocal support that Humphrey would not. Four days before the election, Johnson was handed conclusive proof that Nixon was sabotaging the Paris talks by encouraging Thieu to spin things out.

This news would have won the election for Humphrey had Johnson stayed within the law, but he hadn't. The evidence came from illegal wiretaps on the South Vietnamese embassy in Washington. Johnson telephoned Nixon and demanded to know if he was undermining the Paris talks. Of course not, said Nixon. Then he hung up the telephone and laughed.[29]

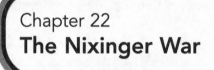

Chapter 22
The Nixinger War

NIXON HAD HINTED THAT HE HAD A PLAN FOR ENDING THE WAR. Looked at closely, though, all he offered was carefully crafted ambiguity, such as, "I pledge to you that the new leadership will end the war and win the peace in the Pacific." So desperate were those who wanted the Vietnam agony to end, the electorate read what it wanted to read into the empty pledges of a man they did not trust. And even though Nixon had won the election, the country had not given him a mandate to do anything drastic in Vietnam, either to escalate or to get out. He had a wafer-thin margin in the popular vote and a Senate and House that were both overwhelmingly Democratic.

By the time of the election, Nixon realized that this was an unwinnable war, yet once he was installed in power, he had no idea how to end it. He and Kissinger fell back on Cold War clichés while a group at RAND, including Daniel Ellsberg, tried to craft an exit strategy. The one they produced shortly before Nixon's inauguration was simple and workable: talk up Vietnamization and use it as a justification for withdrawal.

Nixon supplemented this by hoping, as Johnson had hoped, to persuade the Russians to help him get out. Nearly every step in aid of withdrawal was an extension of Johnsonian war-making policy, especially an unshakable belief that bombing would make the North negotiate and a feeling that success could be brought closer by invading Cambodia and Laos.

The biggest difference between Nixon and Johnson turned out to be the war's objective: Johnson had insisted that the objective was a non-Communist government in an independent Saigon, making it in effect an American protectorate in perpetuity. Nixon was willing to accept whatever the South Vietnamese could agree on, even if it meant a coalition or neutralization. Only when he could implement that idea would withdrawal become possible.

At first, though, Nixon was obsessed with getting the North Vietnamese to take him seriously—more seriously than they had ever taken LBJ. Like Truman and Johnson before him, he loved talking tough, but he tried to pretend that there was a philosophy, of sorts, behind it. Nixon revealed his idea to Harry R. ("Call me Bob") Haldeman, the huckster he had selected as his White House chief of staff. "I call it the Madman Theory, Bob," Nixon announced as they strolled along a foggy beach in southern California one day during the campaign. Nixon had nothing but admiration for Syngman Rhee, the South Korean strongman, who had told him some years earlier that being unpredictable was a powerful tactic when dealing with the Communists. Nixon intended to take unpredictability to new heights.

"I want the North Vietnamese to believe I've reached the point where I might do *anything* to stop the war. We'll just slip the word to them that, 'for God's sakes, you know Nixon is obsessed about Communism. We can't restrain him when he's angry—and he has his hand on the nuclear button'—and Ho Chi Minh himself will be in Paris in two days begging for peace." He had ample opportunity to ape the madman over the years that followed, but neither Ho—who died in 1969—nor any of his successors ever begged Nixon for peace.[1]

Nixon began his presidency trying to impress his vision on the war by expanding it, secretly. In February 1969, the VC and North Vietnamese launched a new offensive. Taking that for a challenge, he began secretly bombing Cambodia. When Johnson launched Rolling Thunder three years earlier, he had seized the low moral ground, as public reaction across the civilized world demonstrated. In starting a bombing campaign against Cambodia, Nixon was seizing it all over again. When the bombing did not bring relief, he invaded Cambodia, to root out the VC "headquarters," in an area known as the Parrot's Beak. The headquarters did not exist, but the bombing and the invasion destroyed the Cambodian government and brought to power a right-wing general named Lon Nol, who enjoyed Nixon's complete backing. With that kind of support, Lon Nol set about rooting out Communists and neutralists. The result was a civil war, from which the murderous Khmer Rouge emerged. The death toll ran into the millions.

Meanwhile, Nixon was trying to mount a fighting withdrawal, beginning with a plan to invade North Vietnam and to bomb the dikes. It was called Operation Duck Hook, and amounted to an invitation to China to put up or shut up. Duck Hook was scheduled to begin on November 1, 1969. Nixon even had a speech written to justify it, and he hinted at what was coming in discussions with the congressional leadership. "All I can tell you is this: I am doing my damnedest to end the war," Nixon told them in September. "I will not be the first President of the United States to lose a war." Kissinger informed the North Vietnamese delegation to the Paris peace talks that they had to make concessions: "If by November 1 no progress has been made, the United States will have to consider steps of grave consequence."[2]

The North Vietnamese response was to tell Kissinger there would never be peace until the Americans dumped Thieu and Ky. As for the threats, so what? They'd heard them all before. Nixon's plan made a much bigger impression on his secretary of defense, Melvin Laird, and his secretary of state, William Rogers. They threatened to resign if Duck Hook went ahead. Public opinion simply would not accept it. And was the president really ready for a war with China? The country wasn't, Congress wasn't, and the world wasn't.

Thwarted, Nixon made a national television address to promote Vietnamization as his plan for ending the war. Secretly, however, he now realized he needed China's help. This would also be an excellent chance for him to try out his Madman Theory on a worthy opponent, because Mao was an expert at this game. In 1958 Mao had told Khrushchev that he was willing to see hundreds of millions die in a war with the United States. The Soviets could provide the missiles and the nukes, and China could provide the manpower. "War is war," Mao calmly remarked. "The years will pass and we'll get people fucking so they produce more babies than ever before." He was not joking. Khrushchev concluded that Mao was insane. He returned to Moscow and canceled plans to build a nuclear reactor for the Chinese.[3]

Nixon had Kissinger sound out the Chinese on a possible summit meeting. He was also trying to get something useful out of the peace talks in Paris, which had begun in May 1968. They drew an enormous amount of press coverage for what was, most of the time, a charade. The talks in Paris were presented to the public by Nixon and the media as talks mainly between the South Vietnamese and Americans on one side, the North Vietnamese and the People's Revolutionary Government (PRG)—the political wing of the Vietcong—on the other. The real talks, though, consisted of secret discussions between the United States and North Vietnam. Nguyen Van Thieu and the PRG counted for nothing much. Their respective patrons did not even bother to inform them of what was being discussed most of the time.

The core narrative on the American side during these secret exchanges consisted of threats to bomb the North on an unprecedented scale. The North's response was invariably to shrug these off as bluster. Bomb, said the chief negotiator, Le Duc Tho, and see where it gets you. One of Kissinger's senior assistants, John Negroponte, became exasperated. The future ambassador to Iraq fulminated that the Vietnamese were "clumsy, blatant, and essentially contemptuous of the United States, tawdry, petty, and at times transparently childish." This patronizing and racist frame of mind was nothing new on the National Security Council, but it was the part about being "contemptuous of the United States" that seemed to get under Negroponte's skin.[4]

Vietnamization was put to the test in February 1971. The project, to create an ARVN that could fight its own battles with nothing more than some sage and timely advice from its American mentors, had been under way since at least 1965. Here was a chance to show what six years and plenty of chance to learn war by making it had wrought. Seventeen thousand elite ARVN troops, the very best Thieu had, invaded Laos, to cut the Ho Chi Minh Trail, in an operation called Lam Son 719. The ARVN had massive American air and artillery support, and on February 17, Nixon went on television to hail the invasion

of Laos as a phenomenal success. "Tonight, I can report that Vietnamization has succeeded," he declared. "The day the South Vietnamese can take over their own defense is in sight."

The North Vietnamese, however, had not yet delivered their
riposte. Over the next two months they smashed the ARVN in a
succession of huge firefights, shot down 168 helicopters, killed or
wounded more than 8,000 South Vietnamese, and drove the survivors
back into South Vietnam. Lam Son 719 ended in complete defeat, to
Nixon's fury.

By this time, the Ho Chi Minh Trail was an eight-lane highway in
places, and North Vietnamese trucks drove down it at night under a
sky filled with American warplanes. Nixon raged at the air force.
"They say, well, these trucks are moving targets; you've got to be able
to see them to hit them. Bullshit. Just, just, just, cream the fuckers!"[5]

Following Lam Son 719, Hanoi began pressing a list of nine demands in exchange for a cease-fire. These included the overthrow of
the Thieu government, no American bases, neutralization of the
South, more than $7 billion in economic aid for rebuilding both
North and South, and a guaranteed American withdrawal within nine
months of the cease-fire agreement. Nixon, with the 1972 election
just over the horizon, agreed to all of the North's demands except for
getting rid of Thieu. Meanwhile, Kissinger was assuring Thieu that
the United States would in fact keep troops and bases in the South
and would intervene decisively if the cease-fire broke down.

There were also developments on the China front. After eighteen
months of being assiduously courted, Mao allowed face-to-face talks
between Kissinger and Zhou Enlai. In July 1971 Kissinger paid a secret visit to Beijing. If China would only help the United States to
withdraw from South Vietnam, Kissinger told Zhou, the United States
would remove two-thirds of its forces from Taiwan. Zhou dismissed
this odd proposition. So long as there was one American soldier on
Taiwan, the United States would have a justification for defending the
Nationalists from attack.

After Kissinger departed, Zhou flew to Hanoi to reassure the North
Vietnamese leadership that there was no space now, and never would
be, between them and China.

Kissinger's visit to Beijing was but a prelude to Nixon's visit in February 1972. Nixon visited the Great Wall; observed, "This is truly a

great wall"; held discussions with Mao; and told Zhou Enlai, "My predecessor sent 500,000 men into Vietnam, and I've taken 300,000 out. I will end American involvement—it's a matter of time." The one outstanding issue, said Nixon, was American prisoners in North Vietnam. And there was one other thing—he was not going to overthrow Thieu. Nevertheless, he assured Zhou that he would do nothing to prevent Thieu's ouster. The general was expendable.

When Rosemary Woods learned of what Nixon had pledged, his longtime secretary was outraged to her true-blue Republican core. "We have sold out to these bastards," she lamented on her way to the elaborate state banquet Mao had organized to regale his American guests.[6]

Nixon reaped acclaim for having somehow "opened" China to the outside world. China, however, already had diplomatic and economic relations with more than forty countries. To the Chinese, Nixon was coming to pay tribute to the Middle Kingdom, showing that after all, the Americans needed China. In time, Mao knew, it would be China that gained most. The Americans would have to recognize China now, and beyond that, China would finally assume its seat on the UN Security Council, a seat that was being squatted by the Nationalist regime.

Nixon looked to this visit to bring a settlement of the war closer by prying Beijing away from Hanoi. The Chinese meanwhile were reassuring the North Vietnamese that nothing had changed. "We are all the same people," Mao told them.[7]

Only weeks after Nixon returned from Beijing, the PAVN mounted an all-out invasion of the South. It was almost a replay of the North Korean attack on South Korea in June 1950: a mini-blitzkrieg, with an armored spearhead. Nixon ordered an aerial offensive from air force bases in Thailand and the five aircraft carriers operating in the Gulf of Tonkin. They mauled the tanks and artillery, blunting the PAVN attack, but Zhou was quick to reassure Hanoi that American air attacks would change nothing. "This certainly will not work," he said. China had supported the North's offensive and "will support the Vietnamese people to carry out the anti-American patriotic war to its end."[8]

Chinese support at its current level was promoted for at least another five years; until, that is, after the 1976 election, when Nixon's days in power would be at an end. With China still ready to provide weapons, food, and troops, the North had no incentive to settle for anything less than its maximum demand: an end to American involvement in Vietnam's civil war. The equation remained—victory for the North was certain, defeat impossible.

The People's Army of North Vietnam had suffered more than a hundred thousand casualties, and Giap was removed from his position as minister of defense. Even so, the North Vietnamese had seized strategically valuable terrain along the Cambodian and Laotian borders and taken control of most of the demilitarized zone (DMZ). They were well placed to mount another attack—aimed straight at Saigon—once the PAVN had made good its losses.

Stopping the North Vietnamese in their tracks had caused Nixon's spirits to soar into the empyrean, where he became detached from mere earthly concerns. Vietnamization was working after all, he told the country, and he decided to repay North Vietnam for the Easter Offensive by mining Haiphong harbor and using B-52s to turn Hanoi into heaps of rubble.

He was also tempted to bomb the irrigation dikes, but he said to Kissinger, "I'd rather use a nuclear bomb."

With a book published in 1957 titled *Nuclear Weapons and Foreign Policy*, Kissinger had made his reputation as a two-fisted brain box. His argument was that nuclear weapons should be used in limited wars. He claimed they would be manageable—militarily and politically—provided they were not used against another country that possessed nuclear weapons. Nuking nonnuclear countries could be a great help in achieving foreign policy goals.

But when Nixon started talking seriously about using them against North Vietnam, the professor was left gasping for air. His voice fell to a whisper, and he was incapable of formulating a coherent response.

"I just want you to think big, Henry, for Christ's sake," said Nixon, disappointed in the chief academic believer in the merits of nuclear bombing.[9]

At a cabinet meeting on May 8 Nixon announced, "We have crossed the Rubicon." He was going to use airpower to destroy the North's ability to continue the war. He boasted that his will was stronger than Johnson's, and in a televised address he let the American people know that he was going to smash North Vietnam to pieces. Off camera, he told his aides, "Those bastards are going to be bombed like they've never been bombed before! . . . the situation is deteriorating—about November of this year, I'm going to take a goddam hard look at the hole card . . . we're gonna level that goddam country! . . . I wanna know how many Japanese died in the nuclear bombardments. How many in the atomic bombings of Nagasaki and Hiroshima."[10]

At this point, the Madman Theory started to work, but not on the North Vietnamese or the Chinese. They awaited the new aerial offensive, Operation Linebacker, with their usual stoicism. The people who were scared of what the president might do when he was in this mood were the Joint Chiefs. Nixon's talk of using every weapon available sounded like a man getting ready to start a nuclear war. They had good reason to be worried. Nixon was telling Kissinger, "I intend to stop at nothing to bring the enemy to his knees." He demanded a plan from the Chiefs that would "destroy the enemy's war-making capacity."

The Chiefs ignored Nixon's hint that they should consider using nuclear weapons, and stuck to cast-iron bombs, plenty of them—tens of thousands of tons every month. The figures made an impressive chapter in the history of airpower, but they changed nothing. For the moment, though, the failed offensive had made the North Vietnamese willing to make a few minor concessions and one big change: Zhou advised them to drop the demand for Thieu's ouster, because once the Americans departed, Thieu would either leave with them or be ousted. Whatever happened, he wouldn't survive. After thinking this over for a couple of months, the North Vietnamese grudgingly dropped their demand that Thieu be ousted, but a coalition government would have to be guaranteed once the cease-fire took effect.[11]

Nixon made a major concession too. Kissinger got the Russians to pass a message to North Vietnam: if the North would only sign a cease-fire, the troops it had sent into the South could stay there. They did not have to be withdrawn. After the PAVN offensive ground to a halt, Nixon announced that he was going to pull out more American troops, leaving only 49,000 in South Vietnam. The 150,000 North Vietnamese troops still in the South would remain where they were, undisturbed.[12]

Thieu was not informed of that. He only found out when a document titled "General Instructions for a Cease-Fire" was retrieved from a VC bunker. Thieu and Kissinger subsequently had a heated discussion. Thieu would never accept such a deal, he said. "If we accept the document as it stands, we will commit suicide—and I will be committing suicide."[13]

Kissinger tried to soothe his fears. The president was certain to be reelected, said Kissinger, so there was nothing to fear. "If they violate [the agreement]," said Kissinger, "we will launch an operation into North Vietnam."

"But where? A landing or an invasion through the 17th parallel?"

No, said Kissinger. They were thinking of mounting an attack into the DMZ.

Thieu was disgusted. "The landing should be in the vicinity of Vinh," a city 150 miles north of the DMZ and halfway to Hanoi.

Kissinger said Thieu had no choice: if he did not sign, Congress would not appropriate the money needed to keep South Vietnam fighting. Thieu shrugged that off. "If you want to give up the struggle," he retorted, "we will fight on alone until our resources are gone, and then we will die." Kissinger managed to keep a straight face. General Thieu the heroic martyr? Not in this world. Like others of his kind, when the end came, he would flee Saigon for an emotional reunion with his stolen millions in foreign banks.

Kissinger returned to Washington to announce, "We believe that peace is at hand!" In fact, he believed nothing of the kind, and the North Vietnamese knew it. The only people he fooled were the American voters, who reelected Nixon to the White House ten days later. Privately, Kissinger was close to despair. Suppose Thieu continued to hold out—what then?[14]

By this time in his career, Kissinger had crafted a sense of self that gave credit for every foreign policy success to himself—a humble, up-by-his-bootstraps immigrant with a Strangelovian accent. In an interview with one of the most remarkable journalists of the time, the beautiful, clever, and courageous Oriana Fallaci, Dr. K overflowed with self-confident assertions that belied his chewed nails and gnawed knuckles. "I have acted alone," he told her. "The Americans love this immensely. The Americans love the cowboy, who leads the convoy [sic] alone on his horse, the cowboy who comes into town all alone on his horse, and nothing else. Perhaps not even with a gun, because he does not shoot. He acts, and that is enough, being in the right place at the right time. In sum, a Western. This romantic and surprising character suits me because being alone has always been part of my style."[15]

When Nixon read this, he raged. "We've got to stop paying the price for Kissinger," he told Bob Haldeman, but he could not bring himself in the end to get rid of someone whose deviousness and dishonesty were useful adjuncts to Nixon's own loner style.[16]

Nixon's reelection emboldened him to look for a way of pummeling the North Vietnamese into a more cooperative frame of mind. He and Kissinger began looking for a way to engineer a breakdown in the Paris talks and then say the other side had done it. Their chance came when Le Duc Tho told them he was returning to Hanoi for further instructions. Nixon and Kissinger portrayed this as a walkout, even though they had known of Tho's plans for several weeks.

Nixon promptly ordered an even bigger air offensive than the last one—Operation Linebacker II. This time he would use B-52s against an urban population. He claimed he was doing it only to force the other side back to the talks, and he informed Admiral Thomas Moorer, chairman of the JCS, "This is your chance to use military power effectively to win this war." The bombing was certain to kill and mutilate thousands of civilians. Bombing residential neighborhoods with B-52s that dropped thousands of cast-iron bombs could have no other result, something that Nixon seemed to relish. He was so angry and—given his drinking problems—possibly so inebriated that he did not give much, if any, thought to how the country, the Congress, and America's allies would react. Nixon boasted that he was going to break the North's will.

After all the negotiations, the trip to China, and the withdrawal of nearly all the ground troops, he was still looking for victory in Vietnam. He was going to destroy all the most valuable military and economic targets North Vietnam possessed—a bridge here, a power plant there, an airfield somewhere else, some railroad yards, small fuel dumps.

For eleven days and nights that December, Hanoi shook and ignited as wave after wave of B-52s dropped one-ton bombs. But like Truman and LBJ before him, in his ranting moments Nixon avoided thinking about China. A commander in chief can feel a lot freer, a lot more powerful that way. Yet as American planes dropped aerial mines into Haiphong harbor, Chinese mine-clearing crews were arriving to fish them out.

The resort to using B-52s on urban neighborhoods was taken by the North Vietnamese as a sign of weakness, not strength. The Chinese agreed. Shortly after the bombing stopped, Le Duc Tho traveled to Paris to talk to Henry Kissinger. En route, he broke his journey in Beijing to see Zhou Enlai. Zhou congratulated Tho on the outcome of Operation Linebacker II. "Their attempt to exert pressure through bombing has failed," said Zhou, and the Americans had just played their last card. There were 150,000 North Vietnamese troops now securely based in the South, and American opinion was demanding complete withdrawal of the 90,000 American soldiers who remained. "Let the Americans leave as quickly as possible. In half a year or one year, the situation will change."[17]

The North Vietnamese agreed to return to the negotiations, which allowed Nixon to claim that Linebacker II had brought North Vietnam to its knees. In the negotiations, however, Nixon eventually conceded every demand the North Vietnamese made, allowing them to claim that they had defeated Linebacker II. The Americans had tried to destroy the people's will, and failed.

There was little left that Nixon could do, and he knew it. Before Kissinger departed for Paris and the next round of talks, Nixon gave him his instructions: "Settle on whatever terms are available." That meant arriving at an agreement without Thieu's assent, and the 150,000 North Vietnamese troops in the South would be free to stay. The main thing was, the Americans were leaving. All Nixon asked in return was the release of six hundred American POWs, most of them pilots and other air crew.[18]

Meanwhile, he was threatening Thieu with an end to American aid if he did not sign a cease-fire agreement. This was no bluff. There was already a move in Congress to pass a resolution that would end all aid for the South and pledged a complete pullout of American troops in exchange for the release of the POWs in North Vietnamese hands. That resolution would pass in the House by a two-to-one vote, said Nixon.

He also assured Thieu that the commitments he and Kissinger were making would be a matter of official record and would oblige Nixon's successors in the White House to follow though. General

Alexander Haig told Thieu, "We plan to keep substantial forces in Southeast Asia for hair-trigger response to violations." But still Thieu balked.[19]

Nixon's assurances about his successors' actions were nonsense, and Thieu knew it. No president can make his successor do anything. All Nixon could offer was a practical commitment while he was in power and pious hopes about what might happen after he departed. The Americans were promising retaliation if the North attacked, Thieu told his cronies, "but who can know for sure?"[20]

The National Liberation Front and the North Vietnamese had begun the talks in May 1968 with a list of ten demands. In the final agreement, they secured nine out of ten, and the key American demands, such as a mutual withdrawal, were abandoned. The sole concession the North made was that Thieu could remain in power, for now. Both the Saigon government and the People's Revolutionary Government of South Vietnam refused to sign the cease-fire agreement.

Thieu's prospects did not look good. Having been lied to on matters large and small throughout ten years of war in Indochina, the people of the United States and Congress had had enough. Nor was it any secret that much of the aid provided was stolen by Thieu and other crooks, large and small.

The day had also gone when Congress would allow Nixon to push American troops back into South Vietnam in the guise of responding to an emergency. What Nixon was really hoping for, however, was a five- or six-year gap—which he termed "a decent interval"—between the withdrawal of the last American combat units in April 1973 and the overthrow of Thieu's government. Kissinger thought the interval would be eighteen months, at most.[21]

In August 1974, Nixon resigned. His crooked vice president, Spiro Agnew, had already been forced to resign as his best hope of staying out of prison. With both Nixon and Agnew out of the picture, Congressman Gerald Ford, Agnew's successor, became president.

There were clashes between North and South Vietnamese troops during the months that followed Nixon's departure, but Congress and the country were so angry at having been lied to by Johnson and Nixon on the subject of Vietnam that after more than a decade of brazen mendacity, patience was exhausted.

When American troops withdrew, they left billions of dollars' worth of weapons and military supplies behind for the benefit of the ARVN. Vietnamization had been under way for nearly a decade. If the ARVN was unable to fight its own battles by this time, it would never be ready. Congress continued to supply money, grudgingly, to Thieu's kleptocracy, but the gravy train's manifest wasn't as generous as in earlier times. Ford asked for a billion dollars; Congress authorized $700 million.

During that winter of 1974, as Ford and his chief of staff, Donald Rumsfeld, tried to find ways to aid Thieu, PAVN staff officers were doing what military planners have done during the winter since time immemorial—planning the spring offensive. It began on March 30, and it was aimed at achieving limited goals. Both the North and South had freely violated the cease-fire from the day it was signed. But this time, without American air support, the ARVN folded and the North pushed everything it could move down Highway 1 to join in the fight.

On April 21, with enemy tanks, self-propelled artillery, and truck-loads of infantry rolling toward Saigon, Thieu resigned and was flown to Taiwan. Thereafter he lived in London and Boston in well-padded luxury, playing the drums in a mohair suit, cut continental-style, looking like a Rat Pack aspirant.[22]

On April 29, 1974, PAVN Tank 390, with a large red flag attached, crashed through the gates of the Presidential Palace in Saigon. On the tank's underside was a small steel plate that read MADE IN CHINA.

Chapter 23
Futurismo

A DARK CLOUD LOURED OVER THE PENTAGON AND THE WHITE House through the fifteen years from 1975 to 1990. Unlike most clouds, this one had a name—Vietnam Syndrome—and the shadow it cast seemed to stretch far into the future. It was a future that would be defined by limits on American power, leading ineluctably to a decline in power, leading to even harsher limits, producing an even steeper decline, and so on, until the United States was just another country in a world composed of countries. What a fate.

The declinists believed the world was running out of scarce resources while the nation was running out of answers. Most declinists were the kind of liberals that Spiro Agnew had dismissed as "the nattering nabobs of negativism," but they also included gloomy nabobs of Republicanism, such as Henry Kissinger and Richard Nixon himself.

It was a depressed and anxious country that elected Jimmy Carter in 1976, in preference to Gerald Ford, who had pardoned Nixon for trying to subvert the Constitution and numerous lesser offenses. Executing Charles I in 1649 had done much to reform the British monarchy. Jailing Nixon, or even giving him a suspended sentence, might have been good for the health of American democracy for generations to come, but that opportunity was cast away, to the audible relief of the Republican Party.

Carter arrived in the White House as the virtual embodiment of declinism. He thus brought with him an aversion to the Truman-Eisenhower-Kennedy-Johnson-Nixon policy of armed intervention across the global south as a way of asserting American leadership. Even so, Carter was an Annapolis graduate and career naval officer. As commander in chief, he did not need to be told that the demoralized and exhausted military forces he inherited had to be rebuilt. At the same time, he hoped to reach an agreement with the Soviets that would reduce long-range nuclear missiles to one hundred on each side—enough for deterrence, not enough to destroy the human race. This proposal was too radical for Congress or the Kremlin, but one of Carter's unacknowledged achievements was that he, the supposedly weak CinC, would leave America stronger militarily than the hawkish Nixon had left it.

Fate had been kind enough to raise Carter from obscurity to power, but then it made up for that by giving him Reza Pahlavi, the shah of Iran. The shah's father, a general in the Iranian army, had overthrown the government back in 1926, with the support of the British, whose interest was oil, not democracy.

The son depended, like his father before him, on British protection. But in 1951, shortly after Reza Pahlavi inherited the throne, the Iranian voters, in their first free election, had installed a rumpled, rambling, and lachrymose doctor turned man of the people, Mohammad Mossadeq, as prime minister. Mossadeq had promised to nationalize the oil fields.

Unable to buy him off or scare him off, the British shut the oil fields down. The British Secret Intelligence Service, MI6, yoked its regime-changing forces to those of the CIA and began plotting to overthrow him. Iran's tiny Communist Party had already rallied to the government's defense, which provided a justification other than oil.

By the summer of 1953, with emotions running high on both sides, pro-Mossadeq supporters organized by the Communists and anti-Mossadeq rioters organized by the British and Americans were plunging Tehran into anarchy. Encouraged by the British and the CIA, the

Iranian army stepped in and arrested Mossadeq. The youthful shah had whiled away the turbulence in the streets around his palace by luxuriating a thousand miles away in all the earthly delights that Rome had to offer. He now returned to Iran.[1]

After the coup against Mossadeq, most Iranians refused to accept the shah as their legitimate ruler. His fate was sealed, and in 1979, unloved, unwanted, and unnecessary, he was overthrown and replaced by the religious leader Ayatollah Khomeini. Shortly afterward the United States embassy was stormed, and sixty-six Americans (mainly diplomatic staff) were seized and held hostage. Carter tried to rescue them in an operation too complicated to have any chance of success. It only added to an increasingly jaundiced view of Carter as commander in chief.

Seized by religio-patriotic fervor and a long-suppressed thirst for revenge, Iranians fired potshots at oil tankers operating in the Persian Gulf. Carter ordered U.S. warships to begin escorting the tankers, and he authorized them to fire back.

His failure to negotiate the release of the hostages doomed Carter in the 1980 election. Reagan's victory that fall brought the release of the hostages after 444 days in captivity, giving him a sensational start to his presidency and a chance to recalibrate relations with Iran.

Reagan's election also marked the beginning of serious resistance to declinism. The Vietnam Syndrome was not going to be contained. It was going to be rolled back . . . somehow. What was beyond doubt was that the anti-declinists had found their beau ideal in Reagan, a man who radiated optimism from the way he walked and the passé way that he dressed—in mid-1950s ventless sack suits, complete with padded shoulders, big cuffs, big cuff links, big ties. It was the Big Man in Rotary look, a look once mercifully swept away by the continental style of the Rat Pack and John Kennedy, but back once more in power.

Reagan believed in American exceptionalism and all that it implied—that the United States was so rich, so strong, and so blessed with talented people it could accomplish anything once the national resolve was focused on a clear goal. He began his attack on the Vietnam Syndrome by launching armed interventions in places where success seemed certain, such as Beirut.

A multinational force, headed by the United States, intervened in

Lebanon in the fall of 1982 after the government collapsed thanks to an Israeli invasion. The Israelis installed a government of Christian Falangists in a predominantly Muslim country.

To many a Lebanese Muslim it appeared that the United States was there to defend the unpopular Falangist government. In April 1983, the U.S. embassy was bombed, killing fifty-three people. The president vowed to remain in Lebanon until the country was stabilized.[2]

Six months later, on October 23, a building being used as a barracks by the marines was leveled by a suicide truck bomber. Two hundred and forty-one marines perished. A French military barracks was also destroyed by a bomb, killing fifty-eight French soldiers.

Both the embassy bombing and the marine barracks bombing were almost certainly the work of Hizbollah, a terrorist organization organized and financed by Iran. Suicide bombing itself was also a new development. The first suicide bomber had been a fifteen-year-old Iranian youth who had blown himself up underneath an Iraqi tank a year earlier, in the Iran-Iraq war.[3]

Dramatic events were meanwhile unfolding on the tiny Caribbean island of Grenada, whose place in the world economy was the provision of nutmegs. An avowedly Marxist-Leninist government had been installed there, taking Cuba as its inspiration. There was also a Cuban construction crew numbering three hundred engineers and laborers building a new airport. When Maurice Bishop, the leader of the People's Revolutionary Government, was assassinated, he was replaced by another Castro admirer, Bernard Coard.

Having anyone who admired Castro installed as the leader of a Caribbean or South American country was taken for a deliberate provocation by Reagan and his national security team. The time to strike was ASAP, before Coard was securely in power.

The presence of several hundred American students enrolled at Grenada's medical school provided some justification. The students, too old or too undistinguished academically to get into medical schools at home, had no idea that they were in danger from Communist depredations, but the president decided they were. The fact that the new airport, designed to welcome long-haul tourists, might also welcome Soviet long-range bombers was another reason for invading. And the presence of the Cuban construction workers was the clincher.

On October 25, Grenada was not simply attacked. It was overrun in a miniature D-day: an air, ground, and sea assault that bewildered Grenadans, students, and Cubans alike. Coard was overthrown, and a group of local businessmen formed a new government under American tutelage.[4]

Grenada, the military operation that became famous for the distribution of medals as if they were Cracker Jack prizes, was a success. All the same, it did not change anything in the power equation: Reagan swiftly withdrew American forces from Lebanon, and the navy bombarded Beirut in what looked like a fit of pique.

A Hizbollah offshoot was kidnapping westerners in Lebanon. Reagan, who was fundamentally kindhearted, decided for emotional reasons rather than reasons of state to pay half a million dollars or more for each American hostage released, provided it was kept secret.

This setback brought a reconsideration of the U.S. relationship with Tehran, and a year later Reagan opened up a back channel to the Khomeini regime in order to secure the release of hostages. Far from becoming simpler, though, the relationship with Iran now took a bizarre turn. Within months Reagan managed to put the United States on both sides in the Iran-Iraq war.

While a dozen laws were being violated in order to provide ransom money to Iran, the United States was providing arms and satellite images of the battlefield to Saddam Hussein. Washington was also urging other countries and major financial institutions to loan billions to Saddam to finance his war machine. Iraq was removed from the list of state sponsors of terrorism even though it was no secret that Saddam had used chemical weapons against the Kurds, many of whom were supporting Iran. In December 1983 Reagan sent a former secretary of defense, Donald Rumsfeld, to Baghdad to assure Saddam Hussein that he could count on American support.

Meanwhile the Iranians began sounding out the Americans on the purchase of antitank and antiaircraft weapons. There was a lot of money waiting to be made—money that could be used for other illicit ventures. Before long, Iranian money was being used to finance the right-wing Nicaraguan Contras in their ongoing guerrilla campaign against the left-wing, pro-Cuban government of Daniel Ortega.

The CIA also aided the Contras in what amounted to terrorist attacks, such as planting mines to blow up Soviet ships that might be carrying arms to the left-wing Sandinista party. Unfortunately, the mines could not tell a pro-Contra ship from a pro-Sandinista ship, or even a neutral ship. CIA employees also got involved in smuggling cocaine into the United States from Latin America as a way of financing the Contras. They were acting without authorization, but in the secret world, nothing much is truly straight.

Reagan had authorized the Iran-Contra program, but he managed to deny it with considerable success until the end of his presidency, and almost to his grave. He had completed the rebuilding of the military that Carter had begun. Reagan also talked openly about spending so much on modernizing the military that the Soviets would go broke trying to keep up. The risk, of course, was that the United States would go broke with it.

When the Soviet Union collapsed, in 1989, Reagan was credited, by Americans at least, with having won the Cold War. His efforts received a considerable boost from Margaret Thatcher. When she first appeared on the world stage in the early 1980s, jaws dropped among the gray men who managed world affairs. She might as well have arrived on a trapeze with her hair on fire. Thatcher became Reagan's friend and ally in helping the Soviet leadership to accept the end of Communism—which expired, happily for the world, with a whimper, not a bang.

Even if Reagan had won the Cold War for America, he had not abolished the Vietnam Syndrome. But he talked a great fight. None better.

His vice president and successor, George Herbert Walker Bush, came to the role of commander in chief with a résumé that could hardly be faulted. Dropping out of Yale only days after the attack on Pearl Harbor, Bush had become a navy pilot, flying a torpedo bomber in the Pacific. It was what happened to fliers who were not good enough to handle fighters, but steady and competent enough to fly a less-demanding warplane.

Bush emerged from the war with the enviable distinction of having seen aerial combat and being shot down, yet he survived with all his body parts intact. After graduating from Yale, he got rich in the oil business, served as a congressman, became director of the CIA, was ambassador to the UN, and spent eight years as Ronald Reagan's vice president.

When Bush became president, in January 1989, the Iran-Iraq war had recently ended in a bloody stalemate that had cost up to a million lives. The Soviet Union had spent ten years fighting an unwinnable war in Afghanistan and was about to withdraw, defeated. The Cold War was in its last days. The tectonic plates of global politics were shifting.

That still left Third World irritants, such as Manuel Noriega of Panama, a military strongman who had seized power in a coup. Noriega's government was a typical criminal enterprise in that part of the world—corruption, bribery, blackmail, beatings, jailing, torture, rigged elections, intimidation, plus a slice of a trade that was still fairly new but rich with promise: drugs and drug money were transiting Panama from neighboring Colombia.

Bush was determined to oust him. The U.S. Army commander responsible for Latin America was not. The new secretary of defense, Richard Cheney, retired the general. While the CIA tried to overthrow Noriega by covert means, Cheney promoted an overt approach to regime change, and that was the one the president accepted.

There was so much friction and so much casual violence in Panama it was certain that Bush would not have to wait long for a pretext to invade. In December 1989, Noriega overturned the results of an election that he had lost, and, in front of television camera crews, one of his principal opponents was given a beating that left him covered in blood. Shortly after this, an American serviceman was shot dead by Noriega's paramilitaries, and another serviceman was seized, along with his wife. Bush could count on public and congressional support for removing Manuel Noriega.

There were already plenty of American troops in Panama, but two thousand Special Forces and marines, plus tanks and attack helicopters, were dispatched to lead the way. On December 20, American forces fanned out from their bases, heading for Noriega's headquarters. Noriega was taking a break at that moment in a brothel outside the capital. He thereby eluded capture. From the whorehouse, he fled to the papal nuncio's residence on Christmas Eve and claimed asylum.

The pope did not want him, nor did the nuncio. Noriega surrendered two weeks after the operation to oust him had begun. He is currently in a federal prison, serving a life sentence for drug offenses.

From his cell, he bombards a wide range of correspondents with letters protesting that he is a political prisoner.

Hardly had Noriega been nabbed before an even bigger villain appeared. In mid-July 1990, Keyhole satellites started beaming back pictures of Iraqi tank columns moving south, toward Kuwait. America's friend of convenience, Saddam Hussein, had run up a huge debt in his war with Iran. His creditors, such as France and Russia, were pressing for payment, and he could hardly ignore Paris and Moscow—they were his principal weapons suppliers. The only solution he could see was to put pressure on Kuwait, one of the richest small states in the world. The Saudis had loaned him billions to help fight the war with Iran. So had Kuwait.

Iraq has been a frontline state for three thousand years, the great barrier between the Persians and the heartland of the Arabs, long before Islam. Much as the Russians saw, and still see, themselves as having protected Europe from the Tartars for five hundred years, so Iraqis saw themselves as the defenders of Arabia.

Tension between the warrior Iraqis and the feudal family that owned Kuwait was hardly new. When the British created Iraq, they had divided the huge Rumailah oil field between southern Iraq and northern Kuwait. Divide and rule. Kuwait was, to all intents and purposes, a British protectorate, entrusted to a single merchant family, the Al-Sabahs. In 1938 Sheikh Al-Sabah's advisory council urged him to seek union with Iraq. The British refused to allow it. No Iraqi government could be trusted with so much oil.

When, in 1961, the British finally granted full independence to Kuwait, Iraq's military government began moving tank columns toward it. The British responded by deploying armor and air units to Kuwait. The Iraqis backed away, but the conviction remained that Kuwait was not a real country. It was a rich province torn away by the colonial oppressors and would one day, God willing, be reunited with the rest of Iraq.

For now, though, Kuwait was a key player in the Organization of the Petroleum Exporting Countries (OPEC). Saddam accused Kuwait and the United Arab Emirates of exceeding OPEC's production quotas. They had kept the price of oil low in order to keep the Americans happy. That was the equivalent, he argued, of stealing $14 billion from Iraq. They had also been pumping oil from parts of the Rumailah field that were owned by Iraq, stealing oil worth billions. To make amends, Kuwait must cancel Iraq's war loans.[5]

George H. W. Bush had long been close to the Saudi royal family, and the Saudi ambassador, Prince Bandar bin Sultan, was an old friend. Whatever Saddam is up to, the prince told Bush, he is not about to attack Kuwait. On the evening of August 1, Bush's national security adviser, Brent Scowcroft, arrived at the private quarters of the White House with a different tale. Scowcroft, a retired air force lieutenant general, was closer to Bush than any national security adviser had ever been to a president—so close that Scowcroft was known behind his back as "the First Companion." The two even took their vacations together. And now Scowcroft had some bad news to deliver: "Iraq may be about to invade Kuwait." An hour later, Scowcroft called to confirm it. "They're across the border." What had begun as a bluff mounted to promote debt cancellation had just turned into a blatant grab for Kuwait's oil.[6]

As an oilman, Bush grasped the price-at-the-pump implications of what Saddam was doing. Saddam would have the leverage to force up gasoline prices, at a time when the world economy was still struggling with the effects of quadrupling oil prices in 1973, an idea that had originated with the supposedly pro-Western Shah Reza Pahlavi.[7]

The next morning, a grim-looking Bush faced the press. Was he going to intervene? "We're not discussing intervention," he said, but he knew what he wanted: "Have this invasion reversed and have them get out of Kuwait." This did not mean intervention, because for now, it was a diplomatic problem. "I'm sure there will be a lot of frenzied diplomatic activity. I plan to participate in some of that myself."[8]

The recently installed chairman of the Joint Chiefs of Staff, Colin Powell, did not think Kuwait was worth a war. Nor did his predecessor, Admiral William Crowe. Nor did any of the current Chiefs. Nor did James Baker III, who had served as Reagan's chief of staff and as secretary of the treasury. Baker was a lawyer from Houston who had become rich and influential from advising oil companies and their executives. To Powell, Crowe, Baker, the Chiefs, and Senator Sam Nunn, the chairman of the Senate Armed Services Committee, the right response consisted of two parts. The first was to assume responsibility for the defense of Saudi Arabia.

The only offensive power Saddam possessed was in his tanks and his air force. He had more than four hundred combat aircraft, mostly Soviet-built, but their pilots were no match for their American counterparts, nor was their technology, their leadership, or their command and control. Ditto the tanks. They were Soviet too, but the United States had spent decades devising ways to kill Soviet tanks. Saddam's armored divisions would not survive long against American combat helicopters, A-10 tank busters, and antitank missiles. The biggest problem in defending Saudi Arabia was going to be getting the Saudis to agree to it.

The second part was to push a resolution through the UN that would impose a stringent sanctions regime. If Saddam could not sell Iraq's oil or Kuwait's, he would gain nothing. He would not, as the president feared, control world oil prices. His oil sales would be blocked, making his creditors less patient than ever. At some point Saddam Hussein would be forced to disgorge Kuwait without a war, because even tyrants need money.

Saddam too was apparently thinking of the UN, but he had a different scenario: the issue would go to the UN, which would spend a decade trying to decide what to do, and in the meantime he would control 20 percent of the world's oil supplies and would be able to push up the price. His creditors would not only get paid, but they would be as eager as ever to sell him weapons and military technologies. Given enough money, he might even be able to build a nuclear weapon. This, though, was the same fantasist who had expected to bring Iran to its knees.[9]

On August 4 Bush had his principal advisers meet with him at Camp David. These included Dick Cheney, Brent Scowcroft, Under Secretary of Defense Paul Wolfowitz, James Baker, and the commander of Central Command, Norman Schwarzkopf. Cheney, Scowcroft, and Wolfowitz were convinced that the Vietnam Syndrome had to be rolled back and that, under Reagan, it had been allowed to dictate national security policy. To rely on diplomatic and economic pressure now would only entrench the Syndrome. There was one thing that worried Cheney about war with Iraq. "The problem is the American people might have a short tolerance for war."[10]

When the president returned to the White House later that afternoon, he strode from Marine One over to a bank of microphones and took reporters' questions. As they pressed him on whether he was go-

Here, at Camp David following his reelection in 1972, President Nixon puts on a show of toughness for the benefit of his national security adviser, Henry Kissinger, and Dr. K's assistant General Alexander Haig. The Chinese and the North Vietnamese had long since called his bluff. *(National Archives)*

Nguyen Van Thieu was a general and the president of South Vietnam. He knew that Nixon was going to hand his country over to the North Vietnamese and the Popular Liberation Front, the political arm of the Viet Cong. He knew too that he could do nothing to stop it. *(National Archives)*

Zhou Enlai was one of the great survivors in modern Chinese history. A soldier, a diplomat, and an intellectual, over the course of forty years of shared struggle and danger Zhou had made himself indispensable to Mao. *(National Archives)*

Here Nixon and his wife, Pat, are awestruck tourists visiting the Great Wall in
February 1972. Nixon was almost speechless. He seems never to have grasped
that what the Great Wall represented was failure: a doomed attempt to hold
the future back with brick and stone. *(National Archives)*

George Herbert Walker Bush, a Yale freshman when the Imperial Japanese Navy launched its attack on Pearl Harbor, dropped out immediately to join the navy. Still a downy-cheeked youth, he became a torpedo bomber pilot and was shot down over the Pacific. *(George Bush Presidential Library)*

The first President Bush seems to have decided to fight a war over Kuwait on the spur of the moment and in a fit of pique. After that, there was no turning back. General "Stormin' Norman" Schwarzkopf gave him a personal tour of the Saudi Arabian desert, terrain much like the sands of Mesopotamia farther north. *(George Bush Presidential Library)*

At the end of the liberation of Kuwait, the president greeted the victory parade as it marched
down Pennsylvania Avenue and took the salute of Schwarzkopf and other Desert
Storm commanders. But over the horizon, Saddam Hussein still ruled Iraq. The
crucial question—what happens after Kuwait?—had never been addressed.
George H. W. Bush had committed his country to
a fifty-year war without realizing it.
(*George Bush Presidential Library*)

On the eve of Desert Storm, President George H. W. Bush and his cabinet bowed their heads in prayer, seeking God's blessing for the military campaign. Truman and Johnson, too, had claimed God's approval for the wars they waged in Korea and Vietnam.
(George Bush Presidential Library)

In the wake of Desert Storm, father and son walked toward the White House with a confident step. What really lay ahead, though, was a fifty-year war against Islamic fundamentalism and suicide terrorism.
(George Bush Presidential Library)

Assigned to pilot training in the Texas Air National Guard under dubious circumstances, George W. Bush asked for a non-combat assignment in the Vietnam War and, as usual, got exactly what he asked for. *(George Bush Presidential Library)*

Vice President Richard Cheney and Secretary of Defense Donald Rumsfeld with President Bush. They were determined to recover what they believed were the "lost powers" of the presidency. With their help, Bush would turn the commander-in-chief clause in the Constitution into a danger to the Constitution itself. (*Department of Defense. Photograph by Helene C. Stikkel*)

A month after the fall of Baghdad, Bush 43 flew in this navy plane to the aircraft carrier *Abraham Lincoln*, in the waters off San Diego. Although he had been no more than a passenger, he emerged in a flight suit, with a helmet tucked under his arm. In that moment, Bush became the CinC that until then only Hollywood had been able to provide: the president as warrior, protecting his people. (*Photograph by Gabriel Piper*)

ing to intervene militarily, his patience snapped. Waving an admonitory finger and becoming emotional, he said, "Just wait. Watch and learn . . . This will not stand, this aggression against Kuwait." He had not made this decision at Camp David; he probably had not made it on the helicopter. To Colin Powell, he appeared to have made it the moment he said it. No discussion, no debate, no plan, but as commander in chief, Bush could do it. Everything from this point would be geared to giving him what he wanted.[11]

Scowcroft supported him to the hilt. So did Margaret Thatcher. Nevertheless, most Americans were opposed to a war for oil or for Kuwait. The administration would have to find ways to turn American and world opinion around. As it would take months to assemble a political and military coalition and then move a large, fully equipped expeditionary force to the Gulf, the president would have time to rally support at home and abroad. Besides, Bush told his polling expert, Robert Teeter, his whole life had given him the background to meet this challenge. "This will be a success," he promised Teeter. But to Powell he delivered a less-confident message: don't let this become another Vietnam.[12]

American forces in the Gulf were augmented while planning and troop movements got under way. Bush made a television broadcast to announce the buildup. "The mission of our troops is wholly defensive," he mendaciously declared. "They will not initiate hostilities, but they will defend themselves, the kingdom of Saudi Arabia, and other friends in the Persian Gulf."[13]

Cheney had, like Bush, made millions in the Texas oil business and was thus used to talking to Saudi royals. He was dispatched to Saudi Arabia to secure their agreement to having American troops deployed to the kingdom. While Cheney made the rounds of Arabic governments that were friendly to the United States, Baker was flying all over the globe, creating a wide-ranging coalition that crucially included the Russians and the French. Baker had tried to dissuade Bush from starting a major war. "I know you're aware of the fact that this has all the ingredients that brought down three of the last five presidents: a hostage crisis, body bags, and a full-fledged economic recession caused by forty-dollar oil." Bush would not be swayed, and Baker loyally set off on his global travels.[14]

The UN Security Council authorized action to expel Saddam Hussein from Kuwait and demanded that he destroy all weapons of mass destruction, meaning his chemical and biological weapons stocks. Saddam had no nuclear weapons, only dreams of one day building some.

The United States and Britain had plenty of tanks and troops for the coming venture. Long deployed to Germany to deter the Soviet Union, they were available, now that the USSR had collapsed, for operations in the desert. Japan, Germany, and Saudi Arabia meanwhile agreed to foot the bill for the war. Dick Cheney also got Saudi Arabia's skittish King Fahd to agree to have American troops in the kingdom. Fahd knew that their presence would only fuel the anger and broaden the appeal of Islamic fundamentalists, who would portray the presence of an infidel army as sacrilege. After all, his proudest title was Guardian of the Two Holy Places, meaning Mecca and Medina.[15]

But didn't President Bush need a congressional resolution? The War Powers Act, passed by Congress in 1973 over Nixon's veto, required the president to consult with Congress if hostilities appeared to be imminent. The second requirement was that if he did commit American forces to a conflict, he would have to withdraw those forces after sixty days unless he obtained a congressional resolution authorizing him to fight on.

The attorney general, William P. Barr, assured Bush that as commander in chief, he was free to ignore the War Powers Act. This situation, said Barr, is like Korea. Truman had not sought a congressional resolution, because he already had one from the UN. All the same, Bush wisely chose to go in person and ask Congress for a resolution on September 11. It wasn't going to be easy. The Democrats controlled both the House and the Senate. During his time in the White House, Bush had never been comfortable with what he called "a hostile Congress."[16]

"Iraq will not be permitted to annex Kuwait. That's not a threat, that's not a boast, that's just the way it's going to be." And once Kuwait had been liberated, "a new world order can emerge—free from the threat of terror."

On December 1, with the bulk of coalition forces deployed to the Gulf, Bush gave Saddam forty-five days to comply with the UN resolution calling for withdrawal from Kuwait. In a positive mood, Bush met with the congressional leadership. "This is not a Vietnam," he assured them. "It will not be a long, drawn out mess."[17]

Bush, Scowcroft, and Cheney seemed to give virtually no thought to the long-term ramifications of what they were about to do. Saddam Hussein would be forced to surrender. "He will, I know he will," Bush told Scowcroft.

In the short term, the prospects looked excellent. There was no chance that Saddam's army, with its ramshackle logistics, poor maintenance, and cowed officer corps, would defeat a large, and largely Western, military force, with its superior equipment, training, leadership, and guaranteed air superiority. The Iraqis would be driven out of Kuwait. But what would happen then? The chances of Saddam's surrendering were zero. He was not another Noriega.

Bush rejected advancing all the way to Baghdad to overthrow Saddam, because that would commit American soldiers "to fight in what would be an unwinnable urban guerrilla war," he wrote in his memoirs. The UN resolution had been crafted so that it limited operations to the liberation of Kuwait, and the coalition was organized within the same limits in order to secure Arab support. Opting for war over containment, Bush had fashioned his own shackles, while containment would still have left the war option open.[18]

Henry Kissinger and James Schlesinger, Nixon's secretary of defense, as well as Jimmy Carter, all saw the Middle East being made more unstable than ever by this emotional rush to war, and more thought was being devoted to getting it started than was ever paid to how to end it.

Jimmy Carter was so horrified that he urged the UN Security Council not to mandate military action unless every possible nonmilitary option had been tried first. Bush was incredulous that a former president would lobby the Security Council to vote against an American-sponsored resolution. Carter, however, was like Kissinger and Schlesinger—trying to stop his country from making a strategic mistake.[19]

When Powell offered the president his best advice, which was that containment was a viable option, Bush dismissed it out of hand. Yet assuming that Saddam survived—and like many another psychopath, he had a dismaying talent for survival—a sanctions regime was inevitable. He would still have an army, still be a threat to Kuwait, still be able to cause turmoil in the Gulf. Liberating Kuwait would not be the end of this struggle.

So what was the plan for after Kuwait? There was none. Bush hoped that Saddam might be toppled if he didn't surrender, but hope is never a plan. The president evaded the hardest question of all, preferring to take comfort in telling his diary, "Saddam Hussein will get out of Kuwait [and] our role as a world leader will once again be reaffirmed."[20]

As a former navy pilot, he also had a flier's belief in airpower. Bush kept musing aloud about how the air force would shatter Saddam's army and force it out of Kuwait as its only hope of escaping annihilation from the air. Powell tried repeatedly, as a good soldier would, to try to steer him away from this dangerous delusion, without a lot of success. "Colin," the president responded, "these guys have never been seriously bombed."[21]

Bush found moral justification in portraying Saddam as one of the greatest villains in five thousand years of history. "Lots of people are calling him Hitler," Bush told his advisers, and he proceeded to do the same. He also talked up wildly exaggerated stories of Iraqi atrocities inflicted on the people of Kuwait. The truth was bad enough, but he made it sound like the Rape of Nanking. This struggle, he insisted, was one of good versus evil, and no mistake.

His old employer, the CIA, obligingly put out stories that there were 250,000 Iraqi troops deployed close to the Saudi border, ready to attack. Satellite images obtained from a company that had access to Russian satellite photographs showed that there were no Iraqi troops anywhere near the border. Instead, there was only empty desert.[22]

And then came Nayira, a young Kuwaiti woman who appeared before the Congressional Human Rights Caucus. "I volunteered at the al-Addan hospital," she declared. She saw Iraqi troops pulling sickly infants out of incubators and dumping them on the floor to die. As witnesses go, Nayira was terrific. Tearful but not weepy; distressed but not hysterical; articulate and direct.

Nayira was, in fact, the fifteen-year-old daughter of the Kuwaiti ambassador. She had rehearsed her testimony under the tutelage of Hill and Knowlton, Washington's biggest lobbying firm, whose well-heeled clients included the government of Kuwait. Hill and Knowlton billed the Kuwaitis nearly $20 million for Nayira's perjured testimony, but it was worth every penny.

On January 12, 1991, the House and Senate voted on the joint congressional resolution. It passed in the House 250 to 183. In the Senate the vote was much closer: 52–47. Six senators spoke of how deeply they had been affected by Nayira's testimony and how it had convinced them to vote for war. Without Nayira, Bush would have lost in the Senate by 53 votes to 46. The country was being duped into a war.[23]

One of the senators who voted against the resolution asked, "Are we supposed to go to war simply because one man—the president— makes a series of unilateral decisions that put us in a box—a box that makes that war, to a greater degree, inevitable?" The senator was John Kerry.

By now the president was reaping the benefits of his assiduous public relations campaign. Polls showed that two-thirds of Americans supported military intervention to force Saddam out of Kuwait.

At the last moment, though, Mikhail Gorbachev crafted a peace proposal for getting Saddam out of Kuwait without a war. By this time, Bush was determined to have a war. He torpedoed Gorbachev's proposal by giving Saddam forty-eight hours to get out of Kuwait, or else. It would have been impossible for the slow-moving Iraqis to get out within that time frame with their tanks, artillery, and military supplies, even in the unlikely event that Saddam attempted to comply.[24]

The war began with a prolonged air campaign against military and military-related targets. It made for great television and low casualties. Colin Powell famously described what the strategy would be in thrilling terms: "First we are going to cut this army off. Then we are going to kill it." As the air campaign unfolded, Bush was troubled by a discomfiting thought. "How do we guarantee the future peace? I don't see how it will work with Saddam in power." Scowcroft had the same glimpse of the obvious at about the same time. "If Saddam withdraws with most of his forces intact, we haven't really won."[25] The war would also exacerbate the split between Muslims who were trying to modernize Islam and those who were trying to Islamicize modernity.

The ground offensive came after six weeks of air attacks and cruise missile strikes. The marines advanced into Kuwait to pin the Iraqis in position while the American, British, and French divisions swung east, into the desert. Outflanking the Iraqis by this maneuver, they then struck them in the flank and rear. Iraqi troops in Kuwait abandoned their tanks and artillery and scrambled desperately to get out before they were completely trapped. More than ten thousand perished in the attempt. Coalition fatalities numbered fewer than 150. "Vietnam will soon be behind us," an exultant commander in chief confided to his diary. The Syndrome was dead. Maybe.[26]

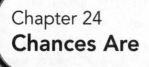

Chapter 24
Chances Are

BUSH HAD CHOSEN THE WRONG YEAR TO WIN HIS WAR. IN THE aftermath of the Iraqi ejection from Kuwait, his approval rating broke the 80 percent mark. Appearing before a joint session of Congress, he got the kind of reception most presidents can only dream about. Entirely devoid of charisma, Bush at that moment seemed magical.

A year later, campaigning for reelection, he was a wounded man. After pledging "Read my lips—no new taxes," budget realities forced him to swallow his words, infuriating his party. Worse, there was a recession. It was coming to an end, but not quickly enough to save him. Enter the most fascinating politician of the boomer generation, Bill Clinton.

On his way out the door, Bush committed American forces to support a UN effort to bring food aid to Somalia. There was no evident American national security interest there that would be secured or advanced by putting marines ashore. This was foreign and defense policy being driven by television, and it went badly wrong, but by then Bush was in retirement and Clinton was in the Situation Room. The

Somalia intervention ended with the deaths of eighteen soldiers. The corpse of one of them was dragged through the streets of Mogadishu, and more than a thousand Somalis were killed in clashes with American troops. Clinton pulled the Americans out, but this too was policy driven by CNN. Not for the last time.

The rise to commander in chief of a former war protestor such as Bill Clinton was so unlikely that only a comic novelist would have dared to use it as a plot device. Clinton had been of draft age during the Vietnam War and was desperate not to serve. In 1969, his draft number came up. Having won a Rhodes scholarship, he was currently studying at Oxford.

Clinton wrote to the commander of the ROTC program at the University of Arkansas, Colonel Eugene Holmes, saying he wanted to enroll in the university's ROTC unit. In the course of a long and tortuous explanation of why he did not want to be drafted, Clinton said he identified with those "fine people [who] have come to find themselves still loving their country but loathing the military." The colonel, understandably, was not to be swayed by sentiments of loathing.

Besides, the ROTC unit was full, with many would-be applicants clamoring to enroll. Clinton was not a student at the university and never had been. On the face of it, he was out of luck. But not quite. The aspiring politician pitched yet another appeal, this time to the state's most senior senator, J. William Fulbright, who had also been a Rhodes scholar.

The senator had never performed military service—too young for World War I and exempt in World War II—and as someone who had come to oppose the Vietnam War after first supporting it, he was sympathetic to Clinton's plea. Phone calls were made. Clinton was admitted into the ROTC unit. Shortly after becoming president, he repaid the debt: he awarded the Medal of Freedom to Fulbright.[1]

Among the active-duty military and many veterans and reservists, Clinton seemed an implausible commander in chief—a peacenik, not a warrior. That impression was reinforced by the ham-fisted attempts early in his administration to allow gays to serve in the military in a two-part deal: the government would not ask recruits about their sexuality, and gay or lesbian recruits would not have to out themselves. If they did, the military was required to discharge them. Called "Don't ask, don't tell," it provided several weeks' worth of material to stand-up comics, and it vanished to the sound of mocking laughter.

Somalia was bad, but the real challenge to Clinton's credentials as CinC arrived on February 26, 1993, when a half-Pakistani, half-Palestinian jihadi named Ramzi Yousef exploded a truck bomb in the basement garage of the World Trade Center. He was trying to bring down one of the towers, making it topple over and crash into the other tower, bringing that down too. Half a dozen people were killed, a huge crater was blown in the concrete floor of the garage, and half a billion dollars' worth of structural damage was caused.[2]

Ramzi Yousef's grandiose plan for the Twin Towers could never have worked as he imagined. Nor was this the first foreign terrorist attack on American soil. German agents had set off an explosion in Jersey City in 1916 that killed a similar number and did comparable damage. The significance of Ramzi Yousef was not what he was trying to do, but what had brought him to the garage under Tower 1.

It was a journey that had begun in Afghanistan when it was still under Soviet occupation. The Saudi government had financed and the United States had directly or indirectly armed tens of thousands of rebels, the mujahideen. The president of Pakistan, the pious General Zia-ul-Haq, accepted millions of Afghan refugees, supported the Afghan mujahideen, and financed religious schools, or madrassas, across Pakistan.

The United States meanwhile helped with the purchase and delivery to Afghanistan of more than sixty thousand tons of arms and ammunition. The CIA helped create training camps in remote valleys for the mujahideen. One of these fighters was Ramzi Yousef. Another was Osama bin Laden, whose father had created one of the biggest construction companies in the non-Western world.[3]

Bin Laden had traveled widely, was well educated and highly intelligent, and had never wanted for anything. Except, that is, for a purpose in life. He found it fighting the Red Army in Afghanistan. To him, as to millions of Muslims, the parlous state of Muslim societies was a cause of shame and anger. Most were ruled by petty tyrants. In the fifty countries where Muslims were in the majority, they were oppressed. Worse, Muslim lands such as Palestine were under occupation.

Bin Laden returned to Saudi Arabia shortly before the Iraqi invasion of Kuwait, leaving behind a mujahideen organization that he called Al Qaeda. It prepared to wage holy war by using the training camps that the CIA had helped construct.

Back in Saudi Arabia, when Saddam invaded Kuwait, bin Laden offered the Saudi government the help of his Arab-Afghans in overthrowing the impious, secular Saddam. The offer was refused. But then Cheney persuaded King Fahd to accept American troops, and bin Laden had a new cause. The presence of the Americans in Saudi Arabia was sacrilege. To the devout, all of Saudi Arabia is holy. By the time Kuwait was liberated huge bases were under construction, to extend the Americans' stay indefinitely. Bin Laden had a new cause. He was going to get them out.

The withdrawal of the Soviets from Afghanistan in 1989 showed that Muslims could fight back. Holy warriors with Kalashnikovs and Stinger missiles had forced a superpower to retreat. God willing, the mujahideen would drive the Americans out of Saudi Arabia. Bush had gone to war with Iraq and put an army into Saudi Arabia to keep the price of gasoline low. The result was going to be the most expensive fuel ever. Osama bin Laden began funding fundamentalist preachers and Islamic terrorists. The Saudi government forced him to leave, and he moved on to Sudan, which welcomed him and his millions.

It is possible that some of bin Laden's money or the money of one of bin Laden's rich supporters found its way to Ramzi Yousef. Whether it did or not, the World Trade Center was a target bin Laden would want to see destroyed. It had been designed by an American architect, Minoru Yamasaki, who had also designed a number of prestigious structures for the Saudi government, including the Dhahran Air Terminal and the building that houses the Saudi equivalent of the Federal Reserve.

The work that Yamasaki had done in the Saudi kingdom was echoed in the Twin Towers. They incorporated numerous religious motifs and references that any pious Saudi would recognize, beginning with a vast square at the base, clearly inspired by the great courtyard of Mecca. It was there, too, in interwoven geometrical patterns that produced a dense, shimmering filigree, something common to some of Islam's holiest sites. To an Islamic fundamentalist, these renowned buildings, owned by a Jewish developer, were likely to be seen as impiety soaring to the heavens, and doubly offensive in being two thumbs up for Western capitalism.[4]

It took the FBI two years to track down Ramzi Yousef. He was caught in Manila when he set himself on fire in his apartment kitchen while experimenting with volatile chemicals. Extradited to the United States, he received a life sentence without possibility of parole.

To Yousef, that was a trifle. What mattered was starting a long, global struggle, and between the World Trade Center explosion and Ramzi Yousef's conviction, Osama bin Laden had been creating Al Qaeda. To signal its disapproval of bin Laden, the Saudi government revoked his citizenship in 1995.

Three years later, nearly simultaneous explosions blew up the U.S. embassies in Dar es Salaam and Nairobi, killing more than two hundred people and injuring more than a thousand. The work of Al Qaeda. Clinton struck back by hitting some of its camps in Afghanistan with cruise missiles. Another cruise missile attack destroyed the only modern pharmaceutical plant in Sudan. The administration claimed that nerve gas was being produced there, but it never offered any proof. What is beyond dispute is that the plant was the principal source of vaccines for children and livestock. To this day, its destruction is the source of anger in Sudan, and the twisted wreckage has become a national museum comparable to the most popular tourist site in Mexico—at least among Mexicans—the Museum of American Aggression, which commemorates the Mexican-American War of 1846–1847.[5]

By this time, the Clinton presidency was engulfed by sex scandals, an investigation by a special counsel, and moves in Congress to impeach the president. Clinton was aware of the rising terrorist threat, but governments can focus on only one crisis at a time. Saving Clinton from impeachment had priority.[6]

While Clinton's attention wandered, a revolution was in the making all around him. The resistance to declinism was growing. The spiritual home of the resisters was the Pentagon, but there was a second home in a proliferating network of right-wing think tanks, such as the American Enterprise Institute, and universities of note, such as Johns Hopkins and Stanford. There were also dozens of well-endowed foundations and institutions that to a greater or lesser degree supported the cause.

The spearhead battalion for those who wanted to put America back on top included two former secretaries of defense, Richard Cheney and Donald Rumsfeld; a former chairman of the JCS, Colin Powell; two former assistant secretaries of defense, Richard Armitage and Richard Perle; an under secretary of defense, Paul Wolfowitz; and a protégé of Brent Scowcroft's, Condoleezza Rice. Some of the intellectual mentors to this movement were former Trotskyites and left-wing radicals. Their conversion to Reaganite Republicanism produced a new creature: the neocon.[7]

Although G. H. W. Bush had done much to advance neocon careers in government, they were disenchanted twice over. First, he had put too much trust in the word of Prince Bandar of Saudi Arabia and King Hussein of Jordan when they told him that Saddam Hussein was not about to invade Kuwait. It seemed blindingly obvious in retrospect that Bush should have made it clear to Saddam than any attack on Kuwait would mean war.

Bush had also bungled the conclusion of the conflict. Given another three days, the Iraqi army would have suffered so much damage that a military coup might have become a serious possibility. Instead, Bush had called a halt to the fighting too soon. Admittedly, he had issued a call for the people of Iraq to resist Saddam's brutal rule, and the result was uprisings by the Shia in the south and the Kurds in the north following the liberation of Kuwait. But there is a nearly foolproof way to crush a revolt, and that is with massacres. The agreement that formalized the end of fighting in Kuwait established no-fly zones over northern Iraq and southern Iraq—zones that were patrolled by U.S. and British aircraft. There was no thought, though, of grounding Iraqi helicopters. Another bungle. Saddam used his helicopter gunships to slaughter Shiites and Kurds in the thousands. The tanks of Saddam's Republican Guard did the rest. Problem solved.

Bush had also authorized covert operations to overthrow Saddam. This move raised the prospects of a tiny organization of anti-Saddam refugees, the Iraqi National Accord (INA), headed by an Iraqi doctor living in London, Ayad Allawi. With CIA funding and encouragement, the INA's project was to create a network within the Iraqi army and security services that would stage a coup and overthrow Saddam.

Phase one would be to undermine the regime by mounting terrorist attacks. These would demonstrate the impotence of a regime that ruled by fear. Aided by the CIA, Allawi brought something new to Iraq—the car bomb. Several car bombs exploded on Iraqi streets, causing a small but indeterminate number of casualties. The INA achieved nothing. Nearly all of the people it recruited within the army and the security services were caught, and those who died quickly were the lucky ones.[8]

Meanwhile, almost in parallel with the Iraqi National Accord, another group of refugees, the Iraqi National Congress (INC), began to enjoy the fruits of American patronage. The INC was the creation of another Iraqi living in London, Ahmed Chalabi. With a Ph.D. in mathematics from MIT, Chalabi brought some Ivy League cachet to the cause, which was to create a network within Iraq that would foment a popular uprising to overthrow Saddam. Besides cachet, however, Chalabi brought something else: the stench of corruption. He had been one of the founders of Petra Bank, a Jordanian venture business that foundered after he looted it. Like Allawi, Chalabi claimed to have access to well-placed informants in Iraq.[9]

To the neocons, Iraq remained an unfinished war. They might not be in power, but they had as much media influence as the Clinton administration. They were also worried about Israel. Terrorist bombings were a growing challenge for the Israelis, but it was Saddam, not a young man in a bomb vest, who could pose an existential threat. By overthrowing Saddam, a strong and assertive United States would secure Israel while striking a blow at declinism.

In the meantime, they set about reshaping American national security policy by organizing the Project for the New American Century (PNAC). Its founders included Donald Rumsfeld, Richard Cheney, former director of Central Intelligence James Woolsey, Florida governor Jeb Bush, an Afghan-American, Zalmay Khalilzad, Dan Quayle, Steve Forbes, Paul Wolfowitz, and various influential journalists and academics. PNAC's "Statement of Principles" began with a clarion call: "American foreign and defense policy is adrift . . . We aim to change this." Convinced of the essential goodness of the United States, they called on it to take control of the world, for the world's— and America's—sake. This was, they reassuringly noted, "a Reaganite policy of military strength and moral clarity." The place to begin was to increase defense spending by 30 percent.[10]

One of PNAC's offshoots was the Committee for the Liberation of

Iraq, and in 1998 Congress passed the Iraq Liberation Act. Bill Clinton signed it into law. The first sentence of this legislation reads: "It should be the policy of the United States to support efforts to remove the regime headed by Saddam Hussein from power in Iraq and to promote the emergence of a democratic government to replace that regime."

Congress voted nearly $100 million to support the Iraq Liberation Act. The Pentagon virtually adopted Ayad Allawi and the Iraqi National Accord, making them rich, while the CIA financed its man Ahmed Chalabi and his Iraqi National Congress, on an equally generous scale.

All this while a sub-rosa war was being fought with Iraq. George H. W. Bush had dismissed sanctions on the grounds that they would not work, because political support for them would not hold up. Nevertheless, sanctions had been imposed shortly after the invasion of Kuwait, and they remained in force. There was an oil-for-food program, essential to American allies such as Jordan, which were dependent on Iraq for their oil supplies. At the same time, the UN was providing most Iraqi households with a basic food ration each week. As always, though, it was the poorest and most vulnerable who suffered—Iraqi children, older Iraqis, sick Iraqis. The lack of medicines and medical supplies caused up to half a million deaths, according to the World Health Organization. When the suffering of Iraqi children was put to Clinton's secretary of state, Madeleine Albright, in a television interview, she replied, "We consider that a price worth paying." The effect of the sanctions on Saddam's rule was zero. He continued to breathe defiance, and in the no-fly zones there were regular exchanges of fire between American and British aircraft and Saddam's air defenses.

Trying to police Iraq from the air was nothing new. It had begun in 1921, when Britain stitched the Kurdish north, the Shiite south, and the Sunni center and west into the country of Iraq. The Iraqis concluded that they had only gotten rid of one colonial power, the Ottoman Turks, in exchange for another, the British. Resistance was commonplace, and in Basra a huge statue of a lion raping a defenseless Iraqi woman expressed the anger of many an Iraqi.

To control Iraq, the British resorted to a policy called "air policing." This consisted of bombing the homes of uncooperative tribal leaders.

Although it was pursued for decades, it did not work; nor did the creation of a constitutional monarchy and the introduction of democratic elections. In 1955 the royal family was overthrown, and most of its members were murdered. Their bloody bodies were put on public display. The new no-fly zones were merely a repackaging of air policing, and they gave Saddam a chance to posture.

So too did the United Nations Special Commission (UNSCOM). Its mission was to search for and destroy biological, chemical, and nuclear weapons. There were limits, too, on Saddam's conventional weapons, and UNSCOM inspectors were also policing those. Saddam, however, had destroyed all of his weapons of mass destruction after he was driven out of Kuwait. He knew that the inspectors would find nothing much. Meanwhile, he could frustrate and bewilder them and maintain a pretense of strength from cardboard ramparts. In the fall of 1998, Clinton and the British prime minister, Tony Blair, launched an aerial offensive, hoping to provoke Saddam into doing something reckless. First, though, they ordered the UNSCOM inspectors out of the country.

While the unfinished war with Saddam rumbled on somewhere on page 5 or 6 of *The New York Times*, the headlines increasingly went to a new twist on Kipling's "savage wars of peace"—namely, humanitarian intervention. Despite the Somalia experience, Clinton supported both the idea and the practice. The principle established by the Treaty of Westphalia in 1648, that the internal affairs of a sovereign nation were not the business of other sovereign nations, was swept aside. Nor did Clinton feel that he had to seek the support of the United Nations. In Kosovo, the United States intervened to stop what the Serbs nauseatingly called "ethnic cleansing" by assembling a coalition of NATO members and ignoring the UN, although when the shooting stopped, the UN came in to manage peacekeeping operations.

The neocons despised the self-indulgent Clinton, but they shared much of his moral outlook. Humanitarian intervention offered "moral clarity" yoked to American power. They wanted to extend humanitarian intervention to Iraq. Clinton was never going to give them that. But if the chance ever came their way . . .

The future did not seem promising, however. The leading Republican candidate for the 2000 election was George W. Bush, son of the president who had gotten a D minus on the Iraqi test. The younger Bush was running for the presidency without any experience of national security and foreign policy. He seemed to be interested in becoming president mainly because Daddy had already done that. He had gone to the same preppy bastion, Andover, as his father; then to Yale, ditto; and he had been initiated into Skull and Bones, ditto all over again. His favorite sport was baseball, just like Dad. When he set about making money, he chose the same field—the oil field—and he opened his office in the same building where his dad operated from. During his military service, he had become a pilot, just like Dad. At times he seemed, to people who were close to him, to be awestruck by his father's achievement.

Just like Daddy, Bush had managed to graduate from Yale without developing any interest in the world of ideas. He mocked his alma mater for its emphasis on the life of the mind and its respect for high intelligence. Attending Harvard Business School only reinforced his preference for action over reflection. Bush père was much the same.[11]

George W. took his father's defeat in 1992 badly. What made it almost inexplicable was the man his father had lost to. Reading up on Clinton after the election, Bush was incredulous. "This guy is mighty fucked up," he told a friend. The best man hadn't won that time.[12]

Bush was also discomfited by the widespread and growing sentiment in the Republican Party that his father had not only lost the White House to the despised Clinton, but had bungled Iraq too. In 1999, while campaigning for the Republican nomination, Bush confided his thoughts on Saddam to Mickey Herskowitz, a writer who was working on his campaign autobiography.

"One of the keys to being seen as a great leader is to be seen as a Commander-in-Chief," said Bush. "My father had all this political capital built up when he drove the Iraqis out of Kuwait and he wasted it. If I ever get the chance to invade, I'm not going to waste it."[13]

Shortly after this, while campaigning in Michigan, Bush met Osama Siblani, the editor of *The Arab American News*, a newspaper in Dearborn, Michigan, home to the largest Arab and Muslim community in the United States. Siblani began talking about Saddam Hussein. "I'm going to take him out," said Bush.

"Let the Iraqi people do it," said Siblani. "Lift the sanctions. People can't make moves on an empty stomach. Once they start establishing a connection with the United States, they will overthrow him."

Bush dismissed Siblani's idea. The thing to do, he told Siblani, was to get the inspectors back in to look for weapons of mass destruction. Getting rid of the WMD would mean getting rid of Saddam.[14]

Why, though, would someone who was going to run as a domestic-issues candidate be so obsessed with overthrowing Saddam? Because in April 1993 his father had paid a triumphal visit to Kuwait to be acclaimed and thanked by the people of Kuwait. In the wake of that visit, the Kuwaiti minister of information, Sheikh Saud Nasir al Sabah, revealed to the world an Iraqi plot to put 175 pounds of Semtex into the car that carried President Bush through the streets of Kuwait City. After that, Saddam Hussein became for George W. Bush "the guy who tried to kill my dad." The source, however, was not above suspicion: the minister of information happened to be the former ambassador to the United States and the father of Nayira. There were other reasons, too, to doubt the story.[15]

Yet George W. Bush was convinced. And it was not only his father who might have been killed in an assassination attempt by the evil Saddam. Laura Bush was in the vehicle traveling immediately behind the president's limousine. She might have perished too.[16]

Bush would never get elected on a pledge to overthrow Saddam Hussein. But if the chance ever came . . .

Chapter 25
Targets

LIKE MANY A SCION DIMINISHED BY THE GLARE OF HIS FATHER'S fame, Bush had trouble finding purpose. What could he ever do that might match, let alone surpass, his father's achievements? He loved his father deeply and claimed, "I would run through a brick wall for my dad." Yet filial expressions of devotion can underline the problem, not resolve it. He took refuge from the unbearable lightness of being George W. Bush by seeking escape in booze and self-pity.

Riding the wastrel road toward self-destruction, he was stopped one night in 1976, at the age of thirty, by a Maine state trooper and charged with drunk driving. Had he been a Kennedy in Massachusetts, this might have been a different story, but George W. Bush pleaded guilty, and his driving license was suspended.

Not even that experience brought sobriety for long. Nine years later, when Bush was on the brink of middle age, George H. W. Bush asked Billy Graham to come to Kennebunkport for a weekend so he could try to talk some sense into his hard-drinking, irresponsible eldest son, who was now thirty-nine, and it was probably now or never.

That weekend, Billy launched one of his most successful campaigns, this time bringing salvation to a single fallen sparrow instead of the multitudes that claimed many a Graham weekend at home or abroad, but with consequences as great as preaching to an entire football stadium of sinners.

By the time Billy left Kennebunkport, the black sheep son had accepted Jesus Christ as his Lord and Savior. He joined a men's Bible study group when he returned to Texas, and became a regular at the First United Methodist Church of Midland. In his office, he placed a religious painting titled *A Charge to Keep*, inspired by a hymn written by Charles Wesley, and at every table where he sat down to eat, meals began with prayers.

Each morning, Bush rose early for that day's reading from *My Utmost for His Highest*, a collection of essays by a British YMCA chaplain, Oswald Chambers, who had ministered to Australian and New Zealand troops in Egypt during the First World War. A collection of readings from the Bible, with a commentary on their significance, the aim of Chambers's book is to help the reader "be the utmost for His highest—my best for His glory."[1]

Straightened up and flying right at last, Bush went into politics, and in 1998 he ran for and was elected governor of Texas. To remind himself of how even the mighty can drift into a world of make-believe, he placed a portrait of Sam Houston in the governor's office. It showed Houston dressed in a Roman toga and pretending to be Gaius Marius, one of the greatest of Roman generals, standing among the ruins of Carthage.

The painting had been commissioned by Houston to show how he had triumphed over his country's enemies—Santa Anna, Mexico, and the Whigs. Gaius Marius had saved Rome by bringing about a revolution in military affairs and producing an unbeatable army. Bush thought the painting showed nothing but a once-great man with an exaggerated sense of himself. "He must have been drunk when this was painted," Bush told visitors to his office, demonstrating his ignorance of Roman and Texan history.[2]

Midway into his gubernatorial term, he was summoned for jury duty. Bush feared that if defense lawyers probed his background and discovered the drunk-driving conviction, his political career might be ruined. He looked to his legal counsel, one of the few Hispanic graduates of Harvard Law School, Alberto Gonzalez. By devising a well-reasoned legal argument for why governors should not sit on juries, Gonzalez got Bush off the hook. A grateful Bush rewarded Gonzalez with a place on the Texas Supreme Court.[3]

Bush had no trouble being reelected governor in 1998. But once his second term ended, what then? Purpose found looked like purpose lost. And then a new prospect appeared—a prospect obvious to all, it seems, except to the man himself.

The answer came during a sermon at the Highland Park United Methodist Church, in Dallas, when Reverend Mark Craig lamented the way America was going. This was an uneasy time. Bill Clinton was fighting off impeachment, and the details of his conduct damaged the idea that people had of the president, the presidency, and the country. The nation was crying out for ethical and courageous men and women, declared Craig, for here was a land "starved of leadership."

When the sermon ended, Barbara Bush turned to her son. "He was talking to you." Bush believed it. Here was a summons, he convinced himself, to a higher calling. A year later, he told a friend, "I believe God wants me to be President."[4]

Ever since he first thought seriously about going into politics, Bush had relied on a political adviser, Karl Rove, college dropout but smart operator. Bush had been a fraternity president at Yale, and that frat boy streak was there for life. Like Franklin Roosevelt, Bush bestowed a nickname on nearly everyone who was close to him without being a family member. And in true frat boy style, most of the nicknames were slightly demeaning. Such were the demands of fraternity house humor. Rove was Boy Genius, an accolade, but one offset by another nickname, Turd Blossom. Good ol' Karl could fall in a bucket of shit and he would come up smelling of roses.

Rove had a clear vision of America, the world, the universe, everything. He saw a Hobbesian existence of perpetual struggle between good and evil, friend and enemy, conservative and liberal. No mercy should be shown to anyone on the wrong side of the equation. Nor should moral scruple be allowed to intrude. Enemies were there to be destroyed, by whatever means necessary. He encouraged Bush to be a very conservative governor and intended that he would be an equally conservative president. Pragmatism was out. Dogmatism was in. You don't compromise with evil—you crush it. Bush, with his preference for action over thought, action without reflection, had no difficulty embracing the Rovian view of America and the world around it.

If he succeeded in his newly found religion-tinged ambition, Bush would become commander in chief, but his record of military service was hardly encouraging. As his four years at Yale drew to a close, Bush became vulnerable to the draft. He applied to serve for six years in the Texas Air National Guard before Selective Service sent him its greetings. He took the required pilot aptitude test, but his score was so low it made him a borderline prospect. Normally, people who scored as poorly as he did were rejected for pilot training. There was also an eighteen-month waiting list even for those who were accepted, yet the son of the ambassador to the UN, George H. W. Bush, was strapped into the cockpit only four months later.

The Texas National Guard maintained an air wing at Ellington Air Force Base, a few miles outside Houston, in order to cater to the children of the Texas elite. It flew obsolescent F-102s, but that was no surprise. In time-honored fashion, the Guard got the junk and the air force got the good stuff, because the air force fought wars. That was fine by Bush. He never indicated any desire to dodge surface-to-air missiles or to fly through quad-mounted 40-mm antiaircraft fire over Vietnamese rice paddies.

And what golden boys his fellow pilots were. They included the son of Senator Lloyd Bentsen, the son of Senator John Tower, and seven football players from the Dallas Cowboys.[5]

Even so, the light duties imposed on Bush at Ellington were taking up too much of his valuable time. He applied for a transfer to an Alabama Air Guard unit that had no airplanes. Bush also failed to appear for a flight physical at an interesting historical moment: the Pentagon had just introduced drug testing as part of routine physicals. His flying status was suspended, but that was the sole consequence of the missed physical.

Transferred to Alabama, Bush visited his new base only occasionally. There was one entire year when he never showed up at all. He was spending most of his time involved in political campaigns or just having fun somewhere. For want of anything better to do, still seeking purpose, he applied to Harvard Business School. Admission was only a formality, and his days as a nonflying flier came to a merciful end: the Guard released him eight months early.

During the Vietnam years, he had what might be termed "a good war," although some years later he would encourage a group of military spouses to be strong, because many of them spent their days dreading the possibility that an army or Marine Corps vehicle might pull into their driveway and a chaplain and another officer would get out, stand at their front door, remove their hats, and say, "We're sorry . . ." Being strong, Bush would tell those spouses, was yet another duty they owed their country because "a time of war is a time for sacrifice." That thought does not appear to have occurred to him during the war in Vietnam.[6]

During his 2000 presidential campaign, Bush campaigned on the need for a strong military. In a short speech that he delivered in Albuquerque, New Mexico, he offered an insight into how he really saw the outside world: "Even though the evil empire may have passed, evil still remains. We're certain there are people that can't stand what America stands for . . . We're certain there are madmen in the world, and there's terror."[7]

He derided the humanitarian interventions that his father had begun and Clinton had continued in places such as Bosnia and Kosovo. "Let me tell you what else I'm worried about," he told a campaign rally in Chattanooga the day before the election. "I'm worried about an opponent who uses nation building and the military in the same sentence. See, our view of the military is for our military to be properly prepared to fight and win wars and, therefore, prevent war from happening in the first place"—the doctrine, in embryo, of preventive war. In a Bush administration, he pledged, there would be none of the peacekeeping, nation building, and the other namby-pamby, do-gooder policies that Clinton and the Democrats loved. The days of wussy foreign policy had to end. "I am a product of the Vietnam world," he told a reporter, and he feared, as the neocons did, that declinism was gaining ground. It must be resisted and ultimately rolled back.[8]

To him, Bill Clinton symbolized all that was wrong in the country, and probably in the world. Change was coming, even though all the polls were pointing to an election that was too close to call. Aboard his campaign plane, with one week to go, he announced to the journalists on board, "I've won."

In the end, it was a different election—in the Supreme Court—

that put him into the White House, on a 5–4 vote, unlike in the general election, where Al Gore got more votes than Bush. He was only the third minority president in American history, but he intended to do big things. What mattered was having the power to do them.

During the campaign, Condoleezza Rice had served as his foreign policy adviser. She shared his contempt for the UN and humanitarian intervention, talking dismissively about what she termed "nation-building done by the 82nd Airborne."[9]

Her tutelage of Bush meanwhile seemed to make no appreciable difference. He did not seem to be learning much and remained uncomfortable and tongue-tied whenever he responded to questions about foreign policy. He also gave an amusing demonstration, on television, of his inability to keep track of who was in charge of various Third World countries that happened to be of some importance to American national security. Bush had hardly ever traveled outside the United States, apart from the obligatory trip to Israel, and made it clear that he had no great desire to shrink that gap in his knowledge.

The only country he showed any serious interest in was Iraq. Saddam Hussein was a menace, Bush told David Nyhan, political editor of *The Boston Globe*, during the campaign. "I'd take 'em out," said Bush, "take out the weapons of mass destruction. I'm surprised he's still there." Similarly, on a political fund-raising trip to California in July 1999, he was introduced to David O. Russell, the writer and director of *Three Kings*, a film that damned George H. W. Bush for encouraging the Shia to rise up against Saddam, only to abandon them to their fate. When Russell remarked that the Shia were still suffering under Saddam's rule, Bush replied, "Then I guess I'm just going to have to finish it," and walked away.[10]

Bush had spent enough time with members of the Saudi royal family that he should have learned the truth about Saddam after the Gulf War.[11] Across the Middle East, the Iraqi ejection from Kuwait was not seen as a defeat for Saddam—it was seen as a victory. His father's expectation—that after Kuwait, Saddam would be overthrown because he had been defeated—was wrong. All he had to do was survive for a year or so. Any Arab leader who survived a war with the United States would be hailed as a hero by fellow Arabs. That was what happened to Saddam, who had outlasted Bush's father, now in retirement while Saddam was still a head of state.

During the transition in the weeks before the inauguration, Vice President–elect Dick Cheney told William Cohen, the outgoing secretary of defense, that Bush wanted to be briefed on Iraq. What the president-elect needed was a range of options for dealing with Iraq.

When the briefing from the CIA came, it focused on the three major national security challenges facing the country: first, the world's biggest terrorist organization, Al Qaeda; second, the proliferation of weapons of mass destruction (WMD); and third, the rapid rise of China. It was not a threat yet, but China might be only five years away from becoming one. It could happen while Bush was still in the White House. There was no briefing on Iraq.[12]

While the nation waited to see what a new president from a different party might bring, a satirical newspaper, *The Onion*, was channeling the future. It offered this forecast of what the inaugural address would promise: "We must squander our nation's hard-won budget surplus on tax breaks for the wealthiest 15 per cent." That would be the main achievement in domestic policy. "And on the foreign front, we must find an enemy and defeat it."[13]

At the start of his first National Security Council meeting, ten days into his presidency, Bush announced a major change in foreign policy. "We're going to correct the imbalances of the previous administration on the Mideast conflict. We're going to tilt it back toward Israel."

"The consequences of that could be dire; especially for the Palestinians," said Colin Powell, the new secretary of state and bearer of the unflattering nickname Balloonfoot.

Bush brushed Powell's objection aside. "Maybe that's the best way to get things back in balance. Sometimes a show of strength by one side can really clarify things." Powell looked shocked. Here was a major change in American foreign policy, but there had been no discussion, no warning, even.

Bush shifted his attention to Rice, serving now as national security adviser. "So, Condi, what are we going to talk about today? What's on the agenda?"

"How Iraq is destabilizing the region, Mr. President."

George Tenet, the director of Central Intelligence, put on a presentation with maps and satellite photographs that purported to show an Iraq that was rearming after losing half of its military equipment during the Persian Gulf War. But in the end, he acknowledged, a lot of what he was saying was interpretation, based on fragmentary intelligence. If the military planners were hoping to use what he had to offer, said Tenet, "We'd be going in there blind."[14]

Throughout this meeting, there was no discussion of whether or not the policy toward Iraq needed to be changed. There was, instead, an unspoken assumption: regime change was coming. But by now Condoleezza Rice had learned something important about Bush: "He knows what he wants to do and what he wants to hear is how to get it done," she told David Rothkopf, a writer who was working on a book about the NSC.[15]

Colin Powell was not persuaded that the United States had to change policy on Iraq. Three weeks after this meeting, he told a television interviewer, "He [Saddam] has not developed any significant capability with respect to weapons of mass destruction. He is unable to project conventional power against his neighbors."[16]

Condoleezza Rice too seemed ready to accede to the fact that however interested in Iraq the president was, hardly anyone else in Washington other than Donald Rumsfeld, Dick Cheney, and Paul Wolfowitz considered Saddam a pressing problem. "We are able to keep his arms from him. His military forces have not been rebuilt," she told CNN on July 29, 2001.

The UN's oil-for-food program, beginning in 1996, had reduced hunger and disease among ordinary Iraqis without doing anything to make Saddam's military stronger. The money raised by these oil sales went into a UN escrow account, while the Iraqi military continued to crumble.

Colin Powell was in favor of increasing the pressure by applying "targeted sanctions," making the sanctions regime both tighter and more sharply focused. Rumsfeld, however, had no patience with sanctions. Like the president, he wanted Saddam out. "What we really ought to think about is going after Saddam," he told the NSC. But for now, this was no more than a pious hope.[17]

That had not discouraged the president from announcing on *Good Morning America* one April day that the Clinton era was truly over. Asked just how far he was prepared to go in defending Taiwan from a Chinese attack, he gave a three-word reply: "Whatever it takes." Clinton had sent aircraft carriers into the Taiwan Strait as a show of force in 1996, but Bush seemed ready for a nuclear war. The tough, uncompromising stance was the new posture in America's relations with the world.

In the months that followed, Bush received a steady stream of memos and reports on terrorist threats, mainly from Al Qaeda or groups inspired by Al Qaeda. He did not like reading reports and seemed averse even to reading short memos. Besides, the one thing that might have grabbed his attention was Iraq, but Saddam never got more than a passing reference.[18]

And then came September 11, 2001. He was reading *My Pet Goat*, a truly dreadful children's book, to a second-grade class at an elementary school in Sarasota, Florida. Karl Rove stepped over and whispered in his ear that a plane had just crashed into one of the towers of the World Trade Center. Bush read on. Probably an accident. After a few minutes, his chief of staff, Andrew Card, whispered in his ear, "A second plane hit the other tower. America is under attack."

Before he left the school, Bush issued a short statement to the local television crews that were covering his visit. "Terrorism against our nation will not stand." He was echoing his father's pledge of eleven years earlier: "This will not stand, this aggression against Kuwait."

By the time he arrived back in Washington at dusk, Bush had spoken with Cheney. They agreed that the old policy of treating terrorism the way the Europeans did, as a challenge to law enforcement, was out. This was war, and it was going to be fought like a war. The United States would not limit itself to going after the terrorists. If it meant anything, this meant that the United States was going to attack the countries that allowed terrorists to operate from their territory—countries such as Afghanistan, where bin Laden was holed up; Sudan, which had sheltered bin Laden for years; Iran, which supported Islamic Jihad and Hizbollah; and minor players, such as Libya, Yemen, and Somalia, a country without a government.

When Bush met with his advisers the next day in the White House Situation Room, Rumsfeld pointed out that international law allowed countries to strike people and states that were about to launch an attack, but it did not sanction retaliation. Bush was incensed. "No," he shouted. "I don't care what the international lawyers say, we're going to kick some ass!"[19]

Rumsfeld was also unenthusiastic about attacking Afghanistan.

The air force could find only forty-two targets worth hitting in the entire country. Let's attack Iraq instead, Rumsfeld advised. Lots of good targets there. But that wasn't what Bush wanted: he wanted regime change in Iraq. Cruise missiles weren't going to deliver that.

After the meeting broke up, Bush remained behind, thinking, frustrated. The major players had departed, but now he summoned some of the counterterrorism experts to come see him. "Look, I know you have a lot to do and all . . . but I want you, as soon as you can, to go back over everything, everything. See if Saddam did this. See if he's linked in any way."

They tried to tell him there was no connection. Richard Clarke, the White House's leading authority on terrorism, told him, "You know, we have looked several times for state sponsorship of Al Qaeda and not found any real linkages with Iraq."

Bush wasn't listening. "Look into Saddam, Iraq," he responded, his irritation plain, and walked away. Afghanistan it would have to be—for now.[20]

The next day, only two days after the World Trade Center attack, Cofer Black, the director of the CIA's Counterterrorism Center, gave a PowerPoint presentation in the Situation Room. The agency had a plan for fighting back against Al Qaeda. "We'll set this thing up so it's an unfair fight for the U.S. military." The plan was an improvised tripartite venture, a pickup team of CIA operatives, the military's Special Forces, and Afghanistan's Northern Alliance. The alliance was composed mainly of Tajiks whose traditional enemy was the Pashtuns of southern Afghanistan, from which the Taliban were drawn.

The Taliban were not a government in the sense that any American understood. Having begun as a student movement, in the anarchy and civil war that followed the Soviet withdrawal they morphed into a ragtag force that managed to capture the capital, Kabul. After that, they set about imposing a harsh and violent theocracy on Afghanistan. The Northern Alliance had been fighting Al Qaeda and its Taliban partners for years.

Law enforcement wasn't the aim anymore, said Black. Killing bin Laden and his followers was. "When we're through with them," he declared, "they'll have flies walking across their eyeballs." Bush wanted to know how long it would take. What he meant, but did not say, was,

"How long before I can take action against Iraq?" Black told him that the flies-and-eyeballs scenario would play out over a matter of weeks. The expression on Bush's face said it all: excellent.[21]

In the days that followed, Bush showed a remarkable talent for losing the propaganda war while bringing a steely reassurance to a grieving nation. Nothing had been so painful, so traumatic since the assassination of John F. Kennedy. In a way, however, this was worse. No one expected another presidential assassination. Nearly everybody expected another terrorist attack.

At the National Cathedral three days after the September 11 attacks, Bush defined America's mission: to "rid the world of evil." And three days after that, he went over to the Pentagon to take a close look at the wreckage. Journalists wanted to know just what he was going to do about bin Laden. "I want justice," said Bush. "And there's an old poster out West . . . Wanted, Dead or Alive."[22]

He also stood on the South Lawn and assured his shaken and grieving countrymen, "It is time for us to win this first war of the 21st century decisively." How? "They hide in caves. We'll get them out."[23]

Again and again Bush said this was a different kind of war. "Conventional warfare is not going to win this," he told visitors. "This is a guerrilla struggle." True, yet he seemed incapable of acting accordingly. Nearly all guerrilla struggles are won, on the rare occasions when they are well and truly won, by reaching a political settlement. He was impatient, too, with advisers such as Colin Powell, who told him that the United States could not fight it alone. Allies might make demands, Bush said, force compromises on him, get in the way. "At some point we might be the only ones left. That's okay with me. We are America."[24]

Every war needs a name. His first effort was Operation Infinite Justice. This was withdrawn after Muslims complained that infinite justice was what Allah was going to bring to the world, not the United States. So for want of anything better, it became the Global War on Terror, abbreviated to "the GWOT." He promised Americans "total victory" in this new struggle, which would end, he said, "at a time and in a manner of our choosing." He was in charge, and the United States was in control.[25]

Bush got off to a poor start, though, by calling the GWOT "this crusade." That did not play well with Muslim opinion either, and he withdrew it. But he had not changed his mind about being on a crusade, because he called it "this terribly important crusade" again, on a visit to Alaska.[26]

How could he not see it in religious terms, however impolitic that might be? To Brent Scowcroft it seemed obvious that Bush now saw his selection to the presidency as a sign of providence. Every cabinet meeting now opened with a prayer, and the president's special assistants were expected to join the White House Bible-study group, even the Jews. Bush's spiritual strivings were further aided and abetted by a Presidential Prayer Team formed after 9/11. It is still in operation and focuses the prayers of millions on the president's needs.[27]

Bush gave the Taliban an ultimatum: hand over Osama bin Laden, or else. They chose the "or else" option. Cofer Black's tripartite attack force proved unstoppable when backed up with American airpower and magnified by the sheer stupidity of the Taliban, who attempted to hold and defend fixed positions. Daisy cutter bombs, cluster bombs, and other high-tech weapons slashed them to ribbons, and the Northern Alliance, on horseback and in pickup truck, pursued the survivors all the way to Kabul, which was captured nine weeks after the attack on the World Trade Center.

It looked like a victory but probably wasn't. Five years later Afghanistan remained the poorest country in the world, according to the UN's Human Development Index. It was also the world's biggest narco-state. The president, Hamid Karzai, had spent so much of his life in the United States that he carried the taint of the stooge, even if that was unfair. He did not dare travel among his countrymen, was surrounded by a Special Forces bodyguard that numbered dozens, and was president only of the presidential palace. When, in October 2005, a parliament was elected, the most powerful people in it were drug lords and warlords. The courts, meanwhile, had started applying Sharia law, and the Taliban was resurgent. Karzai had no real power and virtually no money, as he continually complained to the press.

There were also nearly 20,000 American and 7,500 other NATO troops trying to bring stability to Afghanistan, but all they had managed to control was Kabul. In the mountains, the drug trade flourished and warlords ruled. Suicide bombers were beginning to drive into buildings and convoys. Roadside bombs were beginning to proliferate.

Even the star of the show, Cofer Black, had proved a disappointment. There were no flies walking over the eyeballs of Osama bin Laden or the Taliban leader, Mullah Mohammed Omar. General Tommy Franks, commander of the U.S. Central Command (CentCom), had wanted to put up to 55,000 soldiers into Afghanistan, but the commander in chief would not even consider it, which must have made it easier for bin Laden and the mullah to escape.

The president, however, had a different mission for CentCom's troops than implementing "Wanted—Dead or Alive." When Kabul fell, Bush's attention shifted elsewhere so rapidly it might have been mounted on a swivel. "We've got a job to do with Al Qaeda. We need to look at WMD targets."[28]

Chapter 26
Willful, Mendacious, Deluded

ON FEBRUARY 16, 2002, WITH AMERICAN FORCES RUNNING AROUND the snow-covered mountains of Tora Bora trying to flush out bin Laden and his pediatrician mentor, Ayman al-Zawahiri, Bush signed a secret directive. It established the aims and objectives in the coming war with Iraq. This document provided General Tommy Franks with planning guidance for the invasion. The Afghanistan objective of killing or capturing bin Laden had not been achieved, thanks largely to Bush's refusal to put more than a handful of troops into the hunt. But the president ignored that: "If he's alive, we'll get him. If he's not alive, we already got him," said Bush. He was determined to move on while Americans were still angry and fearful.[1]

Meanwhile, Al Qaeda's top leadership was scattering into Pakistan and across the Muslim world. As it became a flatter, less hierarchical organization, it was also making up for the loss of its physical base in Afghanistan by moving to the Internet. Although Al Qaeda was unable to pull off another spectacular attack comparable to, or exceeding, the carnage of 9/11, the Global War on Terror was already starting to look like the hopeless and highly touted War on Drugs.

Bush seemed not to care about the implications of changing his focus to Iraq. After all, he had never devoted his time or energies to Afghanistan. He preferred instead to continue rallying a shaken nation, and referred to himself as "a war president" in a slightly self-satisfied way, as if it were some kind of promotion. That view, which made him look and sound like an Action Man figure, went to the president's sense of who and what he was. Nearly every day he spent several hours running, working out in the gym, and/or riding his mountain bike. And now Action Man had been matched with historic challenges that demanded action.

By his own admission, Bush shunned introspection, did not read widely, and did not have much patience with people who wanted to talk about ideas. His preferred reading consisted of instruction books or inspirational tomes, preferably a combination of both. The Bible was perfect in that way. Although he had been governor of a major state and was therefore assumed to have executive ability, this may not have been so.

When he was asked how he knew what to do if he read as little as he claimed, his reply was, "My instincts." Even if his instincts were good, that hardly suggested he was the right man for a war of ideas, but he came to the challenge with a clear idea of how to be a successful commander in chief: "As a leader, you can never admit a mistake," he told a writer who was working on a book about his grandfather, Senator Prescott Bush.[2]

Besides, there can be no mistake when you are doing God's will. Brent Scowcroft had known Bush since his wastrel days and had no doubt that Bush saw his selection to the presidency less than a year before 9/11 as a sign of providence: God wanted him there, in the White House, when the crisis came. "Somehow that was meant to be, and his mission is to deal with the war on terrorism."[3]

Even though history now had the United States by the throat, Bush had no more curiosity about the world than before and something close to denial about the character of this new struggle. He repeatedly said that the terrorists were attacking "our values." Powell said much the same. "This is an attack on civilization and an attack against democracy."

What if Suntzu's dictum is correct—that the commander who does not understand his enemy is certain to be defeated? Neither Bush nor any member of his war cabinet would admit that Al Qaeda might be killing people because its adherents were incensed at the occupation of Muslim lands—mainly Palestine and Afghanistan—by Christians and Jews. There was one important advantage to the values argument: it was easy to defend. Occupation was difficult, maybe impossible.

Even David Ben-Gurion had considered the post-1967 Israeli occupation of the West Bank and Gaza Strip to be a political blunder that could eventually lead to the destruction of Israel. There were also thousands of American soldiers and air force personnel stationed in Saudi Arabia. In 1998 bin Laden had published his vehement opposition to the American presence, and 9/11 was the result. His motives weren't exactly a mystery.

In an attempt to turn a war about foreign policy into a struggle over values, Bush fell back on the well-thumbed patriots' chapbook of American exceptionalism, as if he might find answers there. In the months and years to come, Bush spoke, as other politicians had done before him, about the special place reserved by the Almighty for his chosen land and its chosen people, much as Senator Albert Beveridge of Indiana had done a hundred years earlier: "God has marked the American people as his chosen nation to finally lead in the regeneration of the world. This is the divine mission of America, and it holds for us all the profit, all the glory, all the happiness possible to man. We are trustees of the world's progress, guardians of its righteous peace."

Certain that he was doing God's work, the president turned his attention to creating public support for implementing his "territorial strategy" to defeat terrorism. There were only so many places in the world where Al Qaeda might find a welcome. Now that Afghanistan was in the bag, the Joint Chiefs were already at work on plans for the invasion and occupation of seven countries. Iraq first, of course, followed by Syria, then Lebanon, followed by Libya, Iran, Somalia, and Sudan.[4]

Unfortunately, Colin Powell had told *The New York Times* in November 2001 that Iraq was not involved in the World Trade Center attack and posed no threat to anyone. "Iraq isn't going anywhere," said Powell. "It's in a fairly weakened state. It's doing some things we don't like. We'll continue to contain it." There was also Condoleezza Rice's statement on CNN shortly before 9/11 that Saddam Hussein did not pose a threat. Bush was going to have to convince the country, the Europeans, and the UN that Saddam had to be taken out.[5]

His moment and the neocons' had just been spliced together to trigger an explosion. People such as Dick Cheney and Donald Rumsfeld shared much of the neocon view of America's role in the world, but the intellectual godfather of the neoconservatives in the Pentagon was the under secretary of defense, Paul Wolfowitz. He had been a graduate student at Chicago where Leo Strauss, a professor of political philosophy, managed to establish a strange political cult out of threadbare ideas and timeless clichés. Although not a signed-up member of the cult while at the university, Wolfowitz later became one of its high priests.

Strauss had seen all moral authority having only two possible sources—reason or revelation. He distrusted both—but reason most of all. So far, so Phil 101. What Strauss deplored in reason was that political liberals tended to rely on it; yet lacking a firm moral authority, reason drifted into nihilism, putting civilization at risk. But there was hope in conservatism, which made room for revelation.

Strauss also concluded that humanity consisted largely of dimwits, people who should not be allowed anywhere near philosophy. After all, ideas have consequences. Serious intellectual inquiry was the natural preserve of the non-nihilistic thinkers. They were the chosen ones, and their mission was to win the visceral support of the dimwits, which would allow these enlightened souls to take control of events and make the world safe for America and Israel. Strauss taught his students that the two pillars of Western civilization were Athens (reason) and Jerusalem (revelation). Conservative political thinking gave full value to both.

Wolfowitz, a graying vulgarian who licked both sides of his comb before applying it to his wayward mop, possessed a professorial demeanor and the cultist's narrowness. He had come to embrace neoconservative politics, with its near worship of force and threats of force to tame a refractory planet. He had also used his leverage over policy to favor Israel's interests so often and so obviously that unhappy generals were grumbling to sympathetic journalists that the under secretary put the defense of Zionism before the defense of the United States.[6]

Wolfowitz and other neocons, in government and out, did not and could not bring about war with Iraq. Only the president could make that decision, and he had already made it when he was still governor of Texas. What the neocons could do, however, was help him to win the bureaucratic struggle between a skeptical CIA, an even more skeptical State Department, and a Defense Department committed to war. Donald Rumsfeld had wanted to oust Saddam for as long as the president had, and like Bush, had wanted to respond to the World Trade Center attack by attacking Iraq. Having supped with the devil, or at least shaken Saddam's hand and given him a big smile, Rumsfeld may have been seeking atonement for ancient sins. Who knows? But there was no mistaking his determination to remove Saddam. With Rumsfeld, Cheney, and Wolfowitz leading the struggle within the federal bureaucracy, the president could not have found a more willing group of facilitators had he knocked on every door inside the Beltway and handed out a questionnaire.

The biggest problem they faced was the intelligence on Iraq. It showed nothing much. There was no credible intelligence linking bin Laden to Saddam Hussein. Saddam and biological weapons? Nada. Chemical? Zilch. And nuclear? Nothing. Had the true intelligence picture been presented to Congress and the public, Bush would never get his war of maximum choice. The challenge was to ignore the true intelligence, riddled as it was with doubts and disclaimers. Cheney, Rumsfeld, and Wolfowitz met that challenge, ably abetted by Condoleezza Rice and Colin Powell. When reality disappoints, people take refuge in fantasies and dreams. The weapons of mass destruction were the fantasies and dreams of neocons; then they were sold, as often happens with fantasies and dreams, to millions.[7]

Although Bush had been reluctant to create a coalition for Afghanistan, he sought help with Iraq. The country he stood the best chance of persuading was Britain. Tony Blair had pledged as much in the aftermath of the September 11 atrocity when he promised that Britain would stand "shoulder to shoulder, hand in hand" with the United States. Besides, Blair was a devout Christian who was determined to bring light to dark places and bombing to bad people. No world leader—not even Clinton—had believed in humanitarian intervention as forcefully as Tony Blair.

When Blair visited Washington in January 2002, Bush had

sounded him out on an invasion of Iraq. Blair enthusiastically endorsed the idea and pledged unswerving support. That earned him
an invitation to the Bush ranch in Crawford, Texas, in April. It was
rumored that they prayed together, and no one would have been
surprised if that turned out to be true. With Afghanistan deemed
a success, Bush said Iraq was next. Blair reiterated his promise of
British support for any war with Saddam.[8]

A few weeks later, the United States and Britain unleashed a wave
of air attacks on Iraq, to apply pressure on Saddam and degrade Iraqi
air defenses in advance of the coming invasion. These attacks were
outside the no-fly zones, where the UN had authorized combat missions to protect the Kurds and the Shia. That meant these attacks
were, as the British Foreign Office pointed out to Blair, illegal. The
bombing continued anyway until it was determined that Saddam's air
defenses had been degraded by 50 percent.

In July, Sir David Manning, the head of MI6, Britain's equivalent
of the CIA, visited Washington to meet with Bush, Rumsfeld,
Cheney, and George Tenet. On his return to London, Sir David expressed his surprise to Blair; the defense secretary, Geoff Hoon; Jack
Straw, the foreign secretary; and Lord Goldsmith, the attorney general. "Military action is now seen as inevitable," said Manning. Bush
intended to overthrow Saddam by force, using terrorism and weapons
of mass destruction as his justification, "but the intelligence and facts
are being fixed around the policy."[9]

Meanwhile, Bush and those close to him, such as Rice, continued
to insist that no decision had been made. Rice was telling the press,
"The president is looking at all his options but hasn't decided what he
wants to do." This was an unembellished lie. She had just informed
Richard Haas, the neocon head of the State Department's Policy
Planning Staff, that the decision to invade Iraq had already been
taken. State's mission was no longer to help the president decide
whether to attack, but to seek ways of ensuring success in the coming
invasion.[10]

Every four years the government is required by law to produce a
national security strategy (NSS). The National Security Strategy that
was published in the summer of 2002 was written mainly by Condoleezza Rice, but it drew heavily on "Defense Policy Guidance," a
paper drafted by Paul Wolfowitz in 1992, when he was Dick Cheney's

under secretary of defense. New power centers were developing across the non-Western world, wrote Wolfowitz. The United States should respond by making itself so powerful that potential rivals would be sufficiently overawed to accept American hegemony. But if there was a country that refused to roll over, the United States had to be prepared to destroy it. The point of this paper was to get Americans thinking about war with China.[11]

A copy of this paean to American military power was leaked to *The New York Times*. Hardly anyone seemed as enthusiastic as Paul Wolfowitz about fighting a war, almost certainly a nuclear one, with the Chinese. A much weaker, less provocative version of the strategy was finally adopted. It came back, though, bristling with all the old threats, both explicit and implicit, in Rice's draft of NSS 2002. It was signed into law by President Bush without hesitation. The United States was now pledged to whatever it took, including a general nuclear war, to prevent the rise of regional rivals in every part of the world.

China will not be allowed to become dominant in East Asia; Brazil cannot be dominant in South America; Russia cannot be dominant between Eastern Europe and Central Asia; Iran cannot be dominant in the Persian Gulf; and so on in every part of the globe. Only the United States can be dominant anywhere and must be dominant everywhere. Whatever it takes.[12]

The intended subtext was "resistance is futile." In the real world, though, the subtext was going to be "resistance is certain."

The neocons, besotted by the quick solutions that force seemed to offer over international law—something damned by its appeal to liberals—saw a chance to make America the metatext of History. The best any other country might hope for was a mention in the footnotes. That had also been the outlook of Rice's foreign policy hero, Dean Acheson, but he had expressed it in terms of a train, with America as the locomotive and the rest of the world as the caboose, rattling almost pathetically along at the end. That was Acheson's belief until Vietnam derailed his paradigmatic locomotive. Thanks to NSS 2002, Iraqi clerics, Baath Party officers, Mukhabarat agents, Saudi jihadists, and Iraqi nationalists would before long set fire to the wreckage.

Doubts persisted about the coming attack on Iraq. General Anthony Zinni, the former commander of CentCom and Bush's personal envoy to the Middle East, offered a warning. Zinni had been in Somalia when everything fell apart. During his time in Vietnam, he learned Vietnamese. Appointed to CentCom, he learned Arabic. He had drawn something valuable from his Vietnam and Somalia experiences: "War is the easy part."[13]

In a speech delivered to a group of business executives in Florida, Zinni applied that lesson to Iraq. "You could inherit the country of Iraq, if you're willing to do it," said Zinni. "And if our economy is so great that you're willing to put billions of dollars into reforming Iraq. If you want to put soldiers that are already stretched so thin all around the world and add them into a security force there forever, like we see in places like the Sinai. If you want to fight with other countries in the region to try to keep Iraq together as Kurds and Shiites try and split off, you're going to have to make a good case for that." Cheney obviously had not convinced Zinni.[14]

Former national security adviser Brent Scowcroft and former secretary of state James Baker also deplored the coming strategic blunder. They did not believe that Iraq posed a serious threat. Baker wrote an op-ed piece for *The New York Times*, warning the president that Iraq was not Afghanistan. "We had over 500,000 Americans, and more soldiers from our many allies, for the Persian Gulf War." Attempting regime change in Iraq, Baker suggested, would require similar numbers: "If we are to change the regime in Iraq, we will have to occupy the country militarily."[15]

Still, by the time NSS 2002 was published, the government's march to war had the support of more than half the country. Even well-known liberals were signing up in the name of humanitarian interventionism. Abroad, however, and especially in Europe and Islamic countries, public opinion was moving in the opposite direction. The rhetoric of war suddenly became more tightly focused: the emphasis now was on nuclear weapons. Biological and chemical weapons were bad enough, but in their entirety they did not pack the same emotional weight as a single nuke.

On August 22, Dick Cheney told the Veterans of Foreign Wars national convention, "Afghanistan was only the beginning," referring to it as if it were already over. The focus had shifted to Iraq. "There is no doubt that Saddam Hussein now has weapons of mass destruction," Cheney said. More than that, "We now know that Saddam has resumed his efforts to acquire nuclear weapons." He had come terrify-ingly close just before the Persian Gulf War. "After the war we learned that he had been perhaps within a year of acquiring such a weapon."[16]

Condoleezza Rice produced the perfect sound bite. In an interview with CNN she dismissed current questions about why, if Saddam re-ally did possess weapons of mass destruction, there was no "smoking gun." The intelligence wasn't perfect, she agreed, "but we don't want the smoking gun to come in the form of a mushroom cloud."[17]

On October 7, the president prepared to deliver the speech that would bring Congress around to passing a resolution supporting regime change in Iraq. He rehearsed it with his staff that afternoon in the White House family theater, then set off for Cincinnati, Middle America. "The threat comes from Iraq," Bush declared.

> The Iraqi regime . . . possesses and produces chemical and biologi-cal weapons. We've also discovered that Iraq has a growing fleet of manned and unmanned aerial vehicles that could be used to dis-perse chemical and biological weapons across broad areas . . . Al-liance with terrorists could allow the Iraqi regime to attack America without leaving any fingerprints . . . The evidence indicates that Iraq is reconstituting its nuclear weapons program . . . We cannot wait for the final proof—the smoking gun—that could come in the form of a mushroom cloud.[18]

Earlier in the summer, the Italian foreign intelligence agency, SISME, had offered documents to the CIA purporting to show that Saddam had tried to buy uranium, in an unprocessed form known as "yellowcake," from the impoverished African state of Niger. The same documents were offered to the International Atomic Energy Agency. Both the CIA and the IAEA immediately saw these documents for what they were—clumsy forgeries.[19]

The head of SISME, however, persisted in peddling his garbage. Rebuffed by the CIA, General Nicolò Pollari had taken copies to the White House and handed them to Rice's deputy, Stephen Hadley, on September 9. The law said that Hadley had to report his meeting to the congressional committees that oversee intelligence matters. Hadley ignored the law. Had he obeyed it, the documents probably would have become useless. He saved them for another day.[20]

They were published for the first time in a magazine owned by the Italian prime minister, Silvio Berlusconi, which raised questions about his role in their manufacture. Although Berlusconi overtly supported Bush and was willing to commit Italian troops, public opinion across Europe, including Italy, was vehemently opposed to invading Iraq. Berlusconi had even tried to enlist Muammar Gadhafi of Libya to intercede with Saddam and stop the coming war.[21]

When Berlusconi tried to persuade Bush not to invade Iraq, the president assured him there was nothing to worry about. "We have put together a lethal military and we will kick his ass . . . This is going to change. You watch, public opinion will change. We lead our publics. We cannot follow our publics."[22]

The threat that the president was conjuring in his Cincinnati speech was false, in the round and in the details. In August 1995 General Hussein Kamel, the head of Iraq's biological, chemical, and nuclear weapons programs, defected to Jordan. Kamel was married to one of Saddam's daughters, and he despaired at the ruin his father-in-law was bringing on his country.

When he was debriefed by Rolf Ekeus, the head of the United Nations Special Commission, and by experts from the International Atomic Energy Agency, one of the first questions he was asked was, "Is there any continuation of, or present, nuclear activity?"

"No," replied Kamel. "But blueprints are there on microfiche."[23]

There was uranium, which the French had provided for a reactor, but it was tightly guarded by the French, and Iraqis had no access to it. They tried to find some uranium of their own, but what little they found was of poor quality. As for centrifuges, "they had only a few centrifuges." They could therefore produce only a small amount of enriched uranium. Not enough for a bomb.

Kamel was shown a document that suggested Saddam's bomb project was advancing rapidly. He rejected it as a fake. "Dr. Khidir Abdul Abbas Hamza is related to this document . . . He worked with us but he was useless . . . He was even interrogated by a team before he left and was allowed to go." On reaching the United States, Hamza had been helped by the CIA in writing a novel, with the title *Saddam's Bombmaker*. It purported to be nonfiction, and it took pains to conceal the fact that Hamza had been nothing more than a mid-level functionary. He was so terrified of radiation that he sat in an office and read reports rather than going anywhere near the labs where nuclear materials were being stored or developed. Besides, he had been involved with the program for less than a year, and his occupation after arriving in the United States was gas station attendant.

When Ekeus and the inspectors from the IAEA asked what had happened to Saddam's biological weapons, the answer was that they were destroyed in the summer of 1991. "Nothing remained. It was done before you came." But, Kamel assured the inspectors, it was their inspections that had prompted the destruction. "You should not underestimate yourselves. You are very effective in Iraq."

It was the same story with chemical weapons: Saddam had once had sizable amounts, but they had been destroyed. The factory that had produced nerve gas was now turning out pesticides. There were a couple of SCUD launchers somewhere; there were some molds for missile parts, a few centrifuges, computer disks, blueprints, microfiches; doubtless doomed hopes were still animating Saddam, but there was nothing that constituted a threat.

Kamel's patriotism soon cost him his life. Lured back to Iraq with a promise that he would not be punished, and encouraged to accept by his wife, who was homesick, he returned, only to be murdered on Saddam's orders.

After inspections resumed in November 2002, the IAEA concluded that there were no nuclear weapons and no program to build them. That was why the Niger yellowcake story had to be cooked up, in a hurry, with faked documents. Otherwise the "mushroom cloud" that Rice, Cheney, and Bush were using to put fear into the nation would blow away.[24]

On January 28, 2003, in his State of the Union address, Bush returned to the faked documents. They had been passed to the British, who declined to pronounce them forgeries. But a former U.S. ambassador to Gabon, Joseph Wilson IV, had gone to Niger on behalf of the CIA, seen how tightly the yellowcake was controlled by the IAEA, and concluded that the story was false. Despite that, Bush asserted, "The British government has learned that Saddam Hussein recently sought significant quantities of uranium from Africa." Stephen Hadley later claimed that he had put these words into the speech, but he could have done so only with the approval of Condoleezza Rice.[25]

The speech was notable, too, for its yoking Iraq, Iran, and North

Korea in a coalition of their own. "States like these, and their terrorist allies, constitute an axis of evil, arming to threaten the peace of the world . . . [But] I will not wait on events while dangers gather. I will not stand by as peril draws closer and closer. The United States of America will not permit the world's most dangerous regimes to threaten us with the world's most destructive weapons." He was promising three wars, possibly seven.[26]

A week later, the administration thrust Colin Powell into the breach. As a young army officer in Vietnam, Powell had served with the Americal Division and been party to the attempted cover-up of the massacre at My Lai.

When he complained to friends about the wrong and wrongheaded policies of the current administration, Powell referred them to his great hero and role model, George C. Marshall, one of the finest soldiers the United States has produced. Powell could not have chosen a better man. Yet it is inconceivable that Marshall would ever have done what Powell was prepared to do. To have done so, Marshall would have stopped being Marshall.

During a ninety-minute doom-laden presentation to the UN, Powell told a hushed council chamber, "It took years for Iraq to finally admit that it had produced four tons of the deadly nerve agent, VX. A single drop on the skin will kill in minutes. Four tons. The admission only came after the inspectors collected documentation as a result of the defection of Hussein Kamel, Saddam Hussein's late son-in-law." What the documentation had revealed was the fact that what Kamel had told UNSCOM, the IAEA, the CIA, and MI6 was true: it had all been destroyed. Powell did not mention that.

As the neocons at Defense were cranking up the nuclear rhetoric, the Israelis, with whom they had close ties, were urging Bush on. Israel publicly and privately urged Bush to attack Iraq. A newspaper poll in August 2002 showed that 50 percent of Israelis wanted an invasion that would remove Saddam Hussein.[27]

Following the State of the Union address, Israeli prime minister Ariel Sharon tried to raise the stakes, demanding that the governments of Iran, Libya, and Syria must also be overthrown after Iraq was conquered. "These are irresponsible states, which must be disarmed of weapons of mass destruction, and a successful American move in Iraq as a model will make that easier to achieve," Sharon told a visiting delegation of American congressmen. Although Israel was not going to join the coalition that Bush was assembling, "the American action is of vital importance."[28]

All the same, Israeli intelligence had not only concluded that Saddam Hussein did not possess weapons of mass destruction, it was downgrading the threat. On the list it maintained of threats to Israel's survival, Iraq had recently been moved from fourth place to sixth.[29]

By this time, almost everything was in place. Then Kenneth Pollack, an authority on Iran and a booster for the invasion of Iraq, wrote an op-ed piece that appeared in *The New York Times* on February 21, 2003. According to Pollack, Hussein Kamel had revealed "that outside pressure had not only failed to eradicate the nuclear program, it was bigger and more cleverly spread out and concealed than anyone had imagined it to be." This, as Pollack would have known, was untrue, but by now the war drums that he and the other believers were beating had created such a cacophony that truth did not stand a chance. It had become, in effect, irrelevant.

That did not stop the CIA's spokesman, Bill Harlow, from denouncing a cursory account of Kamel's debriefing that appeared in *Newsweek* on March 3. This was the first chance that people had to read any of it for themselves. "Bogus, wrong, untrue," Harlow told the press. Within forty-eight hours, Glen Rangwala, a Middle East scholar at Cambridge University, posted a copy of the entire debriefing transcript on the Internet.

The head of CIA operations in Western Europe, Tyler Drumheller, recruited Saddam's foreign minister, Naji Sabri, to become an informant, in exchange for $100,000 and, in all likelihood, green cards for himself and his family. What about the WMDs? the CIA wanted to know. There are none, said Sabri. They were destroyed ten years ago. Sabri confirmed Hussein Kamel's account of 1995 and the fact that nothing had changed since then.

Drumheller made sure that the president was briefed on Sabri's reports. What he got back was a blunt message: This isn't about the intel. It's about regime change.[30]

In the closing days of the countdown to war, Bush asked Kenan Makiya, an Iraqi exile who taught at Brandeis, to come to the Oval

Office. Makiya had spent years helping to bring about the overthrow of Saddam. The president wanted to put the question directly: What kind of reception will our troops get from ordinary Iraqis?

"They will be greeted with sweets and flowers," replied Makiya.

The president also asked George Tenet, director of Central Intelligence, if there was any doubt about Saddam's WMDs. "It's a slam dunk, Mr. President," Tenet told him.[31]

Shortly after this the president made a trip to Nashville, where an old friend, Pat Robertson, came to see him. It seemed to Robertson that Bush was pumped up. He was radiant with confidence and self-belief, like Mark Twain's "Christian holding four aces." Robertson found the presidential exuberance disturbing. A war was about to begin, and Bush's overweening satisfaction was dangerous. War is just too unpredictable, Robertson reminded himself, and tried to make him look at the harsh realities of what might be just ahead. He told the president that the coming war could turn out to be costly. "Mr. President, you better prepare the American people for casualties."

"Oh, no, we're not going to have any casualties," said Bush.

"Well," Robertson replied, "the Lord told me it's going to be, A, a disaster and, B, messy."[32]

While Bush was making his preparations, Saddam Hussein had been making some of his own. One of his favorite movies these days was Ridley Scott's tub-thumper about the Somalian intervention, *Black Hawk Down*.

Saddam had more than three thousand copies made. They were distributed among senior figures in the military, the Baath, the Mukhabarat, and a new home guard, the Fedayeen Saddam. With the tape went some simple instructions: "Create chaos."[33]

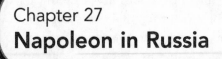

Chapter 27
Napoleon in Russia

WITH THE FIGHTING IN AFGHANISTAN TAPERING OFF, BUSH WAS buoyant. He'd done it. And now, he told Bob Woodward, "I will seize the opportunity to achieve big goals." It soon became obvious what he meant: the overthrow of Saddam in the short term, the transformation of the Middle East into something resembling the Middle West in the long.

Never has the political been more personal. George W. Bush was handed a poisoned chalice. But it was his decision to drain it to the dregs. As a rule, the checks and balances of the federal system would have blocked any president from turning a personal vendetta into a war. Even before securing the Republican nomination, Bush had told at least four people—Mickey Herskowitz, Osama Siblani, David Nyhan, and David O. Russell—that if he became president, he would attack Iraq and oust Saddam Hussein. The justification he gave always went back to his father and Laura Bush. But these weren't normal times. The United States was almost a new country after the Twin

Towers came down, a continental-size binary weapon looking for a place to explode.

The world had long grown used to the United States' chauvinistic sense of exceptionalism. After September 11, that exceptionalism was yoked to a sense of victimhood. Down the ages, when powerful countries have felt they were the victims of history, the results have been calamitous for them, and for others. And in 2002 exceptionalism and victimhood enabled the president to shift the nation's attention from a war still not finished to another unfinished war.

Being commander in chief in wartime is always an exercise in triangulation. Every week George W. Bush had to negotiate with a disparate variety of individuals and institutions to push the country toward Iraq. There were the voters, on whom he would depend for re-election; there was the military, who had to overthrow Saddam without creating a power vacuum; there was the federal bureaucracy; there were the members of the coalition; there were the oil-producing states that opposed the war but were so dependent on American muscle that they could be ignored; there were liberal democracies such as France and Germany that opposed the war, and they were ridiculed; there was the United Nations, which was treated with contempt verging on hostility; and there was the Congress, the media, and the cabinet, all of whom had to be kept on board.

At times it probably felt like a duty to rise to that call in the blood to make somebody pay for 9/11. Afghanistan really didn't satisfy; it might be Muslim, but it wasn't Arabic. Iraq was both. And it made an unintended but perfect fit with the other unwinnable wars. Truman had chosen to fight in Korea at a time when the country was in turmoil over McCarthy's charges of high treason in exalted places and the fury over the supposed "loss" of China to Communism. Lyndon Johnson's decision to turn John Kennedy's "adviser war" in Vietnam into one of the biggest wars of the twentieth century came when he, like the country, was still grieving and angry over Kennedy's assassination. "Whom the Gods would destroy, they first drive crazy." Korea, Vietnam, Iraq—all were made possible by, in, and for a nation that was not its normal self.

As Bush pushed and pulled the country toward Baghdad, he could not have had two more devoted and ruthless assistants than Dick Cheney and Donald Rumsfeld. Cheney was the first vice president to have his own national security staff—fourteen neocons as eager for war as their boss. Cheney was an experienced bureaucratic infighter and a man for whom ousting Saddam was a long-standing personal obsession. He had been working toward it even longer than the president had.

The same was true at the Pentagon. Donald Rumsfeld came back to it as the first returning secretary of defense, having pondered for more than a decade on how to make the Pentagon's military-bureaucratic machinery bend to his will. His previous spell as secretary, during the Vietnam War, had been a tale of friction and frustration. He blamed it on the organization, but any organization foolish enough to fight an unwinnable war is unlikely to provide a satisfying experience.

In the meantime he had become a multimillionaire as CEO at G. D. Searle, a pharmaceutical company and producer of Nutra-Sweet. Rumsfeld had secured total victory for NutraSweet over Equal in the saccharine war by using his influence with Nixon to get the then head of the Food and Drug Administration fired. The FDA had doubts about NutraSweet's safety. The new head of the agency, however, ruled in NutraSweet's favor.

In a speech to the Commonwealth Club of San Francisco in September 2002, Al Gore opposed the invasion of Iraq before the mission in Afghanistan had been completed and Osama bin Laden had been captured or killed. It was obvious to Gore that the venture was likely to fail. What was the plan for stabilizing a broken and defeated Iraq once Saddam was ousted? Gore wondered aloud. Then he quoted Donald Rumsfeld: "That's for the Iraqis to come together and decide."[1] And if they couldn't agree, what then?

Working together, Cheney and Rumsfeld were force magnifiers to one another, making them powerful enough to neuter whatever doubts and hesitations came from the CIA—a place stuffed with liberals—and State, a place that to neocons was almost as pathologically liberal as the United Nations.

Rumsfeld returned to a Pentagon that was debating with itself over wars yet to come. Among defense strategists a new paradigm was taking shape: the "Revolution in Military Affairs." The age of huge tank battles; of infantry divisions pitted against one another in huge, bloody brawls; of armies lumbering toward enemy capitals behind massive artillery barrages—that age was obviously over. What were coming over the horizon were wars that would be dominated by information superiority on the battlefield, information that would guide nimble, fast-moving forces that—although smaller than a standard infantry or armored division—would pack an even bigger punch.

Rumsfeld, Cheney, and Paul Wolfowitz were the neocon and Project for the New American Century representatives at this revolution. They were right about the need to junk the Cold War military paradigm, which had been little more than a tweaking of the military circa 1945.

The lean, mean, fast-moving military they had in mind would be able to take any Third World capital in anything from three weeks to three months. But they more or less ignored the inconvenient legacy of the anticolonial struggle—protracted wars, insurgencies, wars of national liberation. These were the kinds of struggles where large numbers of soldiers would be needed. Fighter pilot Rumsfeld and the draft-avoiding Cheney and Wolfowitz did not think much of the army. Neither did another fighter pilot, George W. Bush. They weren't going to countenance a larger force of grunts.

Rumsfeld pitched himself into the internecine squabbles of the Defense Department with the zeal of a man who saw in himself a natural born bruiser. As captain of the Princeton wrestling team he had been hailed by a campus newspaper as "a speedy takedown specialist," and for all his seventy-plus years, thinning gray hair, and thick spectacles, he saw himself that way still. "I play my game," he boasted. "I play hardball." He also let the warriors around him know that he was every bit as tough as they. Rumsfeld placed a plaque on his desk that declared AGGRESSIVE FIGHTING FOR THE RIGHT IS THE NOBLEST SPORT THE WORLD AFFORDS. And of course, from a fighter plane, high above the blood and the stench of rotting human flesh, it probably does look like sport.[2]

Nor was Rumsfeld able to stop trying to seem clever, at one point describing the Global War on Terror as being like three-dimensional chess. All other wars, he asserted, were like checkers. But he had never played three-dimensional chess. No one has. As similes go, it was not an encouraging one: if three-dimensional chess is an impossible game, wouldn't it make sense to look for a more promising comparison?

Rumsfeld and Cheney found a soul mate rather than a rival in Condoleezza Rice, the national security adviser. Not even they could outdo Rice in unbridled dedication. She too was going to give the president whatever he wanted, whatever the cost to conscience, whatever the consequences for flesh and blood human beings.

During his father's presidency, George W. Bush was known among White House staffers as "the loyalty thermometer." His unofficial assignment was to track down the leakers and in-house critics. Loyalty may well be the most precious and rarest thing in the upper reaches of the executive branch. On the loyalty thermometer, Rice was bubbling over.

She spent much of each day at Bush's side. When he went on vacation, she went with him. At Camp David, she was assigned her own cabin. When the Bush family sits down to dinner on a Sunday evening, she sits down with them.[3]

There was something slightly dubious, though, both in such obvious devotion and in the president's evident need for it. An emotionally needy commander in chief is nothing new. Lyndon Johnson was much the same. But an emotionally needy war president is reminiscent of Tony Soprano, depending on his psychiatrist, Dr. Jennifer Melfi, to shore up his conflicted self as he struggles to be a decent, responsible family man. It just happens that he has to whack the people who don't play by his rules.[4]

When questions were later raised about the president's claim in his State of the Union address that Saddam had tried to obtain yellowcake from Niger, Rice's deputy, Stephen Hadley, claimed that he had put this false assertion into the speech. Condoleezza Rice is probably the true author of those sixteen patently false words.

According to a congressional committee that investigated false and misleading statements that the administration produced before the invasion of Iraq, no one is known to have been more dishonest on the president's behalf. On at least eight occasions, the committee discovered, Condoleezza Rice had made statements that she must have known to be untrue. There were others that were certainly false, but she may have actually believed some of those.[5]

By calling the new challenge a "war," Bush had unwittingly ensured that other global challenges would be pushed to one side. Global warming was one, even though it took tens of thousands of lives each year in unprecedented heat waves, extreme hurricanes, and crop-killing droughts. The War on Terra is likely to prove more important than the War on Terror, but that thought would never occur to Bush or anyone close to him.

Calling it a war also made it possible to win widespread support, in Congress and public opinion, for torture and murder, an opportunity the president was quick to seize. As governor of Texas, he had denied clemency in 152 death penalty cases and granted clemency in just one. Under him, Texas became the execution state par excellence, executing more than twice as many people during those eight years as any other state. His chief legal adviser for many of these cases was Alberto Gonzalez, who produced memos that invariably recommended against clemency.[6]

Bush did not seem to take the memos seriously anyway. He was likely to give a cursory glance at any memo, including these. He also took a malicious delight in approving the execution of Karla Faye Tucker, the first woman sentenced to death in Texas for more than a hundred years. Convicted of a brutal double murder, she became a world famous example of remorse and rehabilitation. The pope was only one of the many thousands who petitioned for commutation of her sentence to life imprisonment.

The night she was executed, in 1998, Bush supporters and death penalty enthusiasts celebrated her death with a party and a barbecue in the parking lot at the penitentiary as she died. Bush was with them in spirit if not in person, giving an impersonation of her toward the end by simpering in a high-pitched voice, "Please, please let me live." Obviously a ridiculous person who deserved to die.[7]

With Bush in the White House, Alberto Gonzalez became the president's special counsel. In January 2002, with hundreds of Taliban fighters and others captured in Afghanistan, Gonzalez told Bush what he wanted to hear. "The war on terrorism is a new kind of war [and] renders obsolete Geneva's strict limitations on questioning of enemy prisoners and renders quaint some of its provisions."[8]

Bush knew he could count on Gonzalez. Even back in Texas, Gonzalez had advised him that as governor, he was not bound by international law. One of the death penalty cases involved a treaty that the Senate had ratified, thereby making it part of domestic law—except in Texas. According to Gonzalez, unless Texas had also ratified the treaty, the governor was free to ignore it. And he did so, putting yet another prisoner to death. Having raised Bush as governor above international law, Gonzalez did the same now that he was president.[9]

This and other memos, from legal counsel in the attorney general's office and the Pentagon, assured him that as president, he was exempt from both international and domestic law, such as the 1996 War Crimes Act. In March 2003 lawyers at the Defense Department advised him further that in his capacity as commander in chief, he could "approve any technique needed to protect the nation's security"—i.e., he could make torture legal. This was followed by other memos that detailed what forms of torture the Rumsfeld legal team had in mind. They were so elastic that anything was allowed—on the grounds of military necessity. This judgment was left entirely to the military, right down to corporals and three-stripe sergeants, who were told, "The gloves are coming off."

In Afghanistan, torture had been routine from the beginning. What happened there would be repeated in Iraq, as would the treatment of detainees—"enemy combatants"—at Guantánamo Bay. The officer commanding there, Major General Geoffrey D. Miller, learned one guiding principle from that experience: "Prisoners are like dogs and if you allow them to believe they are more than a dog, then you've lost control of them."[10]

The president also claimed the right to enforce UN resolutions without UN support. On March 7, 2003, the British attorney general, Lord Goldsmith, had no doubt that such independent action was illegal, as did the lawyers for Kofi Annan, the secretary general of the United Nations. Tony Blair set out to make the British government's lawyer change his mind, and he succeeded. All of the customary procedures for arriving at a judgment on a matter of international law were scrapped. The British Foreign Office's leading authority on international law, Elizabeth Wilmshurst, resigned in protest, but the crucial element was the personal factor. Peter Goldsmith was one of Blair's oldest and closest friends. He had been at private school with Blair, at college with Blair, and in the same legal chambers as Blair when they were training to become barristers. Bowing to pressure, and for the first time in British history, the attorney general on March 17 reversed himself, without producing the detailed legal arguments that normally set out the attorney general's reasoning.[11]

In Blair, the president had a soul mate. Bush continued to link Saddam Hussein with September 11, although the CIA's chief analyst for Middle Eastern intelligence, Paul R. Pillar, could not find any connection between the caves of Afghanistan and the presidential palaces of Baghdad. Blair, meanwhile, insisted that Saddam possessed weapons of mass destruction that could be deployed within forty-five minutes.

This story dominated British front pages at a crucial moment, although it later transpired that the intelligence assessment he cited was referring to mortar shells that might contain small amounts of mustard gas. One such mortar round might carry enough mustard gas to kill a few people, although depending on which way the wind was blowing, it might not even make them sick. Besides, mortar rounds are standard battlefield munitions. But as Blair told the story, southern Europe and the entire Middle East were under threat.

Meanwhile, the president was formulating a doctrine of: preventive war. According to Bush, he had the right, as commander in chief, to attack any country that might pose a threat within the next five years. An attack on Iraq was going to show that he meant it. This was not going to be a preemptive attack, something that would be legal in international law. If a national leader can provide proof that another country is about to strike, he is entitled to make a spoiling attack first.

As mendacious propaganda was being pumped out, Cheney et al. decided what the president would be told and how it should be couched. And both Bush and Blair possessed one crucial character trait—neither one was capable of telling a lie . . . without believing it. Self-delusion, however, is not a distaff version of honesty.

Instead of deploring what Bush and his war cabinet were doing, Blair and his minions were doing the same, distorting and politicizing the intelligence to fit the policy. Yet the right they were asserting—to invade Iraq because it had failed to comply, in their judgment, with UN resolutions from 1991—was obviously absurd. That was a judgment for the UN to make, and it had not done so. If Iran and Venezuela got together and decided to start enforcing UN resolutions without the UN's support, would the United States and Britain uphold their right to do so?

In their self-righteousness, Bush and Blair rejected the sage words of Grandma: The road to Hell is paved with good intentions. Even

Hitler could claim he had nothing but good intentions. Hardly anyone in the history of the world who began a war did so without believing it was for the good of his tribe, his clan, his country. The same was true of mass murderers such as Pol Pot, who thought he was saving the Khmer people, and Mao, who wanted to raise China up even if that meant millions went down, into the grave. In war, what surely matters most is not the intention—it's the result.

Shortly before the "shock and awe" blitz on Baghdad, with Britain ready to put more than twenty thousand troops into Iraq, Bush confided in Blair that this was only the beginning. Iraq would fall quickly. Most of the American and British troops would soon be available for operations elsewhere. "I want to go beyond Iraq in dealing with weapons of mass destruction," he told Blair. He had a list of dangerous states that he was going to bring down: Iran, North Korea, Pakistan, and Saudi Arabia. Blair seemed ready—if not eager—to go along.[12]

While the administration focused its propaganda campaign on weapons of mass destruction, the issue of oil was pushed to one side. Rumsfeld repeatedly asserted, "This is not about oil," yet it would have been highly irresponsible to attack one of the world's biggest oil states and leave oil out of the equation. Before World War II, the United States did not import oil, but by the year 2004 it imported nearly 60 percent of the oil it needed. It was on course to import more than 70 percent by 2025. The implications for America were too serious for any government to ignore, and Bush did not ignore them.

One of his earliest assignments for the NSC was to get it working with an energy task force on future energy needs. The principal recommendation that emerged was that the United States should use its military muscle to push Middle Eastern oil producers into doubling their production from 22 billion barrels a day in 2001 to 45 billion barrels a day in 2025. And if that failed, the document suggested, the United States would have to seize the oil fields and the refineries and do the job itself. If the Arabs thought this was "their" oil, they were wrong. It's ours.[13]

There was planning for Iraq's oil reserves and the billions of dollars that Iraq's oil produced, but not for much else. As the invasion drew near, Rumsfeld drew up a list of all the things he could think of that might go wrong, and devoted some serious thinking, by his own account, to how the Department of Defense might respond. Even so, three contingencies that didn't make his list were:

- Widespread looting
- Theft and concealment of up to a million tons of explosives
- A widespread, deeply rooted insurgency

There were plans galore at the State Department, but Rumsfeld and Cheney had put Colin Powell on the sidelines, and there his department remained. There was no occupation plan worthy of the name. Just as the first President Bush had no plan for after Kuwait, his son maintained that strategic vision. There was no plan for after Baghdad. The army chief of staff, General Eric Shinseki, expressed his anxieties about what would follow the overthrow of Saddam: it would take "several hundred thousand" troops to secure Iraq, he told a congressional committee.

This was Shinseki's way of saying that the operation as planned would probably fail. The army that Rumsfeld had spent two years shaping was too small and had too many other commitments, in South Korea, the Balkans, and elsewhere, to put three hundred thousand soldiers—possibly more—on occupation duty in Iraq. The implication of Shinseki's testimony was that the whole operation was a mistake.

Wolfowitz was incensed, rushing to appear before the same committee the next day. He ridiculed Shinseki's remarks, and Rumsfeld promptly forced Shinseki into retirement, even though he had another year to serve as army chief of staff.

On the evening of March 19, 2003, Tomahawk cruise missiles and fighter-bombers from carriers in the Gulf blew up government buildings in Baghdad and attempted a decapitation strike to kill Saddam Hussein. It made for an unforgettable television spectacle of American military power, the biggest, most expensive fireworks display ever. The president, sitting at his desk in the Oval Office, was as caught up in the drama as anyone, pounding his desk and shouting, "I feel good!"[14]

As the marines and the army raced each other north to Baghdad, the future was there wherever they looked: Saddam had covered the countryside with weapons and explosives. Every few hundred yards along the major roads there were pits filled with rocket-propelled grenades and mortar rounds. Brand-new AK-47s wrapped in plastic bags littered the verges. Government buildings, such as schools, had been turned into ammunition dumps. There were up to three million tons of high explosives, bombs, and artillery rounds. Just back from the roads were underground bunkers. When Saddam said he wanted chaos, local commanders had obliged by spreading the means for it across the landscape. Tommy Franks was hailed for the swiftness with which he had taken Baghdad. But speed isn't everything.[15]

On April 9, with American troops in Firdus Square, Bush summoned Ahmed Chalabi and Kenan Makiya to the Oval Office. Together they watched Saddam's statue decorated with an American flag, then pulled down by a tank recovery vehicle. For all the cheering, though, for all the sense of History these images occasioned, why, Bush wondered, aren't there a lot more people in Firdus Square? Instead of tens of thousands, there were only a few hundred.[16]

What he had just done was to commit the greatest strategic blunder by the leader of a Western democracy in nearly two hundred years. In 1812 Napoleon had invaded Russia, expecting a quick victory once he captured Moscow. He discovered that he now faced two choices. He could remain in Moscow through the winter and watch the Grande Armée die before his eyes. Or he could retreat through the snow and watch the Grande Armée die before his eyes. He chose retreat. If nothing else, retreat offered an illusion of control.

Chapter 28
Armed Missionaries

THE INVASION OF IRAQ WAS A CROSSROADS: EITHER THE CHARAC-
ter of Americans would have to change in order to sustain the policy,
or the policy would have to change in order to sustain the American
character.

Military commanders, in time-honored fashion, turned the advance
from Kuwait to Baghdad into a race between the army and the Marine Corps. The president followed it on television; wherever he went,
he was glued to the screen for much of each day. While he was
watching it at Camp David, a presenter said there were reliable reports that the president was following the advance not by relying on
intelligence reports from the military, but by watching television.
Bush erupted with laughter.[1]

What the screen did not show was that everything needed for
an insurgency was in place. It was not simply a question of a million
tons of munitions and millions of assault rifles and rocket-propelled
grenades. Iraq was probably the most xenophobic country in the
world. That was the legacy of being conquered and occupied by the

Mongols in the thirteenth century, the Turks in the seventeenth century, and the British in 1920. Iraq was about be occupied for the fourth time, a first in the history of Arabic countries. Little wonder, then, that attitude surveys showed more resentment toward foreigners among Iraqis than could be found anywhere else in the world.[2]

Few countries can match Iraq's bloodstained history. For the past three thousand years it has been a frontline state, the barrier between the Persians and the Arab world. And if the United States was serious about installing a democratic government, it would inevitably be dominated by the Shia, reversing fourteen hundred years of Iraqi history and creating a Greater Iran, and a Lesser Iraq. It was debatable whether the Sunni Muslims of the world, by far the majority, would ever accept that.

Following the Soviet withdrawal from Afghanistan, the jihadi movement was split about where to go next. Bin Laden and Al Qaeda wanted to strike "the far enemy," the United States. Most jihadis wanted to strike "the near enemy," namely the oppressive Arab regimes propped up by the United States, from Morocco to Saudi Arabia.[3]

The invasion of Iraq offered something to jihadis on both sides of the argument. In the early months of the occupation, as Iraqis tried to form resistance groups, they lacked experience in guerrilla warfare and there was a shortage of money. Al Qaeda had an abundance of both. It financed much of the resistance and trained both leaders and foot soldiers.

The leader of one group told his followers they should be grateful to the United States for two things: "First, for removing Saddam. Now we can operate freely. And for coming here. Now we can attack them without having to go to America."[4]

There was also a ready-made strategy for the coming insurgency. The Arab strategy for defeating invaders goes back to before the time of Christ, when the Arabs, like the ancient Greeks, had to fight off the Persians. The Arab way is to outlast and exhaust the enemy, whether Persian, Roman, Crusader, Mongolian, or Turkish.

In recent times, following World War I, the British and the French had rushed in to pick up the oily pieces, determined to transform the Middle East by modernizing it and integrating it into the world's political and economic structures. Yet it was Europe that was transformed by that experience, not the Middle East. The Arabs infuriated and frustrated them at every turn. This was common knowledge even among non-Arabists, having been set forth in David Fromkin's *A Peace to End All Peace*, published in 1989 and never out of print. Fromkin's book was an international bestseller, yet no one in the White House, the Pentagon, or on the NSC appears to have read it, despite the long-standing obsession of George W. Bush and Paul Wolfowitz with Iraq.

Even expert voices within the government were rejected. The CIA produced a report saying that an invasion would probably provoke ethnic strife. Wolfowitz rushed into the breach once more to stop this dangerous idea from spreading. Iraq wasn't like Saudi Arabia, he told the National Public Radio audience. "The Iraqis are by and large quite secular. They are overwhelmingly Shia . . . and they don't bring the sensitivity of having the holy cities of Islam on their territory."[5]

By this time, Wolfowitz had made himself the master of the overly confident pronouncement that rests on wishful thinking. It was hardly a secret that to millions of Iraqi and Iranian Shiites, the shrine cities of Najaf and Karbala are two of the holiest places on Earth, but Wolfowitz, a former professor of international relations at Johns Hopkins, was evidently unaware of it.

It seems safe to assume that as under secretary of defense, he would have been familiar with the debriefing of Hussein Kamel. Toward the end of that debriefing, Kamel said that he had defected to Jordan because following the Gulf War, Saddam Hussein had turned Iraq away from secularism and was courting Sunni clerics. To a career Baathist like Kamel, the mosque was a rival power center. "And now," he lamented, "Baath Party members have to pass a religious exam . . . They even stopped party meetings for prayers."

Wolfowitz shared the fantasy that American troops invading Iraq would be greeted as liberators. It would be like the liberation of France, he assured the doubters. His knowledge of World War II was not much better than his knowledge of the shrine cities of the Shia or the merger of mosque and state under Saddam Hussein.

Shortly after the fall of Baghdad, Senator Joe Biden went to see the president to tell him that he feared it was going to be some time before peace and stability were established. From the satisfied expression on Bush's face, it was obvious that he thought everything was going well and would only get better. Biden asked him straight-out, "Mr. President, how can you be so sure when you don't know the facts?"

Bush got up from his desk, stepped over to Biden, and put a hand on his shoulder. "My instincts," he said. "My instincts."[6]

Those instincts, however, were shaped by dogma; they were too rigid to be of much use. With the fall of Baghdad, the Iranian government tried to establish a dialogue with the Bush administration. Its aim was obvious: help the Americans establish a democratic government in Iraq, and the Shia would come to power, finally, after 1,400 years. The Iranians offered to recognize Israel, disarm Hizbollah, and accept stringent limitations on their nuclear research program. In exchange, they wanted American diplomatic recognition and an end to American economic sanctions. Bush wasted no time in rejecting the Iranian proposal.[7]

Contrary to later assertions, there *was* planning for the day after Baghdad fell, but it was planning of a new kind, dominated by neocon convictions. At the end of military operations plans, a civil/military annex had always been attached. That was standard operating procedure. These annexes were written by the State Department and the military's civil affairs officers, and they went back to World War II.

They dealt with security for the people in occupied areas; they provided for the protection of national treasures; they assured the provision of basic services such as policing, water, electricity, and medical care; and above all else, they were designed to create bridges and minimize unpleasantness between occupiers and occupied, both of whom were going to be operating in a new world, where impatience and frustration could provoke an insurgency. Operation Iraqi Freedom had a plan to take Baghdad, but there was no civil/military annex this time. Donald Rumsfeld had frozen out those annex-writing wimps over at Foggy Bottom.[8]

Instead, there was a neocon plan to privatize everything and sell off Iraq's oil fields to American oil companies. Lawrence Lindsey, the former chairman of the Council of Economic Advisers, had assured the president that once the United States controlled Iraq's oil fields, it would be able to drive down the price of oil. "You could add three to five million barrels a day to world supply," said Lindsey. "The successful prosecution of the war would be good for the economy."[9]

Bush, the sometime oilman, was sold, but he had been only a small player, and his ventures in the oil business invariably ended with his father's rich friends having to bail him out. Now he failed to grasp that the majors, such as Exxon, had no desire to see the price of oil come down. The majors sabotaged this pipe dream, but not before Bush made a major change in the coming occupation.

The day Baghdad fell, a retired army general, Jay Garner, was preparing to go into Iraq and lead the humanitarian mission that would rescue the country. Garner had done something similar among the Kurds at the end of the Gulf War. It seemed obvious to him that a new Iraqi government would have to be installed within weeks if the country was going to be stabilized. But at the last moment, he received a phone call from the White House: he had just been supplanted. The president's man in Baghdad was going to be L. Paul ("Call me Jerry") Bremer, sometime foreign service officer but mostly a neocon businessman with a non-humanitarian mission: Bremer was going to privatize everything in sight.

Within weeks, the Bremer creed was being promoted across Iraq, at the same time providing Baathists and rebellious clerics with a powerful recruiting pitch: "Look, we are losing our country. We're losing our resources to a bunch of rich businessmen who want to take over and make our life miserable."[10]

Meanwhile, looting on a massive scale had broken out. The same had happened in 1918, when T. E. Lawrence, a British army officer, masterminded an Arab revolt. Lawrence could hardly credit the scenes of wholesale and methodical looting that erupted across Iraq and Syria when Turkish rule collapsed. And here it was again.

Donald Rumsfeld demonstrated once more his inability to see below the surface of events, crafting weird bromides instead: "Freedom's untidy, and free people are free to make mistakes and commit crimes," he declared. "Stuff happens." The last time this kind of stuff happened in Iraq, it presaged the revolt that drove the Ottomans out. And now the collapse of order and security was providing cover for a handful of clerics, Baathists, former secret police (the Mukhabarat), and former militia, the Fedayeen Saddam, to start organizing loosely linked or stand-alone insurgent cells, and for young Muslim men staring in anger at television screens across the world to start thinking about going to Syria or Jordan, slipping into Iraq, and making jihad. What these groups and individuals lacked was money to get there. Al Qaeda gladly provided it.[11]

At the urging of Ahmed Chalabi, the Pentagon's wannabe and nominally Shiite ruler of Iraq, Bremer dissolved the Iraqi army. It was obvious why Chalabi would want the army dissolved and the Baath Party uprooted: one day he could find himself hanging from a lamppost if the army or the Baathists managed to pull off a coup. The man had sold his soul, and likely his country, in exchange for $4 million a year.

After the insurgency took hold, Bremer was widely criticized for dissolving the army. This overlooks the fact that by the time he acted, most of the army had gone home or had departed to join the embryonic insurgency. During the weeks leading up to the fall of Baghdad, the four Republican Guard divisions that were supposed to defend the city melted away. The buses were still running, and after a few nights of heavy bombing, soldiers took off their uniforms, got on buses, and rode away from the five-hundred-pound bombs.

Not only was there no army to speak of by May 2003, but over the course of ten years, the UN sanctions regime had hollowed out the Iraqi state. Once the most educated, secular, and Westernized country in the Arab world after Lebanon, Saddam's rule had produced a government competent only in the arts of repression. The people were dependent on UN food rations, and in their misery they had turned increasingly Islamic. Tens of thousands of doctors, teachers, engineers, scientists, and professors had decamped for other countries. It was not going to take much to bring down the facade that was the Iraqi state. When General Tommy Franks gave the order to invade, declaring, "It's hammer time," all it took was a single sharp blow. Bremer's plans for the reconstruction of Iraq were predicated on there being a functioning state. There wasn't one.

Had Iraq been blessed with a competent and honest civil service that enjoyed popular support, it would have been possible for Bremer to turn to it at almost any time and order it to reconstitute the army.

What had held Iraq together was the fear of the millions and the will of one man. There really was no functioning state. The United States would have to create one. Meanwhile, Chalabi, Allawi, and their friends and family members were returning to complete the looting of Iraq.

With Baghdad taken and Saddam in hiding, American forces moved into Saddam's palaces and Iraqi military bases. They had virtually no contact with ordinary Iraqis, and that's the way they liked it. Two months after launching Operation Iraqi Freedom, the president donned a flight suit and was flown out to an aircraft carrier, the USS *Abraham Lincoln*, returning from its deployment to the Persian Gulf.

The carrier was within sight of shore, off San Diego. A helicopter could have taken Bush to the carrier. But what the country craved was the commander in chief as First Warrior. So far, only Hollywood had provided that, in *Air Force One* and *Independence Day*. Here, a political dream life was brought to pass. The television cameras were carefully positioned to show nothing but ocean, no hint of land off the starboard bow. But there was a huge banner draped across the carrier's tower to provide the flavor of victory: MISSION ACCOMPLISHED.[12]

Iraqi insurgents had a different narrative. By July, they were taking potshots at American troops across much of Iraq. Bush, irritated by a reporter's questions about what he proposed to do about that, responded by welcoming these attacks: "Bring 'em on!"[13]

Bush loved to talk tough, like Truman and like Johnson, but at Andover and Yale his involvement with the football team was limited to cheerleading, not proving his toughness on muddy fall days. Anyway, Paul Bremer was assuring him that the insurgents did not pose a serious threat: "Largely isolated attacks by small groups of Baathists and Fedayeen Saddam groups of five to ten men. I wouldn't characterize it as an organized resistance."[14]

Neither would Bush, but in August the insurgency announced its intentions by blowing up the Jordanian embassy and the United Nations headquarters in Baghdad, an attack that killed forty-two people. The UN pulled nearly all its survivors out. However, Rumsfeld refused to take these attacks seriously. He chose instead to deride insurgents as no more than a wearisome nuisance that the U.S. military had dealt with in the past and invariably crushed. "The dead-enders are still with us," he told the VFW convention in August 2003. "Those remnants of the defeated regimes who'll go on fighting long after their cause is lost . . . They will be defeated."[15]

The new commander in Iraq, General Ricardo Sanchez, had a strategy for achieving that: search and destroy. Sanchez was going to begin where William Westmoreland had ended. Insurgents were setting off roadside bombs, sending rockets and mortar fire into the bases, and killing American troops. With the president's blessing, the military struck back with a wave of attacks on towns and homes. They rounded up thousands of Iraqis and subjected many—possibly a majority—to torture in some form, including rape, murder, and dog attacks at Abu Ghraib, Camp Victory, Camp Crocker, and other prisons.

After military and civilian interrogators were informed in August 2003, "The gloves are coming off," that was taken, as anyone might expect, as a license to do anything to any Iraqi. One of the casualties of this endorsement of unbridled ferocity against prisoners included a captured Iraqi major general, Abed Hamed Mowhoush, who was tortured and beaten for sixteen straight days, until he died. The CIA meanwhile was recruiting Kurdish and Shiite militias into an organization called the Scorpions. Their task was to torture and murder prisoners, most of whom were Sunnis.[16]

In the United States, the military sometimes turned to a CIA manual published in the 1960s for guidance in interrogation techniques, but what they relied on far more was a Soviet manual from World War II, itself based on the practices of the Soviet secret police, the NKVD. The point was not the extraction of information, but the extraction of confessions. A false confession was as good as a true one, often better. Under Stalin, some of his most loyal lieutenants were forced to confess to crimes that were impossible, such as putting powdered glass into millions of gallons of milk. Such confessions were a measure of how completely they had been destroyed as human beings—no minds of their own any longer, no willpower, no pride, no resistance.[17]

The Soviet manual was the basis of a training program at Fort Bragg. Its methods were carried from North Carolina to Guantánamo Bay and from there to Iraq. Dick Cheney and Donald Rumsfeld also provided guidance to commanders in the field on how they were to implement the president's directives on torture. They were making sure that torture would become inevitable and systematic. Colin Powell tried to intervene, but he was helpless to do anything about what had become a terror regime at places such as Abu Ghraib and Bagram Air Base in Afghanistan.[18]

With the president's doctrine of "military necessity" and the encouragement of the vice president and secretary of defense, anyone from private to general who felt that military necessity called for beating someone to death or having a German shepherd attack a naked Iraqi could do so. A blank check, taken out on human flesh.

When the Senate moved to ban all torture, Bush allowed Dick Cheney to seek an exemption for the CIA, and when Bush was asked about torture at a press conference in Panama, he crafted an ambiguous response: "Any activity we conduct is within the law. We do not torture."[19]

"But now it's all over Iraq," army interrogator Anthony Lagouranis told PBS's *Frontline* program on November 14, 2005, only a week after the president's statement. "The infantry units are torturing people in their homes. They were using things like burns. They smash people's feet with the back of an ax head. They break bones, ribs . . . serious stuff."

The memos crafted by Alberto Gonzalez and other government lawyers that said the president, while acting as commander in chief, was bound by no law, domestic or international, had not been revoked or repudiated. And no country in the world, including countries such as Zimbabwe and Uzbekistan, admits it practices torture. Like Bush, their leaders, too, assert, "We do not torture." But torture is irresistible for a nation that is conducting a war, because it is a win-win proposition: even if the information extracted turns out to be worthless, the knowledge that torture is being inflicted is sure to spread. For every unlucky wretch who's tortured, hundreds, possibly thousands, will be cowed into an impotent passivity. Thus does Bush feel free to say, "We do not torture." He has a war on his hands and a stack of memos telling him that whatever he does is legal. It goes back a long way. The king can do no wrong.

Far from curbing the insurgency, however, torture was helping to fuel it. Across the Islamic world, evidence of torture was a valuable recruiting tool, yet more proof that Muslims were being oppressed, more proof of the need for jihad. The United States had lost the propaganda war by repeatedly providing just what the new Al Qaeda needed.

Winning the propaganda war may now prove to be impossible. Jihadis are more than willing to film, then show on the Internet, the worst of their deeds. The Pentagon and White House are at pains to excuse or to minimize the worst of American deeds. The result is more censorship on our side than on theirs in the information war. That gives them an advantage.

The opening campaign of the Global War on Terror had been to go after Al Qaeda's command and control system and strike it where it was strongest, in Afghanistan and Pakistan. In a matter of months, Bush and Rumsfeld claimed success, even though Osama bin Laden remained at large, as did Mullah Omar. Still, many of the most important figures were dead or in captivity, and the Taliban had been ousted from power.

Meanwhile, though, Al Qaeda had rebuilt its command and control system so that it was virtually invulnerable. By moving to the Internet, it really did have global reach. At a stroke, Al Qaeda had also discovered how to fan anti-American hatred across the *umma* by filling computer screens with infuriating images from Iraq and publishing instructions on how to make poisons, how to cross the borders of Syria and Iran to join the fight in Iraq, how to navigate by the stars in the desert at night, how to make bombs from bleach and other products on sale at almost any 7-Eleven. In September 2001 there were a few hundred terrorist-linked Web sites. After the invasion of Iraq, there were thousands, with plenty of material to choose from.[20]

Nor was there any shortage of volunteers, who were willing—sometimes eager—to blow themselves and a line of police or army recruits to smithereens. Suicide bombing mushroomed across Iraq. And bin Laden won a major victory.

In the fall of 2003, to the immense relief of the Saudi government, nearly all of the American troops were pulled out of Saudi Arabia. Yet the termination of their incendiary presence was already more than compensated for by the occupation of Iraq. The GWOT might be won without ever understanding the enemy, but that seems unlikely. Occupation was and would remain the single most important recruiter of suicide bombers and Iraqi insurgents.

In October 2003 even Rumsfeld was becoming apprehensive. In a memo to Paul Wolfowitz and others, he asked, "Are we winning or losing the Global War on Terror? . . . We are having mixed results with Al Qaeda . . . a great many remain at large . . . Today, we lack metrics to know whether we are winning or losing . . . the coalition can win in Afghanistan and Iraq in one way and another, but it will be a long, hard slog."[22]

While Rumsfeld worried about the metrics, George H. W. Bush was demonstrating what he thought of his son's war. Each year, Texas A&M confers the George Bush Award for Excellence in Public Service. The former president decides who will receive it. In October 2003 the award went to Senator Edward M. Kennedy, one of the war's fiercest critics, the man who had called the president's case for war "a fraud got up in Texas."[23]

The insurgency was also gaining ground because of a deeply rooted American indifference to Iraqi casualties. Dead and mutilated Iraqis were dismissed as "collateral damage" not only by the military but by much of American public opinion. World opinion—and Iraqi opinion—rejected that view, and so did the families of those killed or mutilated. They wanted revenge, and in a nation where the killing of a young man puts an obligation on all of his male first cousins to seek to avenge him, that might be worth taking seriously. But it wasn't.

Contempt for Iraqis, a.k.a. "ragheads," was demonstrated, too, by having soldiers break into homes late at night, pull people out of their beds, steal whatever money they might have, humiliate the men as a prelude to arresting them, and take them to a fate unknown. Thefts by Americans were so common that Iraqis began calling them Ali Babas. More desire for revenge. Foot patrols were conducted on the same basis: any Iraqi male between adolescence and dotage stood an excellent chance of being hauled off and beaten if he did not become abjectly submissive in the presence of gun-toting Americans. Even more desire for revenge.[24]

Shortly before his head was cut off, Maximilien Robespierre forecast what was in store for France as it prepared to send its soldiers abroad spreading the message of the Revolution. He feared for the future of his country because "people resist armed missionaries." From the execution block, he saw Waterloo.

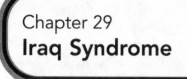

Chapter 29
Iraq Syndrome

IN JUNE 2003, GEORGE BUSH REACHED FOR A POLITICAL COUP, ONE that might pay off in Iraq: he tried to broker a peace deal between Israel and the Palestinians. A summit with Israelis and Palestinians at the Red Sea resort of Aqaba generated some positive publicity, but no breakthrough, nothing to halt the collapse of security in Iraq. The president evidently expected a better result. After all, he was doing God's work. Talking to the Palestinian foreign minister, he boasted about it. "I'm driven with a mission from God," said Bush. "He told me, 'George, go and fight those terrorists in Afghanistan.' And I did. And he told me, 'George, go and end the tyranny in Iraq.' And I did."[1]

This is the language of no other commander in chief in American history. It is the language of Benny Hinn, the Armenian-Palestinian-Canadian Greek Orthodox Pentecostal, the most successful faith healer of modern times. God is always telling Benny Hinn what to do next. It seems to work. Benny's fame, wealth, and crowds grow from one year to the next.[2]

Unfortunately, though, God does not seem to have offered any advice on what to do about stability in Iraq, and Bush looked on as what had once been a functioning country spiraled on down. In early November, the president received a report from the CIA's station chief in Baghdad warning that the security situation in Iraq was close to collapse. "None of the postwar Iraqi political institutions and leaders have shown an ability to govern the country," the station chief informed him. The Iraqis seemed incapable of doing even basic tasks, such as organizing an election.[3]

Still, there was one election that was definitely coming, and that was the 2004 presidential contest. Bush had exactly one year to show that he was winning the War on Terror and succeeding in Iraq. He had little choice now but to try something he had rejected at the start.

Jerry Bremer's predecessor, Jay Garner, had intended to organize an Iraqi election early in the occupation. There was a basic register of voters in the records of the UN's food distribution program. Virtually everyone in Iraq was receiving essential foodstuffs, such as flour and cooking oil, courtesy of the UN. The most powerful figure in the country, the Grand Ayatollah Ali Sistani, the senior Shiite cleric, had urged Garner's replacement, Bremer, to organize an election on the basis of the UN's food data bank.

Bremer refused to do it. He was more interested in building schools where parents would have to pay for their children's education; with building clinics where the sick would have to pay for treatment. Schools and clinics were built, but they remained unused. Iraqis were too poor to support Bremer's vision. Instead of organizing an election, he chose to organize a provisional government of stooges, headed by Ayad Allawi, the car-bombing mastermind who had spent many years on the CIA payroll.

Bremer intended to rule by having provincial and city councils created from among those Iraqis who supported the occupation—or at least were prepared to tolerate it for now. The provisional government was expected to work through the various councils, taking directions from Bremer.[4]

The people he had chosen to govern were drawn mainly from Iraqis much like Allawi, who had spent more than twenty years abroad. Although they had returned to Iraq, their families remained safely ensconced in Paris and London, Washington and New York. These exiles returned to complete the looting of Iraq.

On the advice of Ahmed Chalabi, Bremer helped them by removing nearly all of the senior civil servants. That meant that important posts were now stuffed with the well-meaning but inexperienced, or the ill intentioned and crooked.

Even as Bremer prepared to install his handpicked government, Ehud Barak, the former prime minister of Israel, was giving Dick Cheney the benefit of his experience. Barak was a career soldier and a supporter of the Iraq invasion. But by November he decided that the United States had already lost. He told Cheney, "You cannot win an occupation. All you can do now is choose the size of your humiliation."[5]

Bremer nevertheless was striving to win the occupation or, as he put it in a television interview, to "impose our will," and he seemed to be making progress. In December 2003 Saddam Hussein was betrayed by a hostage whom the army had seized, an Iraqi male who was related to Saddam's cook. Because the information was extracted under duress, the $10 million reward that had been offered for information leading to Saddam's arrest was never paid. "We got him!" Bremer announced, and the president went on television to celebrate the moment. "The capture of Saddam Hussein does not mean the end of the violence in Iraq," he acknowledged. "We still face terrorists [but] they will be defeated."[6]

Things seemed to be coming around, and Bremer had a new gimmick up his sleeve. It was called "the return of sovereignty." This jewel of national self-respect was going to be formally handed over by the generous Americans to Iraqis who would now rally around a new flag (another gimmick) and start building a new Iraq. The flag turned out to be so unpopular that it was soon junked, and the return of sovereignty came close to being a hoax on the uninformed.

A nation's sovereignty is not vested in its government; it is vested in its people. That principle was established across democratic countries in the eighteenth and nineteenth centuries and carried to the rest of the world in the twentieth. That is why no invader can claim the right to rule another country. A regime can be changed, but sovereignty does not then fall into the hands of the occupier. Although Bush's contempt for international law was manifest, Iraq's sovereignty did not shift from Saddam's bloodstained hands into his. What the occupation did was make it impossible for the Iraqis to exercise their sovereign rights—but they still owned them.

The highly publicized "return of sovereignty" was a sham for another reason. Even after Iraq had an elected government, it did not control its own territory. The country remained an American protectorate, much as Kuwait was before the British granted it full independence in 1961. If the United States chose to use Iraq as a base from which to launch attacks on Syria and/or Iran, the Iraqis could not prevent it.[7]

American forces had taken the hardest part of the occupation: Baghdad and the four Sunni-majority provinces. The Kurds had been left to rule themselves. In the Shiite south, coalition forces from Britain, Spain, Japan, Italy, and other countries had taken responsibility for providing security. That left Basra, a city of more than a million people, in the hands of fewer than ten thousand British soldiers. Outnumbered by more than a hundred to one, the British inevitably failed to provide security, electricity, clean water, or anything else the Iraqis needed.

The south became a power vacuum, one that the mosques and militias moved into. The most powerful of the Shiite militias, the Badr Brigade, had been organized, trained, and financed by Iran. For many years it appeared on the State Department's list of terrorist organizations. A year after the invasion, southern Iraq resembled Iran: the women were forced to cover up, the liquor stores were forced to close, the video stores went out of business.

Sistani, like the Iranian government, had a strong interest in maintaining order in southern Iraq. After nearly fourteen hundred years, security might bring elections that would install the Shiite majority in power. A young Shiite cleric, Muqtada al-Sadr, rejected Sistani's strategy of election first, Americans out afterward. He wanted the Americans out first, and then an election. He also had a militia of his own, the Mahdi Army, numbering around ten thousand armed followers.

In April 2004 Bremer decided to rid himself of this troublesome cleric. American forces were ordered to kill or capture Muqtada al-Sadr. Al-Sadr called for an uprising. For a week or so, the occupation was on the brink of collapse as American forces scurried into Kuwait and Kurdistan. The Mahdi Army was joined by thousands of angry, impatient young Sunnis. No one wanted the Americans out more than they did. Sunni-Shiite differences could be settled later.

The president chose this moment to do what he had sworn not to do—micromanage the war. Four American contractors were ambushed in Fallujah. Their bodies were mutilated, and two corpses were hung from a bridge. The images brought into American homes shook the country. Was this another Somalia? The invasion of Iraq was looking like the same thing, only worse. Bush was reported to have erupted with anger, saying, "I want heads to roll!"⁸

The marines were told to go into Fallujah, seize the culprits, and bring them to justice. But what if they were no longer in Fallujah? And how would the marines recognize them even if they found them? The town, not the culprits, became the real target. The marines proceeded to inflict collective punishment on a Sunni town of 300,000 people, roughly 300,000 of whom had nothing to do with the deaths of the contractors.

Six hundred people were killed, thousands were wounded, and a large part of Fallujah was wrecked. The mass grave came back to Iraq: Fallujah's dead were buried in its biggest soccer field. Anger and disgust swept through European countries. Even greater anger swept through Muslim ones. Bush called a halt to the operation, but the marines were fuming. They wanted to finish what they had started, to prove that the marines always win.

Throughout that summer, there were clashes between American troops and the Mahdi Army, mostly in and around the shrine cities of Najaf and Karbala. The government of stooges proved to be useless, and Bremer's assignment ended. Having failed comprehensively in Iraq, he returned to receive the Medal of Freedom. When the president draped it around his neck, Bremer burst into tears.

His replacement, John Negroponte, was a man who had made much of his career in the State Department as an apologist for and defender of some of the world's most murderous regimes, especially the Guatemalan military junta that killed more than two hundred thousand of its own people and practiced torture on an industrial scale to prop up its corrupt rule. A firm believer in the iron fist, Negroponte switched much of the money earmarked for Iraq reconstruction over to security. This played into the hands of the insurgents.

There was already less electricity being generated and less clean water being provided than in the days of Saddam Hussein. More security was needed, but so was more reconstruction.

The president had created for himself the very dilemma that had undermined Lyndon Johnson and nearly everyone else in recent times who has had to fight an insurgency against a foreign occupation. There can be no political solution without first achieving a military success, but there can be no military success without first achieving a political success. In the twentieth century, every insurgency against a foreign occupier ultimately succeeded. It might take decades, but the national liberation movements have always won. The one major exception is supposed to be Malaya, but the British promised to leave once the Chinese insurgency there ended. Besides, there were more than 150,000 soldiers and paramilitary police fighting only 8,000 insurgents, and it still took twelve years and a pledge to withdraw before the insurgency ended.

As happens in most Third World countries, Iraq's new government existed mainly on television. Its ethereal presence was no threat to the insurgency. Much of the stooges' energies went into placing their relatives and friends in well-paying government jobs. Bremer facilitated that by removing the top four tiers of the Iraqi civil service.

Left to improvise, the president was clutching at every straw drifting past. If he was going to be reelected in 2004, he had to show that he was winning the War on Terror, especially in Iraq. The soi-disant "return of sovereignty" was a help, as was caving in to yet another demand from Sistani for an election. It turned out that the UN food ration data base was good enough after all as a voter roll simulacrum.

The Marine Corps was allowed its all-out assault on Fallujah in November 2004, driving three hundred thousand people into the desert; destroying their homes and their businesses; blowing up every hospital and clinic, both train stations, the electricity grid, and the three water treatment plants; and killing thousands of people who had no links with the insurgency. Fallujah became the first martyr city of the twenty-first century and drove many Sunnis to support the insurgency. The commander of the 1st Marine Expeditionary Force, Lieutenant General John Sattler, nevertheless boasted, "We have broken the back of this insurgency." What the marines had really done was spread it.[9]

Most of the insurgents pulled out. The creed of the insurgent has not changed in two thousand years: "He who fights then runs away will live to fight another day." Many headed for Mosul, where they drove the police out and seized tens of millions of dollars' worth of weapons. This could have been predicted: modern guerrillas often arm themselves by capturing enemy weapons. The marines did not seem aware of that.

Marine lieutenant general James Mattis took a different lesson back to San Diego, where he told an audience of military families, "Actually, it's quite fun to fight them . . . It's a hell of a hoot. It's fun to shoot some people," especially Muslims. "Guys like that ain't got no manhood anyway. So it's a hell of a lot of fun to shoot them." If this really was, as the president claimed, a war between civilization and barbarism, it wasn't clear which side General Mattis was on.[10]

The promise of elections and stepped-up military action allowed Bush to keep Iraq largely out of his reelection campaign, except to suggest repeatedly that Iraq had been involved in the attacks of September 11. It worked. A clear majority accepted his claims and everything they implied—the torture, the fictions, the self-defeating policies.

As things stood at that point, the United States president claimed to be above the law whenever he was acting as commander in chief; the United States claimed it had the right to attack any country it suspected might pose a threat up to five years into the future; and the U.S. government had the right to seize, imprison, torture, or kill anyone in the world. A Lebanese journalist remarked, "Well, at least they still let us decide who we'd like to marry."

Any country that chose to opt out from the Global War on Terror was promised the hostility of the United States. The consequences could be serious. No country was permitted to be dominant in its own neighborhood. Any who tried to do so, and refused to back off when Washington blew the whistle, could be attacked, and that definitely included China.

"We had our accountability moment," the president gloated. His reelection confirmed the people's support for this new and threatening America. This was a different country, one that horrified millions of Americans and infuriated much of the world. But so what? *Vox populi, vox dei.*[11]

These unwinnable wars had changed the presidency itself, by creating an over-mighty commander in chief, something the Founders
thought they had precluded by ruling out a monarchy. As the character of the presidency changes, so does the character of the country.
Large numbers of Americans now support torture, increasing restrictions on civil liberties, unprovoked attacks on other countries, and a
president placing himself above the law by declaring, even as he signs
a new law, that he will not be bound by that law's provisions. Thomas
Huxley, one of Darwin's staunchest defenders, used to tell Victorians
an apocryphal story to illustrate Darwin's argument about the adapt-
ability of creatures: A frog was placed in a pan of cold water, said
Huxley, and the temperature of the water was increased by one degree every few days. The frog boiled to death without ever attempting
to jump out of the pan.

In January 2005 the Iraqis managed, with help from the UN, to organize an election, although it was little more than an ethnic census:
the Shiites would collect at least 60 percent of the vote, the Kurds
at least 20 percent, and the Sunnis might account for the remaining
20 percent. With the Sunnis boycotting the election, however, the
voting percentages of the Kurds and the Shiites exceeded their shares
of the population. American troops had organized get-out-the-vote
drives. They put up political posters, controlled access to polling stations, and provided security for the ballot boxes. Whatever happened,
the election was going to produce no surprises.

The installation of the new government was hailed as the third
turning point in the war. Numbers one and two were the fall of Baghdad and the capture of Saddam Hussein. It had a mandate for one
overriding task—to write a constitution. Turning points four and five
would be a referendum on that constitution in December 2005 and
the election of a permanent government early in 2006. And none of
these turning points, singly or together, was going to make any difference to the outcome of this unwinnable war.

The constitution-writing government, like the provisional Allawi
version before it, was established at an American military base, the
Green Zone (otherwise known as the Emerald Kingdom) in Baghdad.
Its members would be defended collectively by American soldiers,

while being treated with contempt by the troops at the heavily guarded checkpoints they passed through each day.

As the insurgency raged on there were questions in Congress and the press about the strategy. There did not seem to be one. But in October 2005 Condoleezza Rice, promoted by Bush to be secretary of state, was able to inform a congressional committee, "Our strategy is to clear, hold and build." The echoes of an earlier war reverberated through the marble corridors. "Clear" means search and destroy; "hold" is the new logo for pacification; and "build" is Vietnamization in a different uniform. The administration was going to fight the new unwinnable war with the same strategy as the old unwinnable war.

The only significant difference was that it would be done by fomenting ethnic strife and promoting a civil war in Iraq. A Kurdish militia, the *peshmerga* formed the backbone of the new Iraqi army. The Shiites' Badr Brigade infiltrated the Iraqi police to fight the Sunnis, with American air support, artillery support, and armor support. A wave of attacks was unleashed in the fall of 2005 across the Sunni towns of western Iraq. As the Sunnis had once done to the Kurds and the Shia, so the Kurds and the Shia now did to them, with American help. And thus they guaranteed that the insurgency would never run out of men, money, or munitions.

To cheer up the troops, Rice made a visit that November to Mosul, for Veterans Day. She informed her audience, serried ranks in desert camouflage, that, "if Iraq does not succeed, and should Iraq become a place of despair, generations of Americans will be condemned to fear." She was placing the burden of making Americans feel safer on the shoulders of Iraqis. Outsourcing was fashionable among American businesses. It was now being extended by the government to cover national security.[12]

Rice seemed unaware that in the world beyond the U.S. military base where she spoke, Iraq was becoming the school of an Afghan jihad. Hundreds, possibly thousands of young Afghan men had volunteered to go to Iraq. There were hundreds, if not thousands more, drawn from countries bordering Afghanistan, such as Uzbekistan and Pakistan. To be accepted, the recruits had to be in excellent health and have the consent of bin Laden's representative in Iraq, a veteran jihadi with the nom de guerre of Abdul Hadi al-Iraqi. They also had to be fluent in Arabic.

On arrival in Iraq, they received three months of basic military training at the "Camp of the Lovers of Virgins in Paradise." They learned how to use small arms, mortars, and rocket-propelled grenades, but the most important part of the course was making, hiding, and detonating bombs—car bombs, truck bombs, roadside bombs, bombs buried beneath roads, bombs in trash containers, bomb belts, bomb vests, bombs as booby traps, bombs that will bring down large buildings, bombs that can be carried in shopping bags . . . The list goes on.

Meeting Iraqis who had volunteered to be suicide bombers inspired them. More moving still, though, was meeting Iraqi parents who had volunteered a teenage son for a suicide mission. The Afghan recruits who volunteered for suicide missions were nearly always rejected. There was no shortage of volunteers for those. Go home, they were told, and spread what you have learned to others. Make bombs for them; make Afghanistan another Iraq. In the fall of 2005, Iraq-style suicide bombings became a feature of life in Afghanistan. The death toll from the fast-growing Afghan insurgency has since risen from a dozen or so deaths each month to roughly 150, with every prospect of going higher. The struggle for Afghanistan is still in its infancy.[13]

In pursuit of "metrics" rather than prosaic figures or numbers, Donald Rumsfeld had meanwhile created an Iraq Room at the Pentagon. "Here we track a whole series of metrics," he informed the National Public Radio audience. "We probably look at 50, 60, 70 different types of metrics and come away with an impression. It's impressionistic more than determinative." One thing the metrics seemed to add up to was defeat for the United States. "The coalition is not going to defeat the insurgency," he conceded. "It strikes me that it will have to be the Iraqi people that will have to do this."[14]

What others called numbers suggested that the Iraqi people were failing to do their part. Three months after Rumsfeld's interview, CentCom claimed that it was killing or capturing between 1,000 and 3,000 insurgents every month. Even so, the number of attacks had risen from 35 a day during the second Fallujah offensive to more than 70 a day six months later.[15]

That did not deter the vice president from going on television to announce, "I think they are in the last throes, if you will, of the insurgency." Porter Goss, the new director of Central Intelligence, more or less endorsed Cheney's assertion. "Not quite in its last throes," he told *Time* magazine, "but I think we are very close to it."[16]

And thus the president repeatedly told military groups that the United States was going to win "total victory" in the War on Terror, in which Iraq was the principal battleground. His strategy carried historic echoes, and not only from Vietnam. Here is the outline strategy for an earlier invasion and occupation of a Muslim country that had generated a strong insurgency:

1. Stabilize the country by garrisoning the major roads, major cities, air bases, and logistics hubs.

2. Relieve government forces of garrison duties and push them into the countryside to battle the insurgents.

3. Provide logistic, air, artillery, and intelligence support to government forces.

4. Seek to minimize friction between occupation troops and local people.

5. Strive for minimal casualties among occupation units.

6. Strengthen the government forces, so that once the resistance is defeated, our army can be withdrawn.

This was the outline strategy drawn up by the Red Army for bringing its invasion and occupation of Afghanistan to a satisfactory conclusion.[17]

When Rice made her November 2005 flying visit to Iraq (she did not spend the night there), the insurgency was bigger than it had ever been. T. E. Lawrence had organized and led insurgencies in Syria, Jordan, and Saudi Arabia. He concluded that any insurgency that could enlist 2 percent of the population would never be defeated. Just 2 percent of the Sunni population of 4.5 million would yield 9,000 insurgents. Every estimate from the Pentagon and others puts the number of insurgents at 10,000 to 20,000. Yet if the CentCom claim of 1,000 to 3,000 killed or captured each month is even in the ballpark, the insurgency was destroyed between November 2004 and November 2005.

What, then, is the size of the insurgency, and where do the insurgents come from? There were roughly 100,000 members of the

Mukhabarat, Saddam's secret police; the Fedayeen Saddam was a militia organized and commanded by one of his sons and numbered 40,000 men; there are the Sunni officers of the old Iraqi army, of whom there are at least 175,000, many of them outraged at Iran's gains in Iraq; and, finally, there is the steady but comparatively small infusion of foreign jihadis. There are therefore more than 300,000 people who have the training and experience to become effective guerrillas. Beyond that, there are surely tens of thousands more who will be ready to join and undergo on-the-job training. The most careful, independent study of the size of the insurgency has been made by John Robb, an authority on networks. He puts the minimum figure at 47,500 and the maximum at 338,500. The likely figure, Robb calculates, is somewhere around 140,000.[18]

This would accord with the best published account from inside the insurgency, which places the number of active fighters at 30,000 to 40,000. They can draw on a network of at least 100,000 enablers. There are more than 70 insurgent groups, numbering from a dozen or so fighters up to the 4,000 claimed members of Al Qaeda in Iraq.

Suicide bombing, Iran's gift to fundamentalist terrorism, has brought a new dimension to insurgency. It is not random; nor is it nihilism. It is a rational strategy to create and spread chaos. Above all, it works. It drove the Americans out of Beirut, the Israeli army out of Lebanon, and Israeli settlers out of the Gaza Strip. Why should insurgents not believe it will eventually drive the Americans out of Iraq?

They do not all have the same goals, and there are times when they fight one another. Al Qaeda in Iraq, and its late leader, Abu Zarqawi, have alienated many Iraqis by attacking civilians not linked to the government or the occupation. But it too is in for the long haul. Al Qaeda has no illusions about seizing control of Iraq. Its objective is to keep the United States mired there for many years. That will make it easier for Al Qaeda cells in other countries, such as Britain, to mount attacks and provide endless propaganda material for the Internet. So long as the occupation continues, his organization will survive. Guerrillas win by not being defeated. And given that nearly 90 percent of Sunni Arabs express support for attacks on Americans, Iraq's insurgents have a secure future. They can make the country ungovernable until the Americans leave. Then they will ensure that it remains ungovernable, making it a secure base for Salafi jihadists—a second Afghanistan.[19]

Bush had little interest in history or the world beyond America's shores. To make Americans secure seemed a simple task, though: make the rest of the world resemble America. Yet when it came to securing the "total victory" he promised, neither Bush nor any of the other war promoters could offer any advice beyond patience.

How, though, does a commander in chief sell an unwinnable war? Short answer: he doesn't. It can't be done beyond more than a year or two, and as Truman discovered, it might be even less than that. The unwinnable war is where the president learns the true limits of his power. This war is virtually unlimited when it comes to destruction, but push a failing war too hard, and the president, along with the country, is likely to abandon its ideals. It finds itself killing for the sake of killing, killing rather than admitting a mistake, killing for revenge, killing for anything but justice. The world will not accept being led in that way. Nor will many Americans. Good intentions are often hard to deliver, but when the heap of corpses becomes too large, good intentions drown in blood.

And in the end, the corpses and blood have done nothing for American security. The United States has defeated itself in Iraq: too much ideology, not enough pragmatism. The war has produced joint winners—Iran and China. Power is not a category, unlike factual truth or personal goodness, beauty or love. Power is a relationship. For some to be strong, others must be weak, or at least weaker. China has won in Iraq because the longer the war continues, America's ability to use its power will diminish and China's freedom of action will grow. If you were a Chinese general or senior politician, which would you prefer—America mired in Iraq for a decade or out of Iraq in a year? The same question and answer apply to the generals of Iran.

America's failure in Iraq is part of China's rise, and it is Iran's great opportunity to tie Iraq's oil to its own. Iran will overtake Saudi Arabia as the biggest oil producer in the world. Even before that point is reached, the United States will probably shrink from attacking it, for fear of oil at $150 a barrel. China too is exempt from American pressure. It is once more in command of its destiny.

American hegemony was acceptable in many parts of the world

because it promised stability. Iraq has shown that the United States cannot provide stability, despite occupying the country with more than 150,000 soldiers and spending hundreds of billions of dollars. The likely final cost will exceed a trillion. It cannot even provide stability on its doorstep, in Haiti, a country in which it has intervened repeatedly. There is a different America now, and a different world.

The mask has slipped, and people at home and abroad have seen a face on American power they will not soon forget. In this new world, dozens of countries are looking for a return to balance of power foreign policy. The result may be more anarchy and chaos, fear and despair, but there seems a good chance that large-scale killing may be avoided. The world is moving away from war. Across the globe, there is less fighting than at any period since the French Revolution.[20]

There are not many people in advanced countries who believe any longer that the solution to the world's major problems is war. The United States and Israel are the only advanced countries that still believe in war as a progressive force. Even the British draw the line at killing on an industrial scale. In time, the American addiction to military force is likely to change; policy seems certain to change; and Americans, already turning strongly to espresso, may become more like Europeans, while Europeans, facing economic stagnation, will become less like Americans. It seems likely that Europe will make a virtue out of its economic weakness. Obliged to consume less, Europeans will embrace the threat of global warming as the moral equivalent of war, and in war, sacrifice is necessary. It seems likely, too, that within a decade, fears about global warming will dwarf the War on Terror, because this may be an existential threat to the entire human race. The GWOT is beginning to look like yesterday's war.

Wars between nation-states are virtually over. The United Nations was created to prevent or to end wars between states. It has succeeded in that mission. There are UN peacekeepers in eighteen countries, and only one war. The United States under George W. Bush has placed itself at the wrong end of history, with the aid of a supine Congress and a people subjected to patriotism abuse.

Chances are that political stability, not anarchy, will spread as regional powers such as India and China and the European Union challenge a failing America to leave regional matters to the people who live there. Nobody wants to be dependent on an America that talks loudly about how indispensable it is, yet stages coups, makes threats, overthrows governments, democratic or not, and kills many of the world's poorest people, to the amusement of some generals.

Much of the world already fears and loathes the United States, while China is getting the benefit of nearly every doubt. It has few enemies to speak of. The United States has them in abundance. The Chinese have already outmaneuvered the Americans over North Korea's nukes, over Iran's nuclear program, over Taiwan, and over Sudan. There is more on the way. The Chinese leadership concluded in 1995 that any country foolish enough to fight in Vietnam after being warned of China's possible intervention was a nation in terminal decline. Nothing since has caused a rethink.

Withdrawal from Iraq will be followed by an Iraq Syndrome. The age of armed intervention is over for the United States. Unable to play its ace—the ability to fight and win a major war—it will no longer be feared. No developing country needs nuclear weapons now to deter the United States. The distribution of assault weapons and explosives and the creation of an embryonic network of insurgents will do the job at much lower cost. Venezuela is already doing that. Others will follow.

China is the only country to have gained strategic advantages from America's three unwinnable wars. The United States has gained nothing, not even the gratitude of South Korea. "We are living through historic times," says President Bush. How true. Iraq will break American power. Hello, China.

Conclusion

THE BUSH ADMINISTRATION HAS DIVIDED THE COUNTRY MORE THAN
any since the early days of the New Deal, and for similar reasons.
Franklin Roosevelt and the people close to him considered themselves revolutionaries; they did not take office in order to perpetuate
the political order that helped to produce the Depression.

Bush's mission, too, is to destroy in order to build. It embraces the
economists' theory of "creative destruction," which says that business
failures are good. Bankruptcy weeds out the inefficient producers and
promotes the growth of new, vigorous businesses in their place. On
the eve of the war with Afghanistan the president told his advisers
what he wanted first and foremost: "Create chaos." Both there and in
Iraq, he got what he asked for.

The other theory around which his mental universe spins is that of
"the unitary executive." Since taking office in 2001, the president has
issued "signing statements" in the course of signing nearly eight hundred laws into effect. These statements declared that the president

will not feel bound by this article or that section of the law, especially if he decides it conflicts with his powers as commander in chief.

Down the generations presidents have issued such statements, mainly to ensure that presidential power and prerogatives are passed intact to their successors. From James Madison to George W. Bush, there were 322 signing statements, an average of eight per president. During six years in office, George W. Bush has produced nearly eight hundred.

Many of these seek justification for asserting his right to ignore the very law he has just signed on the theory of "the unitary executive." This doctrine took root in the Federalist Society during the Reagan administration, and adherents since then have included Justices Antonin Scalia, Clarence Thomas, and Samuel Alito. The chief justice, John Roberts, also has ties to the Federalist Society. The doctrine of the unitary executive is now only one Supreme Court vote away from becoming the law of the land. And if that happens, it will be a different land.

For all intents and purposes, the doctrine of the unitary executive holds that in his role as CinC the president cannot be constrained by the separation of powers. This does not mean that George W. Bush is going to suspend the Constitution and rule by decree. But if there is a major terrorist attack on the scale of, or even exceeding, the atrocity of September 11, there is now almost nothing that would block a president from declaring the Constitution suspended and ruling by emergency decree. Neither Congress nor the courts would be able to stop him. Hello, chaos.

Notes

1. Too Much Too Soon

1. Robert Ferrell, *The Dying President* (Columbia, MO, 1998), 89–90, 151.
2. Diary, April 19, 1946, Charles G. Ross Papers, Harry S. Truman Library (hereinafter cited as HSTL); Harry Vaughan Oral History (hereinafter cited as OH), HSTL; Merle Miller, *Plain Speaking* (New York, 1973), 183, 185. He also told his assistant press secretary that until late July 1944 he had never expected to be president. The change came, by implication, in August. Diary, May 26, 1945, Eben Ayers Papers, HSTL.
3. Jonathan Daniel, *Man of Independence* (Philadelphia, 1950), 259.
4. Miller, *Plain Speaking*, 181–82.
5. Robert Ferrell, ed., *Off the Record: The Private Papers of Harry S. Truman* (Columbia, MO, 1980), 23; James McGregor Burns, *Roosevelt: The Soldier of Freedom* (New York, 1970), 533.
6. Mathew Connelly OH, HSTL.
7. Thomas M. Campbell and George C. Herring, eds., *The Diaries of Edward R. Stettinius Jr., 1943–1946* (New York, 1975), 313–14.
8. Diary, April 25, 1945, Henry L. Stimson Papers, Sterling Library, Yale; Harry S. Truman, *Memoirs* (Garden City, NY, 1955), I, 10.
9. Eben Ayers OH, HSTL; Ferrell, *Off the Record*, 16.
10. George Aiken OH, LBJ Library.
11. Ferrell, *Off the Record*, 23; Journal, May 13, 1945, Joseph E. Davies Papers, Library of Congress (hereinafter cited as LC).
12. Clifford and Holbrooke, *Counsel to the President*, 58; Athan G. Theoharis, *The Yalta Myths* (Columbia, MO, 1970), 10–38.
13. Francis H. Heller, ed., *The Truman White House* (Lawrence, KS, 1980), 9.

14. William Rigdon, *White House Sailor* (New York, 1962), 183.
15. *New York Times*, June 24, 1941. The Russians would have researched the new president and been aware of his sentiments. Stalin had almost certainly been informed.
16. Diary, May 25, 1945, Eben Ayers Papers, HSTL; John Morton Blum, ed., *The Price of Vision: The Diaries of Henry Wallace* (Boston, 1973), 436.
17. Truman, *Memoirs*, I, 82.
18. Albert Resis, ed., *Molotov Remembers* (Chicago, 1993), 55. Cf. Charles Bohlen, *Witness to History* (New York, 1973), 23; Diary, April 22, 1945, Eben Ayers Papers, HSTL.
19. Diary, April 27, 1945, Joseph E. Davies Papers, LC.
20. George Elsey OH, HSTL.
21. Diary and Journal, May 13, 1945, Joseph E. Davies Papers, LC.
22. Journal, June 6, 1945, Joseph E. Davies Papers, LC.
23. Ferrell, *Off the Record*, 21; Memorandum of Conversation, Oct. 24, 1951, Eben Ayers Papers, HSTL.
24. Martin Gilbert, *Winston S. Churchill* (London, 1988), VIII, 6–7.
25. Ibid., 8.
26. Journal, Joseph E. Davies Papers, May 21, 1945, LC.
27. This is the figure that Truman in his memoirs says Marshall provided, and there is indirect confirmation. The army's Operations Division (OPD) was responsible for producing such estimates, and its head, in the last six months of the war, was Lieutenant General John Hull. The casualty estimates that the OPD produced for invading and conquering Japan "ran from a few hundred thousand to a million." John E. Hull oral history, U.S. Army Military History Institute Archives.
28. James Reston, *Deadline* (New York: 1991), 494–99; Walter Isaacson et al., *The Wise Men* (New York: 1986), 293–97. Reston reproduces McCloy's written recollection of these events.

2. Man and Moment

1. Diary, July 1, 1945, Eben Ayers Papers, HSTL.
2. Miller, *Plain Speaking*, 325.
3. Diary, May 25, 1945, Eben Ayers Papers, HSTL.
4. Harry Vaughan OH, HSTL.
5. Ferrell, *Off the Record*, 49.
6. Wallace Graham, 1989 OH, HSTL.
7. Miller, *Plain Speaking*, 203.
8. Vaughan OH, HSTL.
9. Memorandum, "Eisenhower, Truman and Politics," July 25, 1945, Joseph E. Davies Papers, LC; diary, August 16–17, 1945, Eben Ayers Papers, HSTL.
10. *Public Papers of the Presidents* (hereinafter cited as *PPP*), *1945, Truman*, 14.
11. Diary, January 18, 1946, Eben Ayers Papers, HSTL.
12. "Conference with the President," September 19, 1945, President's Secretary's File, HSTL.
13. Diary, September 10, 1945, Eben Ayers Papers, HSTL.
14. Dean Acheson OH, HSTL.

15. George Elsey OH, HSTL.
16. Monte Poen, ed., *Strictly Personal and Confidential* (Boston, 1982), 34; David Gallen, ed., *The Quotable Truman* (New York, 1994), 163.
17. Diary, Jan. 19, 1948, Eben Ayers Papers, HSTL.
18. Ibid., Feb. 21, 1946.
19. Allen E. Roberts, *Brother Truman* (Highland Springs, VA, 1985), 100–101.
20. Diary, Feb. 15, 1946, Charles Ross Papers, HSTL, and Greene OH, HSTL.
21. Wallace A. Graham 1976 OH, HSTL; Edward T. Folliard OH, HSTL.
22. Matthew Connolly OH and George Elsey OH, HSTL.
23. Miller, *Plain Speaking*, 428–29.
24. George Elsey OH, HSTL.
25. Ferrell, *Off the Record*, 38.
26. Diary, March 20, 1946, Eben Ayers Papers, HSTL.
27. Wallace Graham 1989 OH, HSTL. There are two oral histories by Dr. Graham at the Truman Library. The first, conducted in 1976, contains no reference to Truman's need for "snake oil." The second, conducted shortly before Graham died, discusses the subject at length, but he declined to specify what the chemical compound was that made Truman feel confident and in control.

3. Position of Strength

1. Blum, *The Price of Vision*, 451; Department of State, *Foreign Relations of the United States, 1945* (Washington, DC, 1960), II, 378, 973–96, 984. (Hereinafter cited as *FRUS*.)
2. Ferrell, *Off the Record*, 44.
3. Rigdon, *White House Sailor*, 188.
4. *New York Herald Tribune*, July 17, 1945.
5. *New York Times*, July 17, 1945.
6. Ferrell, *Off the Record*, 52.
7. Vladislav Zubok and Constantine Pleshakov, *Inside the Kremlin's Cold War* (Cambridge, MA,, 1996), 31.
8. Ian Kershaw, *Hitler* (New York, 2000), II, 831–33.
9. Diary, July 21, 1945, Joseph E. Davies Papers, LC.
10. Journal, Aug. 1, 1945, Davies Papers, LC.
11. John Snyder OH, HSTL.
12. Ferrell, *Off the Record*, 53; Diary, July 18, 1945, Joseph E. Davies Papers, LC.
13. Diary, July 17, 1945, Davies Papers, LC.
14. Ibid.
15. *Washington Herald*, Aug. 18, 1945; Diary, Dec. 19, 1945, Eben Ayers Papers, HSTL.
16. Martin Gilbert, *Winston S. Churchill* (London, 1988), VIII, 69.
17. In his *Memoirs*, Truman claimed that Stalin said he hoped the Americans would make good use of this weapon against the Japanese. Pavlov, however, said that Stalin merely nodded, and Anthony Eden, standing a few feet away, said that Stalin nodded and said "Thank you." The most reliable witness is probably Pavlov, who would have translated Truman's statement into Russian and then, if Stalin said anything in return, would have translated that too. David Holloway, *Stalin and the Bomb* (New Haven, 1994), 117.

18. Resis, *Molotov Remembers*, 55–56; Bohlen, *Witness to History*, 237; Diary, April 22, 1945, Eben Ayers Papers, HSTL.
19. Andrei Gromyko, *Memoirs* (New York, 1989), 109.
20. Diary, July 28, 1945, Davies Papers, LC.
21. Ferrell, *Off the Record*, 49.
22. Journal, July 17, 1945, Joseph E. Davies Papers, LC.
23. Department of State, *FRUS, 1945*, II, 313.
24. Memorandum for Admiral Leahy, July 1, 1945, George Elsey Papers, HSTL.
25. Zubok and Pleshakov, *Inside the Kremlin's Cold War*, 31; Milovan Djilas, *Conversations with Stalin* (New York, 1962), 114.
26. Diary, July 25, 1945, Joseph E. Davies Papers, LC.
27. *FRUS, 1945*, II, 1475.
28. Diary, July 28, 1945, Joseph E. Davies Papers, LC.
29. Ibid.; Blum, *Price of Vision*, 447.
30. Diary, July 25, 1945, Davies Papers, LC.
31. William D. Leahy, *I Was There* (New York, 1950), 430.
32. Rigdon, *White House Sailor*, 207.
33. *PPP, 1945, Truman*, 198.
34. Blum, *Price of Vision*, 474.
35. Memorandum of Conversation, Oct. 24, 1951, Eben Ayers Papers, HSTL.
36. *PPP, 1945, Truman*, 203.
37. Ayers Diary, August 7, 1945, Eben Ayers Papers, HSTL.
38. Henry L. Stimson and McGeorge Bundy, *On Active Service in Peace and War* (New York: 1946), 645.
39. Dean Acheson, *Present at the Creation* (New York, 1969), 123; Blum, *Price of Vision*, 483.
40. Walter Millis, ed., *The Forrestal Diaries* (New York, 1951), 95.
41. Townsend Hoopes and Douglas Brinkley, *Driven Patriot: The Life of James Forrestal* (New York, 1992), 284.
42. Zubok and Pleshakov, *Inside the Kremlin's Cold War*, 43–44; George Zhukov, *Recollections and Reflections* (Moscow, 1969), 732.
43. David Lilienthal, *The Journals of David E. Lilienthal* (New York: 1964), II, 118; Robert S. Ferrell, "Harry S. Truman: A 50th Anniversary Commemoration of His Presidency," written for an exhibition organized by the state government of Missouri in 1998. Truman's doctors agreed to let his former attorney general, Tom Clark, spend five minutes with the dying Truman in December 1972. Truman held Clark for forty-five minutes talking about the bomb. This essay can be found at www.sos.mo.gov/archives/history/truman.asp

4. Location, Location, Location

1. Harry Vaughan OH, HSTL; Gilbert, *Winston S. Churchill*, VIII, 159.
2. Robert L. Messer, *The End of an Alliance* (Chapel Hill, NC, 1982), 181–82.
3. Ferrell, *Off the Record*, 49. He wrote this on July 7, 1945.
4. Heller, *The Truman White House*, 10.

5. Cold War International History Project, "New Evidence on the Iran Crisis 1945–46," cwihp.si.edu; Resis, *Molotov Remembers*, 74.

6. John Snyder OH, HSTL. Snyder was Truman's secretary of the treasury and an old friend from St. Louis. Snyder probably got this from Byrnes, but it is possible that he got it from Truman.

7. Truman, *Memoirs*, I, 548–49; James Byrnes, *Speaking Frankly* (New York, 1947), 237; David Robertson, *Sly and Able* (New York, 1994), 454–55.

8. Ferrell, *Off the Record*, 79–80.

9. Dean Rusk, *As I Saw It* (New York: 1990), 125–26. Rusk was Byrnes's assistant at the time.

10. Zubok and Pleshakov, *Inside the Kremlin's Cold War*, 35.

11. Svetlana Aliluyeva, *Twenty Letters to a Friend* (New York, 1967), 176; Adam Ulam, *Stalin: The Man and His Era* (Boston: 1989), 633–34.

12. Diary, Feb. 9, 1946, Joseph Davies Papers, LC.

13. *FRUS, 1946*, VI, 696–707.

14. George Kennan, *Memoirs: 1925–1950* (Boston: 1967), 294–95.

15. Diary, Feb. 15, 1946, Charles Ross Papers; Diary, Feb. 25, 1946, Eben Ayers Papers, both HSTL.

16. Diary, March 9, 1946, Charles Ross Papers, HSTL; Clifford and Holbrooke, *Counsel to the President*, 102. For some reason, Clifford has "talons of war" in place of the fasces.

17. Randolph S. Churchill, ed., *The Sinews of Peace* (London, 1948), 93–105.

18. Ulam, *Stalin*, 639.

19. Diary, March 18, 1946, Charles Ross Papers, HSTL.

20. Ferrell, *Off the Record*, 32.

21. Clifford and Holbrooke, *Counsel to the President*, 110; Offner, *Another Such Victory*, 134; Vojtech Mastny and Malcolm Byrne, *A Cardboard Castle? The Inside History of the Warsaw Pact* (New York, 2005), 17–19.

22. Diary, March 25, 1946, Charles Ross Papers, HSTL.

23. Millis, *The Forrestal Diaries*, 72–73; Townsend Hoopes and Douglas Brinkley, *Driven Patriot* (New York, 1992), 273, 275.

24. Hoopes and Brinkley, *Driven Patriot*, 270–73.

25. Edvard Radzinsky, *Stalin* (New York, 1996), 499.

26. Joseph Jones, *The Fifteen Weeks* (New York, 1955), 63–65; Acheson, *Present at the Creation*, 195–96.

27. John Garry Clifford, "President Truman and Peter the Great's Will," *Diplomatic History* (Winter 1980).

28. Truman diary notes, May 22, 1946, HSTL.

5. World Island

1. Memorandum, June 2, 1966, Herbert Feis Papers, LC.

2. George Elsey OH, HSTL.

3. Clifford and Holbrooke, *Counsel to the President*, 123–24.

4. *PPP, 1946, Truman*, 457–63.

5. Cf. Marc Sadoun, ed., *Le Démocratie en France* (Paris, 2000), 2 vols.

6. Offner, *Another Such Victory*, 166.

7.   Ibid., 143.
8.   Acheson, *Present at the Creation*, 219.
9.   *New York Times*, March 2, 1947; John T. McNay, *Acheson and Empire* (Columbia, MO, 2001), 6–7.
10. Joseph Jones, *The Fifteen Weeks* (New York, 1955), 140.
11. James Chace, *Acheson* (New York, 1998), 165–66. Acheson's version of this meeting, in *Present at the Creation*, has Vandenberg saying, "Mr. President, if you will say that to the Congress and the country, I will support you and I believe that most of its members will do the same." Acheson, by his own admission, was not interested in the truth so much as in the uses to which the truth can be shaped to serve particular ends. The version I have chosen to quote comes from Loy Henderson, who is almost certainly more reliable.
12. *PPP, 1947, Truman,* 167–72.
13. Ibid., 178–79.
14. Ibid., 238–41.
15. David H. Close, ed., *The Greek Civil War* (London: 1993), 135 passim; Lawrence S. Wittner, "American Policy towards Greece during World War II," *Diplomatic History* (Spring 1980).
16. Ulam, *Stalin*, 652–53.
17. Chace, *Acheson*, 169; Milovan Djilas, *Conversations with Stalin* (New York, 1962), 181–82.
18. Byrnes, *Speaking Frankly*, 313.

6. Chinese Checkers

1.   Blum, *Price of Vision*, 520.
2.   *Time*, Jan. 22, 1945.
3.   Eben Ayers diary, November 29, 1945, HSTL.
4.   Blum, *Price of Vision*, 519.
5.   David S. McClellan, *Dean Acheson: The State Department Years* (New York, 1976), 188.
6.   Gayle B. Montgomery and James W. Johnson, *One Step from the White House: The Rise and Fall of William Knowland* (Berkeley, CA, 1998), 302–304.
7.   *Congressional Record*, XCIV, 80th Congress, 2nd Session (1948), 3329.
8.   Cabinet Notes, March 7, 1947, Matthew Connolly Papers, HSTL.
9.   Robert Payne, *The Marshall Story* (New York, 1948), 311.
10. Robert Dennison OH, HSTL.
11. Cabinet notes, Nov. 26, 1948, Matthew Connolly Papers, HSTL.
12. "Military Situation in the Far East," Hearings Before the Committee on the Armed Services and the Committee on Foreign Relations, U.S. Senate, 82nd Congress, 1st Session, 1671–72.
13. Dennison OH, HSTL; Hoopes and Brinkley, *Driven Patriot*, 308–309.
14. Arthur H. Vandenberg, Jr., ed., *The Private Papers of Senator Vandenberg* (Boston, 1952), 530–31.
15. H. Bradford Westerfield, *Foreign Policy and Party Politics* (New Haven, 1955), 347.
16. Sergei Gonchov et al., *Uncertain Partners* (Stanford, CA, 1993), 144 passim.
17. Resis, *Molotov Remembers*, 60.

18. Department of Defense, *United States–Vietnam Relations, 1945–1967* (Washington, DC, 1971), VIII, 245.
19. *Military Situation in the Far East*, Part 3, 2664–78.
20. *Washington Post*, July 14, 1949.
21. Diary, January 5, 1950, Eben Ayers Papers, HSTL; "Memorandum Concerning Statement by the President on January 5, 1950," George Elsey Papers, HSTL; *New York Times*, January 6, 1950.
22. *FRUS 1950*, VI, 349–50. There is no mention of this in Rusk's memoir. On the contrary, he claims that no one recommended intervening to save Formosa. Dean Rusk, *As I Saw It* (New York, 1984), 157.
23. Ronald M. McGlothlen, *Controlling the Waves* (New York, 1993), 125–27.

7. National Home

1. Ferrell, *Off the Record*, 41.
2. Blum, *The Price of Vision*, 607.
3. George Elsey OH, HSTL.
4. Cornelius J. Mara OH, HSTL; Douglas Frantz and David McKean, *Friends in High Places* (Boston, 1995), 61.
5. Ibid., 73–74.
6. Blum, *Price of Vision*, 606.
7. Robert J. Donovan, *Conflict and Crisis* (New York, 1977), 322.
8. Diary, November 30, 1945, Eben Ayers Papers, HSTL.
9. H. W. Brands, *Inside the Cold War* (New York, 1991), 187–88.
10. Arthur Krock, *Memoirs* (New York, 1968), 253.
11. Loy Henderson OH, HSTL
12. Eben Ayers OH, HSTL.
13. Wallace Graham OH, HSTL.
14. Miller, *Plain Speaking*, 217; letter, Eddie Jacobson to Josef Cohn, April 1, 1952, in Dennis Merrill, ed., *Documentary History of the Truman Administration* (Bethesda, MD, 1995), XXIV, 236–48.
15. Edwin M. Wright OH, HSTL.
16. *New York Times*, March 19, 1948.
17. Clark Clifford OH, HSTL.
18. James Schoenbaum, *Waging Peace and War* (New York, 1988), 171.
19. Loy Henderson OH, HSTL.
20. Clifford's account is in *FRUS, 1948*, V, 1976; *New York Times*, March 25, 1948.
21. *PPP, 1948, Truman*, 254.
22. Michael Medved, *The Shadow Presidents* (New York: 1979), 225.
23. *FRUS, 1948*, V, 972–75; Forrest C. Pogue, *George C. Marshall*, IV, 372–73.
24. Frantz and McKean, *Friends*, 76.
25. Wright oral history; Miller, *Plain Speaking*, 215.

8. Panic Attack

1. Memorandum, Clark Clifford to HST, November 19, 1947, Clifford Papers, HSTL.

2. *Wall Street Journal*, September 12, 1947.

3. *New York Times*, February 6, 1948.

4. *FRUS: 1947*, IV, 232–35.

5. Walter Bedell Smith to Marshall, March 1, 1948, *FRUS, 1948*, IV, 766–67. Millis, *The Forrestal Diaries*, 384–85.

6. *FRUS: 1948*, IV, 766 passim.

7. Frank Kofsky, *The War Scare of 1948* (New York, 1993), 96–133.

8. *New York Times*, March 13, 1948.

9. *FRUS: 1948*, IV, 735–36.

10. Jean Edward Smith, *Lucius D. Clay* (New York, 1990), 466.

11. *Washington Post*, April 6, 1948; Kofsky, *War Scare*, 118.

12. *PPP, 1948, Truman*, 178; Millis, *Forrestal Diaries*, 322.

13. *Washington Post*, March 17, 1948.

14. Department of State, press releases 218 and 221, March 19, 1948; *New York Times*, March 20, 1948.

15. *Wall Street Journal*, March 26, 1948; *Saturday Evening Post*, November 1948.

16. *New York Times*, March 25–26, 1948; *PPP, 1948, Truman*, 193.

17. *American Magazine*, February 1948; Kofsky, *War Scare*, 152–58, 162.

18. Letter, Truman to Nourse, March 25, 1948, HSTL.

19. *New York Times*, March 31, 1948.

20. Kofsky, *War Scare*, 166.

21. *FRUS, 1948*, IV, 847–850.

22. *Washington Post*, Oct. 22, 1963; Peter Grose, *Operation Rollback* (Boston, 2000), 4–8.

23. C. Thomas Thorne, Jr., and David S. Patterson, eds., *The Emergence of an Intelligence Establishment* (Washington, DC, 1996), 684 passim.

24. Bennett Kovrig, *The Myth of Liberation* (Baltimore, 1973), 116.

25. Ferrell, *Off the Record*, 145.

26. Lucius D. Clay OH, HSTL; Bohlen, *Witness to History*, 277.

27. Memorandum, August 9, 1952, George Elsey Papers, HSTL.

28. *FRUS, 1948*, II, 1196–97.

29. Robert S. Norris and Hans M. Kristensen, "Global Nuclear Stockpiles, 1945–2002," *Bulletin of the Atomic Scientists* (Nov.–Dec. 2002).

30. John T. McNay, *Acheson and Empire* (New York, 2001), 35.

31. Lucius Battle OH, HSTL; Dean Acheson OH, HSTL.

32. Daniel Ford, "B-36: Bomber at the Crossroads," *Air and Space/Smithsonian Magazine* (April–May 1996).

9. Talking Tough

1. Gene Smith, "Brisk Walk and Brusque Talk," *American Heritage* (July–August 1992).

2. Robert Dennison, OH HSTL.

3. Miller, *Plain Speaking*, 392.

4. *Collier's*, August 26, 1944. The chances that Truman actually wrote this article are zero. Truman could not even write his own memoirs. He repeatedly claimed he had written them, although a journalist, William Hillman, was the principal author. When Truman threatened to sue the Kansas City newspaper

that revealed this fact, the newspaper offered to publish its proof, including eyewitness testimonies. Truman backed off.

5. Memorandum, "Plan for Universal Military Training," June 23, 1945, Truman Papers, HSTL; Harry Vaughan OH, HSTL; Clifford and Holbrooke, *Counsel to the President*, 56; Michael J. Hogan, *A Cross of Iron* (New York, 1998), 135.

6. Cabinet Minutes, Aug. 31, 1945, Matthew Connolly Papers, HSTL.

7. Diary, June 4, 1945, Eben Ayers Papers, HSTL.

8. Demetrios Caraley, *The Politics of Military Unification* (New York, 1966), 134–35.

9. Memorandum, "Records of a War Council Meeting, October 17, 1946," Robert Patterson papers, LC.

10. David Lilienthal, *The Journals of David E. Lilienthal: The Atomic Energy Years* (New York, 1964), III, 388–89.

11. Diary, Oct. 15, 1947, Eben Ayers Papers, HSTL.

12. Millis, *Forrestal Diaries*, 160–61; Careley, *Military Unification*, 136.

13. Diary, April 21, 26, 1948, Eben Ayers Papers, HSTL.

14. Undated memo, "National Defense—Armed Forces Unification," George Elsey Papers, HSTL.

15. Eugene Zuckert OH, HSTL.

16. Diary, September 24, 1945, Eben Ayers Papers, HSTL.

17. Greg Herken, *The Winning Weapon* (New York, 1980), 36.

18. *FRUS, 1946*, I, 838–40, 846–51; Lilienthal, *Journals: The Atomic Energy Years*, 125; Acheson, *Present at the Creation*, 155.

19. Chace, *Acheson*, 235.

20. Stephen Zanichowsky, "The Beauty of the Bomb," *Invention and Technology*, Summer 2005.

21. *FRUS, 1950*, I, 141–42.

22. *FRUS, 1950*, I, 176–92.

23. Diary, May 24, 1949, Eben Ayers Papers, HSTL; Robert Dennison OH, HSTL.

24. Tyler Abell, ed., *The Drew Pearson Diaries, 1949–1959* (New York, 1974), 9.

25. Alfred Croft, "The Case of Korea," *The Nation*, June 25, 1960; *New York Times*, Jan. 5, 2005.

26. *FRUS, 1948*, VI, 1079 passion.

27. Ronald M. McGlothlen, *Controlling the Waves* (New York, 1993), 63.

28. Miller, *Plain Speaking*, 273.

29. Cabinet Notes, September 7, 1945, Matthew Connolly Papers, HSTL.

10. Zeitgeist Wins

1. R.A.C. Parker, *Chamberlain and Appeasement* (New York, 1993), 156–74.

2. Paul Stehlin, *Témoignage pour l'Histoire* (Paris, 1964), 76–81.

3. Winston S. Churchill, *Their Finest Hour* (Boston, 1949), 320.

4. Memorandum, "Blair House Meeting," June 25, 1950, George Elsey Papers, HSTL.

5. Acheson, *Present at the Creation*, 406.

6. *FRUS, 1950*, VII, 161–62.

7. Douglas MacArthur, *Reminiscences* (New York, 1964), 320, 329.

8.   *FRUS, 1950*, VII, 157–61.
9.   Offner, *Another Such Victory*, 374.
10.   Ferrell, *Off the Record*, 119.
11.   L. Brent Bozell, *McCarthy and His Enemies* (Chicago, 1954), 45. Bozell was a speechwriter and helped draft this speech.
12.   Geoffrey Perret, *A Dream of Greatness* (New York, 1979), 205.
13.   "Message from General MacArthur, 2512200Z," June 25, 1950, White House Central Files, HSTL.
14.   Wallace Graham, 1989 OH, HSTL.
15.   Rusk, *As I Saw It*, 124.
16.   Bruce Cumings, *The Origins of the Korean War* (Princeton, 1992), II, 568–75.
17.   David Holloway, *Stalin and the Bomb* (New Haven, 1994), 277.
18.   Sergei Goncharev et al., *Uncertain Partners* (Stanford, CA, 1993), 260–64.
19.   Shen Zhihua, "Sino-North Korean Conflict and Its Resolution During the Korean War," Cold War International History Project (hereafter CWIHP), *Bulletin* 14/15; Charles R. Schrader, *Communist Logistics in the Korean War* (Westport, CT, 1995), 25–26.
20.   Memorandum, "President Truman's Conversation with George M. Elsey," June 26, 1950, George Elsey Papers, HSTL.
21.   Beverly Smith, "Why We Went to War in Korea," *Saturday Evening Post*, Nov. 11, 1951. Truman and other major figures in the Korea decision cooperated in the production of this article.
22.   Memorandum, July 16, 1951, George Elsey Papers, HSTL.
23.   Smith, "Why We Went to War."
24.   J. Lawton Collins, *Lightning Joe* (Baton Rouge, 1973), 360–61; Edward Almond OH, U.S. Army Military History Institute; Poen, *Strictly Personal and Confidential*, 49–50.
25.   Richard Lee Strout OH, HSTL.

11. War of Maneuver

1.   Miller, *Plain Speaking*, 276; Dean Acheson OH, HSTL.
2.   Harry S. Truman diary, June 17, 1945, HSTL.
3.   Memorandum, Adjutant General's Office to Burdette M. Fitch, August 25, 1939, RG 407, National Archives.
4.   Diary, Dec. 8, 1945, Eben Ayers Papers, HSTL.
5.   Geoffrey Perret, *Old Soldiers Never Die: The Life of Douglas MacArthur* (New York, 1996), 531.
6.   Barton J. Bernstein, "New Light on the Korean War," *International History Review* (April 1981).
7.   Telegram, MacArthur to Truman, July 19, 1950, HSTL.
8.   Edward Folliard OH, HSTL.
9.   Arthur Krock, *Memoirs*, 260.
10.   George Kennan, *Memoirs, 1950–1963* (Boston, 1972), 91.
11.   Acheson, *Present at the Creation*, 412.
12.   Edward Almond OH, USAMHI.
13.   Heller, *The Truman White House*, 13.
14.   D. Clayton James, *The Years of MacArthur* (Boston, 1985), III, 458.

15. Vernon Walters, *Silent Missions* (Boston, 1978), 197; Perret, *Old Soldiers Never Die*, 546.

16. Truman, *Memoirs* (Garden City, NY, 1955), II, 351–52.

17. Truman, *Memoirs*, II, 356; Memorandum for File, Aug. 26, 1950, George Elsey Papers, HSTL; *Washington Evening Star*, Aug. 30, 1950.

18. Rudy Abramson, *Spanning the Century* (New York, 1992), 445.

19. Memorandum for Record, September 13, 1950, George Elsey Papers; Eben Ayers OH, HSTL.

20. Ferrell, *Off the Record*, 192–93;

21. George Elsey OH and Charles Murphy OH, both HSTL.

22. *Time*, Oct. 23, 1950.

23. Walters, *Silent Missions*, 209.

24. Memo for Record, April 6, 1951, Eben Ayers Papers, HSTL.

25. K. M. Pannikar, *In Two Chinas* (London, 1955), 109–110; Acheson, *Present at the Creation*, 452; Truman, *Memoirs*, II, 362.

26. Truman, *Memoirs*, II, 363–65. Charles Murphy OH, HSTL.

27. Rusk, *As I Saw It*, 168–69.

28. Perret, *Old Soldiers Never Die*, 553–58.

29. Memorandum, compiled by Omar N. Bradley, "Substance of Statements Made at the Wake Island Conference on October 15, 1950," HSTL, and Vernice Anderson OH, HSTL.

30. *Time*, Oct. 23, 1950.

12. What Goes Up . . .

1. *FRUS, 1950*, VII, 649 passim; *PPP, 1950, Truman*, 605–608.

2. Cabinet Notes, Sept. 29, 1950, Matthew Connolly Papers, HSTL.

3. *PPP, 1950, Truman*, 609–14; John Spanier, *The Truman-MacArthur Controversy* (Cambridge, MA, 1959), 99–100.

4. Acheson, *Present at the Creation*, 453.

5. *FRUS, 1950*, VII, 826.

6. Alexander Y. Mansourov, "Stalin, Mao, Kim and China's Decision to Enter the Korean War," Cold War International History Project, Woodrow Wilson Center, Washington, DC, *Bulletin* 17/18.

7. Ibid.

8. Shen Zhihua, "The Discrepancy Between the Russian and Chinese Versions of Mao's October 2, 1950, Message to Stalin," CWIHP, *Bulletin* 17/18.

9. Cable, MacArthur to JCS, Oct. 24, 1950, MacArthur Memorial and Archive (hereafter MMA).

10. Robert Frank Futrell, *The United States Air Force in Korea, 1950–1953*, rev. ed. (Washington, DC, 1983), 244–47.

11. Acheson, *Present at the Creation*, 464.

12. John Hersey, *Aspects of the Presidency* (New York, 1980), 27–30.

13. Cabinet Notes, Nov. 28, 1950, Matthew Connolly Papers, HSTL.

14. Farrell, *Off the Record*, 202–203.

15. Acheson, *Present at the Creation*, 481–84; *FRUS, 1950*, VII, 1462–65.

16. Rusk, *As I Saw It*, 69.

17. *New York Times*, March 24, 1951.

18. Perret, *Old Soldiers Never Die*, 567.
19. D. Clayton James, *The Years of MacArthur* (Boston, 1970), III, 591–92.
20. Rusk, *As I Saw It*, 171.
21. Miller, *Plain Speaking*, 305; Frank Pace OH, HSTL.
22. Rusk, *As I Saw It*, 172.
23. CWIHP, *Bulletin* 6/7 (Winter 1996), 116.
24. Kathryn Weathersby, "New Evidence on North Korea," CWIHP, *Bulletin* 14/15.
25. Ibid.
26. Ibid.
27. Cumings, *The Origins of the Korean War*, II, ii, 60.

13. Wars of Choice

1. CWIHP, *Bulletin* 14/15, "Russian Documents on the Korean War," 372–73; Shu Guang Zhang, *Mao's Military Romanticism* (Lawrence, KS, 1995), 247–60.
2. See "Aggressors for Peace" speech, Sept. 1, 1950, Francis B. Matthews Papers, HSTL.
3. Geoffrey Perret, *Eisenhower* (New York, 1999), 479.
4. *The Guardian*, Sept. 27, 2003.
5. Wilbur Crane Eveland, *Ropes of Sand* (New York, 1982); Roger Warner, *Back Fire* (New York, 1995); *New York Times*, Dec. 31, 1997. Eveland handed over some of the briefcases personally to Chamoun.
6. Piero Gleijeses, *Shattered Hope: The Guatemalan Revolution and the United States* (Princeton, NJ, 1991), 228–30.
7. Cabinet Minutes series, Feb. 28, 1954, Dwight D. Eisenhower Library.
8. Richard Immerman, *The CIA in Guatemala* (Austin, TX, 1982), 137–38; Richard Bissell OH, Columbia Oral History Project, Columbia University.
9. Alexander George and Richard Smoke, *Deterrence in American Foreign Policy* (New York, 1974), 274.
10. Ibid., 280.
11. *PPP, 1955, Eisenhower*, 762–66.
12. William J. Duiker, *Ho Chi Minh* (New York, 2000), 304–308, 331–34.
13. Ibid., 442.
14. Perret, *Eisenhower*, 467.
15. Bernard B. Fall, *Hell in a Very Small Place* (Philadelphia, 1967), 415–16.
16. Lloyd Gardner, *Approaching Vietnam* (New York, 1988), 341.
17. John Mecklin, *Mission in Torment: The U.S. Role in Vietnam* (New York, 1965), 57–58.

14. Getting a Grip

1. Elbridge Durbrow OH, Lyndon B. Johnson Library (hereafter LBJL).
2. Memorandum, "Topics Suggested by Senator Kennedy for Meeting," Jan. 19, 1961, Anne Whitman File, Eisenhower Library; "Memo for Record," Jan. 19, 1961, and Clark Clifford memorandum to JFK, Jan. 24, 1961.

3.   Arleigh Burke OH, JFK Library (hereafter JFKL).

4.   Arthur Schlesinger Jr., *A Thousand Days* (New York, 1965), 276.

5.   Duiker, *Ho Chi Minh*, 649.

6.   Harold P. Ford, "Calling the Sino-Soviet Split," *Intelligence Studies* (Winter 1998–99).

7.   Roger Hilsman, *To Move a Nation* (New York, 1969), 344.

8.   Walt Rostow OH, JFKL; "Memo for Record," May 5, 1961, Arthur Krock Papers, Princeton University.

9.   Peter Grose, *Gentleman Spy: The Life of Allen Dulles* (Amherst, 1996), 512–13.

10. W. W. Rostow, "Beware of Historians Bearing False Analogies," *Foreign Affairs* (Spring 1998).

11. Michael Beschloss, *The Crisis Years* (New York, 1991), 129.

12. *The Pentagon Papers* (Gravel edition), II, 57–58; Stanley Karnow, *Vietnam: A History* (New York, 1983), 214.

13. *Pentagon Papers*, II, 59; *FRUS, 1961–1962*, I, 152–53.

14. David L. DiLeo, *George Ball, Vietnam and the Rethinking of Containment* (Chapel Hill, NC, 1991), 57.

15. Schlesinger, *A Thousand Days*, 546–47; *FRUS, 1961–1963*, I, 391–92, 561–63, 605–607.

16. Ang Chen Guang, *Vietnamese Communists' Relations with China and the Second Indochina Conflict, 1956–1962* (Jefferson, NC, 1997), 215.

17. Kai Bird, *The Color of Truth* (New York, 1998), 223.

18. Lloyd C. Gardner and Ted Gittinger, eds., *Vietnam: The Early Decisions* (Austin, TX, 1997), 164–85.

19. Bird, *Color of Truth*, 222.

20. Lloyd C. Gardner, *Pay Any Price* (Chicago, 1995), 62.

21. Karnow, *Vietnam*, 309.

22. David Halberstam, *The Best and the Brightest* (New York, 1983), 208.

23. David Halberstam, *The Making of a Quagmire* (New York, 1964), 158–60.

24. Don Oberdorfer, *Senator Mansfield* (Washington, DC, 2003), 194–98.

25. Kenneth O'Donnell, *Johnny, We Hardly Knew Ye* (Boston, 1970), 15.

26. Geoffrey Perret, *There's a War to Be Won: the U.S. Army in World War II* (New York, 1991), 284–97, 483.

27. Gil Dorland, *Legacy of Discord* (Dulles, VA, 2001), 97–98.

28. Gardner, *Pay Any Price*, 72.

29. See David M. Toczek, *The Battle of Ap Bac, Vietnam* (Westport, CT, 2001).

30. *FRUS, 1961–1963*, III, 628–29.

31. Dorland, *Legacy*, 102–103; *FRUS, 1961–1963*, IV, 3–6, 69–74.

32. Gardner and Gittinger, *Vietnam*, 167.

33. George McT. Kahin, *Intervention* (New York, 1986), 169.

34. Ellen J. Hammer, *A Death in November* (New York, 1987), 243; *FRUS, 1961–1963*, IV, 393.

35. Paul B. Fay, Jr., OH, JFKL.

36. Lyndon B. Johnson OH, LBJL.

37. Bird, *Color of Truth*, 260.

15. Hard Choices

1. Tom Wicker, *JFK and LBJ* (New York, 1968), 161.
2. William Bundy OH, LBJL; Wicker, *JFK and LBJ*, 205.
3. *FRUS, 1961–1963*, IV, 637–40.
4. *PPP, 1963–1964, Johnson*, 4.
5. Michael Beschloss, ed., *Taking Charge* (New York, 1997), 123.
6. Samuel Anderson OH, Historical Research Agency, Maxwell AFB.
7. Ronnie Dugger, *The Politician* (New York, 1964), 245–49; Clark Newlon, *LBJ* (New York, 1966), 98–101.
8. Diary, July 26, 1942, Harold Ickes Papers, LC, 300–301.
9. Perret, *Old Soldiers Never Die*, 299–301.
10. Dugger, *The Politician*, 371.
11. H. R. McMaster, *Dereliction of Duty: Lyndon Johnson, Robert McNamara and the Joint Chiefs of Staff, and the Lies That Led to Vietnam* (New York, 1997), 522–23.
12. Ray Cline OH, LBJL.
13. *FRUS, 1961*, I, 147–57.
14. Beschloss, *Taking Charge*, 95.
15. *New York Times*, May 1, 1966.
16. Robert Mann, *A Grand Delusion* (New York, 2001), 307.
17. *FRUS, 1964–1968*, I, 12–13.
18. Ibid.; Beschloss, *Taking Charge*, 73–74.

16. The Green Mountain

1. Booth Mooney, *LBJ: An Irreverent Chronicle* (New York, 1976), 173.
2. Leonard Luree, *Party Politics* (New York, 1980), 236.
3. Robert F. Kennedy OH, JFKL.
4. Beschloss, *Taking Charge*, 162.
5. Cable, Feb. 22, 1964, Lodge to Johnson, LBJL.
6. Memo, March 13, 1964, McNamara to to Johnson, LBJL.
7. Cable, Bohlen to Rusk, April 2, 1964, LBJL.
8. Memo, May 25, 1964, Bundy to Johnson, LBJL.
9. Beschloss, *Taking Charge*, 200.
10. Ibid., 249, 257.
11. Memos, Feb. 26, 1964, and March 14, 1964, Bundy to Johnson, LBJL.
12. Beschloss, *Taking Charge*, 213.
13. Ibid., 258, 263.
14. *FRUS, 1964*, I, 147–48.
15. *FRUS, 1964*, I, 244–48.
16. Memorandum, June 25, 1964, Bundy to Johnson, LBJL.
17. Beschloss, *Taking Charge*, 338.
18. Ibid., 370.
19. Memo, March 13, 1964, McNamara to Johnson, LBJL.
20. *FRUS, 1964*, I, 437–40, 457–58.
21. Unpublished, untitled manuscript, William Bundy Papers, LBJL.
22. Letter, Lodge to LBJ, June 5, 1964, LBJL.

23. Beschloss, *Taking Charge*, 416, 426.
24. *Washington Post*, June 16, 1964.

17. Trading Places

1.   Lawrence W. Beilenson, *The Treaty Trap* (Washington, DC, 1969), 38.
2.   *The Pentagon Papers* (Gravel edition), I, 212.
3.   DiLeo, *George Ball*, 59.
4.   *FRUS, 1964*, I, 351–55, 394–96; Lyndon B. Johnson, *The Vantage Point* (New York, 1971), 67.
5.   Karnow, *Vietnam*, 387.
6.   Daniel Ellsberg, *Secrets* (New York, 2004), 14.
7.   Edwin E. Moïse, *Tonkin Gulf and the Escalation of the Vietnam War* (Chapel Hill, NC, 1996), 77–84.
8.   Beschloss, *Taking Charge*, 496–97.
9.   Bird, *Color of Truth*, 289.
10. Moïse, *Tonkin Gulf*, 143–44.
11. Beschloss, *Taking Charge*, 529.
12. Lyndon B. Johnson OH, LBJL.
13. Irving Bernstein, *Guns or Butter: The Presidency of Lyndon Johnson* (New York, 1996), 13; Jan Jarboe Russell, *Lady Bird* (New York, 1999), 244–45.
14. *PPP, 1963–1964, Johnson*, II, 1011.
15. Moïse, *Tonkin Gulf*, 252.
16. Duiker, *Ho Chi Minh*, 543.
17. *New York Times*, Aug. 7, 1964.

18. Thunder and Lightning

1.   Frank Cormier, *LBJ: The Way He Was* (New York, 1977), 123–34.
2.   Robert McNamara, *In Retrospect* (New York, 1995), 96–97.
3.   *PPP, 1963–1964, Johnson*, II, 1165.
4.   William Bundy mss., 1–4, LBJL.
5.   Cecil B. Currey, *Victory at Any Cost* (Washington, DC, 1997), 249.
6.   Quang Zhai, *China and the Vietnam Wars, 1950–1975* (Chapel Hill, NC, 2000), 134.
7.   Yang Kuisong, Working Paper 34: "Changes in Mao Zedong's Attitude Toward the Indochina War, 1949–1973," CWIHP.
8.   *FRUS, 1964–1968*, I, 1057–59.
9.   Memorandums to the President, McGeorge Bundy to Johnson, Jan. 4 and 27, 1965, LBJL.
10. Memorandum to the President, Annex A, Feb. 7, 1965, McGeorge Bundy to Johnson, LBJL.
11. Jeff Shesol, *Mutual Contempt* (New York: 1997), 265.
12. Document 112a, Part 10, "Memos to the President," undated, LBJL.
13. Quang Zhai, *China*, 133.
14. Ibid., 139.
15. Item 107a, May 31, 1965, Memorandums to the President, LBJL. There is only a brief, heavily redacted version of Chen Yi's remarks in the *Foreign Rela-*

tions of the United States, and it amounts to little more than a footnote. In this form it does not convey, for example, the threat to revive the Korean War if China intervened in Vietnam. This warning was just as important as the one China had issued in the fall of 1950 to intervene in Korea, a warning that had been rejected as bluster by Truman, Acheson, and MacArthur. The entire document deserves to be published in its entirety. Only four people ever saw it—LBJ, Rusk, McNamara, and Bundy—a sure sign of how important it was.

16. Item 107a, May 31, 1965, Memorandums to the President, LBJL. There is only a brief and carefully edited version of Chen Yi's remarks in the *Foreign Relations of the United States.* It fails to convey the comprehensive nature of China's threat to enter the Vietnam War, yet it is that threat that is at the heart of Chen Yi's wide-ranging remarks.

17. Quang Zhai, *China,* 138–39.

19. All-Out Limited War

1. Scott Sagan, "SIOP-62: The Nuclear War Plan Briefed to President Kennedy," *International Security* (Summer 1987); Perret, *Eisenhower,* 563.
2. Ellsberg, *Secrets,* 52–53. Ellsberg was the principal author of SIOP-62.
3. H. R. McMaster, *Dereliction of Duty* (New York, 1987), 54.
4. Hanson Baldwin, "The Targets if the Vietnam War Grows," *New York Times,* December 11, 1964.
5. Brian Van DeMark, *Into the Quagmire* (New York, 1991), 94–95.
6. Lady Bird Johnson, *A White House Diary* (New York, 1970), 248.
7. Carl T. Rowan, *Breaking Barriers* (Boston, 1991), 258; Curtis LeMay OH, LBJL.
8. Memorandum, Aug. 2, 1965, McGeorge Bundy to LBJ, Bundy Papers, LBJL.
9. *Washington Post,* Aug. 11, 1964; *Congressional Record,* Aug. 12, 1965, A4497.
10. McKinley Kantor, *Mission with LeMay* (New York, 1965), 565.
11. Karnow, *Vietnam,* 419.
12. George Herring, *LBJ and Vietnam* (Austin, TX, 1994), 91–96.
13. William Conrad Gibbons, *The U.S. Government and the Vietnam War* (Princeton, NJ, 1986), III, 240.
14. Memorandum, July 20, 1965, McNamara to Johnson, LBJL.
15. Memorandum, July 21, 1965, Clark Clifford to McGeorge Bundy, LBJL.
16. Yang Kuisong, Working Paper 34: "Changes in Mao Zedong's Attitude Toward the Indochina War, 1949–1973," CWIHP; Quang Zhai, *China and the Vietnam Wars,* 140–41.
17. *FRUS, 1964–1968,* III, 599–600.

20. Trapped

1. Jim Bishop, *A Day in the Life of President Johnson* (New York, 1967).
2. Errol Morris Web site: *Fog of War* transcript.
3. George Reedy, *Lyndon B. Johnson* (New York, 1982), 155; Bishop, *A Day in the Life,* 88.
4. Dugger, *The Politician,* 429.

5. Ibid., 127; Alfred Steinberger, *Lyndon Baines Johnson Remembered* (Austin, TX, 1985), 168.
6. Reedy, *Lyndon B. Johnson*, 149.
7. Lionel Giles, ed., *Sun Tzu on the Art of War* (London, 1910), Rule 14, Chapter Three.
8. Gibbons, *The U.S. Government and the Vietnam War*, IV, 219–20.
9. Carl Solberg, *Hubert Humphrey* (New York, 1984), 277–78.
10. Mark Clodfelter, *The Limits of Air Power* (New York, 1989), 75–76.
11. Robert Dallek, *Flawed Giant* (New York, 1998), 452.
12. Ray Cline OH, LBJL.
13. *FRUS 1964–1968*, III, 35.
14. Bird, *Color of Truth*, 348.
15. Clodfelter, *Limits of Air Power*, 74.
16. Geoffrey Perret, *Winged Victory: The Army Air Forces in World War II* (New York, 1993), 367–69.
17. W. W. Rostow, *The Stages of Economic Growth* (Cambridge, England, 1965), 162.
18. Karnow, *Vietnam*, 485.
19. *FRUS, 1964–1968*, IV, 203.
20. Robert Mann, *A Grand Delusion*, 493.
21. Lyndon Baines Johnson, *The Vantage Point* (New York, 1971), 244.
22. Clodfelter, *Limits of Air Power*, 94, 150–51.
23. W. W. Rostow, Memo to the President, April 5, 1966, LBJL.
24. David Kaiser, *American Tragedy* (Cambridge, MA, 2000), 407.
25. The full text can be found at www.bailey.uvm.edu/special collections; George Aiken OH, LBJL.
26. W. W. Rostow, "Meeting of the President with Thieu and Ky," Oct. 23, 1966, Lyndon B. Johnson Papers, LBJL.
27. Hugh Sidey, *A Very Personal Presidency* (New York, 1968), 151.
28. Louis Heren, *No Hail, No Farewell* (New York, 1970), 133, 180.
29. Clifford and Holbrooke, *Counsel to the President*, 417.
30. Bernstein, *Guns or Butter*, 399.
31. *FRUS, 1964–1968*, V, 423–38.
32. *New York Times*, Sept. 3, 1967.
33. David M. Barrett, *Uncertain Warriors: Lyndon Johnson and His Advisers* (Lawrence, KS, 1993), 98–99.
34. Tom Johnson Meeting Notes, Sept. 26, 1967, LBJL.

21. Back to the Ranch

1. McNamara, *In Retrospect*, 292–94. McNamara did not know this document existed until he came across it the LBJ Library many years later.
2. Bruce Alan Murphy, *Fortas* (New York, 1988), 243–45.
3. Bird, *Color of Truth*, 255.
4. Meeting Notes, Oct. 3, 1967, Tom Johnson Meeting Notes, LBJL.
5. *The Pentagon Papers* (Gravel edition), 580.
6. Chace, *Acheson*, 416–17.
7. Clifford and Holbrooke, *Counsel to the President*, 454.
8. Congressional Briefing, Nov. 16, 1967, Congressional Briefings, LBJL.

9.   Karnow, *Vietnam*, 514.
10.   Heren, *No Hail, No Farewell*, 134, 178.
11.   William C. Westmoreland, *A Soldier Reports* (New York, 1976), 233.
12.   Sidney Blumenthal, "Blinded by the Light at the End of the Tunnel," *The Guardian*, June 23, 2005.
13.   F. Edward Hebert OH, LBJL.
14.   *Washington Star*, Oct. 15, 1967. Clifford does not mention this speech in his memoirs.
15.   Clifford and Holbrooke, *Counsel to the President*, 551–52.
16.   Robert Mann, *A Grand Delusion*, 601.
17.   Memo, Westmoreland to Wheeler, Dec. 20, 1967, LBJL; William C. Westmoreland, *A Soldier Reports* (New York: 1976), 313–14.
18.   Duiker, *Ho Chi Minh*, 557.
19.   Meeting Notes, March 4, 1968, Tom Johnson Papers, LBJL.
20.   Meeting Notes, March 26, 1968, Tom Johnson Papers, LBJL.
21.   Edgar Berman, *Hubert: The Triumph and Tragedy of the Humphrey I Knew* (New York, 1979), 157.
22.   Jan Jarboe Russell, *Lady Bird* (New York, 1999), 279.
23.   *PPP, 1968–1969, Johnson*, II, 469–70.
24.   Westmoreland, *A Soldier Reports*, 119.
25.   Doris Kearns Goodwin, *Lyndon Johnson and the American Dream* (New York, 1976), 349.
26.   Carl Albert OH, LBJL.
27.   Berman, *Hubert*, 189.
28.   Solberg, *Hubert Humphrey*, 373–74.
29.   Dallek, *Flawed Giant*, 586–87.

22. The Nixinger War

1.   H. R. Haldeman, *The Ends of Power* (New York, 1978), 83.
2.   Henry Kissinger, *The White House Years* (Boston, 1979), 277–80.
3.   Strobe Talbott, ed., *Khrushchev Remembers* (Boston, 1974), 255.
4.   Larry Berman, *No Peace, No Honor* (New York, 2001), 211.
5.   Jeffrey Kimball, *The Vietnam War Files* (Lawrence, KS, 2004), 146.
6.   Patrick Tyler, *A Great Wall: Six Presidents and China* (New York, 199), 143.
7.   Odd Arne Westad et al., *77 Conversations Between Chinese and Foreign Leaders*, CWIHP, Working Paper No. 22, 178.
8.   Ibid., 181.
9.   Kimball, *Vietnam War Files*, 217.
10.   Ibid., 162–64.
11.   Westad et al., *77 Conversations*, Documents 67 and 71.
12.   Berman, *No Peace*, 125.
13.   Ibid., 161.
14.   *New York Times*, October 27, 1972.
15.   Oriana Fallaci, *Interview with History* (Boston, 1977), 40–41.
16.   H. R. Haldeman, *The Ends of Power* (New York, 1978), 63.
17.   Westad et al., *77 Conversations*, Document 64; Berman, *No Peace*, 1–2.
18.   Larry Berman, *No Peace, No Honor* (New York, 2002), 222.

19. Berman, *No Peace*, 218.
20. Ibid., 213.
21. Ibid., 8.
22. *New York Times*, Oct. 1, 2001; BBC News report, Sept. 30, 2001.
23. *The Guardian*, April 29, 2005.

23. Futurismo

1. Perret, *Eisenhower*, 478–79.
2. Caspar Weinberger, *Fighting for Peace* (New York, 1990), 160, 167; George Shultz, *Turmoil and Triumph* (New York, 1993), 228–30.
3. Robert Baer, *See No Evil* (New York, 2003), 72, 266–67.
4. Hugh O'Shaughnessy, *Grenada: Revolution, Invasion and Aftermath* (London, 1984), 39–53.
5. Craig Unger, *House of Bush, House of Saud* (New York, 2004), 132.
6. *New York Times*, Feb. 21, 1991.
7. George H. W. Bush and Brent Scowcroft, *A World Transformed* (New York, 1998), 392, 399.
8. *Washington Post*, Aug. 3, 1990.
9. David Ignatius, "Saddam Hussein Revisited," *Washington Post*, Sept. 14, 2004.
10. Bush and Scowcroft, *A World Transformed*, 328.
11. Bob Woodward, *The Commanders* (New York, 1992), 261.
12. Ibid., 314–15, 324.
13. *New York Times*, Aug. 9, 1990.
14. James Baker, *The Politics of Diplomacy* (New York, 1995), 277.
15. *Time*, Jan. 7, 1991.
16. Woodward, *Commanders*, 339.
17. Bush and Scowcroft, *A World Transformed*, 464.
18. Ibid., 414.
19. Douglas Brinkley, *The Unfinished Presidency: Jimmy Carter* (New York, 1998), 336–37.
20. Bush and Scowcroft, *A World Transformed*, 418.
21. Unger, *House of Bush*, 139.
22. Colin L. Powell, *My American Journey* (New York, 1995), 476.
23. John MacArthur, *Second Front: Censorship and Propaganda in the 1991 Gulf War* (Berkeley, CA, 2004), 58–61.
24. Powell, *My American Journey*, 516–17.
25. Bush and Scowcroft, *A World Transformed*, 471, 473.
26. Ibid., 484.

24. Chances Are

1. *Congressional Record*, July 30, 1993, H: 5550–51.
2. Daniel Benjamin and Steve Simon, *The Age of Sacred Terror* (New York, 2002), 7–10.
3. Stephen Reeve, *Ramzi Yousef, Osama bin-Laden and the Future of Terrorism* (London, 1999), 38 passim.
4. Laurie Kerr, "The Mosque to Commerce," *Slate*, Oct. 1, 2002.

5. Mark Lacey, "Look at the Place!" *New York Times*, Oct. 20, 2005.
6. John F. Harris, *The Survivor* (New York, 2005), 336–38.
7. James Mann, *The Rise of the Vulcans* (New York, 2003), 112–26.
8. Joel Brinkley, "The Reach of War: New Premier," *New York Times*, June 9, 2004.
9. Jane Mayer, "The Manipulator," *The New Yorker*, June 6, 2004.
10. "Statement of Principles," June 3, 1997, Project for the New American Century.
11. Ron Kessler, *A Matter of Character* (New York, 2004), 23–33, 50.
12. James Moore and Wayne Slater, *Bush's Brain: How Karl Rove Made George W. Bush Presidential* (New York, 2003), 210.
13. Russ Baker, "War on My Mind," Guerrilla News Network, Oct. 27, 2004.
14. "Democracy Now," National Public Radio broadcast, March 11, 2005.
15. Seymour Hersh, "Case Not Closed," *The New Yorker*, Oct. 27, 2002.
16. *Daily Telegraph*, March 18, 2003.

25. Targets

1. Paul Kengor, *God and George W. Bush* (New York, 2004), 239.
2. Moore and Slater, *Bush's Brain*, 218.
3. Ibid., 276–78.
4. Kessler, *Matter of Character*, 80; Deborah Caldwell, "An Evolving Faith: Does the President Believe He Has a Divine Mandate?" *Christian Ethics Today*, Spring 2005.
5. Moore and Slater, *Bush's Brain*, 304–306.
6. Cecil Adams, "Did George W. Bush Go AWOL?" *The Chicago Reader*, April 11, 2003; White House press release, Oct. 24, 2005.
7. *Washington Post*, May 31, 2000.
8. Terry M. Neal, "Bush Backs into Nation Building," *Washington Post*, Feb. 26, 2003; Bob Woodward,"Bush at War," *Washington Post*, Nov. 18, 2002.
9. Jay Nordlinger, "Power and Values," *National Review*, Aug. 12, 2002.
10. Andrew Gumbel, "David O. Russell," *LA CityBeat*, June 24, 2004.
11. Russ Baker, "War on My Mind," Guerrilla News Network, Oct. 27, 2004.
12. Bob Woodward, *Plan of Attack* (New York, 2004), 12.
13. *The Onion*, Jan. 18, 2001.
14. Ron Suskind, *The Price of Loyalty* (New York, 2003), 71–73.
15. David Rothkopf, "The Committee That Runs the World," *Foreign Policy*, May/June 2005.
16. State Department press release, Feb. 21, 2001.
17. Suskind, *Price of Loyalty*, 85.
18. Ibid., 149.
19. Richard Clarke, *Against All Enemies* (New York, 2004), 24.
20. Ibid., 32.
21. Bob Woodward, *Bush at War* (New York, 2002), 51–52; Suskind, *Price of Loyalty*, 185.
22. CNN.com, Sept. 17, 2001.
23. White House press release, Sept. 16, 2001.
24. Woodward, *Bush at War*, 81.

25. Department of Defense, *National Defense Strategy of the United States*, March 2005.
26. White House press release, Feb. 16, 2002.
27. David Frum, *The Right Man* (New York, 2003), 3–4; Paul Kengor, *God and George W. Bush*, 239–42.
28. Woodward, *Bush at War*, 310.

26. Willful, Mendacious, Deluded

1. Gary Berntsen and Ralph Pezzullo, *Jawbreaker: The Attack on Bin Laden and Al Qaeda* (New York, 2005), 260 passim; Rowan Scarborough, *Rumsfeld's War* (Washington, DC, 2004), 45.
2. Russ Baker, "Exclusive: Bush Wanted to Invade Iraq If Elected," Guerrilla News Network, Oct. 27, 2004.
3. Rothkopf, "The Committee."
4. Wesley K. Clark, *Winning Modern Wars* (New York, 2004), 130.
5. Bill Keller, "The World According to Colin Powell," *New York Times Magazine*, Nov. 25, 2001.
6. Scarborough, *Rumsfeld's War*, 36.
7. Paul R. Pillar, "Intelligence, Policy and the War in Iraq," *Foreign Affairs*, March/April 2006. Pillar was the CIA's chief analyst for intelligence on the Middle East.
8. *The Times* (London), June 12, 2005; *The Guardian*, Oct. 7, 2005; Philippe Sand, *Lawless World* (New York, 2005). A piquant detail: Sand is a lawyer in the same law practice as Cherie Blair.
9. Memo, "Iraq: Prime Minister's Meeting," July 23, 2002.
10. *The New Yorker*, March 31, 2003; Jay Nordlinger, "Power and Values," *National Review*, Aug. 12, 2002.
11. James Mann, *The Vulcans* (New York, 2003), 209–15.
12. *The National Security Strategy of the United States*, 2002. The full text is available on the Department of Defense Web site. It should be read in conjunction with "Full Spectrum Dominance" also of the DOD Web site. This sets out the military doctrine for implementing the National Security Strategy, and the Project for the New American Century Web site is a useful guide to the thinking that shaped this strategy.
13. BBC News, Nov. 30, 2001.
14. The transcript of this speech to the Florida Economic Council on Aug. 23, 2002, is available on the NPR Web site.
15. James A. Baker III, "The Right Way to Change a Regime," *New York Times*, Aug. 25, 2002.
16. White House press release, Aug. 22, 2002.
17. "Wolf Blitzer Reports," CNN.com, Jan. 10, 2003.
18. White House press release, Oct. 7, 2002.
19. James Bamford, *A Pretext for War* (New York, 2004), 298–307; Ian Masters, "Who Forged the Niger Documents," AlterNet.org, April 7, 2005. This is the transcript of an interview with Vincent Cannistraro, for many years head of counterterrorism at the CIA, including the period of Hussein Kemal's debriefing.

20.   Laura Rozen, "La Repubblica's Scoop, Confirmed," *The American Prospect Online*, Oct. 25, 1995; Juan Cole, *Informed Comment*, Oct. 25, 2005.

21.   *The Guardian*, Oct. 31, 2005.

22.   Woodward, *Plan of Attack*, 296.

23.   This document, headed "UNSCOM/IAEA Sensitive: Note for the File" is available on the Internet.

24.   Joseph Wilson IV, "What I Didn't Find in Africa," *New York Times*, July 6, 2003. White House press release, Jan. 29, 2003.

25.   White House press release, Jan. 28, 2003; David Frum, *The Right Man* (New York, 2003), 239.

26.   *The Guardian*, Aug. 17, 2002.

27.   *Haaretz*, Feb. 18, 2003.

28.   Bamford, *Pretext for War*, 320–21.

29.   CBS News, "A Spy Speaks Out," *60 Minutes*, April 23, 2006. Cf. Paul R. Pillar, "Intelligence, Policy and the War in Iraq," *Foreign Affairs*, March/April 2006.

30.   Tenet later called this expression "the two dumbest words I ever said." CNN.com, April 28, 2005.

31.   Woodward, *Plan of Attack*, 265.

32.   Alan Cooperman, "Bush Predicted No Iraq Casualties," *Washington Post*, Oct. 21, 2004.

33.   "Conversations with History: Robert Scales, Jr." Major General Scales is the coauthor of an account of the Iraq War, but this reference to Saddam Hussein does not appear in his book. He learned of Saddam and *Blackhawk Down* after the book was published. See www.globetrotter.berkeley/edu.

27. Napoleon in Russia

1.   Al Gore, "Iraq and the War on Terrorism," Sept. 23, 2002, www.common wealthclub.org.

2.   Bill D. Moyers, *Moyers on America* (New York, 2004).

3.   David Rothkopf, "The Committee That Runs the World," *Foreign Policy*, March/April 2005.

4.   "West Wing Loyalty," *Christian Science Monitor*, Dec. 17, 2002.

5.   U.S. House of Representatives, Committee on Government Reform, "Iraq on the Record," March 16, 2004, 29.

6.   Alan Berlow, "The Texas Clemency Memos," *The Atlantic*, July/Aug. 2003.

7.   Tucker Carlson, "Devil May Care," *Talk*, Sept. 1999.

8.   *Newsweek*, May 24, 2004.

9.   *Slate*, June 15, 2004.

10.   Adrian Levy and Cathy Scott-Clark, "One Huge U.S. Jail," *The Guardian*, March 19, 2005; *Independent on Sunday*, May 8, 2005.

11.   *The Guardian*, May 25, 2006.

12.   Richard Norton Taylor, "Bush Told Blair of 'Going beyond Iraq,'" *The Guardian*, Oct. 15, 2005.

13.   Jane Mayer, "Contact Sport: What Did the Vice President Do for Halliburton?" *The New Yorker*, Feb. 16 and 23, 2004; transcript of Lawrence Wilker-

son talk to the New America Foundation, Oct. 19, 2005, at www.thewashing
tonnote.com

14.   *Chicago Tribune*, March 20, 2003. This footage of Bush pounding the desk
       was never shown on television in the United States, although it was shown in
       the UK.

15.   Eric Wright, "How Much Is That Uzi in the Window?" *New York Times*, June
       17, 2004.

16.   *Newsday*, Oct. 2005; Woodward, *Plan of Attack*, 408.

28. Armed Missionaries

1.   Elizabeth Bumiller, "The President: No Matter Where, Keeps Battlefield
      Close," *New York Times*, March 30, 2003.

2.   University of Michigan News Service, "Democracy Must Rise from Security,
      University of Michigan Study Shows," Sept. 25, 2005; Richard Morin, "Un-
      welcome Neighbors," *Washington Post*, July 3, 2005.

3.   Fawaz Gerges, *The Far Enemy: Why Jihad Went Global* (Cambridge, England,
      2005).

4.   *The Guardian*, May 14, 2004.

5.   David Morgan, "US Ignored Forecasts of Iraqi Ethnic Turmoil," Reuters, Oct.
      12, 2005; Department of Defense, "News Transcript," Feb. 19, 2003.

6.   Ron Suskind, "Without a Doubt," *New York Times Magazine*, Oct. 17, 2004.

7.   Gareth Porter, "Iran Proposal to U.S. Offered Peace with Israel," Inter Press
      Service, May 24, 2006.

8.   TomDispatch.com, "Ann Wright on Service to Country," Nov. 11, 2005.

9.   Toby Harnden, "Ousting Saddam Would Be 'Good Business,'" *Financial
      Times*, Sept. 17, 2002.

10.   Greg Palast, "Secret Plans for Iraq's Oil," BBC News, March 18, 2005.

11.   CNN.com, April 12, 2003.

12.   CNN.com, May 1, 2003; Dana Milbank, "Explanation for Bush's Carrier
      Landing Altered," *Washington Post*, May 7, 2003.

13.   CNN.com, July 3, 2003.

14.   "Breakfast with Frost," BBC News, June 29, 2003.

15.   Department of Defense press release, Aug. 23, 2003.

16.   Josh White, "Documents Tell of Improvisation by GIs," *Washington Post*,
      Aug. 3, 2005.

17.   Juan Cole, "Informed Comment," May 16, 2005; M. Gregg Bloch and
      Jonathan H. Marks, "Doing Unto Others as They Did Unto Us," *New York
      Times*, Nov. 14, 2005.

18.   Agence France Press, "Cheney's Staff Backed Policies That Led to Prisoner
      Abuse," Nov. 3, 2005; Dan Froomkin, "White House Briefing," *Washington
      Post*, Nov. 5, 2005.

19.   Associated Press, Nov. 7, 2005.

20.   Steve Coll and Susan B. Glasser, "Terrorists Turn to the Web," *Washington
      Post*, Aug. 7, 2005; Ashraf al-Taie, "U.S. Nabs al-Qaida Web site Producer,"
      MSNBC.com, Oct. 16, 2005.

21.   Robert A. Pape, "The Strategic Logic of Suicide Terrorism," *American Political*

Science Review (Aug. 2003). There is also a useful interview with Pape: Scott McConnell, "The Logic of Suicide Terrorism," *Asian Tribune*, July 14, 2004.

22. The memo is dated Oct. 16, 2003. It was published in *USA Today*, May 20, 2005.

23. Georgie Anne Geyer, "Bush Sr.'s 'Message' to Bush Jr." *Boston Globe*, Oct. 18, 2003.

24. *Project on Defense Alternatives*, "Vicious Circle: The Dynamics of Occupation and Resistance in Iraq," May 18, 2005.

29. Iraq Syndrome

1. Norma Percy, "An Almighty Splash," *The Guardian*, Oct. 24, 2005.

2. There are numerous Benny Hinn Web sites, including a CBC documentary that shows Benny, dressed entirely in white, wrestling Satan. You might have thought Satan would know better.

3. Seymour Hersh, "Plan B," *The New Yorker*, June 28, 2004.

4. L. Paul Bremer III, *My Year in Iraq* (New York, 2006), 78 passim.

5. Hersh, "Plan B."

6. White House press release, Dec. 14, 2003.

7. See the interview with Jalal Talabani at *Middle East Online*, Nov. 2, 2005.

8. Matthew Gutman, "Will Rolling Heads Crush Rebellion, or Iraq Itself?" *Jerusalem Post*, April 11, 2004.

9. *Washington Times*, Nov. 19, 2004.

10. CNN.com, Feb. 4, 2005.

11. *Washington Post*, Jan. 16, 2005.

12. *Washington Post*, Nov. 12, 2005.

13. Sara Daniel and Sami Yousafzay, "Terrorisme: Le Retour de Talibans," *Le Nouvel Observateur*, Nov. 3, 2005.

14. NPR Web site, March 29, 2005; Department of Defense press release, March 29, 2005.

15. *Boston Globe*, June 10, 2005.

16. CNN.com, June 20, 2005; *Time Online*, June 19, 2005.

17. Mohammed Yahya Nawroz and Lester W. Grau, "The Soviet War in Afghanistan," Foreign Military Studies Office, Fort Leavenworth, Kansas, June 1996.

18. John Robb, "How Big Is the Iraqi Insurgency?" Oct. 14, 2005. This is posted on Robb's "Global Guerrillas" Web site. A summary can be found in Robb's op-ed "Open-Source War," in *New York Times*, October 15, 2005.

19. Mahan Abedin, "Iraq's Divided Insurgents," *Mideast Monitor*, February 2006.

20. *Human Security Report, 2005*, Parts I and V.

Acknowledgments

Books such as this could not be written without the treasure trove of documents and images held in presidential libraries and without the expert guidance of the archivists who make them available to researchers. My greatest debt is to the staffs at the Dwight D. Eisenhower Library in Abilene, Kansas; the Harry S. Truman Library in Independence, Missouri; the LBJ Library in Ausin, Texas; the George H. W. Bush Library in College Station, Texas; and the National Archives staff of Archive 2 in College Park, Maryland, who are responsible for the Richard M. Nixon presidential materials that are destined, eventually, to be deposited at the Nixon presidential library.

I have also benefited from the help of librarians and archivists at Harvard University, the New York Public Library on Forty-second Street, the U. S. Army Military History Institute in Carlisle, Pennsylvania, and the Library of Congress.

In the course of writing and researching this book I have had two editors: John Glusman, who was there at the beginning, and Thomas LeBien, who was there at the end, ably assisted by June Kim.

Others who have helped me along the way have been two old friends, Bob and Carol Hopper, who invaribly made me feel welcome in their home on numerous research trips to Washington, and Joe and Susan Coppola, who have similarly made visits to Boston a pleasure.

I have also, for the first time but surely not the last, found the Internet valuable for serious research. Two Web sites in particular have proven helpful. One is *TomDispatch*, compiled and written by my friend Tom Englehart. The other is Jaun Cole's *Informed Comment*. They have navigated a path through the toils of the Iraq War that I found invaluable.

Finally, I wish to thank my agent, Michael Congdon, who has been supportive and helpful throughout.

Index

Abu Ghraib, 371, 372
Acheson, Dean, 32, 52, 55, 58, 65–66,
    72–77, 83, 95, 116–18, 126, 188,
    189, 212, 275, 282, 345, 398n11;
    China and, 83, 86–91, 136; Korea
    and, 129–32, 135–37, 144, 150,
    153, 154, 156, 157, 160, 164, 171,
    175; Palestine issue, 95, 97, 98; as
    secretary of state, 116–18, 131;
    Truman and, 116–18
Adams, John, 146
Afghanistan, 5, 317, 319, 334, 373,
    383–84; insurgency, 383–84; Soviet
    invasion of, 305, 317, 318, 365, 385;
    Taliban, 335, 337, 338, 358, 373; tor-
    ture in, 359; U.S. invasion of, 5,
    334–38, 339, 340, 341, 343, 346,
    353, 355, 375, 391
Africa, 74
Agnew, Spiro, 297, 299
Aiken, George, 268, 271
Air Force, U.S., 110, 111, 115, 120,
    121, 122, 123, 128, 248, 335; Gulf
    War, 312, 313; in Vietnam, 250–56,
    266, 290
Alaska, 131
Albania, 113–14
Albright, Madeleine, 322
Alito, Samuel, 392
Allawi, Ayad, 320–21, 322, 370, 376,
    382
Almond, Edward, 157, 167
Al Qaeda, 318, 319, 332, 334–38,
    339–41, 365, 373–74, 386; Iraq con-
    nection invented by Bush, 335,
    342–43, 354, 360
Al-Sabah, Sheikh, 306
al-Sadr, Muqtada, 378
Al-Zawahiri, Ayman, 339
American Enterprise Institute, 319
American Legion, 28, 29
Anderson, Samuel, 204, 205
Anglo-American Committee, 98, 100
Annan, Kofi, 359

Anti-Ballistic Missile Treaty, 224
Ap Bac, 239
appeasement myth, 133–34, 144
Aqaba, 375
Arab American News, The, 324
Arabs, 104, 105, 179, 306, 317–18, 324, 365–66; partition of Palestine, 100–105
Arbenz, Jacobo, 180
Armenia, 56
Armitage, Richard, 320
Army, U.S., 111, 120, 122, 128, 196–97, 213, 248, 362, 394n27; CentCom troops, 338, 384; in Iraq, 362–63, 364, 384; in Korea, 152–53, 155, 166, 169, 171; in Vietnam, 250–56, 279
Army of the Republic of Vietnam (ARVN), 195–200, 209, 217, 239, 253, 269, 289–90, 298
atomic bomb, 7, 8, 18, 53; Hiroshima, 50–53; Manhattan Project, 19, 27, 40, 43–45, 50, 124, 127, 139; Nagasaki, 51; Soviet, 53, 67, 124–28, 142, 177, 218, 246; Truman and, 19–20, 25–27, 40, 43–45, 50–53, 66, 116, 122, 124–28, 170–71, 396n43; U.S. test fire in New Mexico, 27, 40, 44, 45; *see also* nuclear weapons
Atomic Energy Commission (AEC), 122, 125
Attlee, Clement, 48, 170–71; Potsdam Conference, 49
Austin, Warren, 101
Australia, 98, 204, 205, 225, 226, 268
Austria, 247
Azerbaijan, 56

Baath Party, 10, 366, 368, 369
Badr Brigade, 378
Baghdad, 6, 311, 354; Green Zone, 382; UN headquarters bombing, 370; U.S. invasion of, 361, 362, 363, 367, 368
Baker, James III, 307, 308, 309, 346
Baldwin, Hanson W., 248
Balfour, Arthur, 93–94
Balfour Declaration, 99
Balkans, 25, 77, 362
Ball, George, 193, 226, 274, 276, 278

Bandar bin Sultan, Prince, 307, 320
Bao Dai, 91
Barak, Ehud, 377
Barr, William P., 310
Baruch, Bernard, 125–26
Basra, 378
Bataan, 204
Bay of Pigs, 188, 191, 224
Beijing, 88, 90, 238, 290–91
Beirut, 180, 301, 386
Ben-Gurion, David, 341
Bentsen, Lloyd, 329
Berlin, 39–41, 112, 186; blockade and airlift, 114–18; all of Berlin Wall, 64
Berlusconi, Silvio, 348
Bible, 35
Biden, Joe, 366–67
Binh Gia, 239
bin Laden, Osama, 317–18, 319, 334–38, 339–40, 341, 355, 365, 373, 383; escape of, 338, 339
biological weapons, 343, 349
birthrates, Third World, 7
Bishop, Maurice, 302
Black, Cofer, 335–38
Black Hawk Down (film), 10, 352
blacks, 99; desegregation of military, 121; segregation of, 121, 231
Blair, Tony, 343–44; Bush and, 343–44, 359–61
Bohlen, Charles, 214–15
Bonesteel, Charles, 129, 141
Bosnia, 330
Boston Globe, The, 331
Bradlee, Ben, 187
Bradley, Omar, 109, 136, 143, 156, 173, 275, 282
Braun, Eva, 41
Brazil, 345
Bremer, L. Paul, 368, 369–70, 376–77, 379, 380
Brezhnev, Leonid, 234, 238, 242
Buck, Pearl, 80
Buddhism, 183, 198
Bulgaria, 48, 55–58, 77
Bundy, McGeorge, 188–89, 193, 209, 212, 262–63, 275; Vietnam War and, 209, 212, 216–20, 229, 213, 239–40, 245, 251–54, 262–63, 282
Burma, 87, 187

Bush, Barbara, 328
Bush, George Herbert Walker, 4, 5,
    304–15, 329, 331, 334, 353, 357;
    failure to overthrow Saddam, 320,
    324, 325, 331; Gulf War and, 4, 5, 6,
    307–13, 320, 324; interventionism,
    305–15; in Kuwait, 325; military
    service, 304; 1992 election loss, 315,
    324; Panama and, 305–306; as vice
    president, 304; views on Iraq War,
    374
Bush, George W., 3, 4; Afghanistan war,
    334–38, 339, 340, 341, 343, 346,
    353, 355, 375, 391; Tony Blair and,
    343–44, 359–61; changes focus to
    Iraq, 340; contempt for UN, 331,
    350, 354, 359, 360; death penalty
    views, 358; drinking and partying of,
    326–27; emotionalism of, 4–5, 328,
    340, 353, 357, 367; Geneva Conven-
    tions rejected by, 224–25, 358–59; as
    governor of Texas, 327, 328, 343,
    358; "instincts" of, 340, 367; intellec-
    tual limitations of, 324, 331, 340;
    interventionism, 330, 335–38, 341;
    Iraq and, 324–25, 331–35, 339–52,
    353–89; Iraq-9/11 connection in-
    vented by, 335, 341–43, 354, 360; Is-
    rael and, 332, 342, 350–51; loyalty
    demanded by, 357; military and, 329–
    30, 354, 356, 362, 371–72; "military
    necessity" doctrine, 372; "Mission
    Accomplished" photo op, 370; in Na-
    tional Guard, 329; Niger yellowcake
    story, 347–50, 357; 9/11 response,
    334–38, 340, 354; preventive war
    doctrine, 360–61; religion of, 327,
    328, 329, 337, 340, 341, 344, 375,
    376; Saddam and, 324–25, 335, 342,
    344, 353–55, 360; score to settle for
    his father, 4–5, 324–25, 331; signing
    statements issued by, 391–92;
    Supreme Court and, 392; torture pol-
    icy, 358–59, 371–72; tough-guy per-
    sona, 333–34, 336, 340, 348, 352,
    358, 370; 2000 election, 323–24,
    330–31; 2004 election, 376, 380,
    381; unilateralism, 10–13; "unitary
    executive" theory, 391–92; "Wanted
    Dead or Alive" speech, 336, 338; war
    on terrorism, 334–38, 339–41, 354,
    356–58, 373–74, 380, 381, 388,
    392; WMD argument, 343–52
Bush, Jeb, 321
Bush, Laura, 325, 353
Bush, Vannevar, 53
Byrnes, James, 16, 17, 19, 24, 27, 39,
    40, 45–46, 47, 49–50, 52, 55–58,
    70, 72, 77–78, 141

Cabot, John M., 242, 244
Cairo Conference (1943), 87, 129, 140
Cambodia, 87, 187, 225, 235, 260, 265,
    287, 292; bombing and invasion of,
    287–88; civil war, 288
Canada, 98, 226–27
Card, Andrew, 334
Carter, Jimmy, 299, 300–301, 304, 311;
    Iran hostage crisis, 301
Castro, Fidel, 188, 191, 193, 246, 302
Catholicism, 183, 188, 200
Cedar Falls, 269
Celler, Emanuel, 99–100, 104–105
Central Intelligence Agency (CIA), 88,
    108, 178, 180, 190, 191, 200, 218,
    270, 300, 312, 317, 355; covert aid to
    Nicaraguan Contras, 303–304; cre-
    ation of, 112–13; Iraq and, 347, 351,
    366, 371; Vietnam and, 250, 262,
    272–75
Chalabi, Ahmed, 321, 322, 363, 369,
    370, 377
Chamberlain, Stephen J., 109
Chambers, Oswald, My Utmost for His
    Highest, 327
Chamoun, Camille, 179–80
Charles I, King of England, 299
chemical weapons, 303, 310, 343, 349
Cheney, Richard, 4, 305, 320, 321, 333,
    334, 343; draft avoided by, 356; Gulf
    War and, 308–11; Iraq and, 308–11,
    343, 346–47, 354–57, 371–72, 377,
    384–85; neocon views, 320–21, 342,
    354–57; as secretary of defense, 305;
    as vice president, 332, 343, 354–55
Chen Yi, 242–45, 252, 253, 263,
    407n15, 408n16
Chicago Tribune, 172
China, 4, 6, 10, 11, 13, 48, 74, 79–92,
    216–17, 247; birthrate, 7; George W.

China (*cont.*)
   Bush and, 332, 345, 387; civil war, 4,
      80–92, 137; communism, 80–92,
      140, 142, 190, 218, 238, 256; econ-
      omy, 87, 90, 91, 174, 233, 238, 254–
      55; Eisenhower and, 180–84, 190;
      GMD government, 80–92, 136, 154–
      56; Great Leap Forward, 194, 238;
      Johnson and, 213–20, 216–20, 253–
      54; Kennedy and, 199–200; Korean
      War and, 129, 136, 141–44, 154–56,
      160–62, 163–75, 256, 260; military
      industrialization, 254–55; Nixon and,
      288–93; nuclear weapons, 7, 243,
      250, 289; People's Republic estab-
      lished, 90; rise of, 387, 388, 389;
      Roosevelt and, 79–80, 87; Soviets
      and, 80, 86–88, 91, 131–32, 136,
      144, 160, 165–66, 165–75, 181,
      190, 218, 260, 288–89; Third Front,
      254–55; Truman and, 79–92, 142,
      154–56, 164, 169, 213; UN Security
      Council seat issue, 135, 142, 291;
      Vietnam and, 183–84, 189, 190–91,
      215, 220, 226, 233–34, 238–45,
      249–50, 253–56, 259–68, 281,
      290–93, 295–96, 298, 408nn15–16
China White Paper, 84–85, 89
Churchill, John, Duke of Marlborough,
      146
Churchill, Winston, 20, 24, 25, 41, 48,
      54, 79, 134, 146, 170; "iron curtain"
      speech, 61–63, 65; Potsdam Confer-
      ence, 41–49, 140; Truman and, 43–
      44, 48, 49, 50, 54, 60–63; voted out
      of office, 48, 49; at Yalta, 20, 25, 129
civil liberties, increasing restrictions on,
      382
Civil War, 147, 166, 254
Clark, Tom, 396n43
Clarke, Richard, 335
Claudius, Emperor, 9
Clay, Lucius D., 108–109, 115, 152
Clayton, Will, 76
Clifford, Clark, 68–70, 72, 75, 95–105,
      106, 122, 275, 276; Johnson and,
      278–79; Palestine issue, 95, 97–105;
      as speechwriter, 75, 95; Vietnam War
      and, 254, 278–79, 282
Clifford-Elsey report, 68–70

Cline, Ray, 207
Clinton, Bill, 315–23, 324, 333, 343;
      draft avoided by, 316; humanitarian
      intervention policy, 323, 330; Iraq
      and, 322, 323; military and, 316–17;
      1992 election, 315, 324; 1993 World
      Trade Center bombing, 317–19; sex
      scandal and impeachment, 319, 328;
      Somalia and, 315–16, 317, 323
Coard, Bernard, 302–303
Cohen, William, 332
Cold War, 4, 12, 175, 177, 260, 261,
      275, 286, 356; beginnings of, 64;
      Eisenhower and, 176–85; end of,
      304, 305; in Europe vs. Asia, 189–90;
      Kennedy and, 190–91; Korea and,
      144, 175; 1948 war scare, 106–13,
      115–16; NSC-68, 127–28; Truman
      and, 64, 67–70, 106–18, 124–28,
      138–39, 144; Vietnam and, 254;
      X article, 63–64
Collier's magazine, "Our Armed Forces
      Must Be Unified," 120, 400n4
Collins, J. Lawton, 137, 157
Colombia, 224, 305
colonialism, 6, 12, 70, 117, 322; British,
      12, 93–94, 102–104, 268, 306, 322,
      365, 380; French, 70–72, 91, 137,
      182
commander in chief, 145–46; war pow-
      ers and, 145–47
communism, 4, 6, 48, 55, 70–72, 117,
      138, 175, 206, 207, 261; Chinese,
      80–92, 140, 142, 190, 218, 238, 256;
      end of, 304; espionage, 139; Korean,
      129, 141; Soviet, 42, 59–66, 67–78,
      106–18, 124–28, 177, 304; Viet-
      namese, 71, 91, 136, 182–85
Conant, James Bryant, 128
Congress, 4, 6; George W. Bush and,
      347, 354, 388; Gulf War and, 310,
      312–13; Iraq and, 322, 347, 354;
      Johnson and, 217, 226, 230, 231–32,
      264–65; Korea and, 129, 131, 144–
      48; Truman and, 18–19, 35, 47–48,
      75–77, 85–87, 106, 108–11, 129,
      138, 145–48; Vietnam War and, 217,
      231–32, 247–48, 251, 264–65, 268,
      281, 294, 296–98; on war powers,
      146, 147, 310

Congressional Medal of Honor, 32, 151
Constitution, U.S., 145–47, 224, 392
containment, 64, 112, 127–28, 138,
    163, 244, 264
Council of Foreign Ministers (CFM),
    42, 48, 49, 55, 57
Crimean War, 164
Cronkite, Walter, 281
Crowe, William, 307
Cuba, 8, 186, 188, 191, 193, 224, 246–
    47, 302; Bay of Pigs, 188, 191, 224
Cuban Missile Crisis, 8, 197, 212,
    246–47
Czechoslovakia, 107–108

Dardanelles, 46, 47, 64, 65
Dar es Salaam, 319
Darfur, 13
Darwin, Charles, 382
Davies, Joseph E., 22–23, 42, 43,
    47, 49
death penalty, 358
declinism, 299–300, 301, 330
Defense Department: neocon views,
    320–35, 343–52, 354–63; Truman
    and, 111, 122–24, 129, 164
de Gaulle, Charles, 20, 209, 214–15,
    274
democracy, 12, 128, 163
Democratic Party, 16–17, 100, 145, 201
Dewey, Thomas, 17, 84, 99–100
Diem, Ngo Dinh, 183–84, 189–200,
    203, 209–10, 214, 217, 221–22
Dien Bien Phu, 182, 183, 186, 189
Donovan, William, 112
Drumheller, Tyler, 351
Dulles, Allen, 191
Dulles, John Foster, 181, 183, 247
Durbrow, Elbridge, 194
Dyson, Freeman, 127

Early, Steve, 17, 18
Easter Offensive, 292
East Germany, 114, 115
Egypt, 104, 179
Einstein, Albert, 33, 269
Eisenhower, Dwight D., 24–25, 30, 39,
    51, 66, 106, 120, 121, 151, 173,
    186–87, 202; China and, 180–84,
    190; interventionism, 177–85, 187,

208; Korean War and, 176–77, 236;
    as president, 176–85; Soviets and,
    181–85; Vietnam and, 182–85, 187,
    190, 208, 209, 221–22, 223, 273
Ekeus, Rolf, 348, 349
Ellsberg, Daniel, 286
Elsey, George, 68–70, 74, 143, 158–59
Ertegun, Mehmet Munir, 65
Europe, 10, 11, 13, 74, 98, 189, 190,
    221, 247, 365; post–World War II,
    43–52; see also specific countries
European Union, 10
Exxon, 368

Fahd, King, 310, 318
Fallaci, Oriana, 294
Fallujah, 379, 380, 384
fascism, 6, 48, 117
Fedayeen Saddam, 369, 370, 386
Federal Bureau of Investigation (FBI),
    319
Federal Loyalty-Security Program,
    138–39
Finland, 107, 247; pact with Soviet
    Union, 107
Forbes, Steve, 321
Ford, Gerald, 297, 298, 299
Foreign Affairs, 63
Formosa, 85, 87–92, 131, 136, 137,
    140, 145, 154, 168, 181; U.S. de-
    fense of, 87–92, 168, 170; see also
    Taiwan
Forrestal, James, 52–53, 58, 62–65, 70,
    84, 88, 95, 98, 99, 104, 108, 115,
    121, 194; indecisiveness as secretary
    of defense, 123–24, 128; 1948 war
    scare, 108–12; suicide of, 128
Forrestal, Michael, 194, 201
Fortas, Abe, 273–74, 278, 282
France, 29, 30, 61, 79, 146, 154, 214–
    15, 225, 226, 260, 306, 314, 348;
    colonialism, 70–72, 91, 137, 182;
    communism in, 71, 72; post–World
    War II, 71–72; Revolution, 374, 388;
    war in Indochina, 70–72, 136, 137,
    161, 182–85, 189, 209, 214–15,
    225, 226; World War I, 29–30, 46,
    47, 94; World War II, 133, 134
Franco, Francisco, 48
Franks, Tommy, 338, 363, 369

Fromkin, David, *A Peace to End All Peace*, 366
Fulbright, J. William, 231, 316

Gadhafi, Muammar, 348
Galbraith, John Kenneth, 195, 274
Garner, Jay, 368, 376
Gavin, James M., 121
Gehlen, Reinhard, 113, 114
Geneva Accords (1954), 183, 184, 186, 189, 194, 208, 209, 225, 233, 241
Geneva Conventions, 173–74; George W. Bush and, 224–25, 358–59; Truman and, 174
George II, King of England, 146
Germany, 20, 39, 65, 110, 147, 310; Berlin blockade and airlift, 114–18; deutsche mark, 114; Nazi, 20–24, 69, 74, 109; post–World War I, 47; war surrender and reparations, 24, 43–51; World War I, 46; World War II, 20–24, 39, 43, 69, 74, 143, 264
Ghana, 260
Giap, Vo Nguyen, 237, 239, 292
Gilpatric, Roswell, 224
global warming, 10, 357–58, 388
Global War on Terror (GWOT), 3, 7, 10, 336, 339–40, 356–58, 373–74, 380, 381, 388, 392
Goldsmith, Peter, 359
Goldwater, Barry, 228, 230, 236–37
Gonzalez, Alberto, 328, 358–59, 372
Gorbachev, Mikhail, 313
Gore, Al, 331, 355; against Iraq War, 355
Goss, Porter, 385
Graham, Billy, 326–27
Graham, Wallace H., 36–37, 95, 137, 140, 395n27
Great Britain, 12, 20, 146, 154, 181, 225, 226, 299, 304; Al Qaeda in, 386; Churchill's "iron curtain" speech and, 61–63; colonialism, 93–94, 102–104, 268, 306, 322–23, 365, 380; Gulf War, 310, 314; intelligence, 113–14, 178, 179, 300, 344; Iran and, 178, 300; Iraq and, 310, 314, 322–23, 343–44, 359–61, 365, 378; Korean War and, 170–71; Kuwait and, 306; Palestine and, 93–94, 99,

102–104; post–World War II, 48–49, 113–16; rearmament program, 134; World War I, 46, 47; World War II, 43–44, 133–34
Greece, 44, 72–77, 83, 129, 130, 216, 365; civil war, 72–77; Truman and, 72–77
Greene, Wallace, 248
Grenada, 302–303
Groves, Leslie, 19, 53
Guantánamo Bay, 359, 371
Guatemala, 180, 379
guerrilla warfare, 7–8
Gulf of Tonkin, *see* Tonkin Gulf
Gulf War (1991), 4, 5, 6, 307–15, 320, 324, 349, 368; beginning of, 313; events leading to, 307–13; UN role, 308, 309–11
Guo Min Dang, 242

Haas, Richard, 344
Hadley, Stephen, 347, 349, 357
Haig, Alexander, 297
Hainan Island, 168
Haiphong, 239, 262, 292, 296
Haiti, 13, 388
Haldeman, Bob, 287, 295
Hamilton, Alexander, 146
Hamza, Khidir Abdul Abbas, 348–49
Hannegan, Robert, 16, 100
Hanoi, 186, 236, 280; bombing of, 262, 292, 295–96
Harkins, Paul D., 194, 196, 197–98
Harlow, Bill, 351
Harriman, Averell, 20, 23, 24, 46, 56, 59, 194, 256, 274, 275, 276; Korean War and, 155–57
Hartke, Vance, 264–65
Hebert, F. Edward, 278
Helms, Richard, 270
Henderson, Loy, 98, 102
Herrick, John J., 227, 231
Herskowitz, Mickey, 324, 353
Herzl, Theodor, 95
Hess, Moses, 95
Hillenkoetter, R. H., 108, 112
Hilsman, Roger, 196–98
Hinn, Benny, 375
Hirohito, Emperor, 51
Hiroshima, 50–53

Hiss, Alger, 139
Hitler, Adolf, 20, 23–25, 40, 41–42,
    53–69, 74, 109, 117, 133–34, 265;
    suicide of, 24, 41
Hizbollah, 302, 303, 367
Ho Chi Minh, 71, 91, 182, 183, 184,
    189, 213, 227, 233–34, 241, 244,
    251, 256, 280, 283, 287
Ho Chi Minh Trail, 233, 289, 290
Hodge, John R., 130, 144
Holocaust, 23, 93, 94
Hong Kong, 87, 90
Hoover, Herbert, 90, 91
Hoover, J. Edgar, 138
House Armed Services Committee,
    250
House of Representatives, 145, 313
House Un-American Activities Commit-
    tee, 138
Houston, Sam, 327
Hoxha, Enver, 113
Hull, John, 394n27
Humphrey, Hubert, 256, 282–83, 284–
    85; Johnson and, 284–85
Hurley, Patrick J., 81
Hussein, King, 320
Hussein, Saddam, 4, 10, 303, 305–15,
    320, 369; George W. Bush and, 324–
    25, 335, 352, 344, 353–55, 360; cap-
    ture of, 377, 382; failed coups
    against, 320–21; Gulf War and, 307–
    15, 320; Kuwait invaded by, 306–10,
    318; overthrow of, 362–63, 370; U.S.
    arms sold to, 303; weapons of mass
    destruction and, 310, 323, 325, 331,
    332, 338, 343, 344, 346–52
Huxley, Thomas, 382
hydrogen bomb, 7, 126

Ibn Sa'ūd, 97, 99
ICBMs, 246
Ickes, Harold, 205
immigration, postwar, 98
imperialism, 117
Imperial Japanese Army, 130
Imperial Japanese Navy, 8
Inchon, 155–58, 163, 166, 171
India, 90, 247, 388
Indochina, 70—72, 91, 136, 137, 154,
    161, 176, 181–85, 216

Inmum Gun, 139, 147, 149–50, 152–
    55, 157–62, 175
intelligence, 8, 109, 178; British, 113–
    14, 178, 179, 300, 344; faked docu-
    ments on Iraq, 343, 347–51, 357,
    360; Truman and, 109, 110–14
International Atomic Energy Agency
    (IAEA), 347–50
International Control Commission, 186,
    227, 230, 241
International Criminal Court, 12
international waters, 228; free naviga-
    tion rights on, 46–47; Maddox inci-
    dent and, 227–33
Internet, 373, 386
interventionism, 9–11, 300; George H.
    W. Bush, 305–15; George W. Bush,
    330, 335–38, 341; Eisenhower, 177–
    85, 187, 208; Reagan, 301–303; Tru-
    man, 9–11, 72–79, 83–92, 117–18,
    132, 148
Irish Republican Army (IRA), 10
Iran, 55, 56, 69, 74, 143, 177–79, 334,
    341, 349, 350, 373, 386; George W.
    Bush and, 345, 361, 367, 387; Carter
    and, 300–301; hostage crisis, 301,
    303; oil, 178–79, 300, 301, 307, 387;
    Soviets and, 56, 58; Truman and,
    56–58
Iran-Contra, 303–304
Iran-Iraq war, 302, 303, 305, 306
Iraq, 7, 10, 179, 306–15, 349; Afghan
    jihad schools in, 383–84; army, 10,
    320, 369–70, 383; birthrate, 7;
    George W. Bush and, 324–25, 331–
    35, 339–52, 353–89; civil war, 383;
    collapse of security in, 374–89; Gulf
    War, 4, 5, 6, 307–15, 320, 324, 346;
    Hussein regime, 10, 303, 306–15,
    320, 369; IAEA inspections, 348–49;
    insurgency, 7, 362, 364–89; -Iran
    war, 302, 303, 305, 306; Kuwait in-
    vaded by, 306–10, 318; Niger yellow-
    cake story, 347–50, 357; 9/11
    connection invented by Bush, 335,
    341–43, 354, 360; oil, 306–308,
    322, 333, 361–62, 367–68, 387; oil-
    for-food program, 322, 333; postwar
    government and elections, 368, 376–
    82; privatization of, 367–68; recon-

Iraq (*cont.*)
struction of, 369, 376–82; "return of sovereignty," 377–78; Russia and, 306, 307, 313; sanctions, 308, 322, 324, 333, 369; UN and, 308–11, 322, 323, 333, 350, 359, 369, 370, 376, 380, 382; U.S. invasion and occupation of, 224–25, 344, 361, 362–63, 364–89; weapons of mass destruction and, 310, 323, 325, 331, 332, 338, 343, 346–52; xenophobia, 364–65; *see also* Iraq War
Iraqi National Accord (INA), 320–21, 322
Iraqi National Congress (INC), 321, 322
Iraq Liberation Act (1998), 322
Iraq Syndrome, 389
Iraq War, 3, 4–5, 11, 12, 13, 224, 344, 364–89; casualties, 374, 384; events leading to, 339–62; Falluja, 379, 380, 384; insurgency and, 364–89; invasion of Baghdad, 362–63, 367–68; oil and, 361–62, 367–68; torture, 358–59, 371–72
Iron Triangle, 269
Islam, 6, 74, 179, 306, 313, 318–19; growth of jihadi movement, 365–74
isolationism, 76
Israel, 95, 342, 367, 386, 388; George W. Bush and, 332, 342, 350–51; creation of, 95, 99, 104–105; intelligence, 351; Lebanon and, 302; occupation of West Bank and Gaza Strip, 341; summit with Palestinians (2003), 375
Italy, 43, 61, 72, 147, 378; intelligence, 347–48
Iwo Jima, 121

Jackson, Andrew, 29, 35
Jacobson, Eddie, 94, 101
Japan, 8, 26, 55, 70, 80, 88, 98, 131, 137, 147, 152, 182, 208, 221, 247, 310, 378; atomic bombs dropped on, 50–53; attack on Pearl Harbor, 8; economy, 87–88, 129; Soviet Union and, 51, 69; surrender, 51–53, 141, 151; World War II, 8, 19, 25–27, 38, 44–45, 48–51, 79, 129, 204–205, 224, 394n27

Jews, 23, 35; Holocaust, 23, 93, 94; homeland problem, 93–105; Katyn Forest atrocities, 23, 42; Truman and, 93–105; vote, 100, 104
Jiang, Madame, 249–50
Jiang Jieshi, 20, 80–92, 129, 136, 140, 154–56, 180, 217, 249–50
jihadi movement, growth of, 365–74
Johnson, Harold K., 248, 249
Johnson, Lady Bird, 232, 249, 358, 283
Johnson, Louis, 88–89, 128–29, 135; Korea and, 129–31, 135–37, 143, 156–58
Johnson, Lyndon B., 3, 4, 287, 354, 370, 380; becomes president, 202–203, 208; China and, 213–20, 216–20, 242–45, 253–54; Congress and, 217, 226, 230, 231–32, 264–65; Congressional career, 206; emotionalism of, 4, 6, 213, 283, 357; health problems of, 232; intellectual limitations of, 258; *Maddox* incident, 227–33; military and, 206–207, 247–51; 1961 trip to Vietnam, 191–92, 207–208; 1964 presidential election, 216, 228, 232–33, 235–37; persona, 258; reelection not sought by, 274–75, 277, 282–85; religion of, 259; resignation speech, 282–83; rivalry with Kennedy, 6, 257–59; SEATO and, 223–26, 267–69; Silver Star of, 205, 206; Soviet Union and, 206, 246; Tonkin Gulf Resolution, 231–34, 253; trapped by Vietnam situation, 261; as vice president, 191–92, 206–208; Vietnam and, 191–92, 203, 207–10, 213–85; Vietnamization strategy, 216, 278–79; vulgar behavior of, 212–13; WOMs' advice to, 275–76, 282; World War II experience, 204–206
Joint Chiefs of Staff (JCS), 123, 131, 172, 206–207, 246–48; Johnson and, 246–50, 262
Jordan, 104, 320, 322, 366, 369
Judd, Walter, 82–83
Junction City, 269

Kabul, 335, 337
Kaesong, 141–42, 175

Kamel, Hussein, 348, 350, 351, 366
Karbala, 366, 379
Karzai, Hamid, 337
Kattenburg, Paul, 274
Katyn Forest atrocities, 23, 42
Kennan, George, 59, 74, 76, 112, 114, 127, 153, 190; Long Telegram, 59–60, 62–66; X article, 63–64
Kennedy, Edward, 374
Kennedy, Jacqueline, 257
Kennedy, John F., 4, 6, 186–201, 204, 207–208, 210, 257–59, 278, 354; assassination of, 4, 201, 202, 203, 273, 336, 354; Bay of Pigs, 188, 191, 224; charm of, 258; China and, 199–200; Cold War and, 190–91; Cuban Missile Crisis, 8, 197, 212, 246–47; media and, 197, 258; 1964 presidential campaign, 201; Dean Rusk and, 211–12; SEATO and, 226; Vietnam and, 186–201, 216, 222, 238, 258–59, 273, 274
Kennedy, Robert, 212, 213, 263; assassination of, 284; 1968 presidential campaign, 282, 284
Kenya, 268
Kerry, John, 313
Khalilzad, Zalmay, 321
Khanh, Nguyen, 214, 216, 217, 218, 221
Khe Sanh, 277, 279–80
Khmer Rouge, 288
Khomeini, Ayatollah, 301, 303
Khrushchev, Nikita, 8, 174, 177, 188, 190, 234, 238, 246; China and, 181, 288–89
Kim Il Sung, 130, 140–42, 148, 149, 152, 165, 168, 174, 175
King, Ernest J., 26, 124
Kissinger, Henry, 286, 311; in China, 290–91; *Nuclear Weapons and Foreign Policy*, 292; Vietnam War and, 286–88, 290, 293–97
Knowland, William F., 82
Kong Le, 187
Korea, 6, 7, 47, 87, 129–77, 209, 215, 226, 244, 261; birthrate, 7; communism, 129, 141; Eisenhower and, 176–77; KPR government, 129–30; reunification efforts, 130, 140; Truman and, 129–32, 135–48, 149–62, 163–75; Yalta accords on, 129; *see also* Korean War; North Korea; South Korea
Korean War, 3, 4, 5, 6, 13, 132, 133–77, 206, 226, 243, 244, 255, 354; beginning of, 132; Chinese role in, 129, 136, 141–44, 154–56, 160–62, 163–75, 256, 260; Eisenhower and, 176–77, 236; end of, 174–75, 176; Inchon, 155–58, 163, 166, 171; nuclear weapon option, 170–71, 176; POWs, 173–74; as prestige war, 175; Soviet role in, 129, 130, 135, 137, 140–44, 153–54, 165–75, 244; 38th parallel, 163–65, 168, 171, 241; truce talks, 173, 182, 260, 279; Truman and, 129–32, 135–48, 149–62, 163–75, 259–60; UN role, 135, 137, 140, 143, 148, 150, 163, 165–68, 171; U.S. enters, 148; win-the-war offensive, 169
Kosovo, 323, 330
Kosygin, Aleksey, 234, 238, 240, 242
Kowloon, 87, 90
Krug, Julius, 83
Krulak, Victor, 195
Kung, H. H., 89
Kurds, 303, 320, 322, 344, 346, 368, 371, 378, 382, 383
Kuril Islands, 38, 55, 64
Kuwait, 4, 5, 306, 320, 325, 378; Gulf War, 4, 5, 6, 307–15, 320; Hussein's invasion of, 306–10, 318; oil, 306–308
Ky, Nguyen Cao, 265, 268, 270, 288
Kyushu, 25, 26

Laird, Melvin, 288
Lam Son 719, 289–90
Laos, 87, 186–89, 207, 219, 225, 227, 265, 287, 292; invasion of, 289–90
Latin America, 180, 221, 303–304
Lawrence, T. E., 368, 385
League of Nations, 16, 35
Leahy, William D., 21, 24, 28, 39, 40, 42, 57, 65
Lebanon, 179, 301–302, 303, 341, 386; Israel and, 302; marine barracks bombing, 302; U.S. embassy bombing, 302

Lee, Robert E., 29
LeMay, Curtis, 248, 249, 250; Vietnam
    War and, 250, 252, 262
Lemberger, Ernst, 259
Lend-Lease, 46, 56, 81
Lenin, Nikolai, 20
Libya, 334, 341, 348, 350
Life magazine, 63, 75
Lilienthal, David, 126
Lincoln, Abraham, 147, 259
Lindsey, Lawrence, 367–68
Li Zongren, 85, 92
Lodge, Henry Cabot, 198, 200, 203,
    206, 209–10, 214, 218, 220–21, 275
London, 23, 178
"Long Live the People's War" (article),
    242
Long Telegram, 59–60, 62–66
Long Tom, 176
Lon Nol, 288
Lovett, Robert, 164
Lowe, Edwin, 155
Lublin, 24
Lucas, Scott, 145

Macao, 87, 90
MacArthur, Douglas, 6, 16, 30, 51, 89,
    136, 140, 204–206; bravery of, 151;
    China and, 136, 154–56; forces split
    by, 166–67; Korean War, 147–48,
    150–62, 163–75; Truman and, 6, 51,
    89, 150–52, 156–62, 166, 172–73
Mackinder, Sir Halford, 73–74
Maddox incident, 227–33
Madison, James, 146
Maginot Line, 134
Mahdi Army, 378, 379
Maisky, Ivan, 47
Makiya, Kenan, 351–52, 363
Malaya, 154, 199, 216; British in, 268,
    380
Malenkov, Georgy, 174, 177
Malik, Yakov, 150
Manchuria, 26, 82, 160, 163
Manhattan Project, 19, 27, 40, 43–45,
    50, 124, 127, 139
Manning, Sir David, 344
Mansfield, Mike, 81, 195, 196, 208–
    209, 274
Mao Zedong, 80–92, 131, 136, 140,
    142, 168, 173, 175, 176–77, 181,
    190, 213, 233, 361; Great Leap For-
    ward, 194, 238; military industrializa-
    tion, 254–55; Nixon and, 291; Soviet
    Union and, 131–32, 165–66, 174–
    75, 181, 260, 288–89; Vietnam and,
    233–34, 241–45, 254–55, 260, 281
Marine Corps, U.S., 121, 123, 155,
    157, 213, 248, 313, 362; in Iraq, 362,
    364, 379–81
Marks, Leonard, 271
Maronites, 179
Marshall, George C., 26, 28, 30–31,
    40, 44, 51, 72–73, 81, 95, 107, 114,
    121, 124, 204, 350; China and, 81–
    85, 136; Korea and, 131, 157–581,
    164–65, 170; Palestine issue, 97, 98,
    101–104; as secretary of state, 72–
    73, 81–85, 107, 116; Soviet war
    scare, 107–109, 112–13, 115
Marshall Plan, 106, 109, 111, 138
Martin, Joe, 47–48
Martin, Joseph, 172
Masaryk, Jan, 107–108
Matsu, 180, 181
Mattis, James, 381
McCarthy, Eugene, 282
McCarthy, Joseph, 4, 139, 145, 196,
    213
McCloy, John J., 26–27
McCluer, Franc L. ("Bullet"), 54
McCone, John, 190, 200, 214
McConnell, John P., 262, 266
McCormack, John, 221
McDonough, Gordon L., 157
McGovern George, 240–41
McLean, Donald, 113
McNamara, Robert, 193–96, 199, 209–
    10, 212, 247; Johnson and, 247–48,
    277–78; Vietnam War and, 209–10,
    212, 216–21, 228–31, 235, 239–40,
    245, 252–58, 262, 266, 269–71, 273
McNaughton, John, 266
media, 7, 11, 108, 172; birth of modern
    political attack ad, 237; George W.
    Bush and, 331, 333, 341–42, 345,
    347, 351, 364, 370, 384–85; on Gulf
    War, 308–309, 313; Iraq and, 308–
    309, 313, 323, 341–42, 347, 351,
    364, 370, 372, 380, 384–85; Johnson

and, 213, 236–37, 248; Kennedy
and, 197, 258; neocons and, 321,
351; on Somalia, 315, 316; Truman
and, 84, 101–102, 147, 157, 170,
172; on Vietnam War, 234, 248, 250,
251, 255–56, 270–71, 275, 281, 289
Mekong River, 187, 188
Mendenhall, Joseph, 195
Mexico, 146, 319
Middle East, 74, 143, 177, 365; Gulf
War, 307–15; Iraq War, 3, 4–5, 344,
361–63, 364–89; Jewish homeland
problem, 93–105; oil, 178–79, 306–
308, 361–62, 367–68, 387
military, 8–11, 109–11, 133; American
addiction to military force, 388–89;
Bush and, 329–30, 354, 356, 362,
371–72; Clinton and, 316–17; Constitution on war powers and, 145–47;
desegregation of, 121; draft, 109, 120,
316; Eisenhower and, 247; gays in,
316–17; Johnson and, 206–207,
247–51; Kennedy and, 247; Korean
War spending, 177; post–World
War II, 120–23; Reagan and, 304;
Truman and, 29–32, 110–12, 115,
119–24, 128, 133, 151; UMT, 109,
121, 122; unification debate, 120–23
Military Assistance Command, Vietnam
(MACV), 194–97
Miller, Geoffrey D., 359
Minh, Duong Van, 200, 203, 214, 216
Missouri, 29, 33, 35, 54, 60, 80
Missouri National Guard, 29, 30, 120
Missouri Reserve Officers' Associa-
tion, 30
Molotov, Vyacheslav, 20–22, 45, 46, 49,
64, 68, 87, 112
Mongols, 365
Montreux Convention (1936), 46
Moorer, Thomas, 295
Morgenthau, Hans, 263
Moscow, 142, 363
Mossadeq, Mohammad, 177–78, 301–
302
Mosul, 381, 383
Mowhoush, Abed Hamed, 371
Muccio, John J., 135
Muslims, 6, 98, 104, 302, 313, 317,
324, 336–37, 385

Mussolini, Benito, 117
My Lai massacre, 350

Nagasaki, 51
Nairobi, 319
Najaf, 366, 379
Napoleon Bonaparte, 166, 363, 374
National Guard, 252; Missouri, 29, 30,
120; Texas, 329
National Security Council (NSC), 115,
126, 186, 199, 274, 289, 332, 361
National Security Strategy (NSS), 10–
11, 344; of 2002, 344–45, 346
Navy, U.S., 109–10, 111, 120, 122,
124, 128, 248, 303; *Maddox* incident,
227–33; Seventh Fleet, 135–36, 137,
154, 180, 181; in Vietnam, 250
Nayira, 312–13, 325
Nazi-Soviet Pact (1939), 69, 107
Negroponte, John, 289, 379
neocons, 320–25, 330, 332–33, 342–
43, 353–63, 367; privatization of
Iraq, 367–68; WMD argument,
343–52
New Deal, 75, 138, 139, 206, 391
New Guinea, 204, 205
Newsweek, 351
New York, 110; 1993 World Trade Cen-
ter bombing, 317–19; September 11
terrorist attacks, 4, 11, 334–35, 340,
341, 354
New York *Daily News*, 157, 170
New York Times, The, 101, 102, 106,
108, 200, 223, 234, 248, 270, 323,
341, 345, 346, 351
New Zealand, 225, 226, 268
Nhu, Ngo Dinh, 198, 200
Nicaraguan Contras, 303–304
Niger yellowcake story, 347–50, 357
nihilism, 6
Niles, David, 99, 103, 104
Nitze, Paul, 127–28, 177
Nix, Karl W. V., 92
Nixon, Richard M., 284, 285, 310; in
Beijing, 290–91; China and, 288–93;
drinking problem, 295; Madman The-
ory of, 287, 288–89, 293; 1968 elec-
tion, 285, 286; 1972 election, 290,
294–95; pardon of, 299–300; resig-
nation of, 297; Vietnamization strat-

Nixon, Richard M. (*cont.*)
    egy, 288–89, 292, 298; Vietnam War
    and, 286–98
Nolting, Frederick, 194, 198
Noreiga, Manuel, 305–306
North Atlantic Treaty Organization
    (NATO), 9, 117, 154, 161, 171, 189,
    225–26, 337
Northern Alliance, 335
North Korea, 4, 5, 6, 130, 131, 135–77,
    244, 261, 279, 349–50, 361, 389; at-
    tack on South Korea, 132, 139–40;
    birthrate, 7; Inmum Gun, 139, 147,
    149–50, 152–55, 157–62, 175;
    Korean War, 132, 133–48, 149–75;
    nuclear weapons of, 175; *Pueblo*
    incident, 279; Soviet aid to, 129, 130,
    135, 137, 140–44, 153–54, 165–75;
    see also Korea; Korean War
North Vietnam, 5, 6, 183–84, 187, 207;
    birthrate, 7; cease-fire agreement,
    297, 298; economy, 227; existential
    challenge of war, 267; infrastructure,
    241; *Maddox* incident, 227–33;
    Rolling Thunder attacks on, 240–45,
    249–56, 261–62, 287–88; Vietnam
    War, 195–201, 208–98; *see also* Viet-
    nam; Vietnam War
Nourse, Edwin G., 111
NSC-68, 127–28, 177
nuclear weapons, 7, 8, 10, 187, 389,
    395n17; arms race, 53, 67, 124–28,
    177, 218, 246–47; Baruch Plan,
    125–26; George W. Bush and, 333–
    34, 345; China and, 7, 243, 250, 289;
    Eisenhower and, 181, 247; ICBMs,
    246; Iraq and, 310, 323, 325, 331,
    332, 338, 343, 346–52; Kennedy
    and, 247; Korean War and, 170–71,
    176; long-range missiles, 128, 246;
    Manhattan Project, 19, 27, 40, 43–
    45, 50, 124, 127, 139; morality of,
    127; Nixon and, 292–93; Soviet, 53,
    67, 124–28, 142, 177, 218, 246; Tru-
    man and, 19–20, 25–27, 40, 43–45,
    50–53, 66, 116, 122, 124–28, 170–
    71, 396n43; Vietnam and, 218, 219,
    236, 245, 292–93
Nunn, Sam, 307
Nyhan, David, 331, 353

Office of Policy Coordination (OPC),
    113–14
Office of Strategic Services (OSS), 178,
    182
oil, 10, 217, 264, 361–62; Gulf War
    and, 306–15, 318; Iranian, 178–79,
    300, 301, 307, 387; Iraq, 306–308,
    322, 333, 361–62, 367–68, 387; Iraq
    War and, 361–62; Kuwait, 306–308;
    Russian, 10, 264; Vietnam War and,
    264
Okinawa, 25–26, 88, 131
Omar, Mullah Mohammed, 338, 373
Ongjin Peninsula, 141, 142, 175
Onion, The, 332
Operation Duck Hook, 288
Operation Iraqi Freedom, 367, 370
Operation Killer, 171
Operation Linebacker, 293
Operation Linebacker II, 295–96
Operation Olympic, 25–26
Operation Plan 34A, 215–16, 219
Operation Rollback, 113–15
Oppenheimer, J. Robert, 44, 53, 126
Organization of the Petroleum Exporting
    Countries (OPEC), 306–307
Ortega, Daniel, 303–304
Ottoman Turks, 322, 365, 368
Outer Mongolia, 87, 90

Pace, Frank, 148, 173
Pahlavi, Reza, 178, 300–301, 307
Pakistan, 225, 226, 317, 339, 361, 373
Palestine, 93–105, 342, 375; British
    rule, 93, 99, 102–104; partition of,
    100–105
Panama, 224, 305–306; overthrow of
    Noriega, 305–306
Panama Canal, 224
Pannikar, K. M., 160
Paris peace talks, 288, 289, 296, 297
Pathet Lao, 187–88
Patterson, Robert, 70
Patton, George, 30, 173
Pearl Harbor, 8
Pearson, Drew, 33
Pearson, Lester, 226–27
Pentagon, 111, 319, 355; Johnson and,
    219; neocon views, 354–63; Truman
    and, 111–12, 122–23, 157

People's Army of North Vietnam (PAVN), 233, 237, 239, 259, 279, 280, 291–93, 298
People's Liberation Army, 243, 255
People's Revolutionary Government (PRG), 289, 297
Perle, Richard, 320
Persia, 65
Peter the Great, 65, 66
Pham Van Dong, 233, 283
Philby, Kim, 113
Philippines, 7, 88, 131, 136, 150, 208, 225, 226
Phoumi Nosavan, 187, 188, 190
Pillar, Paul R., 360
Pleiku, 240
Poland, 21–24, 43, 65, 116, 224, 260; Katyn Forest atrocities, 23, 42; post–World War II, 43, 47, 49, 77, 110; World War II, 23–24, 43, 74, 224
political attack ad, birth of, 237
Polk, James K., 146
Pollack, Kenneth, 351
Pollari, Nicolò, 347
Pol Pot, 361
population growth, 7
Potsdam Conference, 30, 38–51, 80, 82, 140
Potsdam Declaration, 48–49
Powell, Colin, 307, 320, 332, 336, 340, 341; Gulf War and, 307, 308, 311, 313; Iraq and, 307, 308, 311, 333, 350, 362, 371–72
Prague, 108
Prendergast, Thomas, 80
presidential elections, 201; of 1948, 84, 85, 97, 100, 103, 104, 116, 128, 139; of 1964, 200, 201, 216, 228, 232–33, 235–37; of 1968, 274–75, 282–85, 286; of 1972, 290, 294–95; of 1976, 291, 299; of 1980, 301; of 1992, 315, 324; of 2000, 323–24, 330–31; of 2004, 376, 380, 381
prisoners of war, 174; Korean War, 173–74; Vietnam War, 296
Project for the New American Century (PNAC), 321–22, 356
Pueblo, USS, 279
Pusan, 17, 148, 152, 153, 154, 155, 157
Pyongyang, 141–42, 175

Quayle, Dan, 321
Quemoy, 180, 181, 207
Quezon, Manuel, 6–7

radar, development of, 134
Radio Free Europe, 113
RAND, 286
Rayburn, Sam, 17, 204
Reagan, Ronald, 301–304, 308, 320; Grenada invasion, 302–303; interventionism, 301–303; Iran-Contra and, 303–304; military and, 304; 1980 election, 301
Red Air Force, 166
Red Army, 21, 23, 24, 39, 47, 69, 72, 77, 111, 113, 142, 143, 317, 385
Reedy, George, 232
Reinsch, J. Leonard, 19–20
Republican Party, 100, 138, 299, 300
Republic of Korea Army, 131, 136, 141, 143, 148, 149–50, 163, 167–68, 175
Reston, James, 108, 223
Rhee, Syngman, 129–30, 14, 147, 148, 158, 165, 175, 287
Rice, Condoleezza, 320, 331, 332, 333, 341–42, 357; Iraq and, 344, 347, 349, 357, 383
Richards, Charles, 242
Ridgway, Matthew, 171, 173
Rivers, L. Mendel, 250
roadside bombs, 338, 371, 384
Robb, Charles, 259
Robb, John, 386
Roberts, John, 392
Robertson, Pat, 352
Robertson, Walter, 180
Robespierre, Maximilien, 374
Rogers, William, 288
Rolling Thunder, 240–45, 249–56, 261–62, 287–88
Roman Empire, 9, 74, 220, 327
Romania, 48, 55–58, 77, 114
Rome, 9, 40, 74, 121
Roosevelt, Eleanor, 17
Roosevelt, Franklin D., 8, 15–17, 33, 75, 76, 95, 124, 159, 197, 204, 212, 258, 328, 391; China and, 79–80, 87; death of, 8, 17–18; "Four Freedoms" of, 75; Good Neighbor Policy,

Roosevelt, Franklin D. (*cont.*)
  180; Johnson and, 204–205; nonin-
  tervention policy, 9, 117; Palestine
  issue, 97, 99; secret archive of, 20;
  Soviet Union and, 20, 38, 41, 45, 55;
  Truman and, 15–17; Yalta accords,
  20–24, 45, 129, 224
Roosevelt, Kermit "Kim," 178–79
Roosevelt, Theodore, 178, 224
Rosenman, Samuel, 95, 99
Ross, Charlie, 158, 161
Rostow, Walt, 188, 190, 191, 192–93,
  262, 263–64; *The Stages of Economic
  Growth*, 263–64; Vietnam War and,
  263–64, 267, 273, 277
Rove, Karl, 328–29, 334
Rowe, James, 97
Royal Air Force, 134
Rumailah oil field, 306, 307
Rumsfeld, Donald, 4, 298, 320, 321,
  333–35; Iraq and, 303, 354–57,
  361–62, 367–71, 374, 384; neocon
  views, 354–57
Rusk, Dean, 91–92, 129, 141, 161,
  172, 175, 193, 196–97, 207, 211–
  12; Johnson and, 212–13, 274–75;
  Kennedy and, 211–12; as secretary of
  state, 212; Vietnam War and, 213,
  216, 226, 229, 252–54, 260, 270,
  273
Russell, David O., 331, 353
Russell, Richard, 208, 214, 274
Russia (former Soviet Union), 10, 11,
  13, 308, 345; Iraq and, 306, 307,
  313; oil, 10, 264; *see also* Soviet
  Union

Sabri, Naji, 351
Saigon, 185, 207, 209, 218, 251, 265,
  280, 297, 298
Sanchez, Ricardo, 371
Sandinistas, 304
Sattler, John, 380
Saudi Arabia, 97, 307, 309, 310, 317–
  18, 320, 341, 361, 373, 389; Bush
  family and, 307, 309, 331; Gulf War
  and, 309, 310
Scalia, Antonin, 392
Schlesinger, James, 311
Schwarzkopf, Norman, 308

Scorpions, 371
Scowcroft, Brent, 307, 308, 309, 311,
  313, 337, 346
Seaborn, Glenn, 233
seal, presidential, 60
Secret Intelligence Service (SIS),
  113–14
Senate, 16, 36, 145, 313; anti–Vietnam
  War sentiment in, 264–65, 268; *see
  also* Congress
Senate Armed Services Committee,
  110, 111
Senate Foreign Relations Committee,
  85, 87, 228–29
Seoul, 142, 150, 152, 158, 163, 171
September 11 terrorist attacks, 4, 11,
  334–35, 340, 341, 343, 354; Iraq
  connection invented by Bush, 335,
  341–43, 354, 360
Serbs, 323
Sharon, Ariel, 350–51
Sherrod, Robert, 206
Shia, 179, 320, 322, 331, 344, 346,
  366, 367, 371, 378–79, 382, 383
Shining Path, 10
Shinseki, Eric, 362
Shishakli, Colonel Adib, 179
Shoup, David, 274
Siblani, Osama, 324–25, 353
signing statements, 391–92
Sirhan, Sirhan, 284
SISME, 347
Sistani, Grand Ayatollah Ali, 376, 378,
  380
Smith, Harold D., 32
Smith, Walter Bedell, 107, 112, 115–
  16, 225
Somalia, 9–10, 315, 334, 341, 346;
  U.S. intervention in, 315–16, 323,
  352
Southeast Asia Treaty Organization
  (SEATO), 223–26, 267–69
South Korea, 6, 122, 129–32, 135–77,
  362; Korean War, 132, 133–48, 149–
  75; KPR government, 129–30; North
  Korea attack on, 132, 139–40; post–
  World War II, 129–32; ROK forces,
  131, 136, 141, 143, 148, 149–50,
  163, 167–68, 175; *see also* Korea;
  Korean War

South Vietnam, 6, 183–84, 187, 207;
ARVN troops, 195–200, 209, 217,
239, 253, 269, 289–90, 298; cease-
fire agreement, 297, 298; Diem government, 183–84, 189–200, 203,
209–10, 214, 217, 221–22; infrastructure, 220–21; 1963 coup, 200;
1967 presidential election, 270–71,
272; Taylor-Rostow report on, 192–
93; Thieu government, 265, 270, 285,
288–90, 291, 293–98; Vietnam War,
195–201, 208–98; see also Vietnam;
Vietnam War
Soviet Union, 6, 8, 9, 103, 242, 247;
Afghan war, 305, 317, 318, 365, 385;
China and, 80, 86–88, 91, 131–32,
136, 144, 160, 165–75, 181, 190,
218, 260, 288–89; Clifford-Elsey thesis on, 68–70; collapse of (1989),
304, 310; communism, 42, 59–66,
67–78, 106–18, 124–28, 177, 304;
domination policy, 68–78, 106–18;
economy, 184; Eisenhower and, 181–
85; espionage, 85; gulag archipelago,
59, 174; Iran and, 56, 58; Japan and,
51, 69; Johnson and, 206, 246; Korean War and, 129, 130, 135, 137,
140–44, 153–54, 165–75, 244; military, 62; 1948 war scare, 106–13,
115–16; nuclear arms race, 53, 67,
124–28, 177, 218, 246–47; Reagan
and, 303, 304; Roosevelt and, 20, 38,
41, 45, 55; space race, 181; Truman
and, 20–25, 38–53, 55–66, 67–78,
106–18, 124–28, 153–54, 166; U.S.
war surplus sold to, 110; Vietnam
and, 186, 238–39, 240, 260, 265,
293; World War II, 21–25, 38, 69,
74, 134, 224, 371; see also Russia
(former Soviet Union)
Spaatz, Carl "Toohy," 264
space race, 181
Spain, 48, 147, 378
Spengler, Oswald, 73, 74, 127
Sputnik, 181
Stalin, Joseph, 20–24, 117, 176–77,
190, 371; China and, 80, 86–88, 91,
131–32, 165–68, 174; death of, 174,
175, 176; February 9 (1946) speech,
58–60, 61; Katyn Forest atrocities,

23–24, 42; Korean War and, 129,
137, 140–44, 153–54, 165–66, 174,
175; Potsdam Conference, 39–51,
80, 140; Truman and, 41–53, 57–66,
67–78, 106–18, 153–54, 166,
395n17; Yalta accords, 21, 23–24, 38,
45, 129, 224
State Department, 55, 95, 124, 139;
Communists in, 139; Kennedy and,
190–91, 212; Truman and, 55, 59,
84, 102, 103, 113, 131, 145, 157
Steinhardt, Laurence A., 107
Stettinius, Edward, 17, 18, 20, 21
Stevens, Francis, 204, 205
Stevenson, Adlai, 267, 274
Stimson, Henry L., 18, 19, 26, 40, 42,
44, 51, 52, 124, 188
Stone, Harlan Fisk, 18
Strategic Air Command (SAC), 248
Strauss, Leo, 342
Sudan, 318, 319, 334, 341, 389
suicide bombing, 302, 337, 373, 384, 386
Sullivan, John L., 109–11
Sunnis, 7, 179, 322, 365, 371, 378–79,
382, 383, 386
Suntzu, The Art of War, 260
Supreme Court, U.S., 147, 273, 274,
330; George W. Bush and, 392
Swink, 129
Symington, Stuart, 110–11, 115
Syria, 104, 179, 341, 350, 369, 373

Taft, Robert, 90, 91, 139, 144–45
Taiwan, 11, 180–81, 207, 208, 290,
333, 389, see also Formosa
Taiwan Strait, 90, 180, 181, 333
Taliban, 335, 337, 338, 358, 373
Tallal, Paula, 103–106, 244
Tamil Tigers, 10
Taylor, Maxwell, 192–93, 196, 199,
220, 221, 239, 248, 282
Tehran, 178, 300, 303
Tenet, George, 332–33, 344, 352
Tennyson, Alfred, Lord, "Locksley Hall,"
34–35, 79
territorial waters, 229–30; Maddox inci-
dent and, 227–33; three-mile limit,
229–30
terrorism, 3, 7–8, 10, 317–19; Al
Qaeda, 318, 319, 332–38, 339–41,

terrorism (*cont.*)
　373–74, 386; Bush's global war on, 3,
　7, 10, 336, 339–40, 354, 356–58,
　373–74, 380, 381, 388, 392; Clinton
　and, 317–19; growth of Jihadi move-
　ment, 365–89; Internet, 373, 386;
　1993 World Trade Center bombing,
　317–19; September 11 attacks, 4, 11,
　334–35, 340, 341, 354
Tet Offensive, 280–81
Texas, 327–28, 358, 374
Thailand, 87, 187, 188, 207, 216, 225,
　226
Thatcher, Margaret, 304, 309
Thieu, Nguyen Van, 265, 270, 285, 288,
　289, 290, 291, 293–98
Third World, 7, 117, 278; birthrates, 7
Tho, Le Duc, 295, 296
Thomas, Clarence, 392
Three Kings (film), 331
Tibet, 87, 90, 168
Time magazine, 177, 178, 263, 385
Tito, Josip Broz, 63, 77
Tocqueville, Alexis de, *Democracy in
　America*, 68
Tonkin Gulf, 219, 236, 291; *Maddox* in-
　cident, 227–33
Tonkin Gulf Resolution, 231–34, 253
Tora Bora, 339
torture, 224, 371–72, 382; Bush policy
　on, 358–59, 371–72; Soviet tech-
　niques, 371
Tower, John, 329
Trans-Siberian Railway, 135
treaties, 224; broken, 224–25; SEATO,
　223–26, 267–69
Truman, Bess, 18, 33, 34, 96
Truman, Harry S., 3, 4, 9, 15, 197, 202,
　212, 230, 259, 260, 275, 279, 287,
　354, 370, 387, 393n2, 394n27,
　398n11, 400n4; atomic bomb and,
　19–20, 25–27, 43–45, 50–53, 66,
　116, 122, 124–28, 170–71, 396n43;
　becomes president, 17–27; China
　and, 79–92, 142, 154–56, 164, 169,
　213; Churchill and, 43–44, 48, 49,
　50, 54, 60–63; Congress and, 18–19,
　35, 47–48, 75–77, 85–87, 106,
　108–11, 129, 138, 145–48; "cushion
　effect" style of, 24; education of, 32;
　as emotional decision-maker, 4, 6, 20,
　60, 95–96, 139, 148; enters Korean
　War, 148; free navigation rights on in-
　ternational waterways and, 46–47;
　Greece and, 72–77; health problems
　and medications, 36–37, 137, 166,
　395n27; Hiroshima and, 50–53; in-
　tellectual limitations of, 32–33, 258;
　interventionist policy, 9–11, 72–79,
　83–92, 117–18, 132, 148; Jewish
　homeland problem, 93–105; Korea
　and, 129–32, 135–48, 149–62, 163–
　75, 259–60; Long Telegram and, 59–
　60, 62–66; loyalty of, 28; MacArthur
　and, 6, 51, 89, 150–52, 156–62,
　166, 172–73; military and, 29–32,
　110–12, 115, 119–24, 128, 133,
　151; morality of, 117, 174; 1948 pres-
　idential election, 85, 97, 100, 103,
　104, 116, 128, 138; 1948 invented
　Soviet war scare, 106–13, 115–16;
　Potsdam Conference, 39–51, 80; pre-
　ventive war strategy, 133–34; as sena-
　tor, 16, 36; Soviet Union and, 20–25,
　38–53, 55–66, 67–78, 106–18,
　124–28, 153–54, 166; Stalin and,
　41–53, 57–66, 67–78, 106–18,
　153–54, 166, 395n17; Truman Doc-
　trine speech, 75–78, 95; vice presi-
　dency, 15–17, 28, 31; Yalta accords
　and, 20–24, 25, 38, 129
Truman, Lawrence, 31
Truman, Margaret, 18, 96
Truman Doctrine, 75–78, 95, 127, 130,
　138, 156, 177
truth, 117; manipulation of, 117; Tru-
　man's view of, 117
Tucker, Karla Faye, 358
Turkey, 46, 65–66, 72, 83, 179, 216;
　Truman and, 65–66, 73–76

unilateralism, 10–13, 117, 170, 171,
　187
United Arab Emirates, 306
United Nations, 12, 16, 18, 22, 42, 46,
　52, 58, 61, 76, 94, 125, 388; Bush
　contempt for, 331, 350, 354, 359,
　360; Charter, 224; General Assembly,
　20, 58, 70–71; Gulf War and, 308–
　11; Iraq and, 308–11, 322, 323, 333,

350, 359, 369, 370, 376, 380, 382;
Korean War and, 135, 137, 140, 143,
148, 150, 163, 165–68, 171; nuclear
weapons and, 125–26; oil-for-food
program, 322, 333; Palestine partition
issue, 100–103; Security Council, 42,
58, 79, 100–101, 126, 135, 142, 148,
150, 291, 309–11; Vietnam War and,
251, 267
United Nations Convention Against Torture, 224
United Nations Special Commission
(UNSCOM), 323, 350
United States: capitalism, 319; cultural
power, 8, 12; declining global power
of, 8–13, 299–300, 301, 330, 387–
89; economy, 8, 11, 368; interventionism, 9–11, 72–79, 83–92, 117–18,
132, 148, 177–85, 187, 208, 300,
302–303; military power, 8–11; nuclear arms race, 53, 67, 124–28, 177,
218, 246–47; political power, 8; post-
9/11 sense of victimhood, 11, 354;
racism, 189, 231, 258; space race,
181; unilateralism, 10–13, 117; Vietnam Syndrome, 299–314
universal military training (UMT), 109,
121, 122
U Thant, 251
Uzbekistan, 372

Vandenberg, Arthur, 75, 85, 86, 87,
398n11
Van Fleet, James, 77
Vaughan, Harry, 16, 31, 54
Venezuela, 389
Vientiane, 187, 188
Vietcong, 184–85, 189, 195–200, 203,
214, 217, 220, 233, 236, 237, 239,
267, 269, 275, 280, 287, 289, 297;
troop strength, 237, 239
Vietminh, 71, 72, 161, 182, 183, 184,
187–88, 225
Vietnam, 5, 6, 70, 87, 148, 182–85,
186, 225, 345; birthrate, 7; China
and, 183–84, 189–91, 214, 220,
226, 233–34, 238–45, 249–50,
253–56, 259–68, 281, 290–93,
295–96, 298, 408nn15–16; colonial
rule, 70–72, 91, 137, 182; commu-

nism, 71, 91, 136, 182–85; Eisenhower and, 182–85, 187, 190, 208,
209, 221–22, 223, 273; French war
in, 70–72, 136, 137, 161, 182–85,
189, 209, 214–15, 225, 226; Johnson
and, 191–92, 203, 207–10, 213–85,
287, 297; Kennedy and, 186–201,
216, 222, 238, 258–59, 273, 274;
unification efforts, 215, 259; see also
North Vietnam; South Vietnam;
Vietnam War
Vietnamization, 216, 278–79, 286,
288–89, 292, 298, 383
Vietnam Syndrome, 299–314
Vietnam War, 3, 4, 5, 13, 195–201,
208–98, 316, 330, 345, 350, 354,
355, 380; air strategy, 220, 234, 239–
45, 249–56, 262, 266–67, 291–93,
295; antiwar views, 264–65, 270,
282; casualties, 259; cease-fire agreement, 297, 298; Chinese role in, 189,
190–91, 215, 220, 226, 233–34,
238–45, 249–50, 253–56, 259–68,
281, 290–93, 295–96, 298,
408nn15–16; as civil war, 254, 267;
demilitarized zone (DMZ), 292, 294;
denial, 253; escalation, 218–22, 239,
251–56, 261–62, 265–66, 281–83,
287–88; Johnson and, 203, 207–10,
213–85, 287, 297; Khe Sanh, 277,
279–80; Lam Son 719, 289–90;
Maddox incident, 227–33; media
on, 234, 248, 250, 251, 255–56,
270–71, 275, 281, 289; as national
liberation war, 254, 267; Nixon and,
286–98; nuclear option, 218, 219,
236, 245, 292–93; Operation Linebacker II, 295–96; pacification program, 265; Paris peace talks, 288,
289, 296, 297; POWs, 296; as proxy
war, 254, 267; public opinion on,
233, 251, 270, 275, 281, 282, 297;
Rolling Thunder, 240–45, 249–56,
261–62; roots of, 70–72; search-and-
destroy operations, 269, 276, 282; as
social revolutionary war, 254, 267; Soviets and, 186, 238–39, 240, 260,
265, 293; Tet Offensive, 280–81;
Tonkin Gulf Resolution, 231–34,
253; UN role in, 251, 267; U-2

Vietnam War (*cont.*)
    flights, 262; Vietnamization strategy,
    216, 278–79, 286, 288–89, 298;
    Vietnam Syndrome and, 299–314;
    withdrawal of American troops, 298

Wainwright, Jonathan, 32
Wake Island, 159
Walker, Walton, 166–67, 171
Wallace, Henry, 16, 38, 52, 94, 97, 139
Wall Street Journal, The, 106
Wang Guoquan, 241–42, 244
War Crimes Act (1996), 359
War Department, 124
war powers, 145–47, 310
War Powers Act (1973), 310
Washington, George, 35, 146
Washington Post, The, 109
weapons of mass destruction, 310, 323,
    325, 331, 332, 338, 343, 344, 346–
    52; as neocon fantasy, 343–52, 357
Weizmann, Chaim, 100–102, 105
West Germany, 114, 118
Westmoreland, William, 252, 269, 276–
    77, 280–81, 283, 371
West Point, 29, 120, 121, 198
Wheeler, Earle "Bus," 248, 275, 280–
    81, 283
White House, 202, 257; Oval Office,
    35–36, 202, 257
Wilson, Joseph IV, 349
Wilson, Woodrow, 16, 125, 232
Winthrop, John, 3
Wise Old Men (WOMs), 275–76, 282
Wolfowitz, Paul, 308, 320, 321, 333,
    342, 356, 363, 366, 374; "Defense
    Policy Guidance," 344–45; neocon
    views, 342–45, 366

Woods, Rosemary, 291
Woodward, Bob, 353
Woolsey, James, 321
World Bank, 278
World Health Organization, 322
World Trade Center: 1993 bombing of,
    317–19; September 11 attacks, 4, 11,
    334–35, 340, 341, 354
World War I, 16, 29, 46, 73, 94, 125,
    150, 327
World War II, 3, 8, 69, 73, 103, 117,
    121, 129, 264, 304; appeasement
    myth, 133–34; cost of, 47; D-day,
    121; end of, 8–9, 20, 24–25, 51–53,
    73; Hiroshima, 50–53; Pacific the-
    ater, 25–27, 38, 44–45, 48–53, 121,
    196–97, 204–205, 394n27; repara-
    tions, 43–51

X article, 63–64
X Corps, 157, 158, 166, 167, 169,
    171

Yalta accords, 20–25, 38, 45, 55, 129,
    224
Yalu, 167–69
Yamasaki, Minoru, 318
Yemen, 334
Yousef, Ramzi, 317–19
Yugoslavia, 77

Zarqawi, Abu, 386
Zhou Enlai, 86, 87, 160, 166, 174, 180,
    234, 293, 296; Kissinger and, 290–91
Zhukov, Georgy, 58–59
Zimbabwe, 372
Zinni, Anthony, 345–46
Zionism, 93–105, 342